Executive Compensation
A Strategic Guide for the 1990s

Executive Compensation
A Strategic Guide for the 1990s

Edited by

FRED K. FOULKES

Harvard Business School Press

Boston, Massachusetts

Library of Congress Cataloging-in-Publication Data

Executive compensation : a strategic guide for the 1990s / edited by Fred K. Foulkes.
    p.   cm.
    Includes bibliographical references and index.
    ISBN 0-87584-210-0 (hard cover : alk. paper)
    1. Executives—Salaries, etc.—United States. I. Foulkes, Fred K.
HD4965.5.U6E87   1990
658.4'072'0973—dc20

90-44176
CIP

CONTRIBUTING AUTHORS

LOUIS J. BRINDISI, JR.
Senior Partner
Strategic Compensation Associates

SEYMOUR BURCHMAN
Principal
Sibson & Company

PROFESSOR GERALD W. BUSH
Heller Graduate School
Brandeis University

THEODORE R. BUYNISKI, JR.
Senior Consultant
Sibson & Company

FREDERIC W. COOK
President
Frederic W. Cook & Company

PROFESSOR GRAEF S. CRYSTAL
Graduate School of Business Administration
University of California, Berkeley

EVAN B. DEAN
Senior Vice President
Martin E. Segal Company

CARL FERENBACH
General Partner
Berkshire Partners

JAMES W. FISHER, JR.
Director, Organization Planning and Human Resources Development
Air Products and Chemicals, Inc.

RICHARD A. FURNISS, JR.
Vice President
Towers, Perrin, Forster & Crosby

W. DONALD GOUGH
Managing Principal
Sibson & Company

ROBERT W. KEIDEL
    Senior Consultant
    Wharton Center for Applied Research
    University of Pennsylvania

PROFESSOR RICHARD A. LAMBERT
    Wharton School
    University of Pennsylvania

PROFESSOR DAVID F. LARCKER
    Wharton School
    University of Pennsylvania

PROFESSOR EDWARD E. LAWLER III
    University of Southern California
    School of Business Administration

WESLEY R. LIEBTAG
    Former Director of
    Personnel Programs, IBM

DAVID J. MCLAUGHLIN
    President
    McLaughlin and Company

KENNETH MASON
    Former President
    Quaker Oats Company

FRED W. MEUTER, JR.
    Managing Principal
    Fred Meuter, Jr. & Associates

PROFESSOR GEORGE T. MILKOVICH
    Industrial and Labor Relations School
    Cornell University

ROBERT C. OCHSNER
    Director of Compensation
    Hay Management Consultants

BRUCE OVERTON
    Consultant

ARCH PATTON
    Former Director
    McKinsey & Company

ROBERT D. PAUL
    Vice Chairman
    Martin E. Segal Company

PROFESSOR BONNIE R. RABIN
Smiddy School of Business
Ithaca College

J. E. RICHARD
President
J. Richard & Co.

SAMUEL J. SILBERMAN
Director
Gulf + Western, Inc.

RAY STATA
Chairman and President
Analog Devices, Inc.

MATTHEW P. WARD
Consultant
Frederic W. Cook & Company

CONTENTS

ix

C. The Administration of Compensation

D. The Role of the Compensation Committee of the Board

Part III
STRATEGIC EXECUTIVE COMPENSATION AT WORK: APPLICATIONS

A. Executive Compensation in the High-Tech Industry

B. Executive Compensation in Health Care

C. EXECUTIVE COMPENSATION IN FINANCIAL SERVICES

D. EXECUTIVE COMPENSATION IN RESTRUCTURINGS AND BUYOUTS

PREFACE

In 1951, Professor John F. Mee of Indiana University edited a 1,167-page *Personnel Handbook*. The section entitled "Compensation for Executives," written by contributing author Charles W. Lytle, was just six and a half pages long, coming before "Control of Wages and Salaries" and after "Extra-Financial Incentives for Supervisors." Although the fundamental issues of executive compensation have not changed since 1951, both the theories about how executives should be paid and the ways in which they actually are paid require considerably more exposition today.

In early 1986, when I first thought about collecting some of this exposition into a book, executive compensation was causing much concern in the United States, and the anxiety has grown steadily since then. Many criticize the level of executive pay, which they claim has become distorted relative to the past, other employees, and other countries. Others question the forms of executive compensation plans, some of which seem to pay generously no matter how the company performs. Executive pay, critics argue, has become a free ride, much reward with little risk.

Specific executive compensation practices, including some perks, have also drawn heavy fire on the grounds that they are abusive and unrelated to competitive needs. In addition, some observers of the economy as a whole worry that many executive compensation plans actually undermine the long-term competitiveness of companies and the nation. They believe that bonuses and other types of compensation are tied excessively to the short-term instead of the long-term performance of companies. As a result of these concerns and criticisms, compensation committees and boards of directors are increasingly uncertain about how to pay executives appropriately. They want better rationales that make sense not only to the executives themselves, but to other stakeholders, too.

With the field undergoing fundamental change and reevaluation, it seemed essential to gather together an editorial board of leaders in the field from a variety of backgrounds. The diversity of its members turned out to be one of the board's strengths. We met over two and a half years, beginning with discussions of the field and its essential topics. After authors had accepted our invitation to contribute to the book, all members of the board read the initial outlines. Several members of the board also read first and second drafts of each chapter and returned comments about content and style. Three chapters have been published previously and are reprinted with permission.

The authors are all distinguished in the executive compensation field. They, too, come from a variety of backgrounds and disciplines, and include consultants, academicians, and practitioners, as well as a company chairman, a retired company president, and a professional director. They offer a wide range of perspectives about fundamental executive compensation issues.

The volume is divided into three parts. The first, "Executive Compensation: Past and Present," sets the stage. It puts the field of executive compensation in a historical context and raises basic problems. In Part II, "Developing Strategic Executive Compensation," the strategic approach to compensation is defined and developed. The chapters show how to relate executive compensation planning to overall corporate strategy. Topics range from discussions of common mistakes and the awareness that the old methods are not working to the design of benefits and perks to complement salary and bonus packages.

Part III, "Strategic Executive Compensation at Work: Applications," describes the application of the strategic approach in a variety of settings and situations. These chapters explain the requirements of certain particular strategic situations, from high-tech to financial services to LBOs and new ventures.

We intend this book for men and women who are responsible for the key decisions about executive compensation: compensation committee members of the board and other directors, top management, and internal and external advisers to senior management or the board. The book is neither about techniques nor meant for technicians. It is written for those who want to think about the design, implementation, and communication of executive compensation plans that will be strategic, cost-effective, and responsive to the short- and long-term needs of the business. A glossary at the end of the book defines commonly used technical terms.

For help in making this volume what it is, I must thank each of the members of the editorial advisory board. Their counsel and commitment have been superb. They have been dedicated, hard-working, and available, whether for a meeting or for consultation about a particular subject or chapter. They have given their time generously and have read more drafts of chapters than they ever imagined they would see. I also must thank the authors, several of whom are also members of the editorial board. Each one is a recognized expert and a busy person with a hectic schedule. It is our good fortune that these people made the time to reflect on their experiences and share their wisdom.

I must also thank Gay Auerbach, editorial consultant, who did an outstanding job with the manuscript. She not only attended the meetings of the editorial advisory board and reviewed all of the outlines for the individual chapters, but also applied her considerable editing talents to each chapter. Carmen Jacobson, Ellen Bankert, and Diane von Roesgen, too, deserve special thanks for their administrative assistance in the development of this book. Finally, I want to thank the staff of the Harvard Business School Press, especially Paula Duffy, Carol Franco, and Natalie Greenberg for their help and cooperation over an extended period of time. Of course, I take responsibility for all errors and omissions.

F.K.F.

INTRODUCTION

Fred K. Foulkes

SEVERAL YEARS AGO, a CEO from outside the retailing industry took over a troubled department store chain. His immediate goal was to recruit a new top-management team that not only would work well together but would stay together for several years, despite the high rate of top executive turnover in retailing. To do this, the CEO hired a leading executive compensation consultant to help design a pay plan different from any in the industry.

The main provisions of the plan were extremely competitive salaries relative to others in the industry, a bonus program based on company performance, and very large annual stock option grants (worth 200 percent of salary for those at the top) with long vesting periods. Over the next several years the chain became extremely profitable. The company's stock price rose to ten times its previous level, delighting shareholders, including those in management. The new management team, attracted, motivated, and retained by the unique provisions of the executive compensation plan, was considered the major factor in the company's turnaround.

This case illustrates what this book is about: how a company adopts a strategic approach to executive compensation. Instead of aping the pay scales and practices of his competitors, the CEO created an original and aggressive pay plan that was designed to secure the capable people he needed to bring the company back. After attracting the team, he prolonged their commitment to the company by generously rewarding good long-run results.

Progressive CEOs, board members, and executive compensation professionals today treat pay as an important and manipulable variable in the formula for success. They position salary levels in the labor marketplace the way they position prices in the product and services marketplace. They adopt programs with different degrees of risk and reward depending on whether they are staffing a young profit center with high potential for growth or a mature, stable division. They refine the standards for assessing individual performance as well as the methods of measuring corporate (or divisional) performance. Such fine-tuning of compensation policies in order to further the long-term welfare of the company is the essence of the strategic approach.

IS EXECUTIVE COMPENSATION "TOO HIGH"?

It is impossible to discuss executive compensation without acknowledging the criticism that is directed at the apparently exorbitant pay, benefits, and perquisites of some executives, typically CEOs. In "Those Million-Dollar-a-Year Executives," Arch Patton writes that "few people really believe an executive is worth $1 million or more a year. Indeed, there is a growing feeling that top executives are taking advantage of their power over the corporate purse. So industry has a problem—one that is likely to get worse if not given attention." On February 4, 1990, a columnist for the *New York Times* unveiled the latest excesses in perks: the daily delivery of a peeled orange to one advertising executive at a cost to the firm of about $80,000 a year (or $300 an orange) and the solitary flights aboard a company jet of a dog belonging to Ross Johnson, ex-RJR Nabisco chairman. [1]

According to basic economic theory, rational shareholders (or their representatives) who have full knowledge of what the company is spending to pay top managers will set the compensation of executives at a level that accurately reflects their value to the corporation, whether or not that level seems high to the American public. Graef Crystal observes in "CEO Compensation: The Case of Michael Eisner" that no stockholder of The Walt Disney Company complained about Eisner's multimillion-dollar compensation package because he generated billions of dollars for owners of Disney shares. Whether increases in executive compensation actually lead to improvements in corporate performance, however, is a hotly debated issue. George Milkovich and Bonnie Rabin present evidence about the correlation of pay with company performance in "Executive Compensation and Firm Performance: Research Questions and Answers," as do Richard Lambert and David Larcker in "Executive Compensation, Corporate Decision Making, and Shareholder Wealth: A Review of the Evidence."

One possible reason for imperfections (to the extent that they exist) in the "rational economic behavior" of shareholders is that stockholders are not the ones setting executive salaries. In public corporations, executive compensation is usually designed by top management and approved by the compensation committee and the board of directors. Samuel Silberman, former chairman of Gulf + Western's compensation committee, argues that a committee made up of competent people with whom management freely exchanges information can be fair to both shareholders and management. Likewise, James Fisher, Jr., writes that "[d]irectors today have a heightened awareness of the responsibilities . . . of board membership, and are increasingly serious about their duties as compensation committee members." He also notes that outside directors are disciplined by their fiduciary role.

Although these sanguine views may be correct, a more direct way to ensure that outside directors behave like owners is to encourage them to be shareholders. Attempts to require outside directors to own substantial equity in the company whose shareholders they represent, however, are still nascent. In "Remuneration of Outside Directors," Bruce Overton reports that although the use of variable incentive pay for directors is on the rise (about one-third of the *Fortune* 100 pay outside directors at least partly in stock), the vast majority of directors do not own much equity in the companies they serve.

Most of the authors in this book do not dwell on exceptions to the rule that executives will be paid what they are worth to companies. Our subject is more practical: How can companies in a competitive labor market create compensation plans that will draw the most capable managers and encourage them to take appropriate risks? The book deals both with the principles of pay-for-performance and with specific ways decision makers can manipulate the variables of executive compensation to produce intended effects. It will provide guidance to those who want to design executive compensation programs that will help companies implement their corporate and business strategies.

IS THE STRATEGIC APPROACH TO EXECUTIVE COMPENSATION NEW?

Wesley Liebtag adds a historical perspective by pointing out that the problem of motivating executives to act in the best long-term interests of the corporation did not arise until owners stopped being the sole managers of companies ("Compensating Executives: The Development of Responsible Management"). By the early twentieth century, founders of large corporations in the United States were acutely aware that the interests of those who managed the corporation had to be made to coincide with the interests of the corporation itself. Bonuses consisting of percentages of profits were typical by the 1920s. In 1927, the board of Bank of America gave A. P. Giannini 5 percent of the bank's profits, which amounted to nearly $1.8 million in the first year.[2] Thomas Watson, the great leader of IBM, received a set percentage of the company's profits for years.

In the early days of paying for performance, executives generally were rewarded for earning profits after the profits were earned, at the end of the annual cycle. In the past twenty years, however, it appears that the focus of executive compensation has switched in many companies to the beginning of the performance cycle. (David McLaughlin explains the influences of psychological theories of motivation and new strategic management techniques on executive compensation in "The Rise of a Strategic Approach to Executive Compensation" and "Does Compensation Motivate Executives?".) Decision makers today concentrate on the process of attracting the most capable executives and initiating behavior that will lead to the fulfillment of specific strategic goals. This means developing compensation provisions that will "precondition" executives to succeed, in certain defined ways.

HOW IS STRATEGIC EXECUTIVE COMPENSATION APPLIED TODAY?

The credo that guides many who design executive compensation today is that the principal purpose of a business is to create wealth for shareholders; therefore, compensation programs ought to motivate executives to increase shareholder value. The chapters by Louis Brindisi, Jr., Seymour Burchman, and David McLaughlin ("The Rise of a Strategic Approach to Executive Compensation") describe how the adoption of the "shareholder value" standard has affected compensation plan design.

The way to measure increases in shareholder wealth, of course, is to look at changes in stock price; the most direct way to reward managers for positive changes in stock price is to give them stock. In the past ten years the use of stock incentives, particularly long-term stock incentives, has increased enormously. (Options and other long-term stock incentives were worth almost as much as base pay for the average senior executive in 1989, according to a report by Hewitt Associates cited in *BusinessWeek*.)[3] In some cases, single "mega-grants" of stock have contributed to the increase in the equity component of pay, as in the case of Anthony O'Reilly, the chairman of Heinz Corporation, who received options on 2,126,224 shares from 1985–1990. In the summer of 1990, it was reported that

O'Reilly signed a five-year contract negotiated with the board (subject to shareholder approval) that gave him options, which cannot be exercised until 1995, to purchase an additional four million shares of Heinz stock at $29.87, the price of the stock on the day the contract was signed.

Even leaving out unusually large grants, however, we find that the average company gives a much larger fraction of total compensation in the form of equity than it did ten years ago, and companies have spawned many permutations on the outright grant. Theodore Buyniski ("The Past, Present, and Possible Future Role of Executive Stock Compensation") and Graef Crystal ("Selecting and Valuing Short- and Long-Term Compensation") explore the characteristics of today's many stock plans, explaining when each is most appropriate.

The principle governing current executive compensation planning—that executive compensation should motivate executives in such a way that the market value of the corporation increases—is sound, but difficult to apply in the variety of situations in which businesses, components of businesses, and executives actually exist. To illustrate, let us look at performance measurement. As I have said, the way to determine whether a company's value has increased is to examine the change in stock price relative to changes in the price of peer companies' stock. If the company's stock has risen more than that of its peers, performance has been good and should be rewarded. (The same is true if the company's stock has declined less than that of its peers; using relative changes eliminates the problem of punishing or rewarding executives for effects outside their control.)

The problem with applying this straightforward method of measuring performance is that frequently there are no true peers. Very few companies are in the same business, in the same stage of the life cycle, and at the same level of profitability simultaneously; therefore, relative changes in stock price may have little to do with differences in the performance of management in the short run.

I recently reviewed the long-term executive compensation plan of a poorly performing company. The plan attempted to tie the pay of over one hundred participants to shareholder value by paying a rank-specific bonus percentage for each percentage point the company's average total shareholder return exceeded the average total shareholder return for Standard & Poor's 400 industrials for a three-year period. (Senior officers could receive up to 25 percent of their salary as a bonus; the figure for all others was 10 percent.)

This plan violates the principles offered in this book on several counts.

First, the number of executives who have a long-term impact on profitability in this middle-sized company is probably far less than one hundred. Second, the payout possibilities are not high enough to motivate top executives. And finally, the peer group is not appropriate. The S&P 400 industrials represent too large a group, whose businesses have little in common with the company's own.

Partly because of an increasing appreciation of the uniqueness of each particular situation, there is a great deal of variation in executive compensation practices and policies today. The variation reflects differences in industry, performance, and strategic position. In "Recognizing Divisional Differences," Graef Crystal explains what provisions are best suited to various kinds of business units. Each of the chapters in Part III of the book treats a different special situation, from J. Richard's discussion of executive compensation design in the high-tech industry to the four chapters on executive compensation in restructurings, buyouts, and internal ventures.

Differences in philosophy or values also explain many of the variations in executive compensation plans. For example, CEO Warren Buffett and vice chairman Charles Munger of Berkshire Hathaway each receive salaries of only $100,000 a year, in spite of the fact that Berkshire's profits and returns to shareholders for the past two decades have been phenomenal. Buffett and Munger follow Commodore Vanderbilt's policy of taking nothing but the dividends and owning a lot of stock. Richard Ruch, CEO of office furniture manufacturer Herman Miller, startled the industry in 1984 by adopting Peter Drucker's idea of capping top executive pay at twenty times the pre-tax earnings of the average worker in the company. Ruch thought a cap "was a good way to monitor the issue of fairness and equity among employees."[4]

Albert Lee, author of a history of Roger Smith's years at General Motors, observed that workers in Detroit criticized Smith's $2-million salary more than they complained about Lee Iacocca's $17-million salary because at Chrysler and Ford workers received significant profit sharing, while at GM the executives received bonuses even when the company's profit-sharing plan for workers was not paying out.[5]

WHERE IS EXECUTIVE COMPENSATION GOING?

In his chapter on the organizational impact of executive compensation, Edward Lawler explains that the decisions involved in setting executive compensation affect the behavior of employees at all levels of an organization. Berkshire Hathaway's senior executives and Richard Ruch may be in the vanguard of a greater appreciation of the team effort required for business success. Ray Stata writes that the notion "that the purpose of the corporation is to increase shareholder wealth is a narrow and unrealistic view. Although shareholders own the assets, a corporation is really a partnership among shareholders, employees, customers, and suppliers, each of whom has the right to enter into mutually beneficial agreements." Robert Keidel provides ground rules for translating an appreciation of the importance of teamwork into effective compensation practices in "Executive Rewards and Their Impact on Teamwork."

I foresee that a growing attention to strategic executive compensation will accompany greater recognition of the value of the entire company team. Consultants are already tailoring pay plans more than ever before: for different stages of development, for major events such as plant closings or product introductions, for different divisions, for special financial situations such as divestitures or LBOs, and for specific groups of executives with different kinds of missions.[6]

In executive compensation, as in everything else, there is no substitute for good judgment. Experience suggests that it is wiser to fashion an executive compensation program that fits the unique circumstances of a business than it is to base plans on any single market-related formula or industry practice. As David McLaughlin writes:

> Many companies today are building more flexibility into the overall compensation plans by using relative rather than absolute measures, by writing plans so that many administrative provisions can be set or changed by the compensation committee, and by adding after-the-fact assessment to the determination of payment under long-term performance.

Plans must be adaptable to changing circumstances and leave room for the subjective input of management and the board.

NOTES

1. Deidre Fanning, "Butlers and Crystal, As Well as a View," *New York Times,* February 4, 1990, Section 3, p. 29.

2. Gary Hector, *Breaking the Bank: The Decline of Bank of America* (Boston: Little, Brown, 1988), p. 52.

3. Michael J. Mandel, "Those Fat Bonuses Don't Seem to Boost Performance," *BusinessWeek,* January 8, 1990, p. 26.

4. "The $550 Million Question," *Industry Week,* June 19, 1989, p. 85.

5. Michele Lingre, "Who's Over Paid? Ask Money-Minded People," *Boston Globe*, May 22, 1989.

6. For a report on special executive pay plans for special situations, see Claudia H. Deutsch, "Revising Pay Packages, Again," *New York Times*, February 25, 1990, Section 3, p. 20. The article cites Thomas L. Doorley of Braxton Associates, who said that 20 percent of his clients tailor compensation plans to different stages of development, up from 5 percent a few years ago.

PART I

Executive Compensation: Past and Present

PART I-A

Development of Executive Compensation

1

THE RISE OF A STRATEGIC APPROACH TO EXECUTIVE COMPENSATION

David J. McLaughlin

AROUND THE YEAR 60 B.C., a young Roman general set out to build the first truly professional army. He had what we would call today a vision and a strategy. Over several years this military genius, Julius Caesar, formulated new concepts such as the organization of the infantry brigade and the creation of the first military intelligence service, both of which persist to this day. Like many leaders in the centuries since, Caesar developed compensation programs to reinforce his strategy. In 54 B.C., he formalized the army's salary program. In order to retain top talent, he tripled the pay of his centurions. Three years later he adopted an incentive scheme, allocating supplementary bonuses in lieu of booty after successful campaigns (50 dinari for every legionnaire, and 500 for every centurion).

For the past two thousand years, kings, generals, and others in power (including the owner-managers who dominated the early stages of the Industrial Revolution) have used pay to encourage the accomplishment of an end result. Piecework incentives were used on the factory floor in New England textile mills to increase production. Some Western cattle barons gave extra payment to their crews if the cattle drive reached the railhead early or if the drovers lost fewer head than usual. The officers and crews of whaling ships shared in a successful voyage through an elaborate point system that gave them a share of the profits. As retailing chains and large manufacturing companies grew, managers were given cash bonuses. The top executives of the industrial giants of the late nineteenth and early twentieth centuries often had formula-based incentives that generated sizable sums; for example, the CEO of Bethlehem Steel received a $1.9 million bonus in 1928, a tax-free amount that in today's dollars would be about $25 million.

As these cases illustrate, those in charge wanted to attract, retain, and motivate the people who could help them achieve success. Caesar wanted a more stable, professional army, which is why he strengthened the salary system and put in a kind of retirement scheme for older legionnaires. More recently, Lee Iacocca set about turning around Chrysler by building a new management team. Huge stock option grants helped him to replace thirty-three of Chrysler's top thirty-five executives in a matter of months. When Robert Goizueta became chief executive of Coca-Cola, he worried about losing the talented executives already on his staff, given his new team's modest ownership of Coca-Cola stock. In order to retain his top management, Goizueta awarded "mega-grants" of restricted stock worth up to fifteen times the executives' annual salary in conjunction with parallel long-term cash awards to offset taxes. Coca-Cola used ten-year vesting to hold these executives, but the very magnitude of each person's stake was clearly the most important reason for the executives to focus their attention on increasing the stock price over the long haul.

In these cases and in similar situations over the years, the basic dynamics were the same. Good people were in short supply, and they had alternatives. The essence of great leadership was to figure out what needed to be done, get others whose support was necessary committed to that vision of the future, and motivate them to help make it happen.

What has changed is that the tools available to help attract, retain, and motivate others have become vastly more extensive and sophisticated. Just twenty-five years ago, most executive compensation programs consisted of base salaries, restricted stock options, and, in perhaps six out of ten companies, annual bonuses. Today, there are a dozen types of long-term incentives alone, and most companies use at least two or three.

What has also evolved is a stronger and more explicit link between compensation and the goals and performance of the enterprise. Compensation has become strategic. Companies now talk about positioning their salaries competitively in the marketplace; they adopt different mixes of short- and long-term incentives for different divisions; and they try to select measures of sustained performance that reflect an increase in shareholder value. In short, in the past few decades, strategic thinking and strategic measures have come to provide the framework for compensation program design in progressive companies.

The purpose of this chapter is to examine the strategic approach to executive pay and outline a system to access the specific design and application chapters of this book. I will sketch the evolution of business strategy over recent decades and discuss how the concepts and tools of strategy have influenced our approach to executive pay. Then I will describe how companies approach program design and integrate executive compensation with other core management processes. I will also review several special situations, from the turnaround to the joint venture, and discuss how compensation can be used to reinforce broader business goals. The chapter will conclude with a brief discussion of the inherent limitations of executive compensation plans in the real world, where strategy can change faster than the compensation program, where attracting and retaining is far easier than motivating, and where managing the *total work force* (and the way it is paid) promises in the decade ahead to be a more complex and enduring challenge than the issue of compensation for the very top executives.

THE EVOLUTION OF STRATEGIC PLANNING AND EXECUTIVE COMPENSATION

The modern era of executive compensation began about twenty-five years ago, at about the same time American business discovered "strategy."[1] It was inevitable that the ferment in the new field of business strategy would affect executive compensation; indeed, this was not the first time that a powerful set of management concepts dramatically affected pay design. Early in the century, while executing a segmentation strategy against the then-dominant Ford Motor Company, General Motors developed the divisional profit center concept. In a fateful decision, GM also adopted an annual bonus plan that the legendary Alfred P. Sloan, Jr., later claimed "played almost as big a role as our system of coordination in making decentralization work effectively."[2] With bonuses that could reach 200–300 percent of salary in boon years, General Motor's plan certainly captured executive attention, and the bonus concept spread steadily until the depression and World War II interrupted.

The management concepts pioneered by General Motors during the first quarter of the century and refined by such companies as Westinghouse and General Electric forced companies to rethink the role of corporate management. One proposal was that corporate managers take the lead in formulating multiyear plans, which the operating units would then execute. Long-range planning, advocated by Igor Ansoff[3] and others in the early 1960s, became an important new function and for a time it was the rage to develop "five-year plans." Various support groups cropped up (for example, Stanford Research Institute's Long Range Planning Service) and companies developed more data and insight into their disparate businesses. Unfortunately, the process did not seem to lead anywhere. The fancy new long-range plans were rarely more than extended budgets, only tangentially related to market or competitive dynamics. Moreover, corporate management still did not have a method for forcing re-examination of strategy at the unit level, or a good means of allocating resources among a growing number of businesses.

It was at this point, in the early 1970s, that the Boston Consulting Group, a small consulting firm in Cambridge, Massachusetts, made a major breakthrough and began to promulgate some exciting new ideas built around fresh insight into the theory of competition. Bruce Henderson, the founder of BCG, attributed the breakthrough to research in sociobiology,[4] but whatever their source, BCG's ideas had a dramatic impact on American industry. Henderson circulated monographs on the experience curve and other aspects of strategy and invited top management to seminars where such ideas as the "growth share matrix" became new tools for analyzing a company's businesses. Soon everyone was using terms like "stars" and "cash cows" and "dogs" as labels for different business units.

Expanding on BCG's insights, McKinsey and Company developed some powerful tools for analyzing the competitive strengths and weaknesses of each of a company's businesses. McKinsey contributed an analytical framework for making the appropriate trade-off between the competitive position of a firm in each of its businesses and the attractiveness of that business (the industry growth rate, margins, and so forth). Soon, it became conventional wisdom to see a company as a portfolio of businesses with different growth prospects, earning abilities, cash needs, cash-generating capabilities, and strategies.

Companies rushed to apply these tools. They upgraded planning departments to strategic-planning units and hired consultants with a vengeance. The big general management consulting firms, McKinsey and Booz, Allen & Hamilton, rushed to catch up with upstart BCG and other strategy boutiques. But in all too many companies, the primary action taken was to acquire new businesses, which often yielded disappointing results.

In fact, many companies spent most of the 1980s disassembling the very portfolios they built in the 1960s and 1970s. In time, attention shifted from an exclusive focus on the front-end aspects of strategy (mergers and acquisitions) and began to focus on making it all work, or strategy management, as it came to be called.

All this led to a reintegration with executive compensation, which was ripe for some new ideas. Bonus plans had spread like weeds after World War II. By the 1960s, annual incentive plans were being installed in businesses (such as the large integrated oil companies) that were questionable candidates for schemes that encouraged short-term focus. Professor Malcolm Salter of Harvard pointed out the shortcomings of the bonus in a widely read article entitled "Tailor Incentive Compensation to Strategy."[5]

Unfortunately, there was no good alternative to the bonus. Industry was still meandering down blind alleys in the long-term incentive area, searching for an effective vehicle to replace the revered restricted stock option, which Congress had eliminated in 1964. Companies sought a long-term incentive that would work even when stock did not seem to respond to higher profitability.

What finally emerged in the mid-1970s was the long-term performance plan, offered initially in the form of performance shares and later in the form of long-term cash payments dressed up as performance units. The seminal thinking and experimentation in this area was done by McKinsey, whose partners were leading the crusade for strategy management. The first generation of plans often used cumulative earnings per share growth as a measure of performance, a measure which turned out to have little to do with improving shareholder value. The vehicle was soon refined to use multiple measures that did reflect real value-building. By the mid-1980s, over 60 percent of the top 200 U.S. corporations had some form of long-term performance plan.[6]

These performance plans were clearly the single most important strategic pay vehicle developed over the preceding decades. But the broad concepts that emerged were more significant than any single pay device, however useful. Four concepts in particular have influenced how we think about executive pay.

The first notion has become pervasive: that the primary role of management is to create value for shareholders. Companies have measured total return to the shareholder (share price appreciation plus dividends) for years, of course, but with a boost from modern financial theory, strategists have developed new ways to measure value creation.[7] This has been particularly fruitful in analyzing alternative strategies. The basic notion was that you could calculate the value of each business in a corporation separately by analyzing cash flow and cash flow-based returns. This approach not only provided a more stable and accurate value for the corporation as a whole than the market value of the moment, it often led to the same conclusion the takeover specialist might have reached: the pieces were worth more than the whole. This was one of the reasons companies such as General Electric changed the mix of their businesses during the 1980s; GE divested itself of over 250 units and acquired 300 new ones from 1982–1988.

The concept of value creation has had a profound impact on compensation management. Alfred Rappaport of Northwestern University, one of the early advocates of using the creation of shareholder value as a measure of performance, has also been a harsh critic of traditional executive compensation approaches.[8] Rappaport argued persuasively that many incentive plans rely too much on earnings (as opposed to cash flow) measures and that sole reliance on stock price as a long-term measure of value is dangerous. But perhaps the most influential clarion cry came from two McKinsey principals, Jude Rich and Ennius Bergsma. In their widely quoted article, prophetically entitled "Pay Executives to Create Wealth,"[9] Rich and Bergsma present a series of program design features to tie incentives explicitly to strategy execution and wealth creation.

The concern for value creation has affected program design in several ways. It has led to the use of strategic milestones to help evaluate performance for the purpose of determining annual incentives, thereby breathing new life into the oldest type of executive compensation scheme. Most important, the focus on value creation has shifted the emphasis to company stock and long-term incentives generally. It has led to a fundamental rethinking of the role of multiyear performance plans, and altered the measures used in these plans from cumulative earnings per share growth to measures that better reflect increases in shareholder value.

The second major strategic development affecting compensation planning was the increased emphasis given to the individual business unit. At first, the prevailing notion was that corporations would acquire undervalued companies, and then, by supplying capital and professional management, significantly increase the companies' returns. Under "portfolio" theories of management, companies began to use their unit performance results to determine incentive payouts. This typically was accomplished by relating a portion of the divisional bonus pool to the degree to which the division achieved its profit goal. However, long-range incentives were based on overall corporate results and, of course, the stock option also reflected the company's earnings pattern and prospects. An implicit assumption in much of the compensation (and human resource thinking) was that the underlying entities were likely to remain in the corporate fold.

It is now clear that many diversification moves were ill conceived. In a groundbreaking study of the acquisition and startup patterns of thirty-three large diversified corporations that collectively accounted for 3,788 new business entries after 1950, Michael Porter found that by 1986 these corporations had divested more than half of their acquisitions in new fields. [10] The theory that a good manager could run anything also became suspect, as the value of industry-specific knowledge and experience became better appreciated. At the same time, as companies began wholesale divestments, managers began to identify more with the business unit than with a corporate management that might be planning to sell or spin them off.

All of this led to a new focus on unit compensation. In the 1970s, annual incentive plans began to include more business-specific performance measures such as cash flow generation, market share growth, and even more difficult-to-measure results such as product quality improvement or technological innovation. By the 1980s, new forms of unit-specific, long-term incentives appeared such as formula value stock (a form of simulated stock used for private companies or units of public companies, in which stock price is determined through a special formula). [11] Some companies began to use multiyear results in the traditional performance-unit plan as a partial basis of payout. More important than the specific executive compensation techniques, however, was the profound change in attitude of many key personnel, whose loyalty (and financial prospects) shifted from the corporation to their own units. While some companies like 3M, Mobil Oil, Hewlett-Packard, and IBM still worked hard to promote loyalty and affiliation to the whole, an increasing number of companies were moving in the other direction. They were spinning out business units to create more wealth for shareholders and executive/managers, who could wind up owning 10–15 percent of the new public entities.

The third broad concept that promised to have a lasting impact on compensation programs was the notion that the compensation system was a major determinant of the culture of a company, and that changes in it could affect the values and core skills that could in turn be exploited to further certain strategies. The concept of core skills was a fertile one. Companies identified their unique strengths (an excellent distribution system, for example) which could be building blocks in a preemptive strategy, and exploited these strengths in all their business units. Harvard's Michael Porter introduced the idea of "transferring skills" as a fundamental form of corporate strategy. In *Competitive Advantage* he illustrated primary and support activities in a "value chain," and pointed out that it is only at the business-unit level of the business (not the corporate level) that a company could achieve a competitive advantage. [12] A company could achieve this advantage by either (a) transferring skills or expertise about similar value chains in different business units, or (b) sharing service groups or functions (by using the same sales force, for example).

With such a growth strategy, the relative importance of functions may be quite different from traditional job evaluation schemes. Strategic job evaluation is still in its infancy, but under this approach, the impact of jobs and job families on the investment of company resources in the implementation of strategy outweighs size (i.e., revenue, numbers of direct reports). Whatever the growth strategy, however, a company's culture should be recognized as a major determinant of compensation. Compensation, in turn, helps create the "real" culture. There is a growing recognition that strategy, culture, and pay system have to be aligned and mutually reinforcing.[13]

Several decades of strategy development have led to a fourth influence on executive compensation, which can be summed up in one word: skepticism. There is a growing body of evidence and opinion that some aspects of effective competition and business success are largely intuitive and opportunistic. Many experts argue that contemporary planning should focus on enhancing the ability of the organization to adapt to changes.[14] This would lead to a planning process in which objectives are negotiated from a set of reasonable alternatives; where goals are fluid and require team results; where compensation is focused almost exclusively on the longer term (for example, perhaps with no annual bonus, except as a way to vary pay for a few people at the top).

Experience has certainly built a convincing case for flexibility in program design and judgment in the assessment of performance. In a major study of the attitudes of public-company board members, Sibson & Company found that this influential group believes strongly that leadership, management development, and other qualitative aspects of the top job should be given considerable weight in assessing CEO performance,[15] and Rich and Bergsma advised: "Don't assess results solely according to a mathematical formula. Senior management and board compensation committees should leave room for subjective judgment."[16]

Companies are building flexibility into their overall compensation programs by using relative rather than absolute measures of performance, by writing plans so that many administrative provisions can be set or changed by the compensation committee, and by determining payout from long-term performance plans at the end of the performance period rather than using a formula fixed at the beginning of an award cycle.

What has all of this meant for how executive compensation programs actually develop? Let us now examine how companies approach program design from an overall business perspective.

EXECUTIVE COMPENSATION PROGRAM DESIGN

Well-managed companies and conscientious boards of directors indeed assume that top management pay has to relate to the long-term success of the enterprise, and industry is getting better at the art of shaping programs to fit the strategy and needs of the company. There have been times when personnel objectives (attracting and retaining talent) have overridden otherwise good intentions. Rampant inflation, too, has undermined compensation schemes, as it did in the late 1970s. Further, an ever-changing tax environment and new Financial Accounting Standards Board (FASB) rulings have often ruined programs that were extremely useful in motivating executives. But, in the final analysis, more companies are using a business framework as a starting point for program design.

The process is typically initiated by the chief executive in response to changing circumstances such as a new business strategy, a major acquisition, a new top-management team, or evidence that the current program is not working. The CEO usually starts by enlisting the support of the board of directors and its compensation committee for a fundamental review, and involves committee members in the process. Because program redesign is an intensely analytical process involving specialized expertise and outside objectivity, an executive compensation consultant is often hired to work with management and the board.

The program redesign starts with an analysis of the company's business. Exhibit 1–1 lists ten aspects of a company's situation that should be considered, and illustrates some of the issues and their implications for compensation. Through interviews, a review of company material (long-range plans, budgets, management reports, and so forth), and independent analysis, the team develops new program recommendations. This usually involves a series of working sessions and presentations over several months to (a) determine and reach agreement on program requirements, (b) assess how well the current plans meet these needs, (c) develop detailed recommendations on new or revised plans, (d) determine the initial participants and award schedule, (e) cost out the new program, and (f) gain compensation committee and board approval.

There are several fundamental compensation planning concepts in use that owe a great deal to the strategic thinking and tools formulated over the past few decades. First is the practice of *positioning compensation* so

EXHIBIT 1-1
A Framework for Analysis of Program Requirements

Aspects of Company	Representative Factors to Analyze	Compensation Implications
1. Competitive Environment	Number, size, and location of competitors; industry economics	Reference group for performance and pay comparisons; mix/type of performance measures; pay position
2. Business Characteristics	Track record, growth rate, margins, historic returns	Program priorities and performance targets for incentives; time frame/mix of reward structure
3. Ownership Structure	Structure (private, public, joint-venture); stable or changing	Form of long-term incentive; levels of cash compensation; nature of benefits
4. Business Strategy	Strategy approach; implementation timetable; sophistication of planning	Type and mix of long-term incentives; degree of quantitative versus qualitative measures; valuation of core functions
5. Organization Structure	Number and grouping of SBUs; degree of centralization/decentralization of senior management structure	Degree of integration of incentives; use of corporate versus unit long-term incentive; performance measures; common versus tailored salary structures
6. Financial Characteristics	Capitalization; cash requirements; sophistication of financial systems ; major accounting and tax policies	Performance measurement system; type of long-term incentive; program phasing requirements
7. Culture/Shared Values	Company versus unit orientation; role of individual versus team; fundamental human resource beliefs	Participation; degree of hierarchy; group versus individual incentive orientation
8. Management Style	Decision-making process; approach to individual evaluation; risk profile	Nature of annual incentive process; performance assessment; program hierarchy; leverage
9. Staffing Requirements	Amount of executive recruiting/outplacement; vulnerability to raids; depth of management	Pay positioning; program retention features; degree of mobility required
10. Compensation Tradition and Human Resource Capability	Successes/failures with plan approaches; workability of performance appraisal process	Nature of compensation management system; selection/design of incentive vehicles

that pay levels are related to comparable reference groups of other companies, salary and bonus levels meet the needs of the underlying business (for example, the salary component in a mature business might be set higher than in a rapidly growing unit), and the structure of awards (including short- and long-term incentives) delivers a total payout that is above or below the reference group based on the company's relative performance. Companies use a number of basic tools to establish a compensation position: extensive "market pricing" of key positions, computer models to test the implications of various performance scenarios, and a policy road map to spell out the company's objectives and illustrate how each element of compensation relates to business goals.

Another fundamental pay concept is *varying the mix of short- and long-term rewards* to achieve more balance and better reinforce the long-run company strategy. Companies have done this largely by enlarging the long-term piece of the total compensation pie and instituting a plan that depends less on the stock market. (Use of performance units can achieve this end because they are essentially multiyear cash awards that pay out based on the degree of attainment of three- to five-year goals such as a stated rate of compound increase in earnings per share growth or a higher ROI.) One specific way to manage the mix is to establish comprehensive short- and long-term incentive guidelines by salary grade. The CEO with a $300,000 salary, for example, might be eligible for a 50 percent annual bonus (that could increase to 75 percent with superior performance) and a long-term incentive of 100 percent of salary (200 percent of salary under certain superior performance scenarios). Alternatively, a corporate vice president might have 30–40 percent targets that are equal under both plans. Below the vice presidents, key directors and managers may not participate in the long-term performance plan at all.

Another strategic pay practice is *relating the time frame of rewards to the nature of the business and its underlying strategy.* Sometimes the time frame is indeterminate (in a startup, the number of years before the company goes public, for example, or in a leveraged buyout or bankruptcy, the achievement of certain measurable end points, such as payment of bank debt, strengthening of the balance sheet, and so forth). In other cases, the performance period parallels the strategic planning horizons of the business, usually three to five years. Companies use this time frame as the vesting and/or earn-out period for options or other long-term awards and, to a lesser degree, supplemental retirement plans.

One of the most powerful strategic pay principles is *tailoring performance measurement so that it truly gauges success (or failure) to achieve business goals.* This involves figuring out the right mix of performance measures for each business unit; deciding how to weigh group, sector, and overall corporate performance; and determining the right minimum performance targets and fund accrual rates. Increasingly, specific longer-term measures and even separate long-term plans are also appropriate for certain business units.

Another useful practice is *altering the relationship of fixed to variable costs of compensation based on an analysis of the business.* Lowering fixed costs is a common goal, and the actions to achieve it typically must extend below the executive level to have bottom-line impact. Companies are increasing their variable costs by shifting to flexible benefit schemes, broadening the use of incentives, managing salary growth more carefully (the spread of lump-sum increases is evidence of that), and implementing variable pay schemes, such as gain-sharing, at selected business units and locations. These programs, unlike other strategic pay changes, are intended to do more than influence executive behavior; they are used to change the cost structure of the business.

While these strategically driven concepts are useful starting points for overall change, the entire process of compensation design is still more of an art than a science. This is true because of the number of factors that have to be taken into account. The ultimate compensation program must depend on a company's unique strategy, culture, people, and economics. There is no single "right" answer. Because ample time is needed to solicit input, test alternatives, and build a consensus, most companies allow at least three to four months to design a new or modified executive pay program.

In general, companies try to complete any fundamental program rethinking well before the beginning of a new fiscal year to allow time for effective communication to participants and to secure the necessary shareholder approval. The new executive compensation program is actually enacted by dovetailing a series of related management processes that extend over the entire year. Exhibit 1-2 illustrates a typical schedule and highlights specific actions that management and the compensation committee usually take throughout the year.

How many companies have this neat and tidy process, and approach program design and administration in a logical sequence? Most large companies have been through an intense development process two or three times in the past decade, so the fundamentals are in place. Unless a company faces a takeover threat, a major restructuring, or a change in strategy, it should have time to fine-tune its compensation programs each year. However, a substantial number of companies are in the middle of great change, and there are special situations where a distinct response is required and where executive compensation has a special role to play.

Special Situation 1—Entrenched Management in a Deteriorating Situation

Perhaps the most difficult situation to deal with is the company that is performing poorly and either has no real strategy to turn the business

	D	J	F	M	A	M	J	J	A	S	O	N	D	J	F
Full Board Meeting		x	x			x	x					x	x	x	x
Board Compensation Committee Meeting		x	x			x	x					x	x	x	
Annual Compensation Planning	▓	▓	▓												
• Set new salaries and bonus targets															
• Make stock option grants (timing may vary)															
• Finalize performance plan participation															
• Establish incentive schedules for new year															
Long-Range Planning				▓	▓	▓	▓	▓							
• Determine company business plans and strategy															
• Review high potentials															
• Update succession plans															
Annual Planning/Budgeting									▓	▓	▓	▓			
• Develop operating plans															
• Finalize capital and expense budgets															
• Establish unit goals and priorities															
Year-End Assessment												▓	▓	▓	▓
• Review company/unit performance															
• Establish/approve bonus pool payout															
• Assess CEO performance and determine bonus															
• Review executive performance and recommend officer bonus awards															
Periodic Special Tasks	▓	▓	▓	▓	▓	▓	▓	▓	▓	▓	▓	▓	▓	▓	▓
• Initiate overall program redesign/updating															
• Decide on deferred program funding															
Ongoing Tasks	▓	▓	▓	▓	▓	▓	▓	▓	▓	▓	▓	▓	▓	▓	▓
• Approve all stock option/other stock grants															
• Approve deferred compensation and SERP payouts															
• Approve compensation for new executive hires															
• Review and approve executive employment contracts															

around or is busily executing the wrong strategy. Almost inevitably, the CEO must be replaced before meaningful change can take place. In these situations, compensation management is painfully difficult for all parties involved, particularly the board of directors and its compensation committee, whose members are typically the uncomfortable souls evaluating the CEO's performance. In such cases, the problems are almost never totally apparent, judgments of performance are arguable—at least for a while—and the parties involved are colleagues and often friends. In a deteriorating situation, the pressure is greatest to make excuses, find a way to pay despite failure, and, at the extreme, ensure a payoff via golden parachute arrangements or other guarantees. How this kind of a situation—unfortunately, not rare—is handled is the single biggest determinant of recovery and often even survival, as the experiences of scores of companies like CBS and the Bank of America attest.

One procedure that can help everyone focus on the true situation and establish the climate for change is to use the normal compensation planning process to trigger a broader review. One board deftly accomplished this by requesting a review of the comparisons used to establish its executive compensation. The company had been using several general industry surveys that were full of pay information but contained little performance data. The board compensation committee worked with the top management to develop a specific list of twenty comparable companies to use as a reference for assessing pay and performance. This was not a simple task since the company was in several unique businesses and there was no close model, but the exercise revealed the harsh fact that relative performance had deteriorated. This triggered further dialogue that convinced the board that the company did not have a viable growth strategy. The board insisted that the CEO bring in outside help to formulate a strategy and tied his next bonus to the results of that effort. The new strategy, which included a major downsizing, led to the promotion of a talented group executive to chief operating officer and, within two years, his succession to the top job.

Only in an ideal world, of course, can board members always reason with an incumbent CEO and help him or her realize that it is time for change. It requires a conscientious board willing to work with top management to identify the problem. In one company, profits plummeted after fourteen years of steady growth under a brilliant executive who seemed essential to the business. The board set up a special committee to work with him and outside consultants to audit each of the company's ten businesses and rethink the company strategy. After nine months, the committee divested several businesses, took a substantial write-off, fired the designated successor, and persuaded the CEO to bring in a new leader from outside the company. In this case, the CEO's transitional involvement was crucial and special compensation arrangements had to be fashioned to make it work, including a special stock bonus linked to his support role in making the two-year transition successful and early retirement provisions (under a supplemental retirement plan).

Special Situation 2—The Turnaround

Another situation that tests the mettle of compensation planners and boards is the classic turnaround. This usually involves the recruitment of a new CEO, and executive compensation is often a pivotal consideration in the negotiation. The chairman of the board compensation committee or the head of a board search committee is usually the principal negotiator, aided by an attorney and, often, an outside compensation consultant. There often is no time to redesign the compensation program, so the number of option shares available or the specific incentives authorized by shareholders may be limited. The board is aware, too, that any special deals may set precedents for the rest of the organization.

The compensation issues encountered in turnaround negotiations typically involve contractual and other guarantees; lump-sum payments to "buy out" existing benefits and potential payouts; establishment of parameters of salary and bonus treatment during the initial period; and, most important, establishment of the form and level of long-term incentives. Each situation is unique and depends on the age, risk profile, and current compensation guarantees for the candidate; on the attractiveness and risk of the situation; and on the form and level of compensation that the hiring company is willing to pay.

Several years ago, I was involved in the recruitment of a CEO for a large telecommunications company. The candidate was coming with the acquisition of a high-technology spinoff division where he had an iron-clad, three-year employment contract, some $400,000 in deferred incentives, and a generous pension. Since he did not have to move, both the acquiring company and his former employer had to develop a package that would persuade him to become the CEO. In such a situation, money alone, while almost always a factor, is rarely the starting point. To arrive at a workable solution, the goals and dreams of the individual must be understood, as well as what motivates all the involved parties. In this case, the key was the candidate's desire to head a public company, and the most difficult part of the negotiation was getting the CEO and the board of the acquiring company to agree to spin off the division (under certain performance scenarios) within five years. We then developed a "sign-on bonus" ($2 million) that could be invested in the spinoff stock or taken in cash (with a sizable premium) if specific steps toward independence were not taken on a determined schedule (e.g., organization of the division into a new legal entity with its own stock, registration of the stock, preparation of a prospectus, and so forth).

Sometimes the reward in a turnaround is simply a large, long-term stock option grant, as in Lee Iacocca's case, but in almost all turnaround situations, the candidate wants a contract. The form of the contract (i.e., a fixed-term versus "evergreen," or constantly renewing, agreement), the kind of severance protection that will be provided under various circumstances (termination by the board, a change in control, and so forth), the magnitude and format of stock option and other long-term incentives to be offered, and the details of special benefits such as retirement program accruals must be resolved. Usually transitional compensation agreements also have to be negotiated. These can include a lump-sum "joining bonus" and/or a "settling-in" bonus if a move is involved (to cover one-time, extraordinary charges); a predetermination of salary adjustments for at least the first one or two years (such a clause can specify the minimum amount and timing of raises or merely provide for a review); and, sometimes, guarantee of a portion of the first year's incentive and/or guarantee of future stock awards. One thing I have learned in these situations is that *every* case is unique. The candidate and the hiring company should get first-class tax and legal advice from an attorney with *considerable* experience in this area, and often should also seek the services of an experienced senior compensation consultant. This is not a time for on-the-job learning; all manner of inappropriate actions have been taken in these situations.

Special Situation 3—The Spinoff

This used to be a relatively rare phenomenon, but with the current emphasis on maximizing shareholder value, business units are not only being sold, but also being wholly or partially spun off into separate publicly traded entities. The parent company distributes some of the new company's shares to existing stockholders, subsequently decreasing its ownership with secondary offerings. Among the large companies that have effected spinoffs are American Express (which spun off both Fireman's Fund Property and Casualty Company, and Shearson Lehman) and Coca-Cola (which spun off certain bottling franchises into Coca-Cola Enterprises and its Columbia Pictures unit as well). Sometimes a spinoff is the best way to realize value for a division that cannot be sold or that is not a candidate for a leveraged buyout.

There are a number of distinct compensation issues in these situations, primarily concerning the amount, form, and timing of stock for the spinoff's management and employees; the nature of the capital structure that is negotiated; and the kind of compensation program that the new company will utilize. Again, this is a highly specialized area.

In my experience, companies often fail to start compensation planning early enough. In one case, the parent company lost an opportunity to set up subsidiary stock arrangements with the spinoff candidate and had to work out a more expensive equity package for key personnel at the eleventh hour, an arrangement that took 70 percent more stock. In another case, where the parent company could not have anticipated the spinoff decision, top management failed to evaluate alternative ways to structure the program, simply granting options at the initial offering price, which subsequently plummeted in the October 19, 1987, crash. In a third case, the company failed to anticipate the impact of the spinoff on employees in a business with a highly talented labor force, and suffered considerable turnover before it could get a program in place. (This company should have considered an ESOP, for example, as American Express did in the Shearson Lehman case.) Another company did not set aside enough stock for key executives.[17] In several situations, the parent company simply extended incentive plans and benefits rather than taking advantage of the opportunity to rethink the fixed/variable cost structure and fashion a pay program for its unique personnel requirements.

Special Situation 4—Joint Ventures and Other Unique Entities

The joint venture is similar in some ways to the spinoff or acquisition, but there are also some major differences. In most cases, two or more independent companies with radically different cultures, pay philosophies, and compensation programs must be reconciled. Furthermore, for the many joint ventures that start as small enterprises, the payoff for key personnel is often uncertain since growth and profitability can only be forecast and the ultimate ownership structure is not yet clear. Most of the problems in these situations stem from lack of advance planning, failure to reconcile disparate beliefs into a common compensation philosophy, and a fainthearted approach to establishing a long-term incentive.

Let me describe one case in which a joint venture was launched correctly. It involved the establishment of a new technological venture. Ownership was to be shared by two foreign multibillion-dollar giants. Each would contribute existing businesses, giving the joint venture about $400 million in sales the first year. The plan was to take the new company public in no less than five years. The owners recruited two senior executives to serve as chairman and as president/CEO. Ample time was taken to review the compensation and benefit programs of the respective companies and fashion a new, generally leaner program for the new venture. During early planning, the designated CEO had a unique opportunity to develop a compensation approach that reflected his values and the requirements of the marketplace. The success of the effort came from an innovative equity program built around an unusual capital structure in which the two parent companies held preferred stock and management was given all the common stock (equal to 10 percent of the total). By structuring the provisions of the stock and implementing the programs early, an attractive price was offered for key personnel. (In this company, key technical personnel were considered to be as crucial to success as the executive group, and about 150 were ultimately targeted for stock grants.)

STRATEGIC COMPENSATION IN A CHANGING ENVIRONMENT

Compensation can be a powerful instrument for change and, on occasion, a determining factor in the success of a business venture. Executive compensation program design is, or should be, highly specific to each organization, which is not easy to do. The tax, legal, regulatory, and economic environment in which a compensation program must function is constantly changing, and this can undermine or thwart well-intentioned plans. For example, major legislative changes have affected executives' pay about once every three years over the past two decades, and there is no reason to think this will stop. Furthermore, compensation programs are not very malleable, nor are the executives we are trying to motivate. If a company sets salaries at the 75th percentile, it will not be easy to cut back if competitive situations change. Although the bonus is a flexible, annually renewable device, one does not lightly or frequently cut an executive's bonus target or change the bonus pool formula. Compensation consultants like to talk about how they changed the mix of short- and long-term rewards for their clients, but this usually is accomplished by adding new long-term awards; further changes in the mix are gradual. Long-term plans offer more exciting strategic design opportunities than short-term incentives, but, again, no CEO wants to go to shareholders with new plans too often.

Another dilemma facing many corporations is that it usually takes years to execute a new strategy, and it often takes much more than the promise of a payout in the future to hold mobile personnel through the hard and uncertain times. On the what's-in-it-for-me scoreboard, the payoff has to be meaningful, which requires a board willing to do something bold.

Finally, the emphasis on executives is sometimes exaggerated. To be sure, the right leader must be attracted and properly motivated, and a few key individuals *can* make a difference. But, frankly, the legions of other executives swept into current generous reward systems are often a mixed bag, and over several decades, hierarchial pay schemes can overcompensate the wrong group.[18] In my opinion, while executive compensation will continue to be a high priority in most companies (often for the wrong reasons), the near-obsession of the past few decades with executive pay is subsiding. In the new era, executives are regarded as only one of many groups vital to a company's future success.[19] In companies like IBM, for example, *all* employees are eligible for special awards, and as many as 25 percent receive an award each year, based on the nature of the contribution, not the individual's level in the hierarchy.

Another fine company, on the other hand, has come to represent the unworkable old ways for many. For years, General Motors pioneered many exciting management concepts and a number of powerful compensation techniques (General Motors' management incentive plan dates to 1918). But the company has been slow to adjust to a different era.[20] In the denouement of seventy years of bonus history, it announced a $169.1-million payout of cash and stock to 5,000 executives in the same week that it revealed there would not be any profit-sharing payments for blue-collar workers. (Although 1987 profits of $3.6 billion were up 21 percent, the arcane formula negotiated with the UAW did not generate a payment.) The executive windfall turned out to be the last payment under the bonus plan and, at last, General Motors has shifted to a longer-term focus with a restricted stock incentive that vests over several years.

Perhaps there is something to strategic compensation after all.

NOTES

1. Strategy, as used here, is the formula for how a business is going to grow and compete.

2. Alfred P. Sloan, Jr., *My Years With General Motors* (Garden City, NY: Doubleday, 1964), p. 408.

3. H. I. Ansoff, *Corporate Strategy* (New York: McGraw-Hill, 1965).

4. Bruce D. Henderson, "The Concept of Strategy," *The Strategic Management Handbook*, ed. K. J. Albert (New York: McGraw-Hill, 1983), pp. 3–26.

5. Malcolm S. Salter, "Tailor Incentive Compensation to Strategy," *Harvard Business Review* (March–April 1973), pp. 94–102.

6. Sibson & Company, Inc., *Management Compensation Survey and Annual Report on Executive Compensation*, Princeton, NJ, 1988.

7. See Graef Crystal's discussion of this and related concepts in "Recognizing Divisional Differences," Chapter 12 of this book.

8. Alfred Rappaport, "Executive Incentives vs Corporate Growth," *Harvard Business Review* (July–August 1978), pp. 81–88.

9. Jude T. Rich, and Ennius E. Bergsma, "Pay Executives to Create Wealth," *Chief Executive*, Autumn 1982, pp. 16–19.

10. Michael E. Porter, "From Competitive Advantage to Corporate Strategy," *Harvard Business Review* (May–June 1987), pp. 43–59.

11. Claudia Zeist-Poster, "Executive Compensation: Taking Long-Term Incentives Out of the Corporate Ivory Tower," *Compensation Review* (Second Quarter 1985), pp. 20–31.

12. Michael E. Porter, *Competitive Advantage* (New York: Free Press, 1980).

13. Jan P. Muczyk, "The Strategic Role of Compensation," *Human Resource Planning*, vol. II, no. 3 (1985), pp. 225–239.

14. E. E. Chaffee, "Three Models of Strategy," *Academy of Management Review*, vol. 10, no. 1 (1985), pp. 89–98.

15. Sibson & Company, Inc., *Boards, Company Performance and Executive Pay*, Princeton, NJ, 1986.

16. Rich and Bergsma, "Pay Executives to Create Wealth," p. 19.

17. In a special study of twenty-seven spinoffs and leveraged buyouts that I conducted recently, the median amount set aside for management was 12 percent.

18. Rosabeth Moss Kanter, "The Attack on Pay," *Harvard Business Review* (March–April 1987), pp. 60–67.

19. David Sears, "Making Employees' Pay a Strategic Issue," *Financial Executive* (October 1984), pp. 40–43.

20. Ross Perot, "How I Would Turn Around G.M.," *Fortune*, February 15, 1988, pp. 44–50.

BIBLIOGRAPHY

Albert, Kenneth J., ed. *The Strategic Management Handbook.* New York: McGraw-Hill, 1983.

Andrews, K. R. *The Concept of Corporate Strategy.* Homewood, IL: Irwin, 1987.

Balkin, David B., and Gomez-Mejia, Luis R. "Toward a Contingency Theory of Compensation Strategy." *Strategic Management Journal* 8 (1986), pp. 169–182.

———, eds. *New Perspectives on Compensation.* Englewood Cliffs, NJ: Prentice-Hall, 1987.

Brickley, James A., Bhagat, Sanjai, and Lease, Ronald C. "The Impact of Long-Range Managerial Compensation on Shareholder Wealth." *Journal of Accounting and Economics* (April 1985), pp. 115–129.

Brossy, Roger, and Shaw, Douglas G. "Using Pay to Implement Strategy." *Management Review* 76(9), pp. 44–49.

Chafee, E. E. "Three Models of Strategy." *Academy of Management Review* 10(1) (1985), pp. 89–98.

Gluck, F., Kaufman, S., and Walleck, A. S. "The Four Phases of Strategic Management." *Journal of Business Strategy* 2(3) (1982), pp. 9–21.

Gupta, Anil K. "Matching Managers to Strategies: Point and Counterpoint." *Human Resource Management* 25(2) (1986), pp. 215–234.

Gupta, Anil K., and Govindarajan, V. "Business Unit Strategy: Managerial Characteristics and Business Unit Effectiveness at Strategy Implementation." *Academy of Management Journal* 27(1) (1984), pp. 25–41.

Hufnagel, Ellen M. "Developing Strategic Compensation Plans." *Human Resource Management* 26(1) (1987), pp. 93–108.

Kerr, J. L. "Diversification Strategies and Managerial Rewards: An Empirical Study." *Academy of Management Journal* 28(1) (1985), pp. 155–179.

Kiechel, Walter, III. "Corporate Strategy for the 1990s." *Fortune,* February 29, 1988, pp. 34–42.

King, W. R., and Cleland, D., eds. *Strategic Planning.* Stroudsburg, PA: Van Nostrand, 1987.

Lawler, E. E. III. *Pay and Organizational Development.* Reading, MA: Addison-Wesley, 1981.

McLaughlin, David J. "Reinforcing Corporate Strategy through Executive Compensation." *Management Review* (October 1981), pp. 9–15.

Milkovich, G. T., and Newman, J. M. *Compensation.* Plano, TX: Business Publications, 1984.

Muczyk, Jan P. "The Strategic Role of Compensation." *Human Resource Planning* 2(3) (1985), pp. 225–239.

Murthy, K. R. Srinivasa. *Corporate Strategy and Top Executive Compensation.* Cambridge, MA: Harvard University Press, 1977.

Pennings, Johannes M., and Bussard, David T. "Strategy, Control and Executive Compensation: Fitting the Incentive Plan to the Company." *Topics in Total Compensation* 1(1) (1986), pp. 101–112.

Porter, Michael E. *Competitive Strategy.* New York: Free Press, 1980.

———. *Competitive Advantage.* New York: Free Press, 1985.

———. "From Competitive Advantage to Corporate Strategy." *Harvard Business Review* (May–June 1987), pp. 43–59.

Rappaport, Alfred. "Selecting Strategies That Create Shareholder Value." *Harvard Business Review* (May–June 1981), pp. 139–149.

———. "How to Design Value-Contributing Executive Incentives." *Journal of Business Strategy* (Fall 1983), pp. 49–59.

Rich, Jude T., and Bergsma, Ennius E. "Pay Executives to Create Wealth." *Chief Executive*, November 21, 1982, pp. 16–19.

Rich, Jude T., and Larson, John A. "Why Some Long-Term Incentives Fail." *Compensation Review* (First Quarter 1984), pp. 26–37.

Rowland, K., and Ferris, G., eds. *Research in Personnel and Human Resource Management.* Greenwich, CT: JAI Press, 1987.

Snot, C. C. *Strategy, Organization Design and Human Resource Management.* Greenwich, CT: JAI Press, 1987.

Stata, R., and Maidque, A. M. "Bonus System for Balanced Strategy." *Harvard Business Review* (November–December 1980), pp. 156–163.

Zeitz-Poster, Claudia. "Executive Compensation: Taking Long-Term Incentives Out of the Corporate Ivory Tower." *Compensation Review* (Second Quarter 1985), pp. 20–31.

2

COMPENSATING EXECUTIVES: THE DEVELOPMENT OF RESPONSIBLE MANAGEMENT

Wesley R. Liebtag

> *The concentration of economic power separate from ownership has, in fact, created economic empires, and has delivered these empires into the hands of a new form of absolutism, relegating "owners" to the position of those who supply the means whereby the new princes may exercise their power.*
>
> Adolf A. Berle, Jr., and
> Gardiner C. Means

THE ASCENDANCY OF A MANAGING CLASS, those "new princes" of the corporation who seemed to exercise absolute power without the restraints of ownership, has raised serious concerns in many American minds through the years. In 1932, when Adolf A. Berle and Gardiner C. Means documented the separation of ownership and control among the nation's top 200 nonfinancial corporations, they asked whether we have "any justification for assuming that those in control of a modern corporation will also choose to operate it in the interests of the owners." Berle and Means concluded that the answer to this question depended on the "degree to which the self-interest of those in control may run parallel to the interests of ownership."[1]

The development of executive compensation in the United States has in large part been an attempt to make managers feel the kind of responsibility for their business that an owner feels for the family firm. As we shall see when we look at the case histories of the Erie Railroad and the Du

Pont Company, even the earliest business administrators were intent on stimulating professional managers to behave like owners. Today, when the design of executive rewards often has fallen into the hands of professional compensation planners, the highest goal is still to motivate managing executives to identify with the fate of their enterprise.

Before tracing the development of executive compensation in the United States, however, we will take a brief look at executive compensation as it has evolved in Europe and Japan. After we have identified the main characteristics of European and Japanese practice, the unique features of American executive compensation will stand out in bolder relief.

EXECUTIVE COMPENSATION IN EUROPE

Although political systems varied from country to country, the source and form of wealth in Europe since antiquity was based on land and the proceeds from its cultivation. Until the Industrial Revolution began in England in the late eighteenth century, the owning class received income and derived power by selling or trading the output of the land. Broad participation in ownership did not exist. Stockholders or shareholders were generally found only in the banks and trading companies that flourished in the Dutch cities of Antwerp and Amsterdam during the sixteenth century. Even among these financiers, the distribution of stock was limited to the small groups of capitalists who held control. Elitism—that is, the special treatment of a select group with the power to enforce its will— was the norm, and it remains a significant factor today in most European countries.

With the coming of the Industrial Revolution, the pattern seen in agriculture continued. That is, owners retained control of their businesses and their rewards were tied directly to the success of the enterprise. Funds were raised from the owners' purses, reinvested profits, and the banks, or from what we know today as limited partners. The common shareholder did not exist and to this day, although shares are publicly traded in most European countries, the population at large does not participate in share ownership to the degree that it does in the United States. (Recent data indicate that about 30 percent of Americans directly own stock, compared to only 10 percent in Great Britain, the country with the broadest stock distribution after the United States.)[2] In Germany, it is even illegal under most circumstances for an individual to hold shares acquired through a company stock plan in his or her own name. Share ownership continues to be an elitist function, although the large government-regulated pension plans in some countries give the average employee an arm's-length interest in the company's success.

By and large, then, the separation of ownership and control that characterizes American corporations has not proceeded as rapidly in Europe. One result of this historical pattern is that executive compensation in Europe still tends to favor cash, pensions, and perquisites rather than distribution of stock. And because European countries generally have higher marginal and overall tax rates, companies emphasize perquisites, which either are not taxed or on which tax may be avoided, and large pensions, which are simply a form of deferred income.[3]

Another by-product of the smaller diffusion of stock ownership in Europe is less public interest in executives' salaries. The compensation of individuals and the mechanics of compensation programs are more likely to remain hidden from the eyes of the average employee or the general public than in the United States. Negotiating a unique contract with a single executive is still a common practice that is encouraged by the fact that the tax treatment of different forms of compensation is far less specific than in the United States; indeed, in many cases the tax code is silent. In some countries, notably France, the tax official's opinion has the force of law; as a result, there is much negotiation with government officials and often a good deal of effort goes into finding the "right" tax bureaucrat. One result is a wide variety of practices tailored to individual executives, all presumably legal.

In the socialist countries of Europe such as Belgium, there has been an attempt to moderate executives' earnings by imposing a "cap," expressed as a multiple of average or minimum earnings. Most European countries have a number of enterprises that are owned outright by the government or in which the government is a major shareholder, where executive compensation is determined by the board of directors or government officials. In either case, the government's influence on compensation as well as on other aspects of management is far more substantial than it is in private firms.

Within recent years there has been some evidence of change in the executive compensation practices of our major trading partners in Europe. In Britain the vigorous support of successful industries and the willingness to allow mismanaged companies to die have brought change in that country. The return of major industries to the private sector in France and Italy also has had an effect. Tax codes now recognize stock in a variety of forms as compensation. A few firms have introduced the programmatic application of stock and funded executive plans. Compensation practices also are becoming more visible.

EXECUTIVE COMPENSATION IN JAPAN

Unlike Western businesses, Japanese companies do not pay their senior executives sums that are twenty to forty times the pay of their blue-collar employees. The executive salary is more likely to be ten to fifteen times that of the ordinary factory worker. The use of short-term bonus plans is rare, and stock plans, although becoming more prevalent, are still uncommon.

In spite of a lower salary, however, the Japanese executive—still most often a male—is probably as well treated as his Western counterpart. He often receives many valuable perquisites, including a liberal expense account that covers some household expenses normally treated as personal obligations in the United States. In addition, the average executive continues to work or at least continues to draw a salary and receive perks many years longer than in the West. The formal retirement program is far less important in Japan because executives are paid as active employees beyond the typical American retirement age. Finally, executives and managers are likely to be among the 35 percent of the Japanese work force that enjoys lifetime employment.

Japanese management and compensation practices have had two effects on many firms in the West, particularly in the United States. First, observers have noted that Japanese firms place more emphasis on long-term results than do Americans. The success of this approach has caused many U.S. companies to adopt programs that generate rewards based on multiple-year results. Frederic W. Cook & Co. reports that of the top 200 industrial firms in the United States, only 10 percent used restricted stock as a long-term tool in 1978, whereas 45 percent now have such programs. Only 26 percent had long-term performance plans in 1978; that figure has now risen to 75 percent. Stock options by their very nature are long-term rewards and their use has remained in the 85 percent to 95 percent corridor.[4]

The second effect that Japanese pay practices have had in the United States is that a number of firms have become more aware of the team approach to managing businesses. While in some cases the attention paid has been superficial, in other cases it has been real. At IBM, for example, team rewards were given to senior management in the mid-1960s, before the Japanese approach became widely known. The CEO and other top members of the firm were offered a senior management plan based on earnings per share. At the same time, a business-unit bonus plan that rewarded good judgment, measured by a multitude of factors, was instituted. This plan provided for common percentage awards for members of the same team. Three other examples of the team approach that go beyond the executive area are Kodak's wage dividend plan, Lincoln Electric's profit-sharing plan, and Hewlett-Packard's profit-sharing program.

Long-term and broad profit-sharing plans have not been unmixed blessings for the American shareholder, however. Because the participating executives control both plan design and implementation, there is evidence that in some companies the executive plans are revised whenever yields do not meet expectations. In the case of broad profit-sharing plans, some people feel that the shared profits are viewed as a wage add-on with little benefit to the company or shareholder.

Perhaps long-term management is more a matter of understanding, style, and attitude than compensation program design. After all, if Japanese executives have been successful with long-term management techniques, we should recognize that they have done so without long-term performance plans. It may be that their cultural commitment to the nation and their tendency to form a lifetime partnership with their businesses have been more important reasons for their success.

EXECUTIVE COMPENSATION IN THE UNITED STATES

Although some attempts have been made to achieve Japanese performance levels with profit-sharing and team bonus plans, most American businesses still try to provide incentives that will elicit top performance from *individuals* rather than teams in management positions. But, unlike European counterparts, who are apt to design executive contracts privately on a case-by-case basis, American business people operate in an environment where executive compensation, along with many other corporate actions, is thoroughly scrutinized by the shareholders, other companies, and the general public.

The unique visibility of American executive compensation practice is due to the wide distribution of stock among the general population and the existence of a powerful managing class. The relatively broad-based ownership of American corporations began in the first half of the nineteenth century, when Eastern railroads began selling stock in order to finance construction. Although the stock had little value when it was first issued, it became a symbol of participation in one of the country's great enterprises. The railroads' method of raising capital was widely imitated, providing the foundation of today's broad ownership.[5]

The railroads, America's first modern, large-scale enterprises, were also responsible for the creation of a large group of professional managers and for the development of some of the fundamental management principles that still govern American business and that form the basis of executive compensation today.

The Railroads: Pioneers of Management

In the 1850s and 1860s, the railroads became a major factor in transportation, overtaking the canals that had dominated the movement of heavy freight until that time. Because there was no pool of managers experienced in rail transportation, the men in charge of early railroad operations were drawn from other fields of business and from the military, and their experience in these centralized organizations did not prepare them well for the task of managing enterprises characterized by geographically dispersed operations, the need for cooperation by all functions to meet the customers' needs, and competition from the canals in some areas and between different railroads in other areas. These challenges demanded new management approaches, but the railroads were not equipped initially to develop them.[6] Instead, rail organizations tended to be centralized, with each function reporting to a senior executive who was typically located at headquarters. New units that were set up on a strictly local basis lacked common accounting and financial systems. As a result, operations were inefficient, accidents and conflicts were frequent, coordination both internally and externally was difficult, and customers, especially those who were shipping over several divisions or railroads, were unhappy.

Out of this confusion arose the divisional structure. In March 1856, Daniel C. McCallum, general superintendent of the Erie Railroad, was the first to describe in detail the duties of divisional managers and other administrative heads of the Erie.[7] In a letter to the president of the railroad, McCallum stated that one of the principal responsibilities of divisional superintendents would be to collect "a complete daily history" of operations and to prepare monthly reports for the general superintendent in the central office. McCallum observed that a comparison of the reports would reveal which officers conducted their business "with the greatest economy," indicating "the relative ability and fitness of each for the position he occupies." McCallum predicted that such a comparison would "have the effect of exciting an honorable spirit of emulation to excel."

Lower-grade managers would also be subject to a "rigid system of personal accountability" under McCallum's guidelines.[8]

The Pennsylvania Railroad refined the divisional structure adopted by the Erie. It was the first modern enterprise to introduce the distinction between line and staff functions.[9] Managers were accountable for the profitability of their own divisions. A central staff provided long-run strategic planning, financial measurement and controls, and technical advice.

Because of these innovations, management was able to assign responsibility, measure results, and reward accordingly. The day of esoteric compensation plans had not yet arrived, but the basic underpinnings were present. Business could measure meaningful facts—the critical first step in designing compensation incentives.

Du Pont: Developer of Professional Managers

The innovations of the railroads were widely imitated by other emerging corporations (notably, in the steel industry). As firms grew, of course, new structures became more appropriate for some. Du Pont, one of the most successful of these growing companies, served as another milestone in the development of a class of professional managers driven by performance-oriented incentives.

The genius behind the transformation of the Du Pont Company from a family concern to a centralized, vertically integrated one was Pierre S. du Pont, great-grandson of the founder of the original gunpowder business. Not only did Pierre reorganize the company using new administrative approaches, he also played a critical role in the spread of these new techniques when he became president of General Motors in 1920.[10]

The restructuring of Du Pont began in 1902 when Pierre and his cousins Alfred and Coleman purchased the gunpowder business from older family members. Pierre decided almost immediately to consolidate the Du Pont properties into a centrally administered whole. Functional departments were headed by managers, who also belonged to the central executive committee, which was in charge of overall corporate strategy.

Motivated in part by the wish to eliminate the trade agreements that had dominated relations between the many small companies under Du Pont's control and between other companies, Pierre also used the consolidation plan to cultivate skilled managers as department heads. Pierre had been the first in his family to complete a degree, at the Massachusetts Institute of Technology, and had introduced a professionalism to the family business. He insisted on a new relationship between the du Ponts and the firm, demanding that competence rather than family connection determine whether a manager was hired or promoted.[11]

The company moved quickly to provide an incentive plan that would attract and hold the kind of competent manager Pierre sought. In 1904, Du Pont established the first stock bonus plan used in a major U.S. company.[12] Under the plan, which was intended to recognize "merit alone," blocks of stock were reserved for eligible employees. Employees did not actually take possession of the stock until the accrued dividends covered the price of the stock at the time it was awarded. Pierre's goal was to motivate managers to increase profits, and therefore hasten the dividends by which they might pay for their stock. Department heads were responsible for selecting recipients.

Over the next few years between fifty and one hundred salaried managers received stock bonuses, in lots ranging from $1,000 to $10,000 a year.[13] This represented a fairly substantial number of executives compared to the number in other plans, which were limited to a handful of top managers.

Control of data relative to the bonus awards was vested in the financial organization. Salaries, which were purposely kept low so as to leave plenty of room for variable bonuses, were influenced by the personnel department. As a result, there was little danger of salaries, salary levels, and job evaluation procedures inhibiting the size of bonuses. (In 1978, the bonus system was centralized in personnel, but finance continues to have a strong influence.)

The stock plan explicitly excluded members of the executive committee, the top officials at Du Pont who were still mostly family members (and already possessed large holdings). In 1914, however, Pierre instituted a partnership plan for the most senior managers, who by this time included professional associates unconnected to the family. With the stock bought from Coleman du Pont (who sold out in 1914), Pierre formed a holding company called Du Pont Securities (later, Christiana Securities Company). Pierre initially distributed shares in Christiana Securities to five associates, adding more participants later. Although the holding company was to a large extent a means by which Pierre gained absolute control over Du Pont, he later stated that the plan had been responsible for the company's success during World War I: "We had in our organization at the beginning of the war a nucleus of men representing the best talent in their line. Not one of them has deserted the company, though flattering offers of salary and participation in profits were open to all of them."[14]

Pierre saw to the formation of a similar holding company at General Motors. Recipients financed their allocations with a small down payment plus seven annual installments intended to come from the stocks' dividend earnings. GM had the option to repurchase the stock if the recipient resigned or if his performance deteriorated. Although du Pont recommended over 150 initial partners, Alfred P. Sloan, Jr., (CEO at that time) chose about eighty men to receive the same amount of stock. Many ultimately became millionaires.[15]

What can we learn from the examples of the railroads, Du Pont, and General Motors? First, these cases demonstrate that firms must develop clear business objectives, an appropriate organization, and standards of performance measurement before they decide on pay mechanisms and reward levels. Without a sound strategy and structure, a company has no basis for compensation planning. Second, we can observe how strong founders like Pierre du Pont searched for ways to make the interests of nonowning managers coincide with the interests of the owners.

Following the lead of these and other well-managed companies, many, if not most, enterprises in the United States began to seek new and innovative ways of organizing work and attracting and rewarding their executives. Included among those who contributed to this progress were Andrew Carnegie, Alfred P. Sloan, Jr., and Arch Patton (of McKinsey and Company).

This is not to say that many sins were not committed under the guise of making executives accountable for the performance of their firms. In some plans, managers were held accountable for the firm's performance when, in fact, they could have had no influence on the performance, at least as it was being measured. Some managers undoubtedly received (and still receive) rewards when none was warranted. However, even when compensation plans excluded or included the wrong people, the attempt to involve managers, and in some cases an even wider group of employees, in the company's fate contributed to a feeling of belonging to one's enterprise that was valuable.

Meanwhile, the pay practices of companies were becoming increasingly visible in the United States. This occurred naturally as the distribution of stock broadened. The disclosures made during the financial scandals of the first decades of the twentieth century, which included accusations that the top managers of some firms were abusing their power with exorbitant compensation levels, also increased the visibility of corporate pay practices. During the world wars and periods of depression or inflation, when the government imposed wage and price controls, companies were required to demonstrate with financial details that relief was necessary in order to receive exemption from the controls. This requirement encouraged and sometimes forced firms to divulge and exchange data, which, again, reinforced our national habit of subjecting executive pay to public scrutiny.

Let us now turn to a final case history. We will examine how a major, well-known, integrated company moved from a simple executive compensation plan intended for an emerging, small company to a comprehensive plan that embraced and supported the needs of an international enterprise, an enterprise with a coherent and influential set of beliefs. This example is offered for two reasons: because the author has firsthand knowledge of the company, and because the company provides an archetype of the changes many compensation plans have gone through as firms make the transition from small, growing businesses to major industrial enterprises. The path this firm took, although perhaps not the best one for another company or even for this one, is nevertheless representative, and therefore instructive.

IBM: Archetype of Change

When Thomas Watson became president of Computer-Tabulating-Recording Company in 1915, he worked for a salary plus a share of profits (which equaled 5 percent of profits after taxes and dividend payments) under an employment contract. The company was relatively small (sales of $15 million in 1919, the fifth year of Watson's presidency) and had a limited product line; the employees numbered a few thousand. As the company grew and prospered, the percentage of profits that Watson received was reduced at his instigation. Watson gave similar contracts with varying percentages to both line and staff executives.

By the mid-1960s, IBM was active around the world, its product line was broad and sophisticated, and the employee population exceeded 200,000. Although forty executives received stock options, awarded solely at the discretion of the chairman, salary continued to be the primary form of compensation. Ninety executives were on a service contract nearly identical to the one that covered the chairman. Salary administration was simple: there were no corporate guidelines and the chairman made all decisions above the $30,000 level. Because of the control process and because the chairman maintained his own salary at a low level (and reduced his share of the profits on several occasions), salaries tended to be "compressed" within a rather narrow range. There was no formal process for evaluating positions.

Pressures brought about by growth, complexity, and, in some cases, envy began to grow. For one thing, it was clear that not all ninety managers covered by service contracts had a direct impact on the company's results. There were other problems as well: The contracts were tailored to individual executives rather than to their positions; the fractions awarded were based on total corporate results rather than on the performance of separate business units; and, since executive salaries were based on annual results, the pattern of earnings altered considerably as the business moved from lease to sales. Finally, the whole system was largely dependent on the judgment of one person, the chairman.

In the late 1960s, Thomas J. Watson, Jr., who by then had assumed leadership of IBM, stopped everything. A task force leader was appointed, an outside consultant was retained, and interviews of the interested parties were conducted. The company was able to develop a new compensation strategy more quickly than some companies because of its long history of leadership by one strong personality. Even so, change was not easy. Some resisted the new plan, others were unsure about it.

The compensation study, like many similar studies conducted by other firms, included an examination of IBM's "culture," an analysis of the labor market and the law (both current and anticipated), a review of the plans other firms were using, and interviews with about one hundred company executives. As a result of the study, IBM made the following decisions about executive compensation:

- The company would buy out the existing profit-sharing employment contracts. (Many other firms have found this the best way to get out of an unsatisfactory plan.) Its decision was based on the simple perception that the plan was no longer meeting the needs of the business.
- The top executives, about a dozen, would receive from 25 percent to 50 percent of their annual compensation in the form of a performance incentive. Before executives received a payout, earnings per share had to equal or exceed the average of the past three years. In addition, a specified ROE had to be achieved.
- Approximately sixty executives would receive bonuses of from 15 percent to 30 percent of total earnings, depending on senior management's judgment of their overall performance within groups. They were divided into approximately twelve groups, each group identified with a business unit. Individual variations in performance would be dealt with through salary or special awards. The size and composition of the groups would be determined by management's judgment of who had the most direct effect on the business. Titles and reporting relationships were of less importance. Those not in the groups would be rewarded with merit salary increases and by individual spot awards of as much as $100,000, continuing long-standing IBM practice.
- No staff executives (legal, financial, or personnel) would participate.

Such executives were expected to pursue specific objectives, as formulated by senior management, objectives that might be in direct conflict with profit goals, at least in the time frame contemplated for those in the selected groups.

- Payments would be in cash with an opportunity for deferral. (When inflation became a factor, particularly in countries such as Brazil, deferrals were often eliminated.)
- Stock options would be continued. Grants would be made annually, but the recipient would have to requalify in each reward period. In other words, the company eliminated "automatics." At the time, management anticipated that about 1,000 people would qualify for options. There was then, and continues to be, a great deal of discussion about how much is "enough" and how many are "enough." Because stock option grants are not ongoing "rights" but must be earned each year, the size of the group varies from year to year.

  The size of the grants would also vary, depending both on the criteria being met and the individual circumstances. After the plan went into effect, initial grants were often three times earnings, and follow-ons one to two times earnings. A final grant of several times earnings was sometimes given when participants were dropped from the program.
- Base pay would be administered in accordance with recently installed international position evaluation and merit pay systems. The salary system that was adopted made use of an internally developed factor-degree evaluation system, salary grades (initially there were forty-five, but this was subsequently reduced to twenty-three), a performance planning and appraisal system, and salary guidelines that provided for top performers to receive increases of two to three times the size given to those whose work was merely satisfactory. "Annual" increase patterns were avoided.
- The company would continue to avoid loans and perquisites except in some overseas units where the culture and past practices almost dictated their use. Management believed that perquisites were difficult to control, questionable under many tax laws, and unfair to the executive because they deprived him or her of the right to decide how to use his or her compensation.
- A small executive compensation department would be established within personnel and the role of the executive compensation committee of the board of directors would be modified.
- Key elements of the plan would be presented to shareholders.

No long-term performance plan other than stock options was included in IBM's compensation plan. The company believed that the combination of rapidly changing markets, exploding technology, and unpredictable world conditions would force many revisions in a long-term compensation program, thereby destroying the plan's credibility. Long-term compensation programs seemed impractical in a firm that reorganized frequently and constantly moved executives to different positions.

IBM also intentionally limited the number of participants in both its bonus and stock programs. Top management believed that broad bonus plan awards and stock option plans would lead to generalized awards with little to distinguish one group or individual from another.

The decisions IBM made in the late 1960s have remained in place. However, continued expansion of operations overseas, changes in tax laws, and growth in the total business brought the need for some modifications of the plans. These have included the following:

- Salary levels for the top 1,200 executives were abandoned. In general, this change affected those employees who were within three or four levels of the CEO. The company believed that this change enhanced its flexibility while communicating to the executives the company's intent to treat each as an individual. Although few other companies are known to have abolished salary levels for executives, most companies do not adhere to them strictly.
- The group eligible for stock options was enlarged to 1,400 and later reduced to approximately 1,100. The rationale was that the group should not be so large that one or more of the top executives did not know each participant personally.
- Stock options were granted overseas where practical.
- Restricted stock was introduced on a very selective basis, primarily to add emphasis to the company's appreciation of valuable employees. (The term "restricted stock" means a promise by the company to give an individual at a future time a stated number of shares of the company's stock. The executive in turn must remain at IBM to receive the stock.)
- Incentive stock options (ISOs) and stock appreciation rights (SARs) were used selectively for officers. ISOs bestowed certain tax advantages at the expense of flexibility. SARs allowed a company to give cash in lieu of the appreciation on shares of stock, and were introduced primarily to overcome SEC regulations of an officer's or another insider's right to trade stock at certain times.
- Stock-for-stock features that permitted the use of already-owned stock to exercise options were provided in order to ease the exercise process.
- The company believed that incentives were only desirable when there was clear evidence that an individual could affect the bottom line.

The "judgmental" bonus system was extended to a number of overseas business units and this along with modest domestic expansion brought the total covered by the bonus scheme up to about 300.

- In 1980, the executive compensation department began preparing and discussing with each officer a customized, ten-year outlook book that portrayed all the events that would occur during his or her employment, including such things as the dates on which stock transactions would occur. The intent of this program was to provide better information to the executive and thus enhance commitment to the programs, as well as to enable executives to make the most of the rewards provided. (Although executives may use the ten-year outlook book in their own financial planning, IBM does not provide financial consulting for its executives, in the belief that obtaining such advice is the responsibility of the individual.)

Finally, by the mid-1980s there were needs for further revisions. The creation of a separate business unit to conduct the company's business in the United States, the re-missioning of the corporate staff to remove it from the day-to-day operations in the United States, and the vastly increased emphasis on the delegation of authority downward throughout the world created a need for broader use of executive compensation tools. Participation in the stock option plan was increased; support staff members, such as those in personnel, were now included in the incentive plans and the business units worldwide were encouraged to experiment with annual incentive plans for key personnel. The executive compensation department on the corporate staff continues to set broad guidelines, administer the top-management plans, and monitor the various innovations. Management continues to make awards on the basis of informed judgment rather than by formula.

CONCLUSION

The case studies discussed here illustrate how both broad trends and specific company circumstances have contributed to the development of executive compensation. The separation of ownership and control and the growth of a large and powerful managerial class in the United States were two historical influences that led to the creation of compensation plans intended to motivate executives to work for their firms' long-run health. In designing tools to this end, each company was constrained by its characteristic product cycle, its phase of development (whether it was new and expanding or mature and consolidating), the attitude of its labor force, and organizational changes.

All companies have found problems in their executive and management compensation systems. The cost was considered too great, or not enough to provide a real incentive. The group of eligible executives was deemed too small or too large (it is always interesting to ask who thinks so, the CEO, the participants, or those who were excluded). The choice of performance measures was considered unsatisfactory.[16] Business objectives changed, rendering established performance measures obsolete, as when a company decided to concentrate on profitability rather than on market share. Or, a new company was acquired with completely different compensation practices, which either had to be altered or maintained with a loss of flexibility in moving executives in and out of the new division. Tax laws changed, aggressive consultants developed new approaches adopted by competitors in the labor market. The list of problems was long.

Virtually all American corporations outgrew the compensation practices that were installed by their founders. Most experienced a period of study followed by reformulation of their executive compensation plans, which sometimes acquired the imprint of the chairman or another leader in the reform. Out of all this a pattern, a set of beliefs and practices peculiar to each company, emerged.

Executive compensation will probably continue to become more complex. Fads will come and go, executive leadership will change. Some tools will work, others will not. We will not always know why they did or did not succeed.

Nevertheless, in the long run, compensation planners will continue to seek ways to encourage managers to improve the performance of the business. And, based on past experience, it now seems evident that thoughtful planners will focus on plans that ensure that participating executives are held accountable for the success of the firm, accountable to employees and to the shareholders. The wise compensation designer will choose tools and programs that enhance accountability and make less use of those that do not. It is clear that stock options, which link the interest of the executives and the shareholders, and formula-based performance plans that are sound and stable enhance accountability. SARs, golden parachutes, cancellation and reissuance of stock options, and perquisites detract from it.

Accountability continues to be the goal, as yet unreached by all firms, but worthy of our best efforts.

NOTES

1. Adolf A. Berle, Jr., and Gardiner C. Means, *The Modern Corporation and Private Property* (New York: The MacMillan Co., 1932), p. 121.

2. This information comes from a discussion with Frederic W. Cook of Frederic W. Cook & Co. about its publication, "Long-Term Incentive Plans: The Top 200" (New York: Frederic W. Cook & Co., September 1987).

3. The fact that the vehicles of executive compensation in Europe are different from those widely used in the United States makes comparison of remuneration a complicated task, one that has generated much academic and popular debate.

4. Cook, "Long-Term Incentive Plans," p. 18.

5. The complete history of stock ownership in the United States is outside the scope of this chapter. Readers who are interested in learning more about the subject should consult quarterly and annual SEC reports.

6. Much of the summary in this section relies on Alfred D. Chandler, Jr.'s *The Visible Hand: The Managerial Revolution in American Business* (Cambridge, MA: Belknap Press of Harvard University Press, 1977); and *The Railroads: The Nation's First Big Business*, Alfred D. Chandler, Jr., ed. (New York: Harcourt, Brace & World, 1965).

7. Alfred D. Chandler, Jr., and Richard S. Tedlow, *The Coming of Managerial Capitalism* (Homewood, IL: Richard D. Irwin, 1985), pp. 200–208; Chandler, *The Railroads*, pp. 98–99.

8. Chandler and Tedlow, *The Coming of Managerial Capitalism*, pp. 207–208.

9. For a history of the early financing of the railroads, see Chandler's *The Railroads*, pp. 48–58.

10. Alfred D. Chandler, Jr., and Stephen Salsbury, *Pierre S. du Pont and the Making of the Modern Corporation* (New York: Harper & Row, 1971), p. xxi. The section on Du Pont is based on Chandler's account.

11. Ibid., p. 125.

12. According to a National Conference Board report cited by Chandler, there were five employee stock purchase plans in existence before 1901, although they were not necessarily bonus programs. See Chandler and Salsbury, *Pierre S. du Pont and the Making of the Modern Corporation*, p. 135 and footnote 24, p. 639.

13. Ibid., p. 137.

14. Ibid., p. 538.

15. Ibid., pp. 541–543.

16. Performance can be based on an absolute goal, or it can be a relative measure, comparing results to that of other companies in an industry or to the results of the economy as a whole.

3

THOSE MILLION-DOLLAR-A-YEAR EXECUTIVES

Arch Patton

TOP MANAGEMENT PAY reached a new peak in 1983 as scores of executives received more than $1 million for a year's work. While chief executives had broken the million-dollar barrier before, the number doing so and the size of their paychecks touched off a brouhaha in 1984. The business press used such terms as "greedy," "mad," and "outrageous" to describe the compensation decisions made by many company boards of directors. One TV commentator even called the million-dollar-plus payments "obscene."

As the wave of criticism grew, it was surprising how little attention was given the underlying causes of the explosion in top management compensation, the pressures that finally blew the top off the pay volcano. They are many, complex, and subject to interpretation that reflects the "eye of the beholder." It is not likely that chief executives receiving the seven-figure awards, for example, thought that their directors were making a mistake. Yet many competent observers believe top management pay increases have gotten out of hand and that a continuation of present trends will lead to serious stresses between workers and management in many already hard-pressed industries. Some observers, in fact, predict government intervention.

Breaching the million-dollar barrier could hardly have come at a worse time. The top management of many basic industries had asked employees to change work rules and take pay cuts during the recession, yet executive pay continued to rise. Furthermore, a sizable number of important industries—steel, automobile, machine tool, textile, clothing, shoe, to name a few—have petitioned the federal government to ease foreign competition by means of quotas, import duties, or some other protectionist action.

Cries for government help are hardly evidence of great management performance. To be sure, the inflated dollar has hurt profitability, and wages in Taiwan, Korea, and Japan are considerably lower than those in the United States. There is widespread suspicion, however, that successive managements of many companies permitted wages to get out of line, and studies have shown that the foreigner's wage advantage accounts for barely half the production cost differential between U.S. and Japanese companies in the automobile industry, for example, with superior Japanese management accounting for much of the rest.[1]

Manufacturers are not the only ones needing help. Banking executives, for instance, have shown more enthusiasm than judgment in making energy loans, not to mention those to Latin American governments, to the point that the Federal Reserve has had to take a hand. Utility executives, for their part, have had difficulty profitably integrating nuclear power into their systems, while foreign executives seem to have had little trouble.

The federal government has helped industry in other ways as well. A multitude of tax reductions have sharply cut industry's contribution to running the government. In 1965, for example, industry's tax payments were 26 percent of all federal income. In 1983, industry contributed only 6 percent.

Profit is, of course, a critical yardstick of executive performance. By this measure, too, executive performance leaves something to be desired. The net income of companies making up the *Fortune* 500 list would have been lower for the fourth successive year in 1983, according to the magazine, had it not been for the extraordinary earnings of the automobile industry. These huge profits resulted from limits set on Japanese imports, demanded by our government, which permitted higher price tags—hence bigger profits. And sixty of the 500 companies in the *Fortune* list had losses in 1983, the largest number showing red ink since the profit-measurement survey started thirty years ago.[2]

As noted, this record does not reflect outstanding executive achievement, yet directors of the one hundred largest publicly owned industrial corporations increased the salary and cash bonuses of their CEOs by an average of 13.7 percent in 1983, whereas employees' hourly wages increased only 5.9 percent. Furthermore, directors of thirty-two companies rewarded their chief executives with total income in excess of $1 million. Half this group received that much or more in salary and cash bonus alone. Of the other half, twelve had stock option profits large enough to push their total above $1 million, and four received income from other company sources to attain this figure.

Exhibit 3–1 shows the relationship of total 1983 compensation of the one hundred chief executives to company sales. A sizable proportion of the million-dollar executives received payments substantially in excess of this figure. Further, CEOs of smaller companies received the largest in-

Exhibit 3-1
Total Compensation of Chief Executives for 1983 in 100 of the Largest U.S. Industrial Corporations

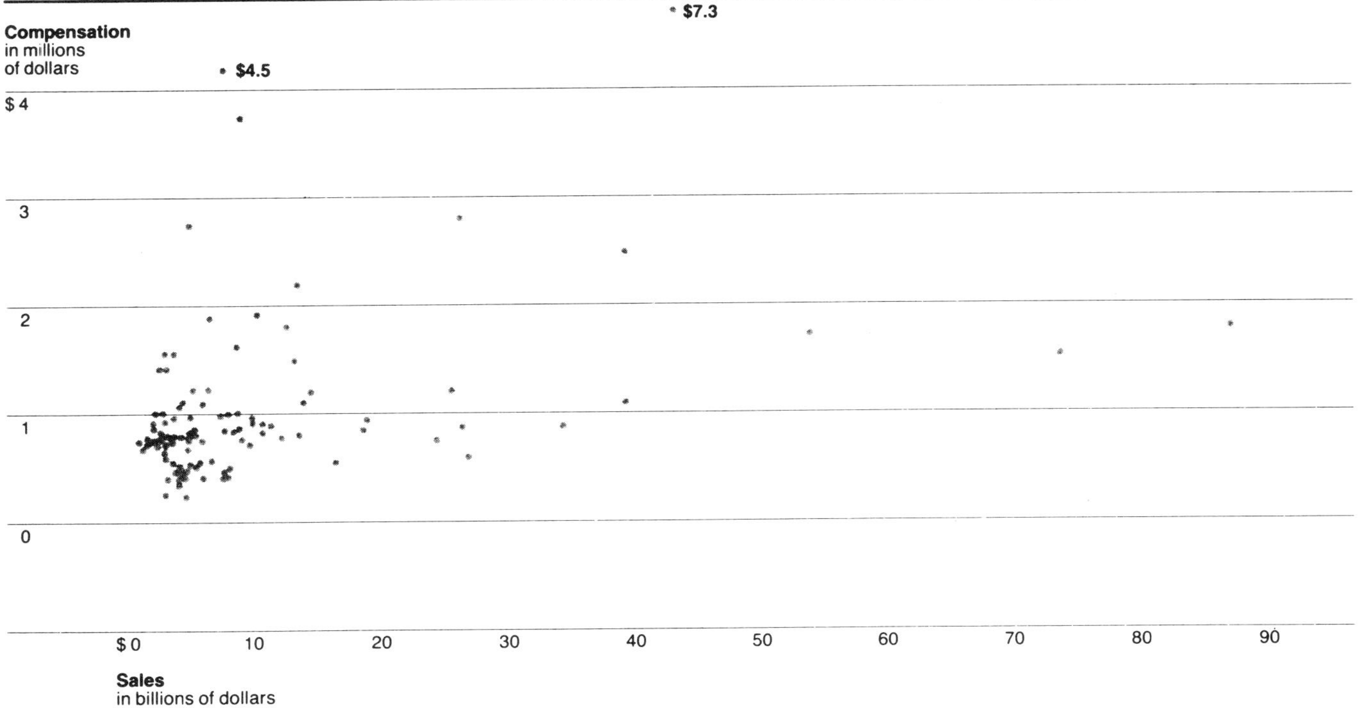

Compensation
in millions
of dollars

$4

3

2

1

0

Sales
in billions of dollars

$0   10   20   30   40   50   60   70   80   90

• $7.3

• $4.5

Source:
Company proxy statements.

come. This finding is apparently no aberration, for a *Forbes* magazine survey reported that seventy chief executives of companies smaller than the one hundred largest topped the $1-million figure in 1983.[3] Many executives subordinate to the CEO also entered the ranks of million-dollar recipients.

Directors approved salary and cash bonus increases for eighty-one of the one hundred chief executives, although one-third of the companies reported lower profits in 1983. (Indeed, twenty-one chief executives received pay increases despite declining company earnings.) The profit of a single year is not a sound measure of executive performance, of course, but this pay-performance anomaly recurs; in 1982, fifty-five of the one hundred largest companies had lower earnings, while half their CEOs received pay increases, and 1981 was little different.

The compensation of newly elected chief executives is interesting and puzzling. When executives are promoted, they usually receive considerably less pay, because of their inexperience, than those they replace. Many boards follow such a policy for new top managers. In the three years 1981–1983, for example, thirty-nine new chief executives were elected by directors of the one hundred largest industrial companies, and approximately half of them were paid 20 percent to 40 percent below the previous chief executives.

The other half, however, were paid more than their predecessors. Some of these increases undoubtedly had logical explanations, but when half the new chief executives were considered worth more than the retired CEOs, one can only wonder why the latter had not been fired. Outside hires were not a factor, for only three of the thirty-nine new chief executives had company tenure of less than four years; most of the rest were company veterans with twenty or more years of service.

Directors of the one hundred largest companies have increased the compensation of chief executives at a rapid rate in the last decade. For example, between 1973 and 1983 the following increases occurred:

Cost of living	+124%
Hourly wages in industry	+116%
Profits of the 100 largest companies	+110%
Salaries and cash bonuses for the chief executives of the 100 largest companies	+131%

Note that deferred or "contingent" bonuses and stock option profits are not included in these comparisons. Contingent bonuses were not reported in 1983, but in 1982 they equaled 23 percent of the salaries and cash bonuses of chief executives of the sixty-two companies using such deferred bonuses. Stock option profits were even larger, soaring to 95 percent of salaries and cash bonuses in the companies whose chief executives took option profits in that year. In 1982, stock option profits were 61 percent of cash pay on the same basis.

FORCES BOOSTING PAY

Why should top management compensation, which clustered in the $300,000 range for most of the one hundred largest industrial corporations' chief executives a decade ago, swoosh above the $1 million mark at a time when millions of people are unemployed, inflation is relatively mild, and industry is recovering from a major recession? Answering this question is not easy. Having dealt with the executive compensation problems of large companies over three decades, however, I think it worth a try.

The causes of the rampant rise in top management pay are, in my view, partly structural, partly poorly used aids developed to assist in the managerial process, and partly changes in the mores and viewpoints of industry's directors and top executives.

Structural Aspects

Among the three causes of rising compensation, only the structural aspects are beyond management control. They are also the easiest to assess. Therefore, I will mention them but briefly in passing. Inflation is the most important. The cost of living, as noted, jumped 124 percent between 1973 and 1983. Compound interest also added its nudge to the upward push of inflation as the years passed. On these factors alone, the $300,000 median 1973 cash compensation for chief executives of these big companies would have risen close to the $700,000 level in 1983.

The Management Aids

To deal with an increasingly complex industrial environment, management sought help from new resources and techniques. One of the earliest was the executive compensation survey. After inflation itself, the compensation survey may well be the most important ingredient in rising executive compensation, for it lends itself to often well-meaning actions that lead to unwarranted compensation increases.

For example, when a survey reports a functional job in a $150,000 to $250,000 salary range, with rare exceptions the $200,000 midpoint becomes the range bottom in the mind of the survey user ("don't we expect above-average performance?") This view almost automatically increases the pay of many executives. Furthermore, the survey uses job title as the measure of value, whereas the responsibilities of the position are the real yardstick. The sales vice president responsible for pricing, for example, is far more valuable than one without this authority. But the job title does not measure this differential, which my experience suggests yields an important upward tilt to executive compensation.

Another aspect of compensation surveys bears directly on CEO pay: the top-down focus of all executive surveys. The CEO sits at the apex of the executive pyramid, from which all top jobs are valued. This approach seemed reasonable thirty-odd years ago when the first American Management Association Executive Compensation Survey was put together but now shows signs of having outlived its usefulness. Top management compensation—with its salary, cash bonus, deferred bonus, long-term contingent bonus, stock options, benefits, and other perks—has simply become an unmeasurable basis of comparison.

Furthermore, the SEC has recently ruled that companies no longer need report some forms of compensation. One of these, the contingent bonus, is becoming popular and substantial. It could readily replace the normal cash bonus, which is reportable, and the contingency can be made easy or difficult to attain at the board's discretion. The ordinary deferred bonus need not be reported either, until paid.

The Japanese compensation system—building the pay structure from the bottom up—has much to recommend it. Indeed, had it been adopted a decade ago, the inflation in management compensation almost certainly would have been under far better control today. The spread between the hourly worker and the U.S. chief executive has widened far more than is generally recognized. In the last decade alone, compensation changes noted earlier indicate that the percentage increase in the average chief executive's spendable income probably doubled that of foremen and hourly workers. Today we tend to forget the relatively low level of the marginal tax rate and the number of devices for adding to executive income.

A wide variety of consultants have assumed an important role in the management process. When executive compensation is involved, two very normal human attributes have tended to boost pay levels. Increasingly, company executives seem to regard raising pay levels good for the company (it means better performance, doesn't it?). For their part, the consultants like to satisfy this well-meaning desire of the executive and frequently have substantial other income from the client to protect. This could create a conflict of interest, for consultant recommendations below the expectations of the executive might not be well received. Further, as time goes on, the consultant may come to regard the executive rather than the company as his client. This attitude has been known to produce results not in the company's best interest.

The shortage of executive talent and the growing number of staff jobs have made the executive recruiter important to many companies that are either growing rapidly or poorly training their executives. Indeed, inadequate executive development is so widespread in industry that long-established companies are the biggest source of income for most recruiting firms, a fact that puts no feather in top management's cap.

Two aspects of the recruiter's work push up the compensation structure of the client: the need to make the offer attractive to the sought-after outside executive and the fact that the headhunter's fee is a percentage (usually one-third) of the final pay package. The pressure further increases if the compensation agreed on is above the company's present structure, as it frequently is. It then becomes necessary to boost the entire structure or suffer morale problems.

The upward pressure on executive compensation stemming from these nonstructural forces does not come into play until directors and top management make decisions involving these forces. However, there is little question that each force has helped ratchet top-level pay as a result of thoughtless and substantial usage in some companies.

The Board of Directors

The board of directors has legal responsibility for setting the compensation of company officers. Since the pay of the entire top echelon tends to move in tandem—and has for decades—the compensation increase awarded the chief executive is reflected all the way down the executive structure. Thus, if they overpay the chief executive and other officers, directors usually inflate the standard for the entire executive organization.

A board often works at a disadvantage when it makes compensation decisions. Most board members come from a variety of industries, each with its own profit-and-loss levers and environments; most have little day-to-day knowledge of individual executives' performance; some are principals in firms doing professional work for the company at substantial fees and hence risk having conflicts of interest.

Board members, therefore, depend heavily on chief executives for guidance in making compensation decisions. In effect, chief executives signal what they think they are worth by the increases they propose for their subordinates. If the executive happens to regard money as *the* measure of success—as many do—it will not take long for the pay structure to reflect this attitude. Since a goodly proportion of board members owe their appointment to the chief executive, with whom they are friends, they tend to accept his or her proposals. This tendency is reinforced when directors are retired or near retirement, for board membership is highly regarded as a retirement activity. Being invited to remain on the board each year means not only keeping active but also bringing in a comfortable income. Directors' fees in the $25,000 to $40,000 annual range are common, and a few companies pay directors pensions for life of half or more of their fees when the directors go off their boards.

One important change in board composition over the years has been the increase in the number of board members who are chief executives of other companies. The attitude often seems to be "you come on my board, and I'll join yours." Directors are honorable men and women, but a risk is obvious: the urge to be mutually supportive is real, for chief executives of big companies have similar problems in this increasingly predatory corporate world. The exchange of board memberships is often accompanied by membership on compensation committees.

As a consequence of these conditions, the attitude of boards toward compensation has changed. Not long ago, the retired president and chief executive became chairman, and one or more family retainers were directors. These board members usually felt company-protective and spent the company's money carefully, as though it were their own. This attitude provided a balance to the power of the president and chief executive. Today, with professional management dominating most boards, the attitude is better described as executive-protective. It is interesting that golden parachutes for executives and pensions for directors came onto the scene at about the same time.

The dominant board member—the chief executive—has also changed in outlook and background. His predecessor of a few decades ago was usually a hands-on line manager with sales, manufacturing, or engineering experience. He seldom served on other company boards. He spent a lot of time visiting plants and customers. Like the successful general, he recognized the leadership value of being with his troops. He involved himself in such nitty-gritty activities as establishing a compensation structure, evaluating executive jobs, and assessing individuals' performance. In those days it was not unusual for the chief executive to spend a week or more seeing to it that executive bonuses reflected penalty as well as reward, a practice the late Alfred P. Sloan, Jr., followed when he was chairman of General Motors.

Today's chief executive is more likely to have a staff background in law, finance, or accounting. He or she deals with a larger organization—a more impersonal one—and usually has only minimal experience in manufacturing, sales, and engineering. If the one hundred largest companies are a reasonable sample, we can see that four out of five chief executives have an average of three outside directorships, and one of these is outside the home city, so the executive spends considerable time on someone else's business.

Most directors will agree that an adequate contribution to the typical board requires at least ten full days a year (if they take preparation for board meetings into account). Major committee memberships add to this total. Thus, it is reasonable to expect the active executive sitting on three boards of other companies to spend thirty or more working days a year on the problems of companies other than his own. That's nearly one-seventh of his or her available working time.

One result of this outside time commitment is that many of today's chief executives do not provide the same degree of personal leadership to their troops as did their predecessors. Plants and customers are visited only occasionally as a matter of ceremony. There is also evidence that many chief executives have retreated from the tedium of trying to reward and penalize subordinates on the basis of personal knowledge of individual performance. These "details" they turn over to their staffs.

The Changed Mores

Every organized group has its customs, and industry is no exception. In the early postwar years company loyalty was a powerful cultural force. Executives expected to complete their careers with the same company; hence, they had every reason to regard company interests as their interests. This made "company money" something to be protected. Since there were no compensation surveys, internal equity in pay relationships was what counted. If business was bad, no pay increase meant that the executives were helping the company and in turn protecting their jobs.

Company loyalty was a key element in corporate discipline and made for the unity of action that characterizes an effective team. Promotion was the number one incentive under these conditions, and executives willingly accepted corporate decisions that disadvantaged them—like moving their families—for the common good.

Inflation, compensation surveys, and the ubiquitous recruiters changed all that. Money became the measure of success to a large and increasing proportion of the executive population at a time when a job change was worth two to five times the salary added by the average company's promotion increase. As a result, promotion lost out to changing employers as the primary incentive and had the effect of putting self-interest ahead of company interest. This self-interest, in turn, weakened company discipline.

In the intervening years, many of these then-young executives had reached the top as chief executives and directors. The compensation decisions of boards in recent years seem to indicate that their belief in money as the measure of success is still strong. No doubt this viewpoint helps explain the willingness of directors to vote for golden parachutes, to cancel high-priced options in favor of lower-priced ones, and to vote pensions for themselves. The rationale, of course, is that these actions are "competitively necessary," as one director put it. Many well-run companies, however, apparently resist taking such steps without suffering in the marketplace.

Somehow, company money seems less sacrosanct these days. The huge option profits that executives are reporting frequently result from large option grants and the replacement of higher-priced options with lower-priced ones when the stock market declines. The year-by-year actions of directors in this regard are not only overlooked in the fine print of proxy statements but lost in the mists of time. Few stockholders are aware of the amount of stock awarded executives over the years. A number of big companies have allocated 15 percent or more of their outstanding shares as options to executives.

WHAT TO DO

Most of us regard a million dollars with awe. This undoubtedly was a major factor in the storm unleashed in the business press by the million-dollar executive and probably explains why few people really believe an executive is worth $1 million or more a year. Indeed, there is a growing feeling that top executives are taking advantage of their power over the corporate purse. So industry has a problem—one that is likely to get worse if not given attention.

The average person respects the contribution the entrepreneur makes to creating jobs and fostering growth and rarely begrudges the millions of dollars the entrepreneur's efforts bring. Similarly, the executive who rescues a nearly bankrupt Chrysler or reshapes the ailing Kresge Company to create the fabulously successful K mart Corporation is widely recognized as being worth millions to the shareholders.

But most chief executives are administrators. They are responsible for managing the affairs of a company whose products and markets earlier executives have developed. Most hold the helm for only a few years, closely following policies that others have established. Yet more than one-third of the largest company chief executives who received $1 million or more in 1983 had held the job for only three years or less. Several of the highest paid had two years or less experience as chief executives.

In light of the foregoing, the disinterested observer can hardly be blamed for believing that a problem exists and that the board of directors is the crux of that problem. Too many directors appear to act as part of top management rather than as monitors capable of and willing to reward and penalize management's performance in furthering company interests.

Disclose Compensation Figures

I suspect that publicity would do more to correct the compensation imbalance at the top-management level than any other single action. Many companies obviously do their best to soft-pedal compensation information in their proxy statements—as though they were embarrassed to discuss it—by using techniques such as fine print, footnotes, and scattering the various compensation devices in a way that makes getting year-to-year comparisons or totals difficult.

As indicated earlier, the SEC has actually encouraged this tendency by permitting deferred compensation—either cash or contingent—to be excluded from reporting requirements until paid. Thus, it is virtually impossible to judge an officer's compensation for a given year. Further, when these deferred items are paid to the executive, they will distort comparisons with both the previous and the following year.

To help shareholders assess company performance, most companies provide a balance sheet record going back five or ten years in their proxy statements. Officer compensation data, however, are limited to one year and make comparisons difficult for the average stockholder. It seems to me that industry—perhaps under the leadership of the Business Round-table—could keep the government from intruding in this area by agreeing to publish a minimum of three-year comparisons that provide the stockholder with fully disclosed and easily understandable compensation figures.

The listing should probably include salary, cash bonus, deferred income, option profits, benefits—the total package. Stock option grants have become so large and so frequently repeated that perhaps companies should also report the total percentage of outstanding shares given as options since the company has started issuing them.

Most senior executives who accept membership on another company's board usually rationalize this action as helpful to their own companies. Since their own companies pay them rather well and they take time off from their own business to help someone else, it seems to me that they should turn over any remuneration received as outside directors to their companies. After retirement, of course, they would keep the money. At the very least, the income that active executives receive as outside board members should be separately reported in their own companies' proxy statements for the scrutiny of shareholders. Some CEOs receive substantial income from outside directorships.

Make Board Changes

Other less important but potentially useful steps could be taken. Suppose, for example, that industry went back to having the president as chief executive, with the chairmanship reserved for the retired CEO. To be sure, the retired chief executive would be looking over the CEO's shoulder, and the new person would probably resent such surveillance. But this step would be helpful in providing some balance to the power of today's CEO with the board.

Knowledge is power, and adding a few well-chosen line and staff subordinates of the chief executive to the board would be of considerable benefit to the outside directors. The improved understanding of operational problems, too, would help restore a more reasonable balance of power to the board. The obvious risk, of course, is that these second-echelon executives would be under the thumb of the CEO. There are risks both ways, however, and it seems to me that operational knowledge is so important at the board level that the chance should be taken. Furthermore, the company would benefit from the incentive that the opportunity for board membership brings to the promotion process.

Having the chief executive of another company on a board of directors has obvious advantages, for that CEO faces similar problems. Swapping board memberships, however, has a coziness reminiscent of the old-boy network that leaves something to be desired. The exchange of compensation committee memberships is also suspect on the same grounds.

Outside board memberships are socially and financially attractive, but they do take time. Since most active executives complain about a lack of time, a policy of no outside board memberships would help. A number of the best-run U.S. companies seem to do quite well with such a policy, as do the Japanese.

Retired executives have several potential advantages as board members. Most important, they can be chosen for their experience and mental vigor. If the search is well done, it is not difficult to find out about people having specific talents from either their competitors or from those with whom they have worked. Too many executives join boards of their friends, whereas retired executives should be sought out for their talents—and their independence.

Retired executives also have time. They no longer have day-by-day responsibilities and can devote more of this scarce commodity to developing an ongoing working knowledge of company activities on an organized basis for the benefit of other board members. Being exposed to second- and third-echelon subordinates in pursuit of such a goal, they would also be helpful in succession planning and compensation decisions.

Other experimental approaches will obviously be needed if boards are to do their job effectively, but the important point is for industry to show signs of putting its house in order before the government steps in. The ineptness of some boards in handling top-management compensation recently is an early warning that industry should not ignore.

The widespread state of mind among executives that money is the measure of success may well be the biggest single hurdle. It took several decades to reach full flower and may yield only as time passes and mores change. In light of the potential stresses between workers and management, however, as well as possible government intervention, making something happen certainly seems worth the effort.

NOTES

1. See, for example, William J. Abernathy, Kim B. Clark, and Alan M. Kantrow, "The New Industrial Competition," *Harvard Business Review* (September–October 1981), p. 68.

2. "The Fortune Directory of the Largest U.S. Industrial Corporations," *Fortune,* April 30, 1984, p. 274.

3. John A. Byrne, "Who Gets the Most Pay," *Forbes,* June 4, 1984, p. 96.

PART I-B

The Impact of Executive Pay on Performance

4

DOES COMPENSATION MOTIVATE EXECUTIVES?

David J. McLaughlin

EXECUTIVES DOWNPLAY THE IMPORTANCE of money in analyzing their own motives, and overemphasize rewards in managing their subordinates. One friend's explanation for accepting a new job typified this ambivalence: "I am going to be getting *a lot* more money, but the real reason I have accepted their offer is that I can expect to become a senior vice president two to three years earlier." He then talked about the compensation package for half an hour. One recalls an admonition of Artemus Ward, the humorist, "When a fellow says it's not the money, but the principle of the thing—it's the money."

Executives are not only ambivalent about money, they are also uneasy about its impact. They realize that compensation can undermine motivation, a central thesis in one of the most widely reprinted articles from the *Harvard Business Review*—Frederick Herzberg's "One More Time: How Do You Motivate Employees?"[1] Herzberg claimed that factors such as achievement, recognition, the work itself, and advancement stimulate employees while other factors lead to dissatisfaction. He categorized salary as a major source of dissatisfaction. Subsequent studies have shown that Herzberg's model was wrong and that most of the factors he listed could either motivate or "demotivate," depending on the circumstances.[2]

The notion persists that money can be a very dangerous instrument in the management process. Edward L. Deci, a psychologist and sociologist who teaches at the University of Rochester, is sometimes cited as a source for the thesis that attaching a reward to a task always undermines a person's motivation. Actually, Deci's findings are more complex. He found that when individuals are *involved* in setting the targets and goals that are the basis for an incentive, *and when the feedback is handled correctly*, pay can be a positive reinforcement:

> [R]ewards, like feedback, when used to convey to people a sense of appreciation for work well done, will tend to be experienced informationally

59

and will maintain or enhance intrinsic motivation, but when they are used to motivate people, they will surely be experienced controllingly and will undermine intrinsic motivation.[3]

Despite such cautions, management is putting even more emphasis on compensation in an effort to stimulate better performance from employees and executives. This book contains a rich array of pay schemes. Today's average executive receives a dozen or more forms of remuneration, most of which are justified in order to "attract, retain, and motivate" key personnel.

Compensation serves many purposes, and it seems to work. Money is certainly a big factor in attracting personnel. While most new MBAs do not take the highest paying offer, they rarely take the lowest. People do move from company to company, sometimes for the money, and almost always with extra compensation or a new reward (like a bonus or stock option). The executive search business is a multibillion-dollar-a-year industry, built on the premise that talent will move from one company to another.

There is also irrefutable evidence that compensation affects retention. Individual executives stay in a job—even when they are desperate to leave—until the year-end bonus is paid, or the pension becomes vested, or the long-term performance plan award is determined.

Anyone who has run a business knows that compensation can affect behavior. What executive has not seen a turnaround in the performance of an individual after a difficult review and compensation discussion? Who has not worried about his or her bonus in a tough year? The thoughtful chief executive is more worried that incentives will provoke the wrong behavior than that incentives will not motivate participants. The allocation of incentive pools and the size of the bonus given different departments contributed to the demise of Lehman Brothers several years ago. The annual bonus plan at General Motors (where payouts sometimes topped 300 percent in the 1960s and 1970s) contributed to a short-term orientation in that company. Even the Chinese communists have learned to be careful about incentives. While I was lecturing on personnel management in China in 1987, several officials recounted the story of an experimental bonus scheme for bus drivers in Hunan province. The idea was to stimulate them to save gas by giving an extra payment to drivers whose fuel consumption was below the standard set for the route. They canceled the program after six months when they discovered that in order to save gas, many drivers avoided stops, turned off the engine to coast down long hills, failed to come to a complete stop, and so forth. Gas consumption dropped, but repair bills skyrocketed and service deteriorated. (If you have ridden on a Chinese bus, this is hard to imagine.)

What does all this mean? Can you motivate executives with money? Is compensation the "hygiene factor" that Herzberg described, or can it occasionally contribute to satisfaction, and even a positive change in behavior and improved performance? What principles guide the effective use of compensation?

This chapter will explore these complex questions in several sections. First, I will critically review the dominant psychological theories of motivation. My principal objective in this section will be to distinguish between *transactional* motivation and *enduring* motivation. The second section will present guidelines on how to motivate employees with compensation at a transactional level. In the third section, I will assess the major forms of reward to determine the motivational value inherent in their design and typical administration. The final section will return to the subject of enduring motivation and the role of remuneration in this largely self-driven process.

MOTIVATIONAL THEORIES

Psychological theories of motivation have contributed to the confusion in industry about money and its effect on employee behavior.

Of the dozens of motivational concepts and models, there is not a single model or theory that explains and can predict what will motivate employees overall. However, even work that is largely discredited often contains important truths. Take B. F. Skinner's theory of reinforcement.[4] Skinner thought that it is possible to understand, control, and manipulate behavior with reinforcement. This is hardly the basis of modern personnel management. Yet some of Skinner's findings are powerful and are not disputed by even the most humanistic of psychologists. For example, positive reinforcement is more effective than negative feedback (a rule many managers have yet to master); variable reinforcement works best; and immediate reinforcement is better than delayed rewards (one of the reasons why special award plans that give immediate feedback and recognition work better than most bonus plans).

An effective motivational template, then, involves an amalgamation of concepts, beliefs, and insights. What is important in establishing company policy and in adopting specific pay schemes is to be deliberate about the assumptions made about people and their behavior. One of the biggest problems with the personnel function in the United States is that many of the assumptions implicit in compensation programs are highly questionable psychologically. For example, job evaluation assumes that people should and normally do fit into jobs that are created by management, evaluated and assigned salary levels by the personnel department, and defined as a set of predetermined duties. This is an industrial engineering construct and lacks a dynamic concept of human growth. It ignores the obvious differences in personality that shape people's approach to work, and it constitutes a control approach to human resource management. Compensation practices are laden with control mechanisms, as I will show. Leaders, like IBM, abandoned grade levels and job descriptions for executives years ago.

Some theories that are useful at one level can be harmful if extended into a broader concept of the management of people at work. The re-inforcement theory cited earlier, for example, advocates a control approach to employees and was formulated about the same time that Frederick Taylor introduced scientific management. The compensation construct of the Taylor/Skinner model of human behavior is built on a theory of reward and punishment, an approach that persists to this day, especially at the executive level. Harry Levinson calls it the "carrot-and-stick philosophy . . . which imprison[s] people psychologically and assume[s] that they are jackasses to be manipulated." [5]

It is important to realize that behind most "motivational" theories is a larger concept of human behavior. The irony is that some of the most useful techniques for short-term management involve a questionable model for an overall human response philosophy. The reverse is also true. Some of the most fertile psychological concepts are of limited use operationally—in the daily management of people—but are of tremendous value in presenting a humanistic model of people at work in an environment that facilitates their development and contribution. Abraham Maslow's five-stage hierarchy of human needs is a case in point. [6] Maslow argued that biological needs must be largely satisfied before safety needs become important, the need for safety precedes the need to belong, and so forth, through the need for esteem, and finally, self-actualization. Maslow's hierarchy proved to be of limited value in explaining specific behavior, and most experts now discount him and other so-called content theorists whose work focused on innate drives and the specific variables that influence behavior. A major criticism of the approach is that it ignores the fact that man is a thinking animal. Despite this skepticism and caution, the business world has embraced and popularized many of the content theories. One reason is that they provide an uplifting growth-oriented view of personnel. Although Herzberg's list of motivators and demotivators cited earlier proved hard to replicate and was wrong on a number of counts, his analysis of the personnel management theories of the 1960s was brilliant and his concepts led to the job enrichment movement. He is credited with being one of the first psychologists to reach a management audience with the message that personal growth stems from the work itself and that psychological growth is a precondition of job satisfaction.

As a practical matter, it seems that people do need to be directed—and occasionally controlled—at a very specific level. In other words, companies need *transactional* tools of motivation that encourage the successful completion of a particular task or goal, as well as a broader, uplifting concept of human development and behavior that provokes *enduring* motivation. Viewed this way, psychological research and motivational models begin to fall into place.

Expectancy theory is a creditable and sound psychological construct that can be applied to specific transactions—a given effort and a given result. One of the most important contributors to this useful theory is Edward Lawler.[7] Expectancy theory argues that the level of effort an individual expends is based on judgments about the likelihood he or she will succeed (expectancies) and the attractiveness (value) of the final outcome. Exhibit 4-1, a schematic of the expectancy theory model, shows factors that influence the judgments and the value of the outcome (say, a salary increase or stock option gain), including feedback loops (first pointed out by Lawler and Lyman Porter) and specific plan features and experiences that the company can influence. Exhibit 4–2 illustrates some of the major assessments that an individual might make in determining the value of a given stock option, and includes both "objective" and "judgmental" considerations: the features of the option itself and personal factors such as prior experience with options.

Although the expectancy theory may seem complicated, human behavior itself is complicated—and the operative implications of the theory make sense: the greater the value placed on the outcome, the greater the effort expended. As Ronald Biggs, the mastermind of the £2.6-million Great Train Robbery, said, "I became a crook because I needed the money."[8] The average executive, too, will work harder for a greater reward.

I will return to the concept of "enduring motivation," but let us first see how far one can take transactional motivation. Although the expectancy theory model may be valid, it is hard to apply to a dynamic work situation

EXHIBIT 4-1
Motivation Under Expectancy Theory
$M = [E \rightarrow P] \times [(P \rightarrow O) (V)]$

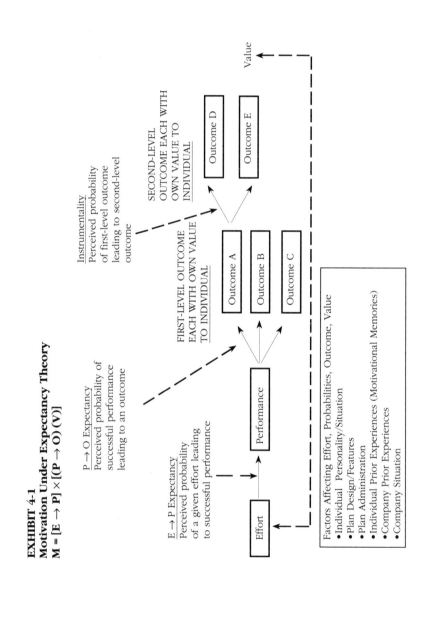

EXHIBIT 4-2
Illustration of Factors Affecting Value Given a Stock Option Award

Objective Considerations

- Earnings history
- Debt equity ratio
- Distribution of stock holdings
- Size and competitive structure of market in which the company competes
- Company and industry PE ratio, BETA, etc.

Judgmental Considerations

- Confidence in CEO and top-management team
- Belief in industry
- Evaluation of where market is going over time frame
- Assessment of what aspects of company will appeal to investor
- Future trends in economy

Probability Assessments

- Adequacy of resources needed to achieve results
- Ability of management to improve performance
- Degree to which improved performance will lead to higher earnings
- Probability that market will recognize improved performance and increased EPS
- Odds of realizing a gain in stock option
- Magnitude of gain

Value Given to Option

Stock Option Details

- Exercise price
- Award size
- Vesting provisions
- Exercise rules upon termination, death, etc.

Personal Factors

- Prior experience with options
- Risk profile
- Importance of building net worth
- Time frame of one's career at company

(or pay decision, for that matter) because of the number of variables and the complexity of their interaction. In my work, it has proved more useful to discuss transactional motivation as a series of rules or guidelines.

Guideline 1: The potential compensation must be real and tangible, and not just a vague promise. This is not as obvious as it appears. Much of executive compensation involves some form of future promise. Often, management cannot formally commit itself to a planned compensation action, particularly in executive-level hiring. There might not be any shares left in the stock option program, for example; or the annual incentive plan might be undergoing redesign; or the awards themselves (under a performance unit plan, for example) may be determined by the board of directors each year, so their value may change from year to year.

A CEO who wants to make an award real but who has to wait for stockholder or board approval should be careful of what he or she says, as the new president of a *Fortune* 500 company learned recently. He granted a sizable stock option to a new hire without getting board approval and was embarrassed six weeks later to discover that the exercise price was going to be 30 percent higher on the real date of grant. These days, boards of directors often do not want to make a permanent, ongoing commitment to certain plans, particularly long-term incentives (one of four such programs change each year). Other executive extras—supplemental retirement plans, for example—often are not formally documented, even in larger companies.

To motivate effectively, make a special effort to document the plan, illustrate the potential value under a variety of scenarios, and make the whole thing tangible by giving the recipient a formal letter, a contract, or a certificate. If you have to make promises, manage expectations carefully. And keep in mind that finalizing a new executive compensation program is like building an addition on a house: It takes twice as long as the most reasonable estimate.

Guideline 2: Be sure the executives understand the ground rules and commit themselves to the process. Tom Watson of IBM once said, "Until there is understanding there is no real basis for motivation."[9] In twenty-five years of consulting, I can remember only a few companies where the executives could explain how their bonus award would change with varying levels of company, unit, and individual performance. Sometimes this was because the plan involved a complex series of multiplications, but usually it was because the program was not clearly communicated and continually reinforced.

A bonus plan is relatively easy to explain, but the new generation of long-term incentives is more difficult. The vesting or earn-out period of most performance unit plans is clear, but the payout schedule is usually more obscure than management would like to think. Simple, you say, if what is required is to achieve a certain earnings-per-share growth during the three-year term of the plan (that is, you get 50 percent of the award at cumulative earnings-per-share growth of 8 percent, 75 percent payout at 10 percent, and full payout at 12 percent). The experience of one of the five largest diversified financial services companies illustrates how "simple" is really complex. A crisis meeting was called a week before the board meeting to establish the first payout under the performance unit plan. Everyone attended: the president, the CFO, the head of human resources, the controller, and the outside auditor. Although the plan (fortunately, devised by another consultant) contained several pages of explanation and definition, this august group could not agree on the precise amount of the first award. No one had documented the statistical ground rules (for example, was compound earnings going to be calculated from point to point, or by using a regression?). But that was not the real problem. In the three years since the plan had gone into effect there had been one acquisition and two divestments, a major write-off in one business, an extraordinary gain in another, and a significant change in accounting policies that reduced short-term income. As a result, there were at least three payouts that could be justified under the plan. Is it any wonder that the executives did not have the foggiest idea what they stood to gain?

The harsh truth is that most executives do not really understand the basis of payout under most long-term incentive plans used today. The latest trends in this area (the use of a performance matrix to relate payout to a combination of earnings growth and improved return on investment, for example) may be accurate and useful performance measures, but they increase complexity and decrease understanding. For this reason, most executives discount the value of the incentive and file the plan in a drawer until the end of the cycle.

I am convinced that you have to simplify compensation schemes if they are going to motivate executives. This is possible even with a performance share scheme. In 1984, a privately held computer peripherals company put in a performance unit plan that is simplicity itself. Each year 1 percent of the pretax income goes into a pool for distribution (with interest) three years later. The board can add up to an additional 1 percent to the pool, based on its assessment of management's success in achieving the company's long-term objectives and strategy. Although the process is complex, all the participants know the factors that are evaluated (e.g., new product development). Communication is timely and simple. Each year the executives know how they are doing and what their potential payout is. This plan has not only been effective in holding key talent in an industry characterized by raids, but it is one of the few long-term incentive programs executives say they understand.

Guideline 3: To be motivated, employees have to believe that they really can influence the results that are to be achieved. One of the reasons that salary increases are not very effective motivators is that even top executives feel that the size of increases is outside their control. In some companies, the bonus plan is based on an esoteric companywide formula. Or, particularly in small, privately held companies, there is no formula at all: The bonus is a "deus ex machina" judgment by the founder. Larger companies have a different problem. Nothing discourages or disheartens a key executive in a highly profitable business unit more than finding out that his or her bonus was severely depressed, or even eliminated, because the overall corporate profits did not clear some hurdle he or she did not even know about. Most companies have addressed this problem by decentralizing the incentive process and basing payout on unit results.

Although goal setting can help a company meet Guideline 2 (promoting understanding) and Guideline 3 (assuring personal control over the results), it is a trickier and more limiting method than most companies acknowledge. It is difficult to set meaningful goals for many jobs in any company, and extraordinarily difficult for all jobs in a rapidly growing enterprise. But the biggest risk is that predetermined goals tied to a budget-driven process do not allow for personal initiative. Psychologist Harry Levinson underscored the dangers inherent in goal setting when he said, "No objectives will have significant incentive power if they are forced choices unrelated to a man's underlying dreams, wishes, and personal aspirations."[10]

Guideline 4: Whatever must be done to receive a reward must involve the right degree of challenge. If a reward is contingent on the achievement of a stated goal (true of most short- and long-term incentives), people will be motivated most effectively if the objective is set at a difficult but achievable level. Set it too low and people coast, too high and they give up.

Research has shown that the more difficult the performance goal, the better the performance, provided the goal is accepted by the individual. This truth leads inexperienced companies to set goals too high, particularly when they are introducing an incentive plan. One compensation committee I recall wondered why its long-term incentive plan was not working. This marginal company, undergoing a massive restructuring and turnaround, had established a return-on-investment goal that was in the upper quartile of the competitive universe. (Companies can get around this dilemma by setting progressively higher objectives for two or three cycles, or by using relative movement against a competitive universe.) Setting corporate or divisional profit objectives is a special gift. Art Maine, who headed the HR function at Sherwin Williams during its dramatic turnaround in the early 1980s, once said, "You have to make people winners and build their confidence."[11]

Guideline 5: Keep the reward open-ended. Compensation planners tend to cap compensation with salary increase limits, bonus maxima, dollar limits on commissions, long-term incentive award ceilings, and so forth. The usual justification is to control costs and prevent runaway payoffs, but the net effect is to diminish motivation. Ross Perot, the founder of Electronic Data Systems Corporation, left IBM principally because the design of the commission formula effectively capped his commissions as a salesman. Psychological research shows that the size of the potential payoff has a great impact on how much employees value an incentive. Warren Buffet, the legendary head of Berkshire Hathaway, uses an incentive plan without a ceiling for each of the individuals who run his businesses.[12]

The discouraging effect of a cap is most apparent in long-term incentives, because capital accumulation is likely to be integral to an executive's long-term objectives and dreams. Ceilings are least appropriate in a new venture, where the ultimate payoff is an initial public offering and the founders hope the company will be another Apple Computer or Xerox. One of the advantages of the stock option is that it is open-ended; only the market sets the ultimate price. Any substitute equity plan in a private company or startup venture of a large public company should be similarly open-ended. Unfortunately, the typical personnel department likes to control and cap. One of the worst examples of this approach occurred several years ago when a large chemical company made an arrangement with the founding management team of a startup division to split the profits above stated return goals and then got nervous when it looked like the payout might exceed $5 million. The proposed cap nearly ruined the venture.

Guideline 6: To motivate, the reward has to be large enough to be significant to the individual. There are no absolute answers on how big is big enough. Most surveys show that there is a common range of bonus targets (from 10 percent to 15 percent of salary at the bottom to 50 percent to 60 percent at the top); there is similar "competitive" data for stock option awards. In establishing the size of an incentive, most companies develop guidelines (usually hierarchical) built around survey data, but that is a narrow way of thinking. Motivation is about what is right and significant for an individual in a given set of circumstances. Companies often show flexibility when they recruit new executives, but then make everybody adhere to rigid guidelines and rules. In general, companies are too fainthearted in establishing the scale of reward.

Another problem with rules is that they are often rigged to reduce the payout if targets are not reached, but fail to raise the payout if goals are exceeded. Speaking of most managers' conservative approach to risk, John Hammond observes, "I strongly suspect the trouble lies in the control systems we have set up to reward and punish managers. These systems are generally hard on the managers if they have short-run failures, or at least the managers think the systems work that way. Moreover, the added reward to the manager for a huge financial success is perceived to be a relatively small increment to the reward for simply 'doing a good job.' "[13]

In establishing the scale of an incentive payout, three questions should be asked. First, what bonuses has the executive received in the past? Second, what will make a difference in his or her standard of living or net worth? Third, what will enable the individual to realize a personal goal? The last question is particularly pertinent to younger, fast-track managers who might be saving for the down payment on a house, for example.

Guideline 7: Pay very well for good performance and significantly extra for truly superior results. Pay-for-performance is the most widely advocated and imperfectly delivered pay dictum in the land. Failure to deliver often erodes motivation. The effect of effort on performance, and of performance on reward, is at the heart of the expectancy model I discussed earlier. Failure to pay a good performer is one of the most commonly perceived inequities. It is a serious problem below the executive level, where companies still rely primarily on salaries, which are difficult to relate to performance except over a long period of time. At the executive level, where there is a richer array of tools, companies often fail to grant large enough increases when someone is promoted, fail to differentiate bonuses sufficiently on the upside of the performance curve, and fail to weed out marginal performers early enough.

The limitations inherent in incentives is particularly troublesome in most executive compensation programs. Ed Lawler laments: "Overall, the United States has become a society in which the profits of companies are at risk as a function of performance, but the pay of individuals is affected only at the extremes of performance."[14] In many companies, even extraordinary results do not lead to the maximum bonus. This was apparent in one $200-million manufacturing company, where I had an opportunity to interview the ten top managers after they had completed a difficult turnaround and delivered profits that were three times the amount expected. Although the board had given generous bonuses, it was shocked to learn how dissatisfied and angry the executive group was. The bonus plan limited payouts to a maximum of 50 percent of pay for officers, which was annoying but accepted as a reality. But even in this, the best of years, no one received the full 50 percent. Instead, bonuses ranged from 45 percent to 48 percent of salary. As one executive put it: "First we walked on water, and then we ran on water. What do they want? It just is not fair."

Guideline 8: Make the reward proximate to the event. One of the most effective pay devices is the special award, the amount of which is less significant than the prompt reinforcement of a significant contribution. This kind of award is consistent with a theory of performance appraisal called "critical incidents," which calls for frequent feedback on performance based on every significant event. Proximate awards are usually random awards; a body of research argues that such spontaneous, immediate reinforcement (called variable ratio reinforcement) is a more powerful influence on behavior than a regular schedule of bonus payments.

In general, companies have been slow to exploit the potential of the special award. IBM has an extended range of "event-driven" special awards that range from dinner for two to $100,000 grants. The bulk of executive plans do not follow the "proximate" principle, however. Most rewards are bestowed according to accounting or operational schedules. But there is no reason a company cannot respond to extraordinary managerial contributions. A California client of mine uses a beer bash to celebrate extraordinary accomplishments such as major new orders. Another client keeps a special pool of restricted stock for chairman's grants. And quite a number of companies give special, out-of-cycle stock option awards.

EFFECTIVENESS OF VARIOUS PAY VEHICLES

How do these guidelines apply to specific forms of reward? Exhibit 4–3 rates the motivational effectiveness of fourteen of the most common forms of executive pay as they are typically designed and administered. The shading represents the extent to which each type of remuneration fully, partially, or rarely meets the criteria discussed in the preceding sec-

EXHIBIT 4-3
Summary Assessment of Ability of

Compensation Plan	Real, Tangible	Clear, Understandable	Controllable	Measurable	Provides Recognition	Uncapped, Open-ended	Large enough	Linked to Performance	Fair, Equitable	Proximate, Timely	Random, Unexpected
Salary					N			N			
Salary Increase			N		N	N	N	N			
Annual Bonus		N	N			N	N				
Formula Incentive									N		
Special Award							N				
Profit Sharing			N		N		N				
Stock Option			N					N		N	
Restricted Stock							N				
Performance Share		N	N			N	N			N	
Performance Unit		N	N			N	N			N	
Deferred Comp.								N		N	
Pension		N	N			N					
SERP	N								N		
Contract		N									

tion. The negative highlights problem areas where there is a high risk that the compensation method will fail to motivate employees.

Note that the most common forms of pay—salary and bonus—run a high risk of causing negative reactions. The salary increase in particular is ineffective because it is outside the recipient's control; usually it is not large enough to provide recognition and, in most companies, performance has little effect on the increase. Moreover, Herzberg proved that salary treatment is often considered unfair and demotivating. The typical bonus has more potential to motivate. In contrast with salary programs,

Executive Compensation Vehicles to Motivate

Comment

Still hierarchical and tied to organization level in most companies. Should be market driven.

Range of increases too narrow in most companies and not tied to performance.

The trickiest pay device known. Can be designed to motivate.

Rare at executive level, but some CEOs have straight percentage profits.

An effective motivational device at all levels, rarely used with officers.

Too remote to motivate.

Executives tend to either over- or undervalue based on market. A big lure to those who do not have them.

The most popular long-term incentive.

Complex senior management vehicle.

Complex senior management vehicle.

Primarily a way to minimize taxes; cash flow/retirement planning vehicle.

Significant lump sum value if you can stay the course and live to collect.

Supplemental retirement can be critical for senior-level executives and executive hires.

More of a protection than a basic motivational tool.

Legend

▨ **Fully Meets Under Most Plans**

▨ **Partially Meets in Typical Design/Administration**

☐ **Rarely Meets**

N **Negative/Frequent Source of Demotivation**

whose limitations are inherent, most of the bonus negatives can be overcome. However, one half to two-thirds of the executive bonus plans in place today do not work, largely because they ignore the sound principles just reviewed.

The formula incentive, like a salesperson's commission, is an effective motivator, but it can be costly and is therefore rare in larger companies. It is often used in a turnaround (like Great Atlantic and Pacific Tea Company) or to "incent" a founder (Reebok International, Ltd.). One plan used by a large real estate developer is typical: The executive group of eight gets 5 percent of the pretax profits. The president gets 25 percent of the pot, and the seven others split the rest. In a good year, the payout exceeds 300 percent of the participants' salary, or over $1 million for the CEO. When rewards approach this magnitude, companies often modify the formula to impose a set-aside (to cover a minimum return for shareholders). This must be done with great skill to avoid dampening the effect of a direct incentive. Michael Eisner, the CEO of The Walt Disney Company, had his formula modified (he now receives 2 percent of net income *after* a 9 percent return on shareholders' equity) but he still earned a $6.7 million bonus in 1988.

Among long-term incentives, restricted stock is probably the most popular vehicle. It is more tangible than the option (there is a built-in floor value) and infinitely more understandable than the performance share or performance unit plan. Most compensation consultants, however, deride the typical restricted stock grant because it vests based on time rather than performance. This is a perfect illustration of how "experts" assume that motivation comes from outside the individual, as if the nature of the reward and the performance measurement system on which it is contingent are the beginning and end of the motivational equation. For some reason, compensation experts always try to design precise rules for processes that are inherently subjective. In fact, compensation is part of a relationship between the company and its personnel, and between a manager and a subordinate. When you have a vehicle whose characteristics make it an effective motivational tool in a world where such vehicles are rare indeed, you figure out how to overcome its limitations. For example, using restricted stock selectively to recognize the most promising young managers builds in performance considerations at the front end. So what if a few of your judgments are wrong?

Most benefits and perquisites are not really motivational devices. They are meant to provide protection, assure a comfortable retirement, or, in some cases, help hold the executive. Of course, just because most of these vehicles are not incentives does not mean that they should be avoided. Benefits are useful for attracting key personnel to the company and making it more expensive to lure them away.

But some companies have escalated their benefits and perks year after year in order to "be competitive." Twenty years ago, Herzberg observed that "people spend less time working for more money and more security than ever before, and the trend cannot be reversed. These benefits are no longer rewards, they are rights . . . unless the ante is continually raised, the psychological reaction of employees is that the company is turning back the clock."[15] Since then, of course, the number of forms of executive pay has at least tripled, and companies are having a hard time controlling the costs of some benefits like medical insurance. Despite the escalating pay, too many top executives are less motivated and often eager to cash out in a takeover. We need to simplify pay schemes and get back to plans with real motivational potential. We should also return to the original purpose of the stock option—to facilitate increased ownership.

More fundamentally, however, American industry must reflect deeply and broadly about stimulating enduring motivation. In 1987, Herzberg characterized most of what passed for motivation as movement, and went on to observe:

> Movement is a function of fear of punishment or failure to get extrinsic rewards. Motivation is a function of growth from getting intrinsic rewards out of interesting and challenging work. While the immediate behavioral results from movement and motivation appear alike, their dynamics, which produce vastly different long-term consequences, are different. Movement requires constant reinforcement and stresses short-term results. . . . Motivation is based on growth needs. It is an internal engine, and its benefits show up over a long period of time. Because the ultimate reward in motivation is personal growth, people don't need to be rewarded incrementally.[16]

The balance of this chapter outlines some of what we know about internal motivation, discusses the role of the company in facilitating and sustaining the "internal engine," and provides a few caveats about compensation management in the well-motivated organization.

ENDURING MOTIVATION

Businesses are not eleemosynary institutions. Their primary purpose is not to provide growth experiences for the people who work there, but to make a profit and deliver an adequate return to their shareholders. To survive and prosper, companies need a viable product/service, an approach to the marketplace that gives them a sustainable competitive advantage, and, most of all, good top leadership. A superior product, an early entry into a new market, and founders with towering skills can do much to attract talent to an organization.

Not all companies build an organization of highly motivated personnel. The companies that do have a special way of nurturing the talent that early success sends their way. They build a distinctive culture with a special set of values that is shared by the people who work there and who see a career in the company as a way to fulfill their own dreams and aspirations. In short, they have a highly motivated work force that is committed to the success of the enterprise.

Some of the large companies I have served over the years that succeeded in inspiring their employees include American Express, the Boeing Company, Bristol-Myers Company, Caterpillar, Inc., J. C. Penney Company, Inc., Merck & Co., Inc., International Business Machines Corporation, Minnesota Mining and Manufacturing Company (3M), and Mobil Corporation. As I reflect on motivation in these companies (and a score of smaller "successes in process"), it strikes me that they all create a purpose and a sustained vision that lifts up their employees and helps make work life important, whether they make aspirins, typewriters, or tractors.

Executive greed can destroy such a culture. The most poignant examples occur when a great old company becomes the target of a takeover. In Time Inc's recent takeover battle, many employees were convinced that money, not the good of the corporation, was the driving force behind the initial Time-Warner Communications deal (symbolized by Steven Ross's projected $180-million windfall). One Time staffer commented, "Maybe I am being naive or idealistic, but I believe that this is a special place, a company that makes a difference in the world, not just a collection of businesses to be busted by a corporate raider. When they tell us they are not in it for the money, they are just insulting us."[17]

Once again, there is evidence that compensation, particularly egregious cases of executive overcompensation, can demoralize not only an individual but also an entire work force. But what about money as a positive influence? Do leading companies do anything special in the compensation arena to foster motivation? Does money play a role in what I have called enduring motivation?

I am convinced that the creation of an effective, well-motivated work force initially has little to do with money. Great companies of any size manifest an overriding philosophy about people and how they treat them. Harry Levinson calls it a "psychological contract."[18] This contract consists of certain assumptions that the founders and managers make about people and is shaped by the values they subscribe to and look for in others. Compensation decisions (including the formative decisions about levels of pay, the extent of variation in salaries, and the approach to bonuses and stock ownership) are influenced by and subordinate to these assumptions. Particularly important are respect for the dignity of the individual, trust, honesty, and open communications. Underlying these values is a conviction that every employee matters.

These companies are more egalitarian in their outlook and share the wealth more broadly than their less progressive peers. The head of a truly great organization worries more about the troops than about the top brass. One of the sad things about the evolution of compensation in this country is that the gap between executives' and line workers' salaries has widened dramatically over the past decade. We are close to convincing this generation of workers that "it's every man for himself." Leading companies are more apt to use broad-based incentives, wide stock ownership, and fair retirement plans for all. Many great companies continue to use profit-sharing retirement plans (Procter & Gamble, for example), even though they can be more expensive and usually do not offer the same degree of leveraged payout for executives and the more common pension offers.

In progressive firms, a more egalitarian philosophy is pervasive. I was reminded of this when I was discussing what form and level of interest to credit to the deferred compensation accounts of the top executives of two *Fortune* 500 companies. In company A, the thought process went: What are other companies doing (i.e., what can we get away with) and what will give us the best return? In company B, the CEO cut the discussion short by saying, "I wouldn't feel comfortable using any other rate than that which was available to all employees in our thrift plan."

Great companies give a lot of attention to selecting raw talent. Goldman Sachs puts it well: "We make an unusual effort to identify and recruit the very best person for every job. Although our activities are measured in billions of dollars, we select our people one by one. In a service business we know that without the best people, we cannot be the best firm."[19] Wise firms are not just trying to get the best and brightest, they are also screening people at all levels for compatibility of values.

Another hallmark of a progressive firm is its fair treatment of those whom it eases out. McKinsey and Company in effect fires nine out of ten of the talented MBAs it brings in each year, through a six-year winnowing process. But it handles those nine in such a way that most show up for annual alumni meetings held all over the country; the former employees are among the firm's greatest salespeople.

The average industrial company does not have the up-or-out policy of the professional firm. Most people who join a business usually expect to stay. The compensation and benefit architecture is designed to retain and reward them for length of service, through vesting provisions. An important part of the psychological contract with employees involves a promise of commitment and security. Although not all firms have IBM's lifetime employment policy, the companies that endure are not places where employees are only as good as their last contribution; employees bank something over time. As a result, there is much less outside influence on compensation: Because they rarely hire outside executives, such firms can maintain internal pay equity relatively easy.

Several practices help leading companies inspire both transactional and enduring motivation. First, although they are strongly oriented toward performance and cultivate a meritocracy, real differentiation in compensation comes gradually, largely as a result of promotion instead of through sharp differences in the annual bonus given to executives at the same level. In other words, they treat their executives, even those who are failing, with dignity and even compassion. Second, there is more emphasis on teamwork in the incentive architecture. A few companies, such as 3M, pay identical bonuses as a percentage of salary to executives at the same organizational level. But even companies that adjust for individual performance give the most weight to group results. Third, progressive firms do not change programs as frequently, as one would expect in companies where core programs reflect enduring values more than tax laws or the latest trends. Fourth, communication is open and complete. Finally, such companies always seem to have a plan that, while it may have the same label as plans in other companies, is in fact a distinctive and integral part of their culture. For example, Bristol-Myers retained a quarterly incentive plan for executives for years, contrary to conventional wisdom, and IBM has always limited participation in its incentive plan to far fewer than would be predicted for a company of its size.

These characteristics do not translate automatically into an effective pay program or a well-motivated executive group. Many large companies have not been successful in maintaining an entrepreneurial environment or in adjusting to changing times. A new compensation program has often been a central tool in effecting necessary change. Coca-Cola's dramatic restricted stock awards are a good example.

Does money motivate? As the fundamental force in most people's lives, of course not. In the final analysis, motivation comes from within a person. The best a company can do is create an environment in which employees feel they can make a contribution and advance as far as talent and ambition will take them. But the compensation system—particularly the values and beliefs it implies—is a major element in the environment.

Compensation is clearly a factor in what propels people to choose some careers over others, to accept a specific job, and to perform at high levels.

It is not easy to motivate transactionally with money. It is even more difficult to administer compensation with a clear eye on motivation when there are so many other legitimate objectives that pay plans must meet.

NOTES

1. Frederick Herzberg, "One More Time: How Do You Motivate Employees?", *Harvard Business Review* (January–February 1968), pp. 109–120.

2. See J. P. Campbell, M. D. Dunnette, E. E. Lawler III, and K. E. Weick, Jr., *Managerial Behavior and Human Performance* (New York: McGraw-Hill, 1970).

3. E. L. Deci and R. M. Ryan, *Intrinsic Motivation and Self-Determination in Human Behavior* (New York: Plenum, 1987), p. 300.

4. B. F. Skinner, *Science and Human Behavior* (New York: Macmillan, 1953).

5. Harry Levinson, *The Great Jackass Fallacy* (Boston: Division of Research, Harvard Business School, 1973), pp. 15–16.

6. Abraham H. Maslow, *Motivation and Personality* (New York: Harper and Bros., 1954).

7. Edward E. Lawler III, *Effectiveness: A Psychological View* (New York: McGraw-Hill, 1971) and *Motivation in Work Organizations* (Monterey, CA: Brooks/Cole, 1973).

8. Quoted in *The Wall Street Journal*, February 2, 1981, p. 1.

9. Thomas Watson, *A Business and Its Beliefs: The Ideas That Helped Build IBM* (New York: McGraw-Hill, 1963), p. 55.

10. Harry Levinson, "Management by Whose Objectives?", *Harvard Business Review* (July–August 1970), p. 12.

11. Art Maine, discussion in a Senior Personnel Executive Forum Conference, Pebble Beach, CA, 1986.

12. Carl J. Loomis, "The Inside Story of Warren Buffet," *Fortune*, April 11, 1988, p. 33.

13. John S. Hammond III, "Better Decisions with Preference Theory," *Harvard Business Review—On Management* (New York: Harper & Row, 1975), pp. 86–116.

14. Edward E. Lawler III, "Paying for Performance: A Motivational Analysis," paper given at New York University Conference on Pay for Performance, New York City, 1985.

15. Herzberg, "One More Time," p. 110.

16. Frederick Herzberg, "Retrospective Commentary" on his 1968 article, *Harvard Business Review* (September–October 1987), p. 118.

17. Geraldine Fabrikaut, "The Anxiety at Time Inc Over Bidding," *New York Times*, July 1, 1989, p. 29.

18. Harry Levinson, *Psychological Man* (Cambridge, MA: Levinson Institute, 1976) and *Men, Management and Mental Health* (Cambridge, MA: Harvard University Press, 1962).

19. Goldman Sachs, *Our Business Principles*.

5

EXECUTIVE COMPENSATION AND FIRM PERFORMANCE: RESEARCH QUESTIONS AND ANSWERS

George T. Milkovich and Bonnie R. Rabin

PUBLIC SKEPTICISM ABOUT EXECUTIVE pay and its relationship to the performance of firms has a long history. Over fifty years ago, President Roosevelt inveighed against corporate executives as part of the forces of "entrenched greed" (*Fortune*, 1939). Four days after his speech, the U.S. Treasury Department published a list of names of individuals reported to be paid above $15,000. In the same year, *Fortune* reported the results of an opinion poll: "Over half of those responding felt executives of large corporations were paid too much." Since then, detailed disclosure of the compensation of the highest paid individuals in publicly held firms has been legally required. And executive pay continues to evoke skepticism in the press.

While preparing this chapter, we sampled fifty years of media accounts and opinion polls on executive compensation. We discovered five recurring themes:

- U.S. corporate executives are "overpaid."
- Corporate policies that determine executive pay ignore the interests of shareholders.
- Employment agreements such as golden parachutes shield executives from the sacrifices and risks faced by other employees and often run counter to the long-term interests of firms.
- Executive compensation simply does not make much sense; factors that might be expected to have an effect on firm performance—company size, the risk of the business, the experience and training of individuals—do matter, but not as much as expected.
- Changes in executives' pay are unrelated to changes in the performance of the firms they manage; their pay continues to rise even when the firms' performance declines.

Contemporary criticism reiterates these fifty-year-old themes. Each spring articles are published with such titles as "Corporate Leaders Took Home Fatter Pay Checks Last Year . . . Did Shareholders Get Their Money's Worth?" or "Top Executive Pay Peeves the Public: Are They Really Worth the Money?" (See for example, *BusinessWeek*, 1984, 1985, 1986, 1988; *The Wall Street Journal* 1985; AFL–CIO, 1988; Crystal, 1988a,b; Loomis, 1984.) *Fortune* recently commissioned a study entitled "The Wacky, Wacky World of CEO Pay" (Crystal, 1988a). According to a Lou Harris poll, (*BusinessWeek*, 1984) over 75 percent of the American public believes that top corporate executives are not worth the compensation they receive. Ironically, the specter of increased congressional and SEC regulation emanates from some of the very consultants who advise compensation committees on executive pay and whose fees are based in part on the billing revenues generated by that advice (Loomis, *Fortune*, 1984).

The earliest critiques are based more on exhortation than evidence. In recent years, however, articles in *BusinessWeek* and *Fortune* present extensive data, including details on the amounts of base pay, annual cash bonuses, and stock options, and employ more sophisticated analysis. Nevertheless, recent writers are just as critical of executive pay practices (Crystal, 1988a,b).

Conflicting views seldom get much coverage, except in academic journals (Ehrenberg and Milkovich, 1987; Baker, Jensen, and Murphy, 1988). Perhaps the lack of wider coverage is attributable to the propensity of academics to write only for each other. Their evidence and conclusions are often embedded in esoteric statistical analysis. Perhaps because they are sensitive to their universities' reward systems, academic researchers seldom translate their studies for the popular press or the public. A few notable exceptions do exist. For example, K. J. Murphy at the Simon School of Management at the University of Rochester summarized his extensive research in the *Harvard Business Review* in 1986, concluding that "On average, compensation policies encourage managers to act on behalf of their shareholders and to put in the best managerial performance they can."

Our task here is to discuss what is known or at least strongly supported by the empirical research on executive compensation. After finishing this chapter, the reader should be able to distinguish facts from opinions about executive pay. We argue that a *strategic* perspective on executive compensation requires research that looks beyond how much executives earn. Research that examines the relationships between risks and returns in executive pay plans, and ways to improve the link between executive pay and the performance of firms strengthens our understanding of the relationship between executives' pay and their firm's performance.

EXECUTIVE COMPENSATION: MORE COMPLEX THAN MEETS THE EYE

At the outset, it is useful to stress that executive compensation is multidimensional (Patton, 1956; Ellig, 1982; ACA, 1988); it involves three dimensions: pay *levels*, *forms*, and *structure*. Embedded within this framework are the *risk* and *return* relationships, also fundamental to understanding executive compensation. According to compensation professionals, the relationships between the risks executives face and the returns they receive determine in part the availability of critical executive talent and the quality of executive performance (Crystal, 1988b; Cook, 1988).

Pay *level* refers to the dollar amount of total compensation paid. It represents the total financial *returns* earned by the executive and it is the dimension of executive pay most often reported by the media. A survey of average total cash compensation (salary and bonus) received in 1987 by the top five executives across U.S. firms is shown in Exhibit 5-1. Level includes the value of *all* forms of pay: base salary and annual cash bonus plus long-term incentives, perks, golden parachutes, and other benefits.

In addition to pay level, executive compensation varies across pay forms: base salary, annual cash bonus, long-term incentives such as stock options, perks such as club memberships, and other benefits. Exhibit 5-2 shows variations in annual bonuses as a percentage of base salary. On average, 12 percent of the chief executives receive cash bonuses equal to 100 percent or more of their base pay; the median bonus for executives is 68 percent of base pay. A critical issue is that pay systems differ in terms of the relative importance of each pay *form*. According to Exhibit 5-2, the middle range of executives receive bonuses that range from 42 percent to 87 percent of base pay. Similar differences are reported in surveys of long-term incentives and perks (Cook, 1988).

Equally apparent is that alternative pay forms differ in the degree of risk and return they offer. For example, pay plans that are highly leveraged with annual bonuses (i.e., those CEOs in Exhibit 5-2 with 100 percent bonuses) are probably more risky than less leveraged plans (i.e., CEOs with 9 percent bonuses).

Pay system *risk* involves the extent of the performance contingency of the pay system, which is defined by the chance of receiving pay *returns*.

EXHIBIT 5-1
1987 Total Compensation
(Salary + Bonus)

Compensation Rank	Median	Differential*	Compensation Rank	Median	Differential* to Highest
Manufacturing (254 firms)			Commercial Banks (93 firms)		
Highest paid	$642,000		Highest paid	$412,000	
Second	400,000	62.3%	Second	260,000	63.1%
Third	320,000	49.8	Third	215,000	52.2
Fourth	283,000	44.1	Fourth	185,000	44.9
Fifth	252,000	39.3	Fifth	166,000	40.3
Trade (33 firms)			Insurance (91 firms)		
Highest paid	$413,000		Highest paid	$398,000	
Second	318,000	77.0%	Second	255,000	64.1%
Third	268,000	64.9	Third	195,000	49.0
Fourth	212,000	51.3	Fourth	167,000	42.0
Fifth	195,000	47.2	Fifth	150,000	37.7
Energy (31 firms)			Utilities (111 firms)		
Highest paid	$525,000		Highest paid	$355,000	
Second	400,000	76.2%	Second	218,000	61.4%
Third	359,000	68.4	Third	171,000	48.2
Fourth	213,000	40.6	Fourth	149,000	42.0
Fifth	200,000	38.1	Fifth	142,000	40.0

*Differential is the ratio of each level to the highest paid within each industry group.
Source: Adapted from Human Resources Briefings, *Conference Board* 4, October 10, 1988, p. 1.

The "risk-return" trade-off of pay systems is illustrated in Exhibit 5-3. Consider two executive pay systems, labelled W and X in Exhibit 5-3. Each potential pay system returns $100,000. Pay system X consists of $50,000 in bonus and $50,000 in base salary, while pay system W consists of $100,000 in base pay. Although pay plans X and W are "identical," W's performance targets make it a more risky plan. The two systems are clearly unequivalent when *risk* and return are considered, all else being equal. For the same return, pay system W offers less risk to the individual than pay system X.

As an additional example of risk-return trade-offs in pay systems, consider two alternative systems, Y and Z, also depicted in Exhibit 5-3. Pay system Y returns $200,000 in base pay and pay system Z returns $250,000 consisting of $130,000 in base pay and $120,000 in a performance-contingent bonus. Pay systems Y and Z may actually be equivalent when pay system risk *and* return are considered. That is, in order to get an executive to undertake the added risk of pay system Z, a greater return may be necessary. Depending on the firm's financial goals and on shareholder and executive risk preferences and tolerance, the levels of risk and return in the executive pay system can be varied accordingly.

EXHIBIT 5-2
Annual Bonus Awards as Percentage of Base Salary

1987 Bonus Awards (Percentage of Salary)	CEOs		Second Highest Paid		Third Highest Paid		Fourth Highest Paid		Fifth Highest Paid	
	Number	Percentage	Number	Percentage	Number	Percentage	Number	Percentage	Number	Percentage
100% or more	38	17%	23	10%	14	6%	14	6%	11	5%
90–99	12	6	12	5	12	5	6	3	4	2
80–89	23	11	18	8	17	8	17	8	9	4
70–79	33	15	34	15	24	11	21	9	16	7
60–69	35	16	27	12	26	12	26	12	31	14
50–59	16	7	40	18	32	14	30	13	28	13
40–49	14	6	19	8	35	16	40	18	39	18
30–39	21	10	17	8	26	12	31	14	25	11
20–29	12	6	16	7	20	9	18	8	29	13
10–19	12	6	18	8	14	6	17	8	26	12
Less than 10%	4	2	3	1	5	2	4	2	3	1
Total	220	100%	227	100%	225	100%	224	100%	221	100%
Median Bonus		68%		60%		53%		50%		48%
Middle 50% Range		42–87%		41–78%		37–74%		34–70%		29–63%

Source: "Top Executive Compensation," 1988 ed., Conference Board, Research Report 920.

The point is that the *risk* of executive pay plans refers to the chances of receiving the pay, which depends on the performance targets—some targets are firm-specific and some are determined by market forces.

When applied to executive compensation management, the risk-return concept can play a role in a *strategic* approach to pay. For example, as part of a strategic pay philosophy, two equally sized firms may desire to equate the risk level of the executive pay system to the risk of their respective shareholders. Both firms have determined that the competitive pay level necessary to attract and retain the CEO is $550,000. However, in the first of the two firms, much more of the total pay level must be placed "at risk," since shareholder returns are characterized by more variability—the beta of the stock. The first firm, perhaps a scientific instruments firm, is twice as "risky" as the second firm. Hence, the first firm may place one-third of total pay returns in a contingent bonus fund linked to a specific financial target. The second firm, perhaps a metal-machinery parts manufacturer with a market beta of half that of the scientific instruments firm, may only place one-fifth of the total pay return at risk. The risk-return concept can assist the firm in making this strategic policy choice more precisely.

The third dimension of executive pay—structure—involves decisions about differentials: among members of the executive team as well as the ratio of the least paid in a company to the highest. Note that in the data shown in Exhibit 5-2, the differentials of the four highest paid executives relative to the highest paid vary by industry. Firms in manufacturing, insurance, and banking maintain wider cash differentials among executives than firms in trade and energy. Similar differences exist in firms within a single industry (Rabin, 1987).

From a strategic pay perspective, pay level, forms, structure, and the relationship of risk to return are important variables in executive compensation. For example, the level of pay offered by competitors for executive talent is believed to affect a firm's ability to attract qualified executives and retain them (Ellig, 1982). Consequently, companies pay a great deal of attention to positioning the level of pay relative to that of competitors. In addition, firms must also address the degree of risk involved in their own pay plan. The risk-return trade-off in a pay system may act as a signal to executives, communicating whether or not the firm values risk-taking behavior as well as the degree of its commitment to pay-for-performance. It also allows the firm to equate executive interests with those of shareholders.

Decisions about the forms of pay a company chooses depend on the

EXHIBIT 5-3
The Pay "Arc": Risk-Return Trade-Offs

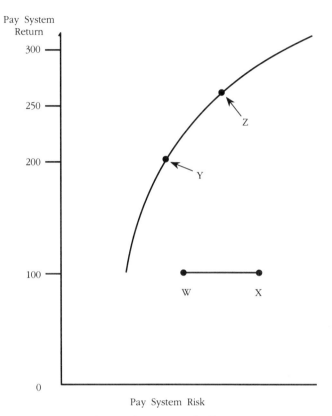

Source: B. R. Rabin, "Risk-Return Tradeoffs in Compensation
Systems," *IRRA Proceedings*, 1988, p. 608

firm's pay-for-performance philosophy, its relative short- and long-term emphasis, and its interest in growth of market share and return on shareholder value. For example, the firm's commitment to pay-for-performance is reflected in the ratio of variable pay to base or total compensation. Its relative short-/long-term emphasis is reflected in the ratio of annual cash bonuses to performance shares. However, different pay forms may produce different results in various organizational settings.

Various pay forms result in differences under various conditions—industry, timing, and financial objectives come into play. Consider an executive compensation agreement that includes base salary, annual cash bonuses based on financial performance, and annual restricted stock grants negotiated for each year of the five-year term covered by the agreement. Under this plan, a "bad" year may not yield a cash bonus, yet the executive might still receive significant returns from the stock grants awarded in earlier years. The effect of the stock grants, negotiated as part of the five-year agreement to attract and retain the executive, may be so large as to swamp any short-term incentive intended by using the cash bonus. All things being equal, the poor financial performance may be reflected in the value of the stock, and the executive does lose the opportunity to earn the bonus. But all things are seldom equal, and the relative value of the stock in any period can offset the value of the lost bonus.

The point is that the mix of pay forms translates into risk-return trade-offs for an executive. A pay plan is analogous to a portfolio of investments, with risks and returns associated with each investment in the portfolio, as well as aggregate risk for the total portfolio. In assessing the risk-return trade-off of a pay system the returns of each pay form must be examined.

The structure of executive pay also concerns the pay hierarchy in an organization. Disparities in the short- and long-term provisions of executive contracts for the various members of a managerial team are one example. From a strategic perspective, egalitarian policies ("we are all in this together") translate into smaller differences in compensation levels or risks among members of the executive team. Less egalitarian policies lead to greater differences; that is, one executive may receive bonuses, while another may receive stock.

Surprisingly, very little is known about the effects of structure on executive behavior or on firms' performance. Some economists have treated executive pay as if it were a "tournament" or competition among players (Lazear and Rosen, 1981). Their analysis focuses on the size of the differentials between the "winners" (top executives) and the rest of the field (presumably all other executives). They argue that sizable differentials for the top position are required to motivate executives to compete and invest in the "game." But top executives often bring in their own teams, and encourage "losers" to play in other organizations. So it is not clear what effect differentials really have. If current findings on high-commitment/high-involvement organizations are accurate, "cooperation" not "competition" among team members is more desirable (Lawler, 1986; Walton, 1985; Klingel and Martin, 1988). Teamwork, commitment, and risk-sharing among production and staff employees apparently has pay-offs; the same may be true for executives.

One highly publicized structural issue is the gap between returns received by executives and those received by other employees. For example,

Michael Eisner, CEO at Disney, received cash payments of over $7 million in 1987. This is ten times more than a ride operator in a Disney theme park earns in an entire lifetime. Many people claim the gap between executive and other employees' pay is "unfair." *Fortune* recently proclaimed a trust gap resulted from executive-employee pay differentials. A recent study reported that in the United States, the average CEO salary is fourteen times that of an entry professional, compared to a ratio of between 7:1 and 8:1 in Europe (Towers, Perrin, Forster & Crosby, 1988). The gap is most obvious when large cash bonuses are paid to executives at the same time concessions are demanded from other employees. Although there is little research on the impact of these differences on work force performance, it is likely that the effects are not positive.

In summary, executive compensation can be examined in terms of the levels of pay, the compensation of different pay forms in the plan (risk-return relationships), and structural ratios. Thus, a strategic issue for executive pay in the 1990s is not only how much executives earn, but what risks are associated with the higher level of pay. Students of compensation must consider the *entire pattern* of pay decisions (Rabin, 1987; Milkovich, 1988). We turn next to what is known about these dimensions of compensation.

THE RESEARCH

Much of the early research on executive compensation focuses on the sales versus profit debate (Ciscel and Carroll, 1980). The earliest research, dating back to the 1950s, examines whether compensation (base salary plus bonus) is more highly correlated with sales or reported profits. The results are mixed. On average, the level of cash compensation is correlated with both the level of sales and profits, although sales tend to be more important in most studies. In one recent study, the data suggest that if a firm increases its sales by 10 percent, it will pay its executives an average of 3 percent more (Baker, Jensen, and Murphy, 1988). The results are less surprising when we consider that the majority of executive pay surveys, tailored for firms' compensation committees, emphasize cash compensation (base plus bonus) in relation to firms' revenues. Hence, the findings of strong relationships between revenues and cash compensation are not surprising.

Another explanation for the correlation between cash compensation and sales is that larger firms may employ more qualified executives and be able to pay them more. The fact that a 10 percent sales growth results in a 3 percent increase in cash compensation leads some researchers to observe "that executives can increase their pay by increasing their firm's revenues even when the increase in size reduces their firm's market value. This could explain some of the vast amount of inefficient expenditures of corporate resources on diversification programs that have created large conglomerates over the last twenty years" (Baker, Jensen, and Murphy 1988, p. 609).

A subsequent wave of studies extended this interest in sales versus profit objectives by analyzing whether other factors were related to executive compensation. Generally, these studies report that the cash compensation paid to executives depends to some extent on the industry in which a firm operates. On average, manufacturing pays the highest, followed by energy, banking, insurance, utilities, and trades (Conference Board, 1989). Firms with mature product lines tend to pay higher cash compensation than those in the startup stages. Startup firms offer large amounts of stock options and ownership possibilities in lieu of up-front cash compensation. Firms controlled by a few dominant stockholders (as opposed to "management-controlled firms") exhibit stronger links between financial returns and executives' cash compensation (Gomez-Mejia, Tosi, and Hinkin, 1987), suggesting the manager-controlled firms are more likely to overpay compared to owner-controlled firms. In sum, the research suggests that executive pay levels are correlated most strongly with levels of revenues, profits, industry, product life cycle, and type of ownership.

However, the research offers little practical guidance for executive pay decision making, and is limited in four serious ways. At best it reports what was or what is but says nothing about how systems would work if pay levels, risk, and structure were altered. Second, these studies usually are restricted to cash compensation levels. They ignore performance-based remuneration such as stock options or performance shares, and fail to take account of employment contract clauses that may reduce or even eliminate the link between performance and pay, reducing risk to the executive. For example, Rabin (1987) found that the use of employment agreements is associated with lower performance levels as measured by return on equity (ROE), shareholder value, and sales. Third, many studies do not attempt to account for differences in the composition of pay forms. In these situations, the degree of risk or the link to performance differs across firms. For this reason, we are unable to determine from the evidence whether firms that utilize more risky pay systems experience better performance. The fourth limitation of much of the existing research involves the passage of time between enactment of pay systems and their consequences. Most analysts observe pay and performance at the same point in time; a time series approach that allows for the lag between policy decisions and results would be more appropriate. If we are interested in the effects on performance of long-term incentives, for example, then we should be examining tomorrow's performance. It is questionable whether looking at the relationship between today's pay and today's performance is appropriate.

In short, to document a correlation between cash compensation today and today's performance is not in itself evidence of the impact of complex executive pay systems on corporate performance. The inquiry must (1) recognize the complexities in executive pay (levels, forms, structures, and risk-return relationships), (2) measure total (not just cash) compensation, and (3) consider the time lags involved.

Recent studies are beginning to overcome some of these shortcomings. Several articles have documented a strong positive relationship between CEO pay (measured as cash compensation) and firm performance (measured by changes in shareholder wealth as well as by accounting methods). The conclusion of one study is that firm performance is associated with relatively small year-to-year changes in CEO pay. Changes in the rate of return on common stock, for example, explains at most 8 percent of the change in CEO bonus and salary (Baker, Jensen, and Murphy, 1988).

Rabin incorporated a series of time lags covering the short, medium, and longer terms, and found that executive pay systems including pay levels, risk, and structure explain a significant portion of the variation in the eventual financial performance of firms. The effects differ by industry, time period, and performance measure. One implication of the findings is that it may be more efficient to emphasize one form of pay over another, depending on the firm's financial objectives and industry. For example, some firms balance relatively low base pay with greater attention to performance-based pay or risky forms of compensation. Rabin also found that in some industries (e.g., machinery manufacturing), the use of employment agreements is associated with a decline in performance over time. Finally, the study revealed that stock options do not seem to have any effect on firm performance and that the level of base pay is negatively related to profits and growth in some industries. These findings support our contention that executive compensation is indeed more complex than depicted in the popular business press.

Several experts have begun to analyze the relationship between executive pay systems and firms' financial *policies* (as distinct from financial *performance*). The premise behind the research is that a strategic approach to executive pay should be related to other corporate policies. Evidence from four separate studies verifies that compensation policy is tied to other corporate decisions. For example, Rabin (1988) found a strong correlation between the dividend policies that firms pursue over time and their mix of and disclosure of executives' base salary and annual bonuses. Other researchers found that debt ratios are negatively related to management shareholding (Friend and Pang, 1988). The authors suggest that this is because debt has a greater nondiversifiable risk to management than to shareholders. Another study discovered a positive relationship between the security holdings of managers and changes in firm performance and financial leverage. Relationships have also been found between the type of accounting schemes and the type of executive bonus plans companies use (Larcker, 1983). According to the evidence, then, executive pay policy is related to financial policy and performance results. It appears that strategic executive compensation *can* support overall business goals.

Virtually all the research confirms that changes in executive compensation are positively correlated with financial performance. The findings refute the belief, widely reported in the press, that executives pursue objectives that are inconsistent with the interests of the owners of the corporation. On the contrary, executives appear to be motivated to improve the economic performance of their firms.

Recent "event studies" focus on whether particular forms of executive pay are associated with improved returns to shareholders by analyzing the stock market's reaction to the announcement of a specific event. The assumption underlying the research is that markets react to managerial decisions that affect cash flows—positive decisions yield increases in shareholder wealth. Researchers have applied the method by monitoring the market's reaction to the announcement of specific short- or long-term incentive schemes, executive turnover and replacements, and golden parachutes (Bhagat, Brickley, and Lease, 1985; Brickley, Bhagat, and Lease, 1985; Larcker, 1983; Lambert and Larcker, 1985). Results indicate that stock prices fluctuate by 1 percent to 2 percent of total shareholder value in reaction to announcements of changes in executive pay plans. There are two possible explanations. The first is that the introduction of new pay schemes does indeed motivate executives and, consequently, increase shareholder wealth. One study finds that the adoption of long-term performance share plans is followed by increases in capital investments (Larcker, 1983). Another possible explanation is that changes in executive pay plans are made in anticipation of improved earnings; therefore, changes in pay schemes signal changes in the firm's financial fortunes. In this view, changes in pay schemes are a form of insider information that signal changes in the firm's financial fortunes. Or the changes in executive pay plans and stock values may be attributable to external influences such as new tax or accounting regulations.

On balance, caution is required before drawing conclusions from event studies. Although their authors do find an *association* between the adoption of particular forms of executive pay (golden parachutes, stock option grants, and so forth) and higher stock market returns, the nature of the relationship is unclear. Note that the incentives the studies discuss are designed to affect the long-term performance of the firm, yet the stock price changes associated with the announcements are measured in the short term. Only Larcker's study of changes in capital investment policies found that executive decisions were altered in the long run by the adoption of different forms of pay (Larcker, 1983).

CONCLUSIONS

A growing body of research evidence supports conclusions that contradict many of the themes found in the popular press. The research demonstrates:

1. *Executives' pay levels are related to their firm's economic performance.* Despite the anecdotes noted in the press, in the majority of firms the level of compensation is, on average, related to a wide variety of performance measures, including shareholder wealth, sales, profits, and return on equity. Changes in pay levels are, on average, related to changes in these measures.
2. *Differences in the riskiness of pay systems are to be related to firms' financial performance.* Employment agreements, percentage of annual bonus, and the use of stock options are all related to differences in financial results. The degree of these relationships vary by industry group and timing of the effects.
3. *Executive compensation plans do matter to the investment community and stockholders.* The introduction of new forms of compensation may signal the overall strategic position of firms to investors. Changes in compensation plans may inform investors of impending changes in the firm's value as well as serve the intended purpose of motivating executives to improve value.
4. *Executive pay levels are related to specific firm characteristics, includ-*

ing revenues, product markets, financial strategies, stage of development, and industry.

Note that we emphasize *association* not causation: the available data do *not* allow us to say that executive pay levels determine corporate performance. On the other hand, corporate performance does determine how much companies can afford to compensate all employees, including executives. Compensation plans with appropriate risk-return links *may* act as incentives that affect executive behavior, but studies do not prove it.

Unfortunately, the research does not offer much guidance on which to base decisions about executive pay. At best, it reports "what was" or "what is," but it has yet to directly examine the "what ifs." For example, *what if* a high-risk/high-return plan (low base pay with high performance targets and incentives) were installed under specific circumstances, or *what if* the gap between executive and employee pay were controlled—what is likely to be their effects? This sort of question is perhaps the most useful, yet the most difficult to answer. Nonetheless, research does suggest that such differences in pay systems have been associated with differences in financial performance. We turn now to a brief agenda for executive compensation research in the 1990s.

RESEARCH AGENDA: WHAT WE NEED TO KNOW

The issue of executive pay and firm performance is clearly far more complex than the media's rhetoric suggests. Not only is pay level important, so are the risks underlying alternative forms of pay. For example, a million-dollar executive may be worth the price he or she is paid if shareholder value is increased. Differences in financial performance from firm to firm, for example, may be traced in part to differences in compensation risks and returns faced by executives. Ignoring the riskiness of pay systems may lead to misleading conclusions about compensation plans. Risk represents a critical component of a strategic approach to compensation design in the 1990s.

The effect of the executive-employee pay differential is inadequately understood. If the executives in an organization are more than a collection of individuals competing for the top job, then we must study the influences of pay structure on performance. As we noted earlier, the impact of significant gaps between the compensation of top managers and that of rank-and-file employees is another topic on which speculation is rife, but research is rare.

It is noteworthy that no studies exist on *how* the level of executive compensation affects economic performance. We do not know, for example, whether offering higher salary levels in order to attract and retain key executives really pays, whether promoting executives from within really pays, whether different risk-return trade-offs in pay-for-performance plans really do attract executives who are more (or less) prone to take risks. And we do not know if any of these subsequently affect firm performance.

The state of knowledge in executive pay research brings to mind the frustration of Harry Truman with his economic advisers: *On the one hand*, we do know that executive pay is related to firm performance; *on the other hand*, very little is known about the complex pay-performance relationship. How does pay affect performance? More is involved than how much an executive gets paid, and much more remains to be learned. The research literature suggests that pay practice in the 1990s should entail careful consideration of executive pay levels and pay system risk in relation to corporate goals.

REFERENCES

AFL–CIO Reviews the Issues. "Executive Pay Soars." Report No. 16 (February 1988).

Agrawal, A., and Mandleker, G. "Managerial Incentives and Corporate Investment and Financing Decisions." *Journal of Finance* 4 (September 1987), pp. 309–322.

American Compensation Association and Peat Marwick. *Executive Compensation Strategies and Trends—The Factual Base.* Scottsdale, AZ: ACA, 1988.

Antle, R., and Abbie, S. "An Empirical Investigation of the Relative Performance Evaluation of Corporate Executives." *Journal of Accounting Research* 24 (Spring 1986), pp. 1–32.

Baker, G. P., Jensen, M. C., and Murphy, K. L. "Compensation and Incentives: Practice vs. Theory." *The Journal of Finance* 43(3) (1988), pp. 593–616.

Balkin, D., and Gomez-Mejia, L. "The Strategic Role of Compensation." *Strategic Management Journal*, forthcoming.

Bhagat, S., Brickley, J., and Lease, R. "Incentive Effects of Employee Stock Purchase Plans." *Journal of Financial Economics* 14 (June 1985), pp. 195–216.

Brickley, J., Bhagat, S., and Lease, R. "The Impact of Long-Range Managerial Compensation Plans on Shareholder Wealth." *Journal of Accounting and Economics* (April 1985), pp. 115–129.

Broderick, R. F. "Pay Policy, Organizational Strategy and Structure: A Question of Fit." Paper for the Research Symposium of the HRP Society, Wharton, 1985.

BusinessWeek. "Executive Pay: The Top Earners—Who Made the Most and Are They Worth It?" May 7, 1984, pp. 88–116; May 7, 1985, pp. 57–69; May 5, 1986, pp. 48–80; May 2, 1988, pp. 50–91.

———. "Top Executives Pay Peeves the Public." June 25, 1984, p. 15.

———. "Executive Pay: Who Made the Most . . . And Are They Worth It?" May 1, 1989, pp. 87–95.

Ciscel, D., and Carroll, T. "The Determinants of Executive Salaries: An Econometric Survey." *Review of Economics and Statistics* (February 1980), pp. 7–13.

Conference Board. "Top Executive Compensation." Research Report 920, New York, 1989.

Cook, F. *Long-Term Incentive Compensation Grants.* New York: Frederic W. Cook & Co., 1988.

Crystal, G. S. "The Wacky, Wacky World of CEO Pay." *Fortune,* June 6, 1988, pp. 68–78.

———. "Where's the Risk in CEO's Rewards?" *Fortune,* December 19, 1988, pp. 62–66.

Eaton, J., and Rosen, H. "Agency, Delayed Compensation and the Structure of Executive Remuneration." *Journal of Finance* 38 (December 1983), pp. 1489—1505.

Ehrenberg, R. G., and Milkovich, G. T. "Compensation and Firm Performance." In M. Kleiner et al., eds. *Human Resources and the Performance of Firms.* Madison, WI: Industrial Relations Research Association, 1987, pp. 87–122.

Ellig, B. *Executive Compensation—A Total Pay Perspective.* New York: McGraw-Hill, 1982.

Fortune, July 27, 1939, pp. 64–66.

Fox, H., and Peck, C. "Top Executive Compensation in U.S.-Based Multinationals." *The Conference Board.* Bulletin 191 (1986).

Friend, L., and Pang, L. "An Empirical Test of the Impact of Managerial Self-Interest on Corporate Capital Structure." *Journal of Finance* (June 1988), pp. 271–282.

Gomez-Mejia, L., and Balkin, D. "The Effectiveness of Individual and Aggregate Compensation Strategies." Mimeo (1986).

Gomez-Mejia, L., Tosi, H., and Hinkin, L. "Managerial Control Performance and Executive Compensation." *Academy of Management Journal* 30 (1987), pp. 51–70.

Hewitt Associates Total Compensation Data Base. "Overview of Long-Term Incentive Valuations." Lincolnshire, IL, 1988.

Jensen, Michael C., and Murphy, Kevin J. "Are Executive Compensation Contracts Structured Properly?" Harvard Business School and University of Rochester. Working Paper (February 1988).

Klingel, S., and Martin, A. A *Fighting Chance: New Strategies to Save Jobs and Reduce Costs*. Ithaca: ILR Press, 1988.

Lambert, R. A., and Larcker, D. F. "Golden Parachutes, Executive Decision-Making, and Shareholder Wealth." *Journal of Accounting and Economics* 7 (April 1985), pp. 179–204.

Larcker, D. F. "The Association Between Performance Plan Adoption and Corporate Capital Investments." *Journal of Accounting and Economics* 5 (1983), pp. 3–30.

Lawler, E. E. *High Involvement Management*. San Francisco: Jossey-Bass, 1986.

Lazear, Edward, and Rosen, Sherwin. "Rank Order Tournaments as Optimum Labor Contracts." *Journal of Political Economy* 89 (October 1981), pp. 841–864.

Loomis, A. M. "Business Is Bungling Long-Term Compensation." *Fortune*, July 23, 1984, pp. 64–69.

Milkovich, G. T. "Restructuring of Compensation Systems." *American Compensation Association Conference Highlights*. Scottsdale, AZ: ACA, 1988.

———. "Strategic Perspectives in Compensation." In G. Ferris and K. Rowland, eds. *Research in Personnel and HR Management* (Greenwich, CT: JAI Press, 1988), pp. 263–288.

Murphy, K. J. "Corporate Performance and Managerial Remuneration: An Empirical Analysis." *Journal of Accounting and Economics* 7 (April 1985), pp. 11–42.

———. "Top Executives Are Worth Every Nickel They Get." *Harvard Business Review* (March–April 1986), pp. 125–131.

Patton, A. "Annual Report on Executive Compensation." *Harvard Business Review* (November–December 1956), pp. 124–129.

Rabin, B. R. "Executive Compensation: The Case of Employment Agreements." Paper presented at the Academy of Management meetings, San Diego (1985).

———. "Executive Compensation and Dividend Policy: A Signalling Model." Paper presented at the Academy of Management meetings, Chicago (1986).

———. "Executive Compensation and Firm Performance: An Empirical Analysis." IRRA Proceedings (1987), pp. 323–331.

———. "Risk-Return Tradeoffs in Compensation Systems." IRRA Proceedings (1988).

Towers, Perrin, Forster & Crosby. "International Compensation Comparisons." New York, 1988.

Walton, R. E. "Form Control to Commitment in the Workplace." *Harvard Business Review* (March–April 1985), pp. 77–84.

6

EXECUTIVE COMPENSATION, CORPORATE DECISION MAKING, AND SHAREHOLDER WEALTH: A REVIEW OF THE EVIDENCE

Richard A. Lambert and David F. Larcker

INTRODUCTION

In recent years the compensation of corporate management has become the focus of a major controversy. The level of executive pay and its relationship to corporate performance are now central issues in a generally heated debate among legislators, corporate directors, economists, financial journalists, and compensation professionals.

As a sampling of the rhetoric generated by this controversy, consider this pronouncement in Carol Loomis's widely cited *Fortune* article entitled (provocatively, if not very judiciously) "The Madness of Executive Compensation":

> In a totally rational world, top executives would get paid handsomely for first-class performance, and would lose out when they flopped. But to an extraordinary extent, those who flop still get paid handsomely.

Moreover, Loomis continues,

> It is widely believed that many compensation committees are rubber stamps, unwilling to be hard-nosed about the pay of top executives, particularly those chaps who are fellow members of the board.[1]

Or consider this more forceful expression of dissatisfaction with corporate compensation committees, which appeared in a recent *Wall Street Journal* editorial:

> Boards of directors, individual shareholders, and large institutions have got to clean up their own acts with respect to corporations that have poor per-

formance and then make that performance even poorer by offering outrageous amounts of compensation to demonstrably incompetent executives.[2]

Finally, in another recent *Wall Street Journal* editorial, entitled "Reform Executive Pay or Congress Will," Peter Drucker calls for executives to limit their compensation to a multiple of the compensation earned by the "rank and file."[3] And, perhaps taking its cue from Drucker's moralistic tone, the American Law Institute has added to the general furor by proposing amendments to the Business Judgment Rule that would change the composition of corporate boards of directors, further restrict the autonomy of corporate managements, and regulate executive compensation.[4]

Executive compensation consultants, while predictably far less hostile, have also been strongly critical of conventional compensation practices. But here the discussion has focused not on the appropriate *level* of executive pay, but rather on the proper criteria, the ideal "scorecard," for evaluating managerial performance and awarding bonuses. The widespread use of short-term, accounting-oriented measures like EPS and EPS growth has come under attack, and a number of alternatives have been proposed to strengthen the unity of interest between management and stockholders. Some consultants have proposed real, or inflation-adjusted, returns on stockholders' equity (that is, the return on equity minus the cost of equity capital) as the ideal basis for incentive compensation.[5] Others have argued that discounted cash flow is the performance measure that corresponds most strongly to the process by which investors price corporate shares.[6]

Meanwhile, as the controversy rages on in political and business circles, academics have begun to explore some of the issues raised above. In contrast to the morass of baseless charge and countercharge in which the public debate has become enmired, researchers in the fields of economics, finance, and accounting have established the beginnings of a scientific inquiry into questions of managerial economics. The result to date has been a small, but rapidly growing body of empirical studies providing insights into matters like the following:

- What are the consequences of the separation of ownership from control in the large public corporation? How effective are compensation contracts in overcoming conflicts of interest between management and stockholders?
- What are the pros and cons of various "scorecards" for evaluating managerial performance and awarding executive bonuses? What is the optimal "mix" of components—stock options, annual cash bonuses,

long-term performance payments, and so forth—in the total compensation package?

- Do compensation contracts "really matter" to executives? That is, do managers respond differently to different compensation plans?
- To what extent is annual executive compensation related (and, furthermore, to what extent *should* it be related) to year-to-year corporate performance and stockholder returns?
- How effective is the labor market for executives—that market which sets a manager's "opportunity wage"—in curbing management's natural tendency to pursue its self-interest at the expense of stockholders?

Our purpose in this article is to review the academic literature on executive compensation. We also discuss some of the more innovative incentive plans introduced by compensation professionals in recent years.

FRAMEWORK FOR EXAMINING EXECUTIVE COMPENSATION

A recent development in the theory of corporate organization, known as "agency theory," has focused attention on the separation of ownership from control in large public corporations. In the context of this theory, management incentive compensation plans are viewed as one of several important means of reducing potential conflicts of interest between management and shareholders. (The others are the existence of a market for corporate control, which disciplines inefficient managers through the threat of takeover, and a market for executive labor, which in theory weighs an executive's past service to shareholders when determining his or her opportunities for alternative employment.) To the extent the separation of ownership from control is a serious problem in the large public corporation (and the recent proliferation of leveraged buyouts can be construed as evidence in support of this supposition), an effective compensation program can add value to the firm by improving the alignment of management incentives with stockholder interests.

There are three principal kinds of conflicts discussed in the agency literature. First, and most obviously, whereas shareholders' primary interest is in having a management team that maximizes their financial return, executives may derive "nonpecuniary" benefits ("perks," in the vernacular) from their control over corporate resources. They may authorize purchase of superfluous corporate jets. Or, with far more serious consequences, they may seek to build a corporate empire through a series of large acquisitions at costly premiums that penalize their own shareholders.[7] (It is important to note that in this context, "perk" means any expenditure that has a higher value to management than to shareholders. Thus, "perks" have a potential value much larger than the sum of costs for club memberships, first class air travel, and so forth.)

Second, management and shareholders can differ sharply in their attitudes toward the risk of potential investment strategies. Whereas shareholders can diversify their wealth by spreading it among different assets, a large portion of a manager's wealth (human capital, compensation earned, and stock in the firm) is tied to the fortunes of the company. Therefore, we would expect managers to be more risk-averse than shareholders. Too great a difference in risk aversion might cause a manager to turn down a project that would benefit shareholders because the perceived personal risks are too high.

Third, there is a potential conflict between the decision-making time horizons of executives and shareholders. For example, an executive's investment decisions may be evaluated by the compensation committee over a shorter time period than shareholders use in assessing the eventual outcome of the same investment decisions. This pressure may in turn cause a manager to evaluate projects based on their immediate impact on profits, rather than according to the present value of cash flows over the life of the investment. A foreshortened decision-making horizon thus may motivate management to turn down profitable long-term investments.

From the perspective of agency theory, then, executive compensation contracts are *not* simply a tax-efficient vehicle for delivering pay to executives (although taxes offer at least a partial explanation for some features of compensation plans).[8] The primary function of incentive compensation plans is to control the kinds of conflicts of interest between management and shareholders described above. And, as we hope to show in the next section, the ability of the agency framework to identify the sources of conflicts between stockholders and executives is useful in determining the "optimal" design of a compensation plan.

COMPENSATION "SCORECARDS" AND CONTRACT DESIGN

How then, are current compensation plans designed to control such conflicts of interest between management and stockholders? And, furthermore, how effective are they in accomplishing this end? In this section, we discuss the implications of the agency issues discussed above for choosing the appropriate performance measure, as well as the structure and components of the compensation package.

Before considering specific contract designs, it is useful to point out some of the difficulties that arise in evaluating managerial performance. For one thing, the separation between ownership and management prevents shareholders from directly observing much of management's activity. Also, because shareholders almost never possess management's familiarity with the operations of the firm, they may not be able to evaluate the consequences of those actions they can observe. As a result, they must often rely on reported *results* (on an accountant's periodic measure of net income, for example, or share price performance) as the basis for evaluating management's performance. Unfortunately, these results are likely to reflect the effects of a large number of factors that are not under management's control. This may make it difficult to determine whether poor results are due to "bad luck" or to poor decisions on the part of management.

Another problem is that the consequences of management's current decisions may extend over many years, and it is often difficult to foresee today their effects on the value of the firm in *future* periods. These difficulties suggest that compensation contracts (or any other disciplinary mechanism) can never be fully successful in resolving agency problems. But, given such limitations, let's see how the contracts are designed to deal with these management-shareholder conflicts.

Executive Expenditures and Risky Investments

One objective of a good compensation scheme is to motivate managers to make expenditure decisions that benefit shareholders. To approach this problem, consider the extreme (and improbable) case of an executive whose compensation is totally independent of his performance. An example would be a manager whose compensation consisted entirely of a *fixed* salary—one that, say, in real terms remained unchanged from year to year. Such a manager would have no incentive to increase shareholder wealth because he does not share in any of the resulting gains. He would be much more likely than other executives to avail himself of perquisites of all varieties, at the expense of his shareholders.

This incentive problem—one which all companies with outside stockholders face to at least some degree—can be reduced by making part of an executive's compensation depend upon the financial performance of the firm. By allowing managers to share in the company's gains, a compensation plan provides them some incentive to develop strategies that will increase shareholder wealth. Also, since the executive now bears some of the costs of "perk" consumption, he will be less likely to evaluate corporate expenditures according to the personal satisfaction—and perhaps, in the case of some major investment decisions, the sense of power or prestige—they offer him.

Given this concern, it may seem that the optimal compensation scheme will bind executive compensation as tightly as possible to changes in the stock price of the firm. The problem with this solution, however, is that stock prices are often affected by factors beyond management's influence. This means that tying management's compensation very closely to the firm's stock price will greatly increase executives' individual exposure to risk. And imposing large personal risks on management can actually *reduce* shareholder wealth—in two ways. First, an increase in management's exposure to market risk will make the compensation scheme less attractive, all other things being equal; and in return for bearing additional risk, executives collectively will require an increase in the general level of their compensation.[9] Second, increasing an executive's exposure to risk may cause him to become more conservative in his investment strategy. An executive may turn down risky projects that promise high expected returns to shareholders and accept only "safe" projects offering stable, but substandard returns.

How can the compensation package be designed to give executives the incentive to increase profits and control expenditures, or "perks," while at the same time encouraging them to pursue risky though profitable investment strategies? One possibility is to supplement stock price movements with other measures of firm performance, thereby providing compensation committees (and shareholders generally) with additional information that makes it easier to separate the effect of executives' actions from other factors that influence the firm's profits. In this way, an executive can be shielded from the "exogenous" or uncontrollable variables that affect the firm's profits, and his individual contribution can be more easily identified and evaluated.

To be effective, however, such measures must reflect the effectiveness of management more clearly than do stock prices; or, at a minimum, they must provide information about managerial performance that stock prices do not. For example, if stock prices were always a fixed multiple of accounting earnings, there would be no benefit to basing executive compensation on both earnings and share price—because both measures would be providing the same information about management's performance. But because stock prices are not fixed multiples of EPS, this means that stock prices and accounting earnings provide somewhat different (although certainly not unrelated) indications of management's effectiveness. By combining several different measures of performance, some of the "noise" contained in each individual measure can be removed, offering a better assessment of managerial performance.[10]

An alternative is to weigh corporate performance against the performance of other comparable companies. In such *relative* performance schemes, executive compensation is set according to how well the company performs relative to a comparison or peer group.[11] The implicit assumption underlying this approach is that the construction of a peer group allows general market or macroeconomic influences and industry-specific influences to be removed from the performance measure, thereby providing a better measure of an executive's distinctive contribution to the firm's profitability. The biggest difficulty in implementing such an approach is finding an appropriate peer group, especially for companies that have many different products. But, for many firms operating in well-defined industries, such as banking, paper, and oil, relative performance measures are becoming commonplace features of the compensation plan.

Another way to encourage managers to take risks, while still controlling "perks," is to structure their compensation in such a manner as to offset their risk aversion. Consider a project that shareholders perceive to be a worthwhile risk (that is, the investment has a positive net present value after discounting at the required rate of return). As suggested, when a manager is more risk-averse than shareholders, he may turn down a positive net present value project because he perceives the adverse consequences *to him* if the project performs poorly to dominate the favorable personal consequences if the project succeeds. The manager's risk aversion can be partially offset if his compensation contract is designed to make the adverse consequences associated with the "downside" less severe, or to make the favorable consequences of the "upside" more attractive. Properly designed stock options, or accounting-based option contracts, may be the answer to neutralizing a manager's risk aversion. Options may be effective in encouraging management to invest in riskier projects because, while they carry no additional downside risk, their value generally increases as the volatility of the company's stock price rises, and they allow managers to share in the upside potential of the firm.

In general, then, agency theory implies that it is desirable to compensate executives on the basis of share price in order to give them incentives to control their expenditures and develop strategies that increase shareholder wealth. But, the choice of how closely to tie management's compensation to share price must also consider the effect of exposing executives to greater market risk. The degree to which the executive's compensation should be tied to share price will therefore depend on the relative importance of these two incentive problems in the particular firm.

Decision-Making Horizon

The agency problem that results from differences in the decision-making time horizon of shareholders and executives can be partially resolved by changing either the "scorecard" or the payoff structure of compensation. The compensation "scorecard" can be changed from a measure with a "short-term" focus (such as yearly accounting earnings) to a measure that has an inherently "long-term" focus (for example, the market price of the common stock).[12]

Consider, for example, the situation where a manager is contemplating a capital investment with a positive expected net present value, but an adverse impact on accounting earnings in the early years of the project. An executive compensated primarily on the basis of yearly accounting earnings may reject this project because of its effect on his "short-term" compensation. If the executive is instead compensated on the basis of share price (through, say, stock or stock options), he will be more likely to accept the project because he expects it to have a favorable impact on his compensation. The implicit assumption of this approach, of course, is that executives believe that the "long-term" performance measure (that is, the stock price) will eventually, if not immediately, reward him by reflecting the "long-term" consequences of his investment decisions.[13]

An alternative, or perhaps complementary, way to lengthen the executive's decision-making horizon is to defer the payoff earned by the executive to some future point in time. Some corporations defer part of an executive's yearly bonus and require that the deferred compensation be paid in common stock. Since the executive's compensation is explicitly tied to the performance of the corporation in subsequent years, this type of bonus deferral will tend to lengthen his decision-making horizon.

In a similar manner, many corporations have also adopted compensation contracts known as "performance plans."[14] These contracts provide payoffs to executives if the growth in specified accounting numbers (generally earnings per share or return on equity) over a three- to five-year performance period exceeds some target. One important feature of performance plans is that the compensation earned from this contract is deferred until the end of this period. Nothing is earned if the executive leaves or is terminated during the term of the performance plan. And this stipulation, of course, could extend a manager's time horizon through at least the duration of the performance period.

DO COMPENSATION CONTRACTS REALLY MATTER?

The next question we want to examine concerns whether executives really respond to the incentives provided by their compensation contracts. If the agency framework is useful in analyzing compensation questions, we should observe that executives compensated with different contracts will exhibit differences in their decision making. We now turn to a review of the empirical evidence on this question.

Academic research has recently begun to examine the incentive effects of compensation contracts. This research is typically conducted in one of two ways. First, researchers look for changes in executive decision making after a *new* compensation contract is adopted. For example, do managers compensated by a new "long-term" contract undertake more "long-term" investment? Second, studies attempt to ascertain whether the variation in existing compensation contracts across firms is associated with differences in executive decision making. For example, do managers receiving a substantial portion of their compensation from a bonus contract make different decisions than managers receiving only a modest bonus? The results of this set of studies provide some insights into agency problems related to executive expenditure decisions, risk aversion, and decision-making horizon.

Executive Expenditure Decisions

A typical funding formula for establishing the yearly bonus pool for executives is diagrammed in Exhibit 6-1. There is generally a threshold level of net income that must be surpassed before any bonus is paid (for example, net income must exceed 5 percent of total capital employed). Most proxy statement disclosures indicate that when net income exceeds this minimum standard, the bonus pool is computed as some percentage of net income above the threshold. The bonus pool also often has an explicit ceiling. For example, in some compensation plans, the bonus may not exceed total cash dividends paid or, perhaps, some target per-

EXHIBIT 6-1
Typical Short-Term Bonus Contract

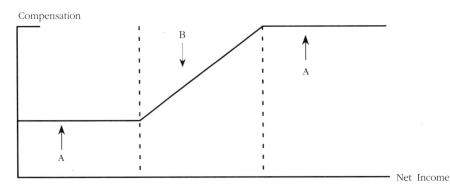

Compensation

B

A

A

Net Income

centage of the total salaries of the executives participating in the bonus plan.

A recent study by Paul Healy has attempted to determine how executives actually respond to the incentives inherent in these kinds of net income-based contracts.[15] Specifically, the question posed by Healy's study is this: Do executives adjust their expenditure decisions in order to increase the payoff from their yearly bonus contract?

The hypotheses of Healy's study can be illustrated using Exhibit 6-1. Consider the case where an executive expects net income to be on the "flat" portion of the contract (denoted as A in Exhibit 6-1). In this case, a manager would have an incentive to accelerate accounting recognition of expenses (say, maintenance) and defer recognition of revenues (for example, by delaying sale of goods until after the fiscal year is closed). Such accrual or deferral decisions would have no effect on the executive's bonus in the present year, but would increase the probability of obtaining a bonus in subsequent periods. By contrast, an executive who expects net income to fall in the "sloped" portion of the contract (denoted as "B" in Exhibit 6-1) faces the opposite set of incentives. His or her bonus for the current period can be increased by accelerating the recognition of revenues and deferring the recognition of expenses.[16]

The results of Healy's study confirm our expectations. As predicted, managers who expect reported net income to fall below the bonus threshold appear to decrease revenues and increase expenses. The opposite pattern of behavior is observed when executives expect net income to fall between the bonus threshold and the ceiling.

A study conducted by Mark Wolfson examines the effects of bonus contracts on the behavior of executives in oil and gas partnerships.[17] Many of these partnerships are organized such that limited partners contribute capital to the enterprise and a drilling agent performs the exploration and development activity. The contracts specifying how the costs and revenues are shared are often designed to take advantage of tax code regulations. In one common sharing arrangement, the limited partners bear all of the drilling costs. After discovery of oil and gas, the drilling agent bears all of the costs necessary to complete the well. The limited partners and the drilling agent then share the revenues earned from the sale of oil or gas.

The arrangement ideally should be structured such that the drilling agent has an incentive to complete every well where the total revenues accruing to *both* parties are expected to exceed his costs to complete the well. An "agency" problem arises, however, because the drilling agent receives only part of the revenues associated with completion while bearing all of the costs. The drilling agent thus has an incentive to complete only those wells for which his share of the revenues exceeds the cost of completion. Thus he is not likely to complete all of the wells that would benefit the limited partners.

If the limited partners view this agency problem to be serious, they will be less willing to invest funds in such partnerships. The drilling agent therefore has an incentive to devise a means of reducing this conflict of interest. One way to counteract this "noncompletion" incentive is to select only highly risky drilling programs, those whose expected outcome is highly variable. In this way, the wells are likely to be "so good" or "so bad" that the interests and objectives of the limited partners and the drilling agent are brought together. In such extreme cases, the fortunes of the drilling agent and limited partners are virtually identical: either they both "win big" or they lose the initial investment by the limited partner.

Wolfson tested this hypothesis, and his results suggest that partnerships with contacts like those described above engage in significantly more risky (exploratory) drilling than partnerships that operate under different sharing arrangements.

A study by one of the present authors examines changes in the level of "perks" associated with the adoption of bonus contracts by major commercial banks.[18] In this study "perks" are defined as occupancy, furniture, and salary expenditures, as well as the number of bank employees. (It is assumed that bank managers prefer to have more expensive working conditions and larger staffs than the level of expenditures desired by shareholders.)

This study determines specifically whether the ratio of management's expenditures on "perks" (as defined above) to operating revenue decreases following the adoption of an annual bonus contract. (This hypothesis follows, of course, from our earlier discussion: a manager compensated with a bonus contract bears part of the cost of expenditures on "perks," whereas a manager with only a fixed salary does not.) The results indicate that banks without bonus contacts had a significantly higher ratio of "perks" to operating revenue than similar banks with bonus contracts. Moreover, there is some evidence that the ratio of nonpecuniary expenditures to revenue decreases following the adoption of the bonus plan. Thus it appears that bonus contracts influence the expenditure decisions of bank managers.

Risk Aversion

Some evidence on the issue of whether executives behave as though they are more risk-averse than shareholders has been provided by Yakov Amihud and Baruch Lev.[19] Their study examines executive motives in conglomerate mergers.

Finance theory maintains that mergers undertaken *solely* for corporate diversification do not benefit stockholders because they can costlessly duplicate such diversification by holding different securities. Executives, however, benefit from corporate diversification because they hold partially "undiversifiable" portfolios, consisting of their compensation claims on the firm and their human capital. The authors hypothesize that because executives are more risk-averse than shareholders, executives undertake conglomerate mergers to decrease the variability of the value of the firm. By decreasing firm variability through conglomerate-type acquisitions, managers can effectively diversify—and thus increase the value of—their own "undiversifiable" portfolios.

Amihud and Lev find in fact that companies with broadly dispersed stock ownership—those in which there is no dominant shareholder to monitor corporate decisions—are more likely to engage in conglomerate or diversifying mergers than firms with concentrated ownership interests.[20]

In a somewhat more direct analysis of the ability of compensation contracts to affect executive risk aversion, we examined changes in firm variability associated with the *initial* adoption of stock option plans.[21] We attempted to determine whether the adoption of a stock option contract motivates managers to increase the variability in equity returns.

Two possibilities are considered in this study. First, standard option pricing models suggest that the value of an option increases as the variability of stock prices increases. This suggests that the adoption of stock options will counteract executives' risk aversion and motivate them to increase firm variability. A second possibility is that standard option pricing models are not applicable to *executive* stock options. Executives cannot sell their options to other investors. Nor can they short their own stock, making it difficult to construct the riskless hedge required for option pricing models to work. In fact, under certain circumstances, stock options may actually *increase* the risk aversion of a manager, thereby motivating him to decrease firm variability.

An explanation of why the standard option pricing formulas may not be appropriate in valuing executive stock options is as follows: Consider the behavior of a risk-averse manager who cannot diversify or hedge the risk associated with the option's payoff. If he expects the options to finish far "in the money" (which is likely because options are usually granted with an exercise price equal to or below the stock price at the date of the grant), he may want to "bank" the value of that option by *decreasing* the variability of the firm's stock price, thus increasing the odds that the options will finish "in the money."

If, however, an executive's options are expected to finish "out of the money," then a manager may have an incentive to increase the variance of the firm's stock price in order to increase the probability that they will become valuable. This suggests that granting options that are initially "out of the money" may be the solution to overcoming managers' risk aversion.

The results of our study indicate that firms whose options are expected to finish "out of the money" tend to exhibit increasing stock price variability following the adoption of stock option plans. In contrast, companies whose options are expected to finish "in the money" tend to exhibit decreases in stock price variability.

Decision-Making Horizon

As discussed earlier, if the decision-making horizon of management is significantly shorter than that of shareholders, this can lead to "underinvestment" by the corporation. For example, if an executive is being evaluated solely according to near-term accounting performance and a profitable investment project under consideration is expected to have an adverse impact on earnings in early years, he will have an incentive to reject that investment.

One possible way to mitigate this problem is to adopt a compensation contract designed to lengthen executives' decision-making horizon. This presumes, of course, that compensation contracts can actually motivate a manager to lengthen his decision-making horizon. Although this issue cannot be examined directly, it is possible to determine whether the investment behavior of executives changes after a contractual change.

In a study published in 1983, one of the present authors examined whether the adoption of "long-term" compensation contracts was associated with increases in "long-term" investment.[22] The specific focus of this study was the adoption of "performance plans," those contracts which provide deferred compensation when certain "long-term" (generally ranging over a three- to six-year period) goals are met. The relative amount of capital investment of companies adopting performance plans was compared to the investment of similar firms without performance plans. The results of the study indicated that firms adopting performance plans had substantial increases in capital investment after the contractual change relative to similar firms without performance plans.

Stockholder Response to New Compensation Plans

The research on whether compensation contracts "really matter" suggests that the design of such contracts influences executive decision making. But how does this influence translate into shareholder wealth? Furthermore, how do investors respond to the adoption of new compensation plans?

Several studies have, in fact, documented that stock prices rise when companies announce the adoption of "long-term" compensation contracts.[23] These studies find that "long-term" contracts are associated with an approximately 1 percent to 2 percent increase in shareholder wealth. (Although these percentages might seem small in absolute terms, it is important to remember that the firms making these contractual changes are extremely large, and these percentages translate into millions of dollars of increases in shareholder value.) In short, compensation contracts do "appear to matter"—to investors as well as management.

THE RELATIONSHIP BETWEEN PAY AND PERFORMANCE

To this point, we have suggested that agency theory provides a framework for analyzing issues in executive compensation. We have also presented evidence that the theory is useful in predicting the "incentive effects" of different compensation contracts. In this section, we bring the theory to bear on the available evidence regarding the relationship between executive compensation and corporate performance.

Much of the controversy surrounding executive compensation tends to focus on whether executive compensation is related to corporate performance. That is, are current compensation contracts really designed to "pay for performance?" Criticism of executive compensation in the financial press is based almost entirely upon intuition and personal observation— what financial economists call "anecdotal" evidence.[24] Although no formal statistical analysis is done, these articles generally conclude that there is little or no relationship between executive compensation and corporate performance or shareholder wealth. Corporate compensation practices are then pronounced "irrational," failing to distinguish between good and bad performance.

Two academic studies presented at the University of Rochester's recent Conference on Managerial Compensation and the Managerial Labor Market address this issue more systematically.[25] Both of these studies examine the correlation between changes in compensation and changes in *shareholder wealth* for large samples of major U.S. corporations; and both show a positive, statistically significant correlation between executive compensation and shareholder wealth. This empirical evidence is, of course, inconsistent with the charges often made in the financial press.

Such findings, however, should not be taken to imply that American corporations have attained the optimum in incentive compensation. In fact, the coefficients measuring the correlation between compensation and shareholder returns, although statistically significant, are rather small. Also, rather modest changes in compensation occur for large changes in shareholder wealth. For example, Kevin Murphy reports that a 10 percent change in the equity value of the firm is associated with only about a 2 percent increase in total executive compensation. Therefore, although there is a statistical association between executive compensation and shareholder wealth, it is difficult to predict changes in executive compensation from changes in shareholder wealth. The correlation results, nevertheless, do suggest that executive compensation in American corporations is not total "madness."

One problem in interpreting these studies is that they typically exclude changes in the value of the executives' stock holdings and stock options from their measure of compensation. Obviously, these components of executive wealth are tied *directly* to changes in shareholder wealth; executives with large holdings in their company's stock are clearly rewarded for good performance and penalized for bad performance through the change in value of their personal stock holdings. And, as other studies show, the stock holdings of top executives in their own companies often constitute a significant portion of their wealth. This suggests that financial press "studies" correlating only annual salary and bonus with accounting profitability measures may seriously understate the real relationship between corporate performance and total compensation.[26]

How Should Compensation Correlate with Shareholder Returns?

Given that a significant portion of the wealth of top executives is already directly tied to stock price performance, we are led to ask: In the best of all possible compensation plans, how *should* the nonstock components of compensation like salary, yearly bonus, and performance plans be related to annual stock price changes?

As suggested earlier, one implication of agency theory is that it may be desirable to base compensation on other measures of the firm's performance in order to "filter out" the effects of random events on stock prices. The "noise" in stock prices may impose too much risk on executives, exposing too much of their compensation to factors beyond their control. Such risks may in turn cause them to become excessively conservative in their investment policy. Therefore, in designing compensation plans, companies can find it necessary to use criteria other than stock price—accounting earnings, return on equity, cash flow, sales, comparisons with industry-average rates of return—to supplement the direct dependence of an executive's stock-related compensation on stock prices. In this sense, the absence of a strong relationship between firm performance and contemporaneous salary and bonus need not be an indication of the irrationality of corporate compensation practices.

To summarize, then, the positive statistical correlations detected in these studies suggest that executive compensation is not total "madness." However, without additional information about the seriousness of "agency" problems resulting from managerial risk aversion in specific firms, it is difficult to determine what the correlation would be between the "optimal" compensation package and shareholder returns. Small positive correlations may represent an "optimal" contract for managers in highly cyclical industries who are thus exposed to some large risks they cannot control. Alternatively, in cases where risk aversion is not a serious concern, the same small positive correlations may imply that current compensation plans fail seriously in motivating management to act in the interest of its shareholders.

THE LABOR MARKET FOR EXECUTIVES

The fact that changes in compensation are correlated with changes in shareholder wealth also tells us little about whether the *level* of executive compensation is correct. Large positive correlations between changes in compensation and shareholder wealth can exist at the same time that executives are being "overpaid" or, for that matter, seriously "underpaid." The level of executive compensation is determined, in theory at least, by the operation of a labor market for executive services. Moreover, to the extent that it effectively determines the relationship between executive performance and *future* levels of executive compensation, this labor market can provide an important means of motivating executives to serve their shareholders.

There are two important aspects of the labor market. First, the labor market sets the executive's opportunity wage, and this provides a lower bound on the amount of total compensation that must be paid to retain him. At the same time, the availability of other executives of comparable experience and ability at this opportunity wage provides some constraint on the level of compensation demanded by executives in their current jobs. This tells us, for example, that executives cannot simply pay themselves any compensation level they desire.

Second, the labor market has the potential to control agency problems.[27] When an executive makes decisions that harm stockholders, the labor market should lower the executive's current opportunity wage (as well as all future period levels of compensation). To the extent executives are penalized in this way for poor decisions, they have less incentive to behave in a manner that benefits themselves at the expense of their shareholders. (This disciplining effect of the labor market assumes, of course, that the labor market has good information about the shareholder consequences of an executive's decisions.)

There have been several empirical studies that have examined aspects of the labor market for corporate executives.

We recently completed a study examining the effects of large corporate acquisitions on subsequent executive pay in an attempt to determine whether the labor market seems to reflect the consequences of executive decisions on shareholder wealth.[28] Specifically, we analyzed the change in real executive compensation (relative to industry standards for firms of a similar size and industry) in the period surrounding the completion of a large acquisition.

Two possibilities were considered. First, there is a strong positive relationship between the level of executive compensation and firm size. This suggests that an executive can increase his compensation simply by increasing firm size, regardless of the impact of this size increase on shareholder wealth. Second, the labor market value of executives should reflect *both* the change in firm size and the effect on profitability caused by an acquisition. If the labor market takes into account changes in shareholder wealth in setting an executive's opportunity wage, we should observe increases in executive compensation only for those acquisitions producing increases in shareholder wealth.

The preliminary results of our study suggest that *real* (inflation-adjusted) executive compensation (relative to industry and size standards) increased following a substantial increase in firm size via acquisition. As predicted, however, virtually all of this increase went to executives making acquisitions that increased shareholder wealth. The managements of companies making acquisitions that reduced their share prices saw no increase in the relative level of their real compensation.

Another study presenting evidence of a rational labor market was performed by Anne Coughlan and Ron Schmidt. They attempted to determine whether changes in shareholder wealth are a good predictor of executive terminations.[29] (To be fired is, of course, to face the most extreme form of labor market discipline, especially when it makes it difficult to obtain another comparable job.) The study finds that terminations are more likely to occur after decreases in shareholder wealth.

A third study of the executive labor market focuses on changes in shareholder wealth at the time of an "unexpected" death of a chief executive officer.[30] The market's response to the announcement of the "unexpected" death of a CEO offers an ideal test of the value of a top executive to a firm. Assuming the search costs of obtaining a new CEO are small relative to the market value of the firm, the effect of an "unexpected" CEO death on shareholder wealth will depend on the stock market's assessment of the value of the former CEO relative to the expected value of the new CEO. From the shareholders' perspective, the value of a CEO is the capitalized value of the CEO's expected future contributions to the value of the firm minus the capitalized value of the CEO's expected future compensation.

If CEOs, as is often alleged by the financial press, have the power to control boards of directors, one would expect the strength of a CEO's control to increase with his seniority. This implies, of course, that the former CEO would have more control over the board than the CEO expected to succeed him. And if such is the case, the former CEO should be paid more (relative to his contribution to the firm's value) than the expected payments to the new CEO. If the relatively "overpaid" CEO dies unexpectedly, the announcement of the death should be accompanied by a positive security market reaction.

The results of the study, however, show a pronounced *negative* security market reaction—at least to the deaths of those CEOs who were not the founders of their companies. [31] This result suggests that CEOs are not overpaid relative to their contribution to shareholder wealth (not at least when compared to alternative managers available in the labor market). [32]

INNOVATIONS IN COMPENSATION DESIGN

The evidence on executive compensation and the market for managerial labor suggests that current executive compensation practices are not total "madness." This discussion should not be construed, however, to imply there is no room for improvement in the design of compensation contracts. In fact, it is interesting to examine some of the recent innovations in compensation contract designs proposed (generally) by compensation consultants and, in some cases, adopted by corporations. Most of these innovative contracts seem designed primarily to deal with the kinds of "agency" problems we have been discussing throughout.

In 1983, for example, Johnson Controls, Inc. developed a unique seven-year performance plan for two of their most senior-level executives (both of whom were then about 60 years of age). In each of the seven years, the base amount of the plan (consisting of $300,000 and $100,000 for the two executives, respectively) is multiplied by a percentage that varies between zero and 150 percent. The determination of each percentage is based upon the *ratio* of the average annual total shareholder return for Johnson Controls (over the ten-year period ending with the current year) to the average total shareholder return for a peer group of *Fortune* 500 companies over the same period. [33] Each of the yearly awards is then invested in a hypothetical portfolio consisting of the stock of Johnson Controls. The payment of the total value of this hypothetical portfolio is deferred until the end of the seven-year performance period.

There are several interesting aspects of this performance plan. First, the term of the contract extends approximately three years beyond the retirement of the two executives. This feature appears to be an attempt to lengthen the decision-making horizons of executives—especially in the case of those near retirement age. This contract explicitly motivates the executives to consider the impact of their decisions on the company after they leave the corporation.

Second, the "scorecard" for the annual changes in the value of the performance plan is formally tied to changes in shareholder wealth over the prior ten years. This is unusual because performance plans are typically based upon earnings per share or return-on-equity growth rates. One explanation for the choice of changes in shareholder wealth is that the board of directors is attempting to lengthen the executive's decision-making horizon by selecting a scorecard that has a longer performance evaluation horizon than yearly accounting numbers.

Finally, the performance plan is based on *relative* changes in shareholder wealth. This appears to be an attempt to isolate that portion of changes in shareholder wealth that is under management's control from economy- and industrywide effects. The choice of a ten-year period for assessing the performance of the company may be an attempt to "wash out" other random elements that affect performance in a single year.

Another example of an innovative compensation scheme is the performance unit plan adopted by TRW in 1983 for twenty-eight of its key executives. Under this plan, the value of each performance unit varies according to how TRW ranks relative to ninety-eight peer companies. More interesting, performance is measured using the ratio of the market value of the firm (equity plus debt) to the *inflation-adjusted* value of net assets (typically referred to as the "q ratio"). The key feature of the TRW contract is that the impact of inflation on accounting measures is explicitly considered. This is important because inflation can severely distort historical accounting measures of corporate performance. For example, corporations (or divisions within corporations) with "old" assets will produce a higher return on assets than otherwise similar corporations (or divisions) with "newer" assets. Since asset age and changes in price level are explicitly considered in the TRW approach, this should produce a more reasonable accounting-based comparison between TRW and peer companies and among the divisions of TRW as well.

A more general, conceptual innovation in compensation design has been proposed by Booz, Allen & Hamilton Inc. The consulting firm's compensation specialists have developed what they call a "Strategic Reward Map" (see Exhibit 6-2). The Strategic Reward Map has two dimensions. The first is called "risk posture." It is measured by the ratio of contingent compensation (i.e., the sum of yearly bonus, stock options, SARs, performance plans, restricted stock, and phantom stock) to yearly salary. This dimension attempts to capture the degree to which an executive's compensation is "at risk." The second dimension is called "time focus." It is measured by the ratio of long-term compensation (i.e., the sum of stock options, SARs, performance plans, restricted stock, and phantom stock) to the annual bonus. This dimension attempts to capture the degree to which an executive's compensation is obtained from long-term (multi-year) performance measures versus short-term (single-year) performance measures. In terms of the agency theory framework, the risk posture and time focus variables are measures of (1) the potentially nondiversifiable risk imposed upon the executive and (2) the executive's decision-making horizon.

The Strategic Reward Map has several potential applications. First, it provides a simple way to synthesize the critical elements and compare compensation practices within a sample of firms. Second, it provides a convenient way to track changes in the "mix" of compensation components over time. Also, it may be possible to develop recommendations regarding contractual design in various portions of the map. For example, consider a firm that has a large market share in a profitable industry with substantial barriers to entry, but where product or service innovation is unlikely to be profitable. For this type of company, it may be desirable to motivate managers to be conservative in their decision making and to be most concerned with the short-term impact of their actions (that is, make few changes and simply manage the existing customer relationships). The executive compensation contracts would accordingly produce a risk posture and time focus in the quadrant labeled C in Exhibit 6-2. By contrast, if the profitability of the firm depends upon executives undertaking risky investments with long-term payoffs, then the compensation plan should be structured so as to fall in quadrant B.[34]

Another approach deserving mention—one that has been widely popularized by executive compensation and management consulting firms— is to measure corporate performance by the "spread" between return on equity (ROE) and the equity cost of capital.[35] One can justify the use of ROE "spread," just as one can justify the use of many financial surrogates, by arguing that this measure provides additional information about managerial actions not contained in stock price changes. But this measure is typically cited as the appropriate scorecard for compensation purposes because of its strong positive correlation with the ratio of the market value of

EXHIBIT 6-2
Strategic Reward Map (Booz, Allen & Hamilton)

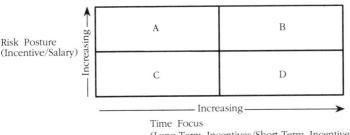

equity to historical book value. This empirical correlation is then used to justify the statement that the most direct way to create shareholder value is to increase the spread between ROE and the equity cost of capital.

There are a number of serious flaws with this argument for using ROE "spread," at least as the sole basis for evaluating managerial performance. For one thing, ROE is an *accounting* measure, one which has all of the inherent problems associated with the historical cost accounting system (e.g., inflation distortions and arbitrary cost allocations). The equity cost of capital, however, is a *market-determined* required rate of return for investing capital in risky projects, and it is at best unclear how the cost of capital is related to the ROE. Moreover, all of the empirical analysis supporting "spread" uses the ratio of market to book as the primary measure of management's success in creating shareholder value. But it is not obvious that shareholders' primary interest is served by managements intent on maximizing their company's price-to-book ratio. The most direct measure of interest to shareholders is the rate of return on their shares. And we are aware of no evidence that indicates that "spread" is directly associated with total shareholder return (or, better yet, with the rate of shareholder return in excess of the normal rate of return given the company's risk).

In fact, it is easy to illustrate that managers compensated on the basis of ROE "spread" may be motivated to decrease shareholder wealth. For example, assume that a manager is considering the adoption of two investment projects, both of which are expected to have a return that exceeds the firm's cost of capital. Assume the ROE "spread" for project A exceeds the "spread" for project B. If the manager is compensated on the basis of ROE "spread" *alone*, he can maximize the "spread" and his compensation by selecting only project A. In this example, the use of "spread" (or any rate of return measure) can have the unfortunate effect of motivating the manager to reject projects that would increase shareholder wealth.[36]

Given this potential problem of "underinvestment" (as well as the potential for manipulating accounting-based measures in general), we recommend caution in using the ROE "spread" as the principal measure of corporate success and as the "scorecard" for computing management incentive awards.

SUMMARY

Our review of the academic research has provided an analysis of a variety of issues concerning executive compensation. We began by using agency theory as an economic framework to identify potential conflicts of interest between management and shareholders. Viewed in this context, the primary function of a corporate compensation plan is to reduce such conflicts by providing management with the strongest possible incentives to maximize shareholder value.

The framework enables us to offer some specific suggestions for reducing management-stockholder conflict through the design of compensation contracts. Empirical tests in the agency literature show that executives respond predictably to the incentives built into compensation contracts. Furthermore, *changes* in compensation plans affect executive decision making in ways consistent with our theory of corporate managers as self-interested economic agents.

The available evidence on the relationship between executive pay and corporate performance documents a positive relationship between senior executives' annual incomes and annual shareholder returns. The correlation becomes especially clear when changes in the value of executive holdings in their own company's stock and stock options (which are often quite substantial) are included in the calculation of income.

The labor market of executives also plays a critical role in curbing management's tendency to pursue its own self-interest at the expense of its stockholders. Research bearing on the executive labor market suggests that an executive's opportunity wage—and, in fact, the ability to retain his job—is related to the effect of his decisions on his shareholders. Also, research showing negative market responses to unexpected deaths of CEOs suggests that most executives are not able to exercise enough control over boards of directors to pay themselves more (relative to their contribution to the firm's profits) than the compensation required by alternative managers.

In general the emerging body of research on the economic consequences of executive compensation suggests, contrary to most discussions in the popular press, that executive compensation is not total "madness." This, of course, does not imply that the conflicts are totally resolved, or that all companies are equally proficient at controlling these conflicts.[37]

The recent trend of corporate reorganizations (spinoffs, leveraged buyouts, and so forth) may also reflect attempts by executives and shareholders to control management incentive problems.[38] One of the more plausible arguments why management groups and investors are paying substantial premiums over market to take firms private is the radical improvement in management incentives. Taking the firm private greatly reduces and, in some cases, eliminates the separation of ownership and control that characterizes most large public corporations. Corporate spinoffs also promise improvements in management incentives. By separating operating units that were previously combined, spinoffs allow the performance of the individual operating units to be evaluated more accurately, thereby improving the ability of the parent company to reward and thus motivate divisional operating managers.

NOTES

1. *Fortune*, July 12, 1982.

2. Graef Crystal, "Congress Thinks It Knows Best About Executive Compensation," *The Wall Street Journal*, July 30, 1984.

3. "Reform Executive Pay or Congress Will," *The Wall Street Journal*, April 24, 1984.

4. On other fronts, although generally only in isolated cases, shareholder activists have levelled charges of "excessive" compensation in attempts to oust incumbent directors in proxy fights. See, for example, the proxy fight discussions regarding Pantry Pride Inc. in *The Wall Street Journal*, Proxy Contest Announcement, November 21, 1984, p. 45.

5. Louis J. Brindisi, "Creating Shareholder Value: A New Mission for Executive Compensation," in Joel M. Stern, G. Bennett Steward III, and Donald H. Chew, eds., *Corporate Restructuring and Executive Compensation* (Cambridge, MA: Ballinger, 1989), pp. 323–338; and Jude Rich and Ennius Bergsma, "Pay Executives to Create Wealth," *Chief Executive* (Autumn 1982), pp. 16–19.

6. See, for example, Alfred Rappaport, "How to Design Value-Contributing Executive Incentives," *Journal of Business Strategy* 4 (1983).

7. For example, it is sometimes argued that founders of firms (e.g., Henry Ford) place such a high value on power and maintaining control over the operations of the firm that these actions decrease their personal wealth and the wealth of the shareholders. In this context, perquisite consumption can be very costly to shareholders. Similarly, the announcement of a "bad" corporate acquisition can decrease the total market value of the acquiring firm's stock by millions of dollars.

8. For some additional discussion of tax/incentive aspects of compensation contracts, see G. Hite and M. Long, "Taxes and Executive Stock Options," *Journal of Accounting and Economics* 4 (1982); M. Miller and M. Scholes, "Executive Compensation, Taxes and Incentives," in W. Sharpe and C. Cootner, eds., *Financial Economics Essays in Honor of Paul Cootner* (1982); C. Smith and R. Watts, "Incentive and Tax Effects of U.S. Executive Compensation Plans," *Australian Management Journal* (1983); R. Lambert and D. Larcker, "Stock Options and Managerial Incentives," working paper, Northwestern University (1984); and M. Scholes and M. Wolfson, "Employee Compensation and Taxes: Links with Incentives and with Investment and Financing Decisions," working paper, Stanford University (1984).

9. A recent study by Rick Antle and Abbie Smith has, in fact, shown that the average level of total compensation (salary plus bonus plus change in the value of stock holdings) is positively related to the riskiness of total compensation. See R. Antle and A. Smith, "Measuring Executive Compensation: Methods and An Application," working paper, University of Chicago (1984).

10. It is, of course, common to observe companies using multiple performance criteria in their compensation contracts. For example, Libby-Owens-Ford Co. has a performance plan tied to increases in return on net assets and increases in sales. In similar manner, Sears, Roebuck, and Co. bases their annual bonus payments on a combination of return on equity, growth in total revenues, net sales, gross profit, and growth in net premiums earned. The subset of performance criteria used by Sears for specific executives varies depending upon the business unit and executive level.

11. For additional discussion of relative performance contracts, see Mark Ubelhart, "A New Look at Executive Compensation Plans," *Cash Flow* (1981); and R. Antle and A. Smith, "An Empirical Investigation into the Relative Performance Evaluation of Corporate Executives," working paper, University of Chicago (1984).

12. Throughout the analysis, we assume that the share price is the present value of the expected future cash flows that accrue to equity holders discounted at the appropriate risk-adjusted rate of return. Therefore, share price has an inherently "long-term" focus.

13. For some evidence that the stock price impounds the consequences of unexpected changes in "long-term" investments, see J. McConnell and C. Muscarella, "Capitalized Value, Growth Opportunities, and Corporate Expenditure Announcements," working paper, Purdue University (1983).

14. For example, 54 of the *Fortune* 100 have performance plans as of 1983. See Towers, Perrin, Forster & Crosby, 1983 *Executive Total Compensation Study*, New York: Towers, Perrin, Forster & Crosby (1983).

15. P. Healy, "The Effect of Bonus Schemes on Accounting Decisions," *Journal of Accounting and Economics* 7 (1985), pp. 85–107.

16. The hypotheses of Healy's study are similar to those developed and empirically examined in D. Larcker and L. Revsine, "The Oil and Gas Accounting Controversy: An Analysis of Economic Consequences," *The Accounting Review* (1983).

17. M. Wolfson, "Empirical Evidence of Incentive Problems and Their Mitigation in Oil and Gas Tax Shelter Programs," in J. Pratt and R. Zeckhauser, *Principals and Agents: The Structure of Business* (Boston: Harvard Business School Press, 1985).

18. D. Larcker, "Short-Term Compensation Contracts, Executive Expenditure Decisions, and Corporate Performance: The Case of Commercial Banks," working paper, Northwestern University (1984).

19. Y. Amihud and B. Lev, "Risk Reduction as a Managerial Motive for Conglomerate Mergers," *Bell Journal of Economics* 12 (1981).

20. For additional discussion of managerial incentives in acquisitions, see B. Lev, "Observations on the Merger Phenomenon and a Review of the Evidence," *Midland Corporate Finance Journal* 1 (1983); D. Larcker, "Managerial Incentives in Mergers and Their Impacts on Shareholder Wealth," in Stern, Steward, and Chew, eds., *Corporate Restructuring*, pp. 311–322; and R. Lambert and D. Larcker, "Golden Parachutes, Executive Decision-Making, and Shareholder Wealth," *Journal of Accounting and Economics* 7 (1985).

21. R. Lambert and D. Larcker, "Stock Options and Managerial Incentives," working paper, Northwestern University (1984).

22. D. Larcker, "The Association Between Performance Plan Adoption and Corporate Capital Investment," *Journal of Accounting and Economics* 5 (1983).

23. For an analysis of the security market response to the adoption of "long-term" compensation contracts, see D. Larcker, "The Association Between Performance Plan Adoption and Corporate Capital Investment;" and J. Brickley, S. Bhagat, and R. Lease, "The Impact of Long-Range Managerial Compensation Plans on Shareholder Wealth," *Journal of Accounting and Economics* 7 (1985). It is important to note that the market reaction to the disclosure of a new compensation plan will reflect not only the market's assessment of the desirability of the compensation scheme, but also the market's assessment of any new strategy changes that are being introduced at the same time.

24. One of the few attempts in the financial press to document its case more carefully is the *Fortune* article by Carol Loomis, which graphed executive compensation (defined as salary plus bonus) versus a single accounting measure of corporate performance. As discussed in more detail shortly, there are two problems with this study. First, instead of the change in shareholder wealth, return

on equity is used as the measure of firm performance. Second, the analysis ignores the stock options and shares owned by the executive, the value of which are of course directly related to shareholder wealth.

25. K. Murphy, "Corporate Performance and Managerial Remuneration," *Journal of Accounting and Economics* 7 (1985); and A. Coughlin and R. Schmidt, "Executive Compensation, Management Turnover, and Firm Performance: An Empirical Investigation," *Journal of Accounting and Economics* 7 (1985), pp. 43–66.

26. For some additional evidence on the importance of equity holdings to managerial decision making, see G. Benston, "The Self-Serving Management Hypothesis: Some Evidence," *Journal of Accounting and Economics* 7 (1985), pp. 67–84; R. Walkling and M. Long, "Agency Theory, Managerial Welfare, and Takeover Bid Resistance," *Rand Journal of Economics* 15 (1984); and W. Lewellen, C. Loderer, and A. Rosenfeld, "Merger Decisions and Executive Stock Ownership in Acquiring Firms," *Journal of Accounting and Economics* 7 (1985), pp. 209–231.

27. For additional discussion of this point, see Eugene Fama, "Agency Problems and the Theory of the Firm," *Journal of Political Economy* 88 (1980).

28. R. Lambert and D. Larcker, "Executive Compensation Effects of Large Corporate Acquisitions," working paper, Northwestern University (1984).

29. A. Coughlan and R. Schmidt, "Executive Compensation, Management Turnover, and Firm Performance: An Empirical Investigation," *Journal of Accounting and Economics* 7 (1985), pp. 43–66.

30. W. Johnson, R. Magee, N. Nagarajan, and H. Newman, "An Analysis of the Stock Price Reaction to Sudden Executive Deaths: Implications for the Managerial Labor Market," *Journal of Accounting and Economics* 7 (1985), pp. 151–174.

31. However, the study does find a significant positive reaction to the announcement of the unexpected death of an executive who was the corporate founder. This is consistent with the hypothesis that corporate founders, who often own a substantial portion of the firm's stock, are able to exercise control over the board of directors that enables them to be paid more relative to their contribution to firm value than their successors.

32. It is important to realize that the security market reaction to a CEO death is more complex than simply the difference in capitalized value of the compensation paid to the new CEO relative to the old CEO. The magnitude of the change in shareholder wealth depends upon the new CEO's contribution to firm value minus compensation paid (in technical terms, the CEO's marginal product) relative to the old CEO's contribution to the firm value minus compensation.

33. Notice that this contract is similar to the market-indexed option suggested by Mark Ubelhart. See "Business Strategy, Performance Measurement, and Compensation," *Midland Corporate Finance Journal* (Winter 1985), pp. 67–75,

and also an earlier article, "A New Look at Executive Compensation Plans," *Cash Flow* (1981). Relative shareholder value compensation contracts have also been adopted by Clevepak Corp. and U.S. West.

34. One must be careful, however, not to impose so much risk on the manager that he becomes too conservative in his decision making.

35. See Louis Brindisi, "Creating Shareholder Value: A New Mission for Executive Compensation," pp. 323–338; and J. Rich and J. Larson, "Why Some Long-Term Incentives Fail," *Compensation Review* (1984) for a discussion of "spread" in a compensation context. One case of adoption of this approach is First Tennessee Corp.'s executive compensation plan.

36. One solution to this problem is to change the compensation contract from one based upon rate of return to one based upon residual income. See C. Horngren, *Cost Accounting: A Managerial Emphasis*. Prentice-Hall (1982), Chapter 20 for some additional discussion of this point.

37. It is important to note that our focus has been primarily directed to the use of compensation contracts and external labor markets to motivate managers to work in shareholders' interests. We have not discussed the disciplining effects of competition within the internal labor market and the market for corporate control. Obviously, the role that compensation contracts play in motivating managers is influenced by the ability of these other mechanisms to discipline managers into selecting actions that increase shareholder wealth.

38. For additional discussion of these issues, see G. Hite and J. Owners, "The Restructuring of Corporate America: An Overview," in Stern, Steward, and Chew, eds., *Corporate Restructuring*, pp. 89–104; K. Schipper and A. Smith, "The Corporate Spin-Off Phenomenon," in Stern, Steward, and Chew, eds., *Corporate Restructuring*, pp. 165–176; and H. DeAngelo, L. DeAngelo, and E. Rice, "Going Private: The Effects of Change in Corporate Ownership Structure," in Stern, Steward, and Chew, eds., *Corporate Restructuring*, pp. 193–206.

PART I-C

The Impact of Executive Pay on Organizations

7

THE ORGANIZATIONAL IMPACT OF EXECUTIVE COMPENSATION

Edward E. Lawler III

REWARD SYSTEMS ARE ONE of the most prominent and frequently discussed features of organizations. Indeed, the literature in organizational behavior and personnel management is replete with the examples of their functional as well as dysfunctional role in organizations.[1] In this literature, executive compensation has been given some attention, but it has received more attention in business magazines such as *Fortune* and *BusinessWeek*. The magazine articles have generally focused on the high level of executive compensation, while the academic literature has focused on how it is determined and on its impact on the executives themselves.[2]

This chapter will focus on how the design choices that are involved in executive compensation affect the behavior of the rest of the organization, that is, the behavior of nonexecutives. My focus is different from that of most of the literature, but one that is important. The argument for its importance rests on the assumption that executive compensation represents a very visible model and symbol of how the organization operates, what it cares about, and what behavior is rewarded. If, as is sometimes true, executive compensation systems are models of how individuals are compensated elsewhere in the organization, then how these systems operate inevitably affects how the other pay systems operate. If they are different from the compensation systems used elsewhere, then the difference may be an important feature of the organization and its culture. In short, no matter what is done with executive compensation, it has important implications for the overall operation of the organization.

IMPACT OF REWARD SYSTEMS

The first step in discussing executive compensation systems is to consider what behavioral impact they can have in organizations. The research on reward systems suggests that, potentially, they can influence six factors.[3]

Attraction and Retention

Research on job choice, career choice, and turnover shows that the kind and level of rewards influence who is attracted to an organization, who will continue to work for it, as well as which jobs individuals will try to obtain.[4] In general, those organizations and jobs that offer the most rewards tend to attract and retain the most people. This seems to occur because high reward levels lead to high satisfaction, which, in turn, leads to lower turnover.

Equity theory argues that employees will feel satisfied enough to remain in a job when their rewards compare favorably with those of people performing similar jobs in other organizations. The emphasis here is on *external* comparisons because turnover means leaving an organization for a better situation elsewhere. Internal equity is also important, but not as likely to affect turnover. If there is internal inequity, employees may not quit, but they are more likely to be dissatisfied, complain, look for internal transfers, and mistrust the organization.

Motivation of Performance

When certain specifiable conditions exist, reward systems have been demonstrated to motivate performance.[5] What are those conditions? Important rewards must be perceived to be tied to effective performance in a timely fashion. Organizations get the kind of behavior that leads to the rewards employees value. People have needs and mental maps of what the world is like. They use the maps to choose those behaviors that lead to outcomes that satisfy their needs. They are inherently neither motivated nor unmotivated to perform effectively; performance motivation depends on the situation, how it is perceived, and personal needs.

The approach that best explains how people develop and act on their mental maps is called expectancy theory.[6] The theory is complex, but, in fact, it is made up of a series of fairly straightforward observations about behavior. Three concepts serve as the key building blocks.

- *Performance-Outcome Expectancy.* Individuals believe or expect that if they behave in a certain way, they will get certain things. For example, if they produce ten units, they will receive the normal hourly pay rate, but if they produce fifteen units, they will receive the hourly rate plus a bonus. Similarly, individuals may believe that certain levels of performance will lead to approval or disapproval from peers or supervisors. Each performance level leads to a number of different kinds of outcomes.

- *Attractiveness.* Outcomes differ in attractiveness for different individuals because outcome values are a result of individual needs and perceptions. For example, some individuals may value an opportunity for promotion because of a need for achievement or power, while others may not want to leave their work group because of a need for affiliation with others. Similarly, a fringe benefit such as a pension plan may have great value for older workers but little for younger employees.
- *Effort-Performance Expectancy.* An individual associates each behavior with a certain expectation or probability of success. For example, employees may have a strong expectancy (e.g., ninety-ten) that if they put forth the effort, they can produce ten units an hour, but that they have only a fifty-fifty chance of producing fifteen units an hour.

Putting these concepts together, it is possible to make a basic statement about motivation. In general, an individual motivation to behave in a certain way is greatest when:

1. The individual believes that the behavior will lead to certain outcomes (performance-outcome expectancy).
2. The individual feels that the outcomes are attractive.
3. The individual believes that performance at a desired level is possible (effort-performance expectancy).

Given a number of alternative levels of behavior (ten, fifteen, or twenty units of production per hour, for example), an individual will choose the level of performance that has the greatest motivational force associated with it, a level indicated by a combination of relevant expectancies, outcomes, and values. In other words, when faced with choices about behavior, an individual considers: "Can I perform at that level if I try? If I perform at that level, what will happen?" and "How do I feel about those things that will happen?" The individual then decides to behave in a way that seems to have the best chance of producing desired outcomes.

Skill Development

Just as reward systems can motivate performance, they can also motivate skill development. The same principle applies: basically, individuals tend to learn those skills that lead to rewards. Thus, reward systems that offer promotion tend to encourage individuals to learn those skills that lead to promotion. In the case of skill development motivation, the key issues are how large the rewards are for different types of skill development (the attractiveness issue), how available the opportunities are to learn the skills, and, finally, how sure a reward is if the skills are learned.

Culture

Reward systems are one feature of organizations that contribute to the overall culture. Depending on how reward systems are developed, structured, and managed, they can help create a wide variety of organizational cultures—human resource-oriented, entrepreneurial, innovative, competence-based, bureaucratic, family-oriented, or participative. Reward systems shape culture precisely because of their strong influence on motivation, satisfaction, skill development, and membership. The behaviors they cause become the dominant patterns of behavior in the organization and lead to perceptions and beliefs about what the organization stands for, believes in, and values.

Perhaps the most obvious connection between pay practices and culture concerns performance-based pay. The absence or presence of this policy can have a dramatic impact on the culture of an organization because it so clearly communicates what the performance norms are. Relatively high pay levels can produce a culture in which people feel they are an elite group working for a top-flight company; innovative pay practices such as flexible benefits can produce a culture in which people are willing to try new ways of doing things; and a system that involves employees in pay decisions can produce a participative culture in which employees are generally committed to the organization and its success.[7]

Reinforcement and Definition of Structure

The reward system of an organization can reinforce and define the organization's structure.[8] Often this feature of reward systems is not fully considered during their design. As a result, their impact on the structure of an organization is often unintentional. This does not mean, however, that the impact of the reward system on structure is usually minimal. Indeed, the system can help define the status hierarchy, determine the degree to which people in technical positions influence line management, and strongly influence the organization's decision structure. The most important structural impact of reward systems is on integration and differentiation.[9] Reward systems are a powerful force for integration and cooperation when they create situations in which individuals share a common fate as far as rewards are concerned. Conversely, they can create differentiation when they pit individuals against each other in competition for rewards, and when they put different parts of the organization on different reward systems.

Cost

Reward systems are expensive. Indeed, pay alone may represent over 50 percent of an organization's operating cost. Thus, it is important in designing the reward system to focus on how high these costs should be and how they will vary as a function of the organization's ability to pay. For example, a reasonable outcome of a well-designed pay system might be an increased cost when the organization has the money to spend and a decreased cost when it does not. An additional objective might be lower overall reward system costs than those of business competitors.

DESIGN OPTIONS

There is almost an infinite number of ways to design and manage reward systems in organizations. The focus in the remainder of this chapter will be on the visible extrinsic rewards that an organization controls and that can, as a matter of policy and practice, be allocated to executives on a targeted basis—pay, benefits, status symbols, and perquisites.

A useful dichotomy in thinking about the design of reward systems is process/content. All organizational systems have a content or structural dimension as well as a process dimension. The structural dimension of a reward system refers to the formal mechanisms, procedures, and practices (e.g., the salary structures, the performance appraisal forms), in short, the nuts and bolts of the system. The process side refers to the communication and decision-making parts of the system. The key issues here are the degree of openness and the degree of participation.

I will begin the discussion of design choices by looking at the key structural choices and then consider the key process choices. Once I have reviewed the design options, I will consider the organizational effects of the choices.

KEY STRUCTURAL DECISIONS

Basis for Reward Levels

Typically, pay and perquisites are based primarily on the types of jobs that people hold. Indeed, with the exception of bonuses and merit salary increases, in most organizations the standard policy at all levels is to evaluate the job, not the person, and then to set the reward level. This approach is based on the assumption that job worth can be determined and that the person doing the job is worth as much to the organization as the job itself. This assumption is in many respects valid since through such techniques as job evaluation it is possible to determine what other organizations are paying for the same or similar jobs. Among the advantages of this system are that it assures an organization that its compensation costs are not dramatically out of line with those of its competitors and it gives a somewhat objective basis to compensation practices. It produces, however, negative results in the areas of costs, skill development, and culture.[10]

An alternative to job-based pay is paying individuals for their skills.[11] In many cases, this approach will not produce dramatically different pay rates than are produced by paying for the job. After all, the skills people have usually match reasonably well the jobs that they are doing. Such an approach, however, can produce different pay results. Often people possess more skills than the job demands; in such cases, individuals are paid more than they would be under a job-based system. Further, individuals do not always have the necessary skills when they enter a job and do not deserve the pay that goes with that job. In these cases, individuals have to earn the right to be paid whatever the job-related skills are worth.

Perhaps the most important changes that occur when skill-based or competence-based pay is used are in organizational climate and motivation. Instead of being rewarded for moving up the hierarchy, people are rewarded for increasing their skills and developing themselves. This can create a climate of concern for personal growth as well as a highly talented work force. It can also decrease the attractiveness of promotion. In factories where the system is used many people can perform multiple tasks, thus creating an extremely knowledgeable and flexible work force.

Role of Performance in Determining Rewards

Perhaps the key strategic decision to be made in the design of a reward system is whether it will be based on performance. Once this decision is made, a number of other features of the reward system tend to fall into place. The major alternative to basing pay on performance is to base it on seniority. Many government agencies, for example, base their rates on the job and then on how long a person has been in that job. In Japan, pay is also often based on seniority, although individuals may receive bonuses based on corporate performance.

Most business organizations in the United States say they reward individual performance.[12] However, a true merit pay or promotion system is often difficult to administer. It is not easy to specify what kind of performance is desired and determine whether it has been demonstrated. Indeed, it has been observed that many organizations would be better off if they did not try to relate pay and promotion to performance and relied on other methods to motivate employees.[13] There is ample evidence that a poorly designed and administered pay-for-performance system can do more harm than good.[14]

There are numerous ways to relate pay to performance. Pay rewards vary widely and can include benefits, stock, and cash. The frequency with which rewards are given can also vary tremendously, ranging from a few minutes to many years. Performance can be measured and rewarded at the individual, group, and organizational levels. Finally, there are many different kinds of performance that can be rewarded. For example, managers can be rewarded for sales increases, productivity volumes, ability to develop subordinates, cost reduction ideas, and so on.

Rewarding some behaviors and not others clearly influences performance. Thus, in decisions about what is to be rewarded, consideration needs to be given to such issues as short- versus long-term performance, risk taking versus risk aversion, division performance versus total corporate performance, ROI maximization versus sales growth, and so on. Decisions about such issues as using stock options (a long-term incentive), for example, should be made only after careful consideration of whether they support the kind of organizational performance that is desired.[15] It is likely that the managers of different divisions of a business should be rewarded for different kinds of performance. For example, growth businesses call for different rewards systems than do "cash cows" because the managers are expected to produce different results.[16]

Market Position of Reward Level

The reward system influences behavior partially as a function of how the reward levels compare to those of other organizations. Organizations frequently have well-developed policies about how their pay levels should compare with the levels in other companies. In the design of pay systems this structural issue is crucial because it can strongly influence the kind of people who are attracted to and retained by an organization, the turnover rate, and the selection ratio. Simply stated, those organizations that adopt a more aggressive stance with respect to the marketplace end up paying more but attracting and retaining more individuals. This strategy may pay off, particularly if turnover is costly and if being successful demands a highly talented work force.

On the other hand, if many of the jobs are low-skilled and easily filled, a high-pay strategy may not be effective. It can increase labor costs and produce minimum benefits. Of course, all jobs do not have to be high-paid. Indeed, some organizations pay well for certain key skills they need and pay average or below average for other skills. This has obvious business advantages in terms of allowing an organization to attract the critical skills that it needs to succeed while at the same time controlling costs.

Although it is not often recognized, the market position a company adopts with respect to its reward systems can also have a noticeable impact on organizational culture. For example, a policy that calls for above-market pay can contribute to the feeling that the organization is elite, that people must be competent to work there, and that they are indeed fortunate to be there. A policy that pays groups different market rates can, on the other hand, cause divisive pressures within the organization.

Degree of Hierarchy in the Reward System

Closely related to the issue of job-based versus competence-based pay is the hierarchical nature of the reward system. Hierarchical systems pay people more money and perquisites as they move up the organizational ladder. This approach strongly reinforces hierarchical power relationships in the organization. Indeed, the reward system itself may have more levels than the formal organization chart has and that can create additional status differences in the organization.

The alternative to a hierarchical system is one in which differences in rewards and perquisites based on management level are dramatically downplayed. For example, in those large corporations (e.g., Digital Equipment Corporation) that adopt an egalitarian stance toward rewards, such things as private parking spaces, executive restrooms, and special entrances are eliminated. People from all levels in the organization eat together, work together, and travel together. Further, individuals can become relatively highly paid by working their way up a technical ladder. A less hierarchical approach to pay and other rewards tends to encourage decision making by expertise rather than by position, and it minimizes status differences in the organization.

As with all reward system options, there is no right or wrong answer as to how hierarchical a system should be. In general, a steeply hierarchical system makes the most sense if an organization needs relatively rigid bureaucratic behavior, strong top-down authority, and a strong motivation for people to move up the organization hierarchy. A more egalitarian approach fits with a more participative management style and the desire to retain technical specialists and experts in nonmanagement roles or lower-level management roles. It is not surprising, therefore, that many of the organizations that have emphasized egalitarianism are in high-technology and knowledge-based businesses.

PROCESS ISSUES AND REWARD ADMINISTRATION

Communication about Rewards

Organizations differ widely in how much information they communicate about their reward systems. At one extreme, some organizations are extremely secretive, particularly about pay. They forbid people to talk about their pay, give minimal information about how rewards are decided upon and allocated, and have no publicly disseminated policies. Of course, in public corporations, even though the pay of most managers is secret, the pay of the top five executives is a matter of public record. At the other extreme, some organizations are so open that everyone's pay is a matter of public record, as is the organization's pay philosophy (many new high-involvement plants operate this way).[17] In addition, all promotions are subject to open job postings and, in some instances, peer groups discuss the eligibility of people for promotion.

The difference between an open and a closed communication policy is enormous, but there is no right or wrong approach. Rather, it is a matter of picking a position on the continuum from open to secret that is supportive of the overall culture and behavior needed for organizational effectiveness. An open system tends to encourage people to ask questions, share data, and ultimately be involved in decisions. A secret system tends to put people in a more dependent position, keeps power concentrated at the top, and allows an organization to keep its options open. Some negative side effects of secret systems are the considerable perceptual distortion about the actual rewards that people get and a low-trust environment in which people have trouble understanding the relationship between pay and performance.[18] Thus, a structurally sound pay system may be rather ineffective because it is misperceived.

Open systems put considerable pressure on organizations to do an effective job of administering rewards. Thus, if difficult-to-defend practices such as merit pay are to be implemented, considerable time and effort need to be invested in pay administration. If they are instituted and run poorly, strong pressure usually develops to eliminate them and pay everyone the same.[19] Ironically, if an organization wants to spend little time administrating rewards but still have merit pay, secrecy may be the best policy, although secrecy in turn may limit the effectiveness of the plan.

Decision Making about Reward Systems

Closely related to the issue of communication is that of decision making. Open communication makes possible the involvement of a wide range of people in the decision-making process. Further, if individuals are to be actively involved in decisions concerning reward systems, they need to be informed about policy and actual practice.

In discussing the decision-making processes used in reward systems, it is important to distinguish between decisions about the design of the systems and decisions about their administration. It is possible to have different decision-making styles for each.

Executive compensation systems are typically designed by a combination of consultants, board members, and the executives. Systems for lower levels are usually designed by top management with the aid of staff support, and administered by strict reliance on the chain of command. The assumption is that this approach provides the proper checks and balances and locates decision making where the expertise rests. In many cases, this is a valid assumption, and it certainly fits well with a management style that emphasizes hierarchy, bureaucracy, and control through the use of extrinsic rewards. It does not fit, however, with an organization that believes in more open communication, higher levels of involvement on the part of the work force, and control through commitment. It also does not fit when expertise is spread broadly throughout the organization.

There have been reports in the research literature of organizations experimenting with involving employees in the design of pay systems.[20] For example, in some instances when employees have been involved in designing their own bonus system, the results have been generally favorable; they raise important issues and provide expertise that is not normally available to the designers of the system. Perhaps more important, once the system is designed, the acceptance level tends to be very high, which often leads to a rapid startup and a commitment to seeing the system survive.

Some companies have experimented with peer groups handling the day-to-day decision making about who should receive pay increases and how jobs should be evaluated and placed in pay structures. The most visible examples of this are in the new participative plants that use skill-based pay.[21] In these plants, the work group reviews the performance of the individual and decides whether he or she has acquired the new skills. Interestingly, what evidence there is suggests that this has gone very well, which is not surprising in many respects, since peers often have the best information about performance and are able to make a valid assessment. The problem in traditional organizations is that the groups lack the motivation to provide valid feedback and to behave responsibly, thus, their expertise is of no use. In more participative open systems, the motivational problem seems to be less severe and, as a result, involvement in decision making seems to be more effective. There also have been isolated instances of executives assessing each other in a peer-group setting (e.g., in Graphic Controls Corporation).

Overall, there is solid evidence that participative approaches to reward system design and administration can be effective. The key seems to be to adopt reward practices that complement the management style of the organization so that the skills and norms to make them effective are already in place.

EXECUTIVE COMPENSATION: STRUCTURE AND PROCESS

Basis for Reward Level

Executive compensation systems are classically job-based systems; at least the formal policies say they are job-based. With the kind of individual deals that are often struck, it can be argued that they are more person-based.[22] In any case, they are not formal skill-based systems. Pay levels are set by comparing senior management jobs to similar jobs in other corporations. The adoption of a job-based system for executives usually means that "the way" to pay all managers is through a job-based system. Most jobs below the executive level are scored on a job-evaluation system that places great weight on the amount of responsibility in the job. Because job-based systems evaluate senior management positions at the high end of the scale, all other jobs in the organization are paid at lower rates. In effect, executive compensation rates are a cap on the entire pay system.

In terms of skill development, job-based pay creates an environment in which the most rewarded skills are those that lead to vertical movement within the organization. This is particularly clear to people because of the public nature of executive salaries. A moderately observant person recognizes that the most highly rewarded individuals in an organization are those at the top and, therefore, that learning managerial skills is the way to get the largest rewards. This is not necessarily a problem in terms of organizational effectiveness, however.

In a traditionally managed organization, the objective may be to motivate the best and the brightest individuals to become managers. In a high-technology organization, however, it is important that many of the best and brightest strive for technical excellence and perhaps stay in lower-level technical or managerial positions.

Another consequence of a job-based system concerns the way people try to restructure their jobs. Since job-evaluation systems pay individuals for the size of the job, there is a clear incentive for individuals to expand their jobs. They are rewarded for taking on more responsibility and increasing their budget, the number of subordinates they have, and the number of management levels under them. This can often lead to empire building and to competition among executives, and those below them, for management responsibilities and budgetary size. It can also drive the entire organization toward a growth culture and high overhead costs.

Finally, one more point should be made about skill-based versus job-based pay. Even those organizations that adopt skill-based pay tend to do it only for nonmanagement personnel.[23] The reason comes from the very top of the organization. Career tracks and pay structures in most organizations are keyed to what happens at the top, and as a result, managers throughout the organization want a career and reward system that is tied to how executives are treated. They resist the suggestion that they be put on a skill-based pay system and treated like production workers. Even in the new participative plants, skill-based pay typically does not cover the managerial employees, and probably never will until skilled-based rewards are used for all management levels.

Role of Performance in Determining Rewards for Executives

The many performance-based approaches to executive compensation have very different impacts on the behavior of executives. My concern, however, is not with this impact but with the impact on the rest of the organization.

In many respects it is difficult to have effective pay-for-performance systems throughout an organization when no such program exists for senior executives, or if the system for the senior executives is poorly administered. If no true pay-for-performance system exists at the senior-management level, it is hard for senior managers to argue credibly for the importance of a pay-for-performance system at the lower levels. This can be a particular problem where pay-for-performance systems designed for the lower levels in the organization are driven by judgment rather than by formula.

Judgment-driven programs rely on performance appraisal inputs and, as is well documented, performance appraisals are difficult to do well.[24] They are particularly difficult to do well when senior management does not demonstrate effective performance appraisal behavior.[25] In essence, effective performance appraisal starts at senior-management levels with good role modeling and flows down through the organization. If appraisal does not start at the top, the senior executives' behavior implies that performance appraisals are only to be done for less important individuals; they are saying, "Do as I say, not as I do." This is not likely to motivate an ambitious manager to do a performance appraisal well. In the case of technical skills, poor role modeling may not be a problem. However, in evaluating performance where much behavior is influenced by norms, values, personal beliefs, and social influences, it can be a significant problem and can discourage managers from doing good performance appraisals.

The types of performance-based pay systems that exist at the senior levels of management indicate to a great extent the kind of behavior expected elsewhere in the organization. For example, if executives are paid primarily on the basis of short-term operating results, the message sent downward through the pay system is quite clear. Emphasize short-term results because that is what the organization values. Inevitably, senior managers will ask for and demand from their subordinates the kind of behavior that is congruent with their own reward systems. Thus, even if the message does not get through to other managers via the formal reward system, it certainly will get through in the formal and informal expectations of senior managers.

Pay-for-performance systems among senior managers that focus on the individual can have a very different impact from those centered on the group and the organization. Again, they communicate different cultures and desired behaviors to individuals throughout the organization. For example, plans that focus on individual rewards tend to foster a climate of individual excellence, competitiveness, and visibility. Plans that are collective in nature tend to encourage senior executives to behave in team-oriented ways and send a message that cooperative behavior is desirable. This, of course, is particularly likely to be true if the same kinds of plans that cover senior management also cover individuals at lower levels of the organization.

Finally, the degree to which executive compensation is based on performance has implications not only for how variable the salary costs of an organization are, but also for the organizational culture and what is seen as fair and equitable at other levels in the organization. For pay to be based on performance at other levels of the organization, it almost has to be at the senior level. Indeed, in most cases logic demands that the portion of pay that is based on performance be greatest for top management because this level has the greatest control over organizational performance. Thus, it is important that a significant amount of senior executive pay be based on performance in organizations that want pay-for-performance to exist at all levels. It would also seem hard for senior executives to run an organization based on commitment and involvement if they personally do not have a considerable amount of compensation tied to business performance, in particular, long-term business performance.[26]

In summary, pay-for-performance at the executive level is important not only because of how it drives the behavior of executives, but also because of how it drives the perceptions and behavior of individuals elsewhere in the organization. Because it is so visible and symbolically important, executive compensation signals to the rest of the organization how important cooperation is, what kind of commitment people are expected to make, and how much of their pay should be based on performance. Finally, it is a first step toward creating an organization in which labor costs are variable based on organizational performance.

Market Position of Reward Levels for Executives

Executive compensation can play a crucial role in determining the market price of jobs throughout the organization and the perceived fairness of that pricing. The pricing of executive jobs relative to the market is visible to all levels of the organization and, therefore, is an important reference point in terms of what employees feel should occur in the rest of the organization. If senior executives are particularly well paid, then other individuals can and will argue that they, too, should be paid well relative to their market. This internal equity argument can be a powerful one.

Of course, because an organization pays high wages at the senior-management level does not mean it has to pay high wages at all levels. Indeed, it can have different policies for different levels of the organization. If it does, however, this raises some important cultural issues. It sends a message that is hierarchical and, in many respects, elitist. It not only sends a strong message that senior managers are more important, it may even imply they take advantage of their position to make sure they are particularly well rewarded. In terms of behavioral consequences, this may not lead to turnover at the lower levels but it certainly can lead to a low level of trust in management, internal conflict, minimal commitment, and feelings of inequity.

If senior executives are restrained in their compensation levels, they are in a powerful position to argue for restraint at other levels. Ken Olsen, the CEO of Digital, has done this for years and it seems to have been relatively effective, even though his low pay is offset by his large ownership position. Other executives who have relatively low pay include Roy Vagelos at Merck and John Akers at IBM. Interestingly, both firms are widely admired for their positive corporate cultures.

If executives do not exercise restraint, they can set off demands for higher pay throughout the organization. This point is illustrated by the union-management discussions in the U.S. auto industry. The executives have tried to focus on the "high wages" of U.S. auto workers, while the union has pointed out that the executives are very highly paid on both a national and international basis. For example, in 1987, Lee Iacocca made $17 million while the CEO of the more successful Honda made $450,000. The CEOs at Ford and General Motors made over $2 million in 1987, while the CEOs of Peugeot and Daimler-Benz made $250,000 and $1.2 million, respectively.

Particularly interesting is the issue of an organizational response to a business downturn. One scenario is to ask for the greatest sacrifice at the lowest levels because that is where costs are highest, and in some cases the individuals there are more highly paid than their counterparts at foreign competitors. A second approach is to emphasize equal cuts throughout the organization. Finally, a third approach emphasizes greater cuts at senior management levels (e.g., Control Data and Hewlett-Packard). Equal or greater cuts at the senior-management level can have a dramatically different cultural impact than greater cuts at the lower levels of the organization. It puts management on a higher moral ground when it comes to asking for sacrifice at other levels. Again, the results may not show up in short-term turnover rates, but they may well show up in terms of culture and long-term commitment to the organization.

Degree of Hierarchy in Reward Systems

In considering executive compensation, it is important to separate three hierarchical features of reward systems. The first is the degree to which total compensation differs from the top to the bottom of the organization. The second is the degree to which symbols, perquisites, and highly visible rewards vary according to management level. The third is the degree to which different reward system practices and policies are in effect at different levels of the organization.

Let us look first at how total rewards differ from the top to the bottom of the organization. As is well documented elsewhere, American organizations tend to be very hierarchical with respect to total rewards. Senior executives get substantially more in total compensation than individuals elsewhere in the organization.[27] Many senior executives in the United States make over $1 million per year—at least fifty times more than the lower-paid employees in their companies. In most cases, this is a much higher multiple than exists elsewhere in the world. One clear impact of this is to make a management position particularly attractive. Thus, from a reward system point of view, individuals have a strong pull to move upward in the organization. As was noted earlier, this may be dysfunctional if a company feels it is important to keep skilled technical individuals at lower levels in the organization.

High executive compensation levels can also have an interesting impact in global businesses. In worldwide businesses, comparisons between pay scales in the United States and other countries are very relevant. This creates an interesting dilemma—or perhaps more accurately, problem—for U.S. executives. Clearly, it is to the competitive advantage of their companies for executives to keep salaries in their organization in line with or below those of the companies they compete with elsewhere in the world. It is difficult, however, for them to do this in a credible way when their own salaries are the ones most out of line with salaries elsewhere.

From a cultural point of view, the issue of visible perquisites and symbols of office is important. If these are plentiful and given out on the basis of hierarchical position, they can contribute strongly to an organization in which power, prestige, and decision making rest in management positions rather than with the individuals holding those positions. This creates and supports a culture of top-down bureaucratic management. It also reinforces the desirability of moving up the management ladder and influences the skill development system of the organization. The U.S. auto companies are prime examples of corporations that have extensive perquisite systems based on hierarchy and top-down management styles. Ford and General Motors are now publicly committed to making their management styles more participative. In order to accomplish this, both may have to abandon their perquisite systems.

Finally, many organizations have different incentive, benefit, and perquisite plans at different levels in the organization. They start at the bottom level, where individuals are put on hourly pay programs. This has the effect of differentiating them from managers and certainly from executives. At the same time, the plans integrate lower-level personnel by giving them a sense of commonality with other individuals at the same level in the organization. In many respects, this can be dysfunctional if management wants to integrate individuals and develop a strong organizationwide commitment to the success of the business.

Creating different performance-based reward systems for different levels in an organization can be particularly powerful in differentiating the organization by hierarchical levels. For example, bonus plans and pay-for-performance plans targeted at executives can separate them culturally and behaviorally from the rest of the organization. Such a separation can lead to serious conflict between individuals in senior-management positions and those elsewhere in the organization, particularly if actions that are good for one group are not necessarily good for others in the organization. This phenomenon has occurred in some widely reported cases where executive bonus systems have paid off extremely well while profit-sharing plans for others have not. General Motors has had union complaints about this and as a result has brought its profit-sharing plan more in line with the executive bonus plan.

An interesting example of symbols concerns the use of so-called parachutes for employees displaced because of mergers and acquisitions. Most organizations offer golden parachutes to a few senior executives. A few organizations have offered silver or tin parachutes to all employees in the organization. A prime example of the latter is Herman Miller, Inc. which has long been admired for its positive work culture. Clearly, these two approaches give very different signals to the work force about who is important to the organization. Golden parachutes are not likely to communicate a sense of concern for all members of the organization and to motivate lower-level employees to develop a strong long-term commitment to the organization. On the other hand, top-to-bottom parachutes indicate very clearly that everyone in the organization is in the same boat and is valued by the organization. Obviously, this approach tends to build a culture of commitment and high involvement.

Communication about Rewards for Executives

In the area of executive compensation, organizations have a limited ability to keep practices and compensation rates secret. The highest paid members of the organization have to be listed in the annual proxy statement. However, for the rest of the executives, pay rates can be, and usually are, kept secret. This creates an odd kind of two-class system in which the top people are separated from the rest of the managers. It can reaffirm their special status in the organization. It can be argued that openness about all executive compensation could reinforce the idea that all executive compensation is defendable and open to scrutiny while keeping it secret suggests that the organization is not interested in doing more than the law requires.

Decision Making about Executive Reward Systems

As noted earlier, there are many ongoing decisions that need to be made in the management and administration of compensation systems. Among the most important of these decisions are those about how highly a job is to be paid and whether someone has earned a performance-related reward. If the management style of the organization calls for these to be made in a participative manner, the decision process at the top becomes particularly critical. That is, senior executives need to do their job evaluation/skill evaluation work very well, to serve as a model of good decision-making processes for the lower levels.

As I mentioned earlier, evaluating performance for the purpose of determining pay changes is an important top-level decision process. If this process is to be done participatively at lower levels, then doing it well at the top is particularly important. It is hard for individuals to make tough decisions in this area because of their potentially strong impact on the well-being of co-workers and, of course, ultimately on themselves. There is always a risk that participation will lead to the "everybody is nice to everybody else" syndrome and no critical evaluation will take place. It is easier to maintain a culture in which valid evaluation occurs if senior executives are willing to take a critical look at each other and make solid participative evaluations. If, however, they engage in poor decision-making practices, and argue that there is a "club" at the top in which everyone must be doing well or they would not have been promoted to that high a position, it is difficult to do good decision making concerning performance or, for that matter, good decision making of any kind at lower levels.

In reward system plan design, the credibility of the decision process is a key factor. Executive compensation decisions typically are not made at levels far above the individuals affected by the systems. Indeed, they are often made by the executives themselves or with the help of an outside consulting firm. The issue of adequate input for executives who are not at the very senior levels of management may arise, but input is rarely an issue with senior-level executives. The issue at that level is one of credibility with lower levels in the organization.

If it is perceived that the decision process at the top level does not involve appropriate checks and balances, then the credibility of the executive compensation system, and indeed the credibility of the executives, is at risk. It is all too easy for lower-level individuals to justify self-serving behavior and to be poor participants in design activities involving rewards if they think that executives take unreasonable advantage of their opportunity to participate in and influence reward system decisions. Executives should have inputs into the system, but final approval of the plan should involve an independent review by a trusted board of directors.

In a traditionally managed organization, the key to a credible decision process lies in having outside directors control the executive compensation decisions. It is not enough to have the compensation committee made up of executives from other corporations; too often their decisions are tainted by self-interest. Higher pay for one executive often leads to higher pay for others in the salary survey-driven world of executive compensation. With overlapping board memberships, many executives determine each other's pay. A compensation committee of the board should be made up of individuals who are not in a position to gain from their decisions and who will represent the interests of the shareholders. In the case of a high-involvement organization a further step is needed. The board should include representatives from all levels in the organization as well as outside members.

CONCLUSIONS

I have argued that executive compensation can have an important impact on how an organization operates and ultimately on its effectiveness, particularly if it is a pay-for-performance system. Executive compensation can also have a major impact on the types of skills that individuals develop in an organization, in particular, on the degree to which employees try to develop management skills and to move up the management ladder.

Executive compensation perhaps has its biggest impact on the culture and structure of an organization. It can signal what is valued and serve as a role model in such areas as performance appraisal, employee involvement, open communication, and putting the long-term success of the organization above self-interest. It can be a major driver of the degree to which the organization is differentiated by horizontal levels. In short, executive compensation systems have an organization impact that goes far beyond their impact on the executives who are directly affected by them.

NOTES

1. See, for example, W. F. Whyte, *Money and Motivation* (New York: Harper, 1955).

2. See, for example, S. Finkelstein and D. C. Hambrick, "Chief Executive Compensation: A Synthesis and Reconciliation," *Strategic Management Journal* 9 (1988), pp. 543–558; and C. A. O'Reilly, B. G. Main, and G. S. Crystal, "CEO Compensation as Tournament and Social Comparison: A Tale of Two Theories," *Administrative Science Quarterly*, 33 (1988), pp. 257–274.

3. E. E. Lawler, "The Strategic Design of Reward Systems," in C. Fombrun, N. Tichy, and M. Devanna, eds., *Strategic Human Resource Management* (New York: Wiley, 1984), pp. 127–147; and E. E. Lawler, *Strategic Pay* (San Francisco: Jossey-Bass, 1990).

4. See, for example, E. E. Lawler, *Motivation in Work Organizations* (Monterey, CA: Brooks/Cole, 1973); and W. H. Mobley, *Employee Turnover: Causes, Consequences, and Control* (Reading, MA: Addison-Wesley, 1982).

5. See, for example, E. E. Lawler, *Pay and Organizational Effectiveness: A Psychological View* (New York: McGraw-Hill, 1971); and V. H. Vroom, *Work and Motivation* (New York: Wiley, 1964).

6. Lawler, *Motivation*; and Vroom, *Work*.

7. E. E. Lawler, *High-Involvement Management* (San Francisco: Jossey-Bass, 1986).

8. E. E. Lawler, *Pay and Organization Development* (Reading, MA: Addison-Wesley, 1981).

9. P. R. Lawrence and J. W. Lorsch, *Organization and Environment: Managing Differentiation and Integration* (Homewood, IL: Irwin, 1967).

10. E. E. Lawler, "What's Wrong with Point-Factor Job Evaluation?" *Compensation and Benefits Review* 18 (2) (1986), pp. 20–28.

11. See, for example, E. E. Lawler and G. E. Ledford, "Skill-Based Pay," *Personnel* 62 (9) (1985), pp. 30–37; and Lawler, *Strategic Pay*.

12. E. E. Lawler, G. E. Ledford, and S. A. Mohrman, *Employee Involvement in America* (Houston: American Productivity and Quality Center, 1989).

13. S. Kerr, "On the Folly of Rewarding A, While Hoping for B," *Academy of Management Journal*, 18 (1975), pp. 769–783.

14. See, for example, Whyte, *Money*; and Lawler, *Pay and Organizational Effectiveness*.

15. See, for example, G. S. Crystal, *Executive Compensation*, 2d ed. (New York: AMACOM, 1978); and B. R. Ellig, *Executive Compensation: A Total Pay Perspective* (New York: McGraw-Hill, 1982).

16. R. Stata and M. A. Maidique, "Bonus System for Balanced Strategy," *Harvard Business Review* 58(6) (1980), pp. 156–163.

17. E. E. Lawler, "The New Plant Revolution," *Organizational Dynamics* 6 (3) (1978), pp. 2–12; and R. E. Walton, "Establishing and Maintaining High Commitment Work Systems," in J. R. Kimberly, R. H. Miles and Associates, *The Organizational Life Cycle* (San Francisco: Jossey-Bass, 1980), pp. 208–290.

18. See, for example, Lawler, *Pay and Organizational Effectiveness*.

19. J. D. Burroughs, "Pay Secrecy and Performance: The Psychological Research," *Compensation Review* 14 (3) (1982), pp. 44–54.

20. I review this literature in *Pay and Organization Development*.

21. See, for example, Walton, "Establishing and Maintaining High Commitment Work Systems."

22. Finkelstein and Hambrick, "Chief Executive Compensation."

23. Lawler, *High-Involvement Management*.

24. E. E. Lawler, A. M. Mohrman, and S. M. Resnick, "Performance Appraisal Revisited," *Organizational Dynamics* 13 (1) (1984), pp. 20–35.

25. A. M. Mohrman, S. M. Resnick-West, and E. E. Lawler, *Designing Performance Appraisal Systems* (San Francisco: Jossey-Bass, 1989).

26. Lawler, *High-Involvement Management*.

27. O'Reilly, Main, and Crystal, "CEO Compensation."

REFERENCES

Burroughs, J. D. "Pay Secrecy and Performance: The Psychological Research." *Compensation Review* 14(3) (1982), pp. 44–54.

Crystal, G. S. *Executive Compensation*. 2d ed. New York: AMACOM, 1978.

Ellig, B. R. *Executive Compensation: A Total Pay Perspective*. New York: McGraw-Hill, 1982.

Finkelstein, S., and Hambrick, D. C. "Chief Executive Compensation: A Synthesis and Reconciliation." *Strategic Management Journal* 9 (1988), pp. 543–558.

Kerr, S. "On the Folly of Rewarding A, while Hoping for B." *Academy of Management Journal* 18 (1975), pp. 769–783.

Lawler, E. E. *Pay and Organizational Effectiveness: A Psychological View*. New York: McGraw-Hill, 1971.

———. *Motivation in Work Organizations*. Monterey, CA: Brooks/Cole, 1973.

———. "The New Plant Revolution." *Organizational Dynamics* 6(3) (1978), pp. 2–12.

———. *Pay and Organization Development*. Reading, MA: Addison-Wesley, 1981.

———. "The Strategic Design of Reward Systems." In C. Fombrun, N. Tichy, and M. Devanna, eds., *Strategic Human Resource Management*. New York: Wiley, 1984, pp. 127–147.

———. "What's Wrong with Point-Factor Job Evaluation?" *Compensation and Benefits Review* 18(2) (1986), pp. 20–28.

———. *High-Involvement Management*. San Francisco: Jossey-Bass, 1986.

———. *Strategic Pay*. San Francisco: Jossey-Bass, 1990.

Lawler, E. E., and Ledford, G. E. "Skill-Based Pay." *Personnel* 62(9) (1985), pp. 30–37.

Lawler, E. E., Ledford, G., and Mohrman, S. A. *Employee Involvement in America*. Houston: American Productivity and Quality Center, 1989.

Lawler, E. E., Mohrman, A. M., and Resnick, S. M. "Performance Appraisal Revisted." *Organizational Dynamics* 13(1) (1984), pp. 20–35.

Lawrence, P. R., and Lorsch, J. W. *Organization and Environment: Managing Differentiation and Integration*. Homewood, IL: Irwin, 1967.

Mobley, W. H. *Employee Turnover: Causes, Consequences, and Control*. Reading, MA: Addison-Wesley, 1982.

Mohrman, A. M., Resnick-West, S. M., and Lawler, E. E. *Designing Performance Appraisal Systems*. San Francisco: Jossey-Bass, 1989.

O'Reilly, C. A., Main, B. G., and Crystal, G. S. "CEO Compensation as Tournament and Social Comparison: A Tale of Two Theories." *Administrative Science Quarterly* 33 (1988), pp. 257–274.

Stata, R., and Maidique, M. A. "Bonus System for Balanced Strategy." *Harvard Business Review* 58(6) (1980), pp. 156–163.

Vroom, V. H. *Work and Motivation.* New York: Wiley, 1964.

Walton, R. E. "Establishing and Maintaining High Commitment Work Systems." In Kimberly, J. R., and Miles, R. H. and Associates. *The Organizational Life Cycle.* San Francisco: Jossey-Bass, 1980, pp. 208–290.

Whyte, W. F. *Money and Motivation.* New York: Harper, 1955.

8

EXECUTIVE REWARDS AND THEIR IMPACT ON TEAMWORK

Robert W. Keidel

CORPORATE COMPETITIVENESS increasingly depends on teamwork. Why? Because only through effective teamwork can a company do well against such crucial performance criteria as innovation, flexibility, adaptability, synergy, and most important, learning capacity. Arie de Geus, who heads up planning for the Royal Dutch/Shell Group of companies, has argued that "the only competitive advantage the company of the future will have is its managers' ability to learn faster than their competitors."[1] There is no way that an organization's managers (and nonmanagers) can learn quickly and efficiently if they are isolated from each other—or arrayed in a hierarchical, bureaucratic pattern. Learning must be spontaneous and shared.

But how can a company ensure that its members and units will cooperate? Two requirements must be met. First, the firm must understand the difference between *strategic teamwork* and other, more common (tactical) forms. Second, it must understand the importance of *systemic rewards*, in which executive compensation is an integral part of organizational design, and not a freestanding "function" that can be managed apart from other design components.

STRATEGIC TEAMWORK

Conventional concepts of teamwork tend to fall into one of two categories. The first is teamwork as an overarching banner. "Teamwork" is championed throughout the corporation in a written document—a vision or mission statement, philosophy, charter, credo, set of guiding principles/ shared values, whatever. This is the "macro" tack. Everyone will, it is hoped, identify with such a lofty purpose and become energized to live the language. The second is the "micro" approach: teamwork stands for interpersonal processes. The focus may center more on behavior than words, but it is the behavior of individuals and small groups that is addressed, not that of the larger organization. Activities consist of understanding group dynamics, establishing a climate of trust, giving and receiving feedback—in a word, teambuilding.

Neither of the conventional notions of teamwork is "wrong." In fact, both may be vital to corporate success. The problem is that neither of these teamwork concepts confronts issues of organizational design— structures and systems. Unless such hard design issues are addressed, soft teamwork will be feckless, because when push comes to shove, power beats process. Or as Woody Allen once said, "the lion and the lamb may lie down together, but the lamb won't get much sleep." The answer, for *strategic* teamwork, is to work on both the lion and the lamb.

SYSTEMIC REWARDS

To view executive compensation systemically, one must go beyond the pay-for-performance issue, i.e., the link between managerial rewards and corporate/unit performance. Executive compensation must be understood in terms of two additional dimensions: (1) the various classes of people within the organization, and (2) overall organizational design.

Too often, executive compensation has been handled as if the organization contained no nonexecutives, or, at least, as if the compensation of senior management could be entirely divorced from the compensation of everyone else. It is as though no others in the company care what kind of money the CEO or the senior management team makes.

At the same time, the executive reward system typically has been treated as a discrete business function, as though other aspects of the organization (its decision system, information system, layout, and so on) are unrelated. Both of these omissions—nonexecutives (i.e., all others in the organization) and nonreward systems (i.e., all other organizational systems)—need to be taken into account if executive compensation is to have a serious, *positive* impact on corporate teamwork.

Jan Carlzon, president of Scandinavian Airlines, uses the concept of "moment of truth" to refer to any instance in which a customer comes in contact with any part of his company, and thereby forms or alters his or her impression of the company. Carlzon cites the 50,000 moments of truth that Scandinavian Airlines faces each day in order to emphasize the importance of continuous attention to customer needs.

If every corporation has myriad moments of truth with its customers, it has far more such encounters with its employees, because employees usually see more of their firm than customers do. To encourage cooperation throughout, a company must address every facet of its design, every piece of the organization that employees experience. It must meld strategic teamwork and systemic rewards.

The reward system is one of *three organizing components that support corporate direction*; the other two components are authority structure and interaction patterns, as shown in Exhibit 8–1. The elements of corporate direction and its supporting components will be considered in turn. I will combine a few basic principles with examples, both positive and negative.

CORPORATE DIRECTION

People need to see not only how their work fits in with the larger organizational mission, but also how it makes a difference. Dun and Bradstreet is a company that has reinforced the latter connection. D&B is committed to providing its clients with objective credit information, but there is no way that the firm could carry out its mission if its employees did not understand the importance of accuracy in every facet of their work. D&B takes pains to make certain that employees do understand. Fast-food chains such as McDonald's and White Castle seek to imbue a similar employee commitment to cleanliness, which is as vital to their corporate success as financial accuracy is to Dun and Bradstreet's.

When it comes to building common objectives among organizational parts, senior managers could learn much from the multishift factory. As anyone who has ever worked in such an environment knows, the only way to maximize performance is to focus on the shifts' *combined* efforts; otherwise, a negative-sum game, in which each shift tries to shine at the others' expense, is inevitable.

Dynamics are no different at higher levels of the corporation. Whether the organizational parts are functions, technical disciplines, business units, or geographically distinct subsidiaries, unless overarching objectives are established, corporate performance will not exceed the sum of the parts' performances—and it may well fall below this.

Another way to develop widespread commitment to the company's strategic direction is through carefully thought-out themes—pledges and slogans that help define the firm's distinctiveness. Some well-known examples:

EXHIBIT 8-1
A Design for Strategic Teamwork

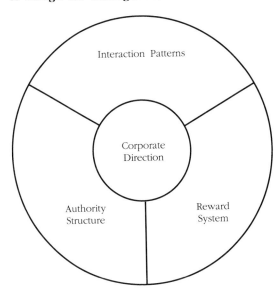

- "We don't cut corners" (quality)—Hartmann
- "We run the tightest ship in the shipping business" (cost/delivery)—United Parcel Service
- "One great idea after another" (technical innovation)—Lotus Development Corporation
- "Everybody is somebody at Dean Witter" (responsiveness to customers)—Dean Witter

One test of the credibility of such language is its life span. But the actual words are less important than the pattern of values that is conveyed; an organization may vary its motto over time yet still express the same core meaning.

An especially powerful test is to establish a quantitative, time-based standard of performance that requires everyone to pull together. Companies such as AT&T (phones) and Navistar (trucks) set out to halve product development time—and succeeded.[2] Other firms have institutionalized time-based indicators of performance—e.g., Caterpillar's 48-hour worldwide spare-parts availability, Deluxe's 48-hour order turnaround, and Domino's Pizza's 30-minute delivery.

REWARD SYSTEM

Do you know what the ratio of the highest pay to the average pay in your company is? In 1988, the ten highest-paid U.S. executives averaged over $19 million in total compensation.[3] Assuming that the average employee in their firms earned $30,000, then the high:average ratio would have been more than 633:1. It is difficult to instill a sense of "all one team" with a disparity of such magnitude. For precisely this reason, Herman Miller, Inc.—America's most-admired furniture manufacturer, according to *Fortune* polls of the last two years—limits the CEO's pay to no more than twenty times that of the average plant worker. Herman Miller's COO makes no more than eighteen times what the average worker makes, and other managerial positions are also capped.

The ratio can, of course, be underdone. Ben & Jerry's Homemade, the ice-cream company, reportedly has had problems recruiting talented managers because of its 5:1 (highest pay:lowest pay) ceiling.[4] Size is also a factor. A sub-$100 million firm is hardly equivalent to a $10-billion corporation.

If anything, however, American companies tend to overdo the gap. In 1960, the average CEO earned forty-one times as much as the average factory worker; by 1988, the ratio had swelled to 93:1.[5] Although there may never be an ideal ratio, a sense of shared concern suggests limits.

Group and organizational bonus schemes, ranging from gainsharing (e.g., Scanlon and Rucker Plans) to profit sharing to stock options, can do much to instill a sense of teamwork. To be effective, however, such programs must have the net effect of integrating the organization. At A. G. Edwards & Sons, the investment services firm, brokers' contributions to profit sharing are matched dollar for dollar, while lower-paid administrative and support workers' contributions are matched $2 to $1.[6]

Nucor Corporation, the fast-growing minimill steel producer, applies the same bonus formula to everyone in the company, in contrast to more typical hierarchical arrangements in which the sharing percentage increases with level. Nucor also illustrates *pain* sharing, or management's willingness to sacrifice during hard times. In fact, percentage pay cuts there increase with hierarchical level. Explains CEO Ken Iverson: "If a company's not successful in one year, excuses don't matter. Management should take the biggest drop in pay because they have the most responsibility."[7]

The last thing to do if organizationwide teamwork is your objective is to reward higher-ups while squeezing lower-downs. The classic demonstration of such a maneuver belongs to General Motors in 1982. On the same day that the United Auto Workers agreed to $2.5 billion in wage concessions, a new senior-management bonus program was put before company shareholders.

One of the most powerful aspects of a company's reward system is its performance appraisal and promotion systems. If teamwork is truly a priority, then cooperative behavior must be an appraisal/promotional criterion. As the CEO of a major electronics firm stated, "In setting the stage for our new corporate culture, we have been very careful to promote those mangers who are comfortable in a participative milieu and to remove those who are not."[8] At Goldman Sachs, one of Wall Street's top performers, collaboration is a central organizational tenet. To become a partner in that firm, an individual must demonstrate the ability to team up with others.

Every company is fraught with status symbols, and many people feel one-down before they have even started work in the morning as a result of passing through hierarchically arranged parking lots, plant entrances, and eating areas. General Motors again provides a recent example of what not to do to encourage a sense of togetherness between management and workers. In 1988, at one of its Inland Division facilities, plant management issued a memo directing salaried employees with non-GM cars to refrain from using the salaried employees' parking lot and instead, park in the hourly workers' lot. The reasoning: because of declining market share, the wrong image would be sent to visitors who park in the salaried lot. This caper did wonders for labor relations. Responded one local union official: "They're punishing these guys by telling them to go out there (and park) with the rest of the dogs. What does that say about us?"[9]

The more forbidding senior managers' quarters are, the less likely that there will be collaboration between levels. The efforts of such CEOs as John Young of Hewlett-Packard and Harry Quadracci of Quad/Graphics demonstrate that physical structures can reinforce, rather than restrict, corporate teamwork. In each case, modesty and accessibility have replaced grandeur. And consider the example set by Trammell Crow, founder of the nation's largest real estate development company. One can walk directly from the elevator to Crow's desk without encountering a single door. And everyone in his organization—senior partner, salesperson, or secretary—has the same size desk.

AUTHORITY STRUCTURE

Minimizing the number of organizational levels reduces communication filtering and distortion and allows more contact among people. These effects can clearly reinforce teamwork and improve performance. But it is not simply the *number* of levels that matters. What is also important is how many people there are at each level. Many companies have deceived themselves into thinking they have decentralized by getting rid of a large corporate headquarters staff but then replicating this staff for each of several business units. Which is really "leaner and tighter": a firm with 1,000 people at corporate headquarters, or a comparable one with 100 at headquarters and four business-unit-based staffs of 350 each?

In terms of decision-making patterns, American managers are most accustomed to mandating, and next-most accustomed to delegating. Their world is vertical: top-down and bottom-up.[10] It is not surprising, then, that collaborating, which represents a horizontal pattern, is the mode used least frequently. Collaborating means either achieving a consensus or, less ambitiously, receiving/providing consulting input. Collaborating also means teamwork. One way to bias the organization in this direction is to establish a norm that people should err on the side of too much collaborative decision making rather than too little. In the language of statistics, this means favoring errors of commission over errors of omission when it comes to team behavior.

A collaborative norm, or expectation, can be generalized across organizational boundaries. U.S. automakers, through "simultaneous engineering," have institutionalized the process of bringing together relevant functions—design, engineering, manufacturing, marketing, and so forth—at the start of the new-car design process, rather than sequentially, as had been the case historically.

Hallmark Cards has implemented a similar change. Formerly, an artist created a design for a particular card, then forwarded it to a writer, who routed the package to marketing where the card's sales potential was gauged. By bringing artist, writer, and marketer together simultaneously to work on a class of cards, Hallmark gained efficiencies and increased the saleability of its cards.[11]

Interdivisional coordination of this sort is equally possible. American Express requires senior managers to specify opportunities for productive collaboration across the corporation in their strategic plans—through interdivisional selling, sharing facilities, and using common systems. Results indicate considerable leveraging of resources.

Or consider Saab-Scania, the Swedish transport manufacturer. In 1983, Saab-Scania formed "Combitech" (for combined technologies) in order to exploit the company's core technical skills. This consortium, made up of several small to medium-sized businesses, has been able to reduce development costs and shorten lead times through a policy of "horizontal cooperation" and continuous information-sharing about R&D projects.

INTERACTION PATTERNS

Physical setting—layout—can make an enormous difference in the quality and amount of teamwork. Yet this issue is routinely ignored in organizational design and change programs. Many office arrangements, like the classic "executive row," mirror factory work flows and therefore rule in certain interactions and preclude all others.[12]

Vertical distances are even more significant than horizontal distances. Berkeley architecture professor Christopher Alexander has estimated that, in terms of the effect on interaction, one flight of stairs is equivalent to about 100 horizontal feet and two flights of stairs to 300 horizontal feet. He concludes that units separated by two or more floors will have almost no informal contact with each other.[13] How, then, can they exhibit teamwork?

Contrast the following uses of "glass" as a medium for retarding or enhancing teamwork.

Case one: an office/factory complex (a company that I observed several years ago). Overlooking the (first-floor) manufacturing area was a second-floor corner office whose glass walls gave managers a window on much of the production process. Managers would congregate in this nest and scrutinize the operation by literally looking down at the workers. While the arrangement saved management the hassle of having to venture out onto the plant floor frequently and interact personally, it also aroused resentment in the workers. The resentment, in turn, gave rise to a number of destructive games around a simple theme: let's see how much we can get away with in plain view! The workers got away with a lot.

Case two: a CEO's office (the office of John Reed, chairman of Citicorp, as described by *Forbes*). "Symbolically, he sits on the second floor of the Citicorp headquarters on Park Avenue, not in the fifteenth-floor aerie used by [ex-chairman Walter] Wriston. Reed's front and back office walls are glass, so that passersby can watch the boss at work. His office is nearly identical to ten others on the floor, each facing an indoor garden. The arrangement is intended to foster accessibility, a collegial atmosphere. In this office arrangement, Reed seems to be saying: No single person can run this show; the chief must rule by example and by inspiration."[14]

Of course, a major constraint on layout is organizational size. Once a company outgrows the basement or garage where it started up, everyone can no longer work in one room at the same time. Fortunately, information technology is making it increasingly feasible to "soft-wire" corporations—that is, to electronically link physically dispersed people. Although such communication will never duplicate the intimacy of person-to-person contact, it can contribute strongly to integrating large, complex, and far-flung corporate enterprises.

Southwest Bell, for instance, used satellite communications to link 55,000 employees just days after the AT&T breakup. According to Chairman and CEO Zane E. Barnes: "The objective was to provide a positive vent for divestiture-related emotions—an electronic catharsis, if you will. And we did, with visible leadership, hard business information, *and* old-fashioned fun, through humor, music, and dance. It was an unprecedented event for us which helped teach the power of shared emotional experiences and nontraditional media."[15]

Many companies are using such electronic capabilities on an ongoing basis. As of late 1988, Cummins Engine had linked 14,000 employees, including production workers, via electronic mail. The effect of such networking is to skirt hierarchical channels that formerly were the primary communication path. Overall, interaction becomes less constrained by level, function, and location.

As Lynn Oppenheim (of the Wharton Center for Applied Research) has pointed out, meeting systems can be a powerful tool for shaping one's organization. A meeting *system* refers to the cycles of preparation, meeting, and follow-up that guide the flow of managerial (and other) work;[16] it also refers to the interrelations among meetings. One high-technology firm, for example, uses a system of overlapping meetings to reinforce the connection between top management and operations: it features a weekly status review and update (three hours); a monthly operational review (three days), and a quarterly review of strategic issues (three days offsite).[17]

In essence, meetings systems can be used either to reinforce teamwork or to frustrate it. When meetings are more inclusive than exclusive, when they are conducted in a more collaborative than authoritarian way, and when they are connected closely with the rest of organizational life, the more likely it is that a company's meeting system will foster teamwork.

One way to supplement the integrative potential of meetings is to combine them with the formation of "diagonal-slice" task forces/project teams made up of individuals from various parts and levels of the organization. These groups typically take a multidisciplinary approach to solving problems (such as a quality defect or a production snag) or to coordinating new developments (such as the manufacture of a new product line or the start-up of a new facility). Like electronic information systems, task forces are able to cut through the organizational boundaries that typically separate people. In so doing, they bring together individuals who otherwise might never collaborate, and they help all members to embrace an organization-wide perspective.

Finally, corporate teamwork can be stimulated by rotating managers (and others) across functions, divisions, and locations. Rotation broadens horizons and increases the variety of people an individual comes to know within the company. American corporations have been criticized—fairly—for their tendency to promote people within functional departments far more than between functions. Similarly, too many corporations that have grown largely through acquisition have failed to move people among units in order to induce a global, rather than local, point of view. I have observed companies made up of multiple distinct subcultures where the primary identification has remained with the subculture because no systematic effort has ever been made to cross-pollinate.

The teamwork guidelines sketched above can be summarized as follows:
Corporate Direction

1. Stress the link between individual/unit behavior and organizational mission.
2. Build in common objectives.
3. Create integrative themes.

Reward System

1. Limit the gap between highest-paid and lowest-paid.
2. Implement group and organizational bonus schemes.
3. Share financial *pain* as well as gain throughout the organization.
4. Make career advancement dependent in part on cooperative behavior.
5. Minimize status symbols that separate people into one-up and one-down categories.

Authority Structure

1. Streamline the hierarchy, especially at high levels.
2. Err on the side of too much collaborative decision making rather than too little.
3. Require organizational units to coordinate their actions through mutual adjustment.

Interaction Patterns

1. Arrange physical configuration—layout—to encourage informal exchanges among those who need to work together.
2. Use information systems to link disparate organizational parts.
3. Develop meeting systems that reinforce cooperation.
4. Create diagonal-slice project teams/task forces.
5. Rotate managers and nonmanagers across functions, divisions, and locations.

CONCLUSION

Corporate competitiveness depends on teamwork, which, in turn, is strongly influenced by executive compensation. For the links to be effective, however, appreciations of teamwork must be strategic, and appreciations of compensation, systemic. In a sense, the entire organization needs to be conceptualized as a team of teams on the one hand, and as a system of reward systems on the other.

Toward this end, I have presented a simple scheme that appears to capture major organizational dimensions while recognizing that there are innumerable ways to model strategy/structure/systems/processes.[18] Of course, corporate direction and its three supporting components—reward system, authority structure, and interaction patterns—overlap. And the injunctions presented within this framework are neither exhaustive nor magical. But they do, it is hoped, provide ground rules that are theoretically sensible and practically useful.

NOTES

1. Arie P. de Geus, "Planning as Learning," *Harvard Business Review* (March–April 1988), p. 74.

2. Brian Dumaine, "How Managers Can Succeed through Speed," *Fortune*, February 13, 1989, p. 56.

3. *BusinessWeek*, May 1, 1989, p. 46.

4. Erik Larson, "Forever Young," *Inc.* (July 1988), p. 58.

5. "Bring CEO Pay Back Down to Earth," *BusinessWeek*, May 1, 1989, p. 146. In this issue, *BusinessWeek*'s annual review of executive pay, top-management remuneration in 1988 was compared with shareholder return and corporate profit. Perhaps in the future, a third index will be reported: the relation of top pay to average and/or bottom pay within the corporation.

6. Ron Zemke with Dick Schaaf, *The Service Edge: 101 Companies that Profit from Customer Care* (New York: NAL Books, 1989), p. 218.

7. Ken Iverson, quoted in "Face-to-Face," *Inc.* (April 1986), p. 44.

8. James. J. Renier, "Turnaround of Information Systems at Honeywell," *The Executive* (February 1987), p. 50.

9. Bradley A. Stertz, "Management Lesson for Today: How Not to Make Workers Loyal," *The Wall Street Journal*, May 19, 1988, p. 37.

10. For a provocative analysis of the pervasiveness of the vertical metaphor in Western society, see George Lakoff and Mark Johnson, *Metaphors We Live By* (Chicago: University of Chicago Press, 1980).

11. Bill Saporito, "Cutting Costs Without Cutting People," *Fortune*, May 25, 1987, p. 28.

12. For a useful discussion of layout options for management teams, see Fritz Steele, "The Ecology of Executive Teams: A New View of the Top," *Organizational Dynamics* (Spring 1983), pp. 65–78.

13. Christopher Alexander, Sara Ishikawa, and Murray Silverstein, with Max Jacobson, Ingrid Fiksdahl-King, and Shlomo Angel, *A Pattern Language* (New York: Oxford University Press, 1977), pp. 410–411.

14. Edwin A. Finn, Jr., and Jack Willoughby, "Teaching Old Banks New Tricks," *Forbes*, June 15, 1987, p. 36.

15. Zane E. Barnes, "Change in the Bell System," *The Executive* (February 1987), p. 45.

16. Lynn Oppenheim, *Making Meetings Matter*. A report by the Wharton Center for Applied Research, Philadelphia, 1988.

17. Homa Bahrami and Stuart Evans, "Stratocracy in High-Technology Firms," *California Management Review* (Fall 1987), pp. 51–66.

18. For a more extended treatment based on team sports metaphors, see Robert W. Keidel, *Corporate Players: Designs for Working and Winning Together* (New York: Wiley, 1988).

PART II

Developing Strategic Executive Compensation

PART II-A
Design of Executive Pay Packages

9

COMMON MISTAKES IN CURRENT PRACTICE

Graef S. Crystal

IT IS TRUE, more often than not, that the perfect executive compensation plan is the one you do not have. In one way or another, many executive compensation plans contain critical flaws. Some trace to a desire to emulate what other companies are doing, even if what other companies are doing is inappropriate. Some trace to a preoccupation with taxation and accounting, issues that, because they are substantive and quantifiable, are easier to grapple with than more important, but more subtle, issues of motivation. Some trace to a tendency to be too easy on executives and, because such plans are too easy on executives, too hard on shareholders. And finally, some trace simply to a failure to think through what one wishes to accomplish.

In this chapter, I will review and comment on these common mistakes.

POSITIONING VIS-A-VIS THE MARKET

Many—indeed, most—companies attempt to articulate where they would like their compensation levels to be vis-à-vis the external market, however they define that market. Hence, you will hear statements such as: "We want our compensation levels to be equal to the median of our seventeen-company comparator group"; or "We want to be at the 75th percentile of the comparator group pay's distribution."

Is there anything wrong with setting levels this way? Shouldn't a company articulate how competitive it wants to be and then move toward that goal?

Indeed it should. But therein lies the rub. For having articulated, say, a 75th percentile pay goal, our hypothetical company, accustomed to achieving its objectives, proceeds to do just that. Hence, it pays at the 75th percentile in normal times, in prosperous times, and in poor times.

Small wonder then that there is so little correlation between company performance and pay in so many studies that have been conducted.

Where did the company go wrong? Quite simply, it forgot to specify the performance circumstances under which it wished to achieve the 75th percentile of the competitive pay distribution. What the company should have done was to declare that it wished to pay at the 75th percentile of the competitive pay distribution only when it achieved, say, a 14 percent after-tax return on beginning equity (or increased its EPS by 10 percent, or had the same ROE as the median company in its comparator group, and so forth).

Now, for the first time, we have a linkage between performance and pay. The company is no longer declaring that its goal is to pay at the 75th percentile, period. Rather, its goal is to pay at the 75th percentile only when its executive group has performed at a requisite level.

But having taken this step, the company is still not finished. By linking performance to pay at a single point in the performance spectrum, the company has left unanswered the question of how pay will reflect all other levels of performance. The company must establish a linkage between performance and pay for any conceivable level of company success or failure. Hence, the company that wished to pay at the 75th percentile for a 14 percent ROE level might declare:

- If ROE is 18 percent or more, we wish to pay at the 90th percentile;
- If ROE is 11 percent, we wish to pay at the competitive median; and
- If ROE is 8 percent or lower, we wish to pay at the 25th percentile.

These are all meaningful performance beacons by which to steer the company's pay ship.

MISINTERPRETING SURVEY RESULTS

Virtually every company participates in multiple pay surveys each year, some of which are conducted by the company itself but most of which are conducted by other companies or third parties such as consulting firms. Although it is technically possible to misinterpret the results of a survey that you conduct yourself, providing details in this area is beyond my scope. Instead, let me discuss the problems of using outside surveys. Three come immediately to mind:

1. Too little attention is paid to the composition of the survey sample. Note that it is the rare survey that contains the *universe* of a com-

pany's competitors. Rather, most surveys contain only a sampling. That would not be erroneous by itself, if every company in a given sample exhibited the same, or almost the same, pay practices. But in fact there is typically a fair amount of pay variability from one company to another. Consequently, the selection of companies to be included in the comparator group sample, or excluded from it, can make a considerable difference in results. So, it is critically important to review the list of companies included in the survey group in order to decide how useful the results are going to be.

Since the survey has been conducted by someone else, there are only two choices available if you do not like the sample: ignore the results or see if you can persuade the authors to rerun the survey with a smaller number of companies. (The latter alternative may eliminate companies you do not want to include. Unhappily, it does not permit you to add companies.)

2. The methodology used may not be appropriate. Suppose, for example, that you are a company with $10 billion in sales and that you are looking at the results of a survey of twenty-five companies with sales ranging from $1 billion to $12 billion and averaging $6 billion. Suppose furthermore that the results only report, for various positions, the simple average or simple median pay level of the twenty-five companies. Given that your company is much larger than the average company and that there may be some relationship between company size and pay, you may be ill-advised to put much weight on the simple average or simple median pay figures from the survey. Once again, you will have to decide whether to discard the survey, to ask the authors to recalculate their results using regression analysis (where size is the independent variable), or to take a chance on the simple averages and medians supplied (thereby implicitly betting that there is no relationship between size and pay).

3. The survey may not include sufficient forms of compensation. For example, the survey may report executive base salaries but omit mention of either short- or long-term incentive pay.

Some companies make the mistake of using one survey from which they get competitive base-salary levels, a second from which they learn about the size of bonuses in relation to base salary, and a third from which they learn about the size, say, of stock option grants as a function of the sum of base salary and short-term incentive awards. These companies are looking for trouble, because the three surveys almost assuredly have different groups of participants, with different pay practices. By combining the average salary from survey one with the average short-term incentive award from survey two and the average long-term incentive award from survey three, the company will end up paying truly average total compensation only by chance.

CONFUSING ECONOMIC INCREASES WITH TRUE MERIT INCREASES

Most companies construct what they call a "merit budget" for a given year. By this, they mean the percentage of salary they intend to spend on so-called "merit increases." Hence, if they appropriate a merit budget of 6 percent of salary and go on to give an employee a 6 percent salary increase, they call this increase a *merit* increase.

Are they correct in their labeling? Except in the rarest of circumstances, they are not.

Consider that the same company may have increased its salary structure (range minimums and maximums) in the same year by 4 percent after looking at its position vis-à-vis its competitors and after taking into account competitors' salary increase plans for the forthcoming year. In this case, therefore, the company is betting that competitive rates of pay will advance at the rate of 4 percent in the next year.

If that bet turns out to be correct, then the first four percentage points of any salary increase an employee receives has nothing at all to do with the employee's personal contributions and everything to do with external economic conditions. An employee who receives a 4 percent "merit increase" has really received a 4 percent "economic" increase and no merit increase. The employee who receives a 6 percent merit increase has really received a 4 percent economic increase and a 2 percent true merit increase.

Why is it important to make a distinction between economic and merit increases? First, although the typical employee may not be a trained economist, he or she has at least some notion that there is something phony about the company's representing a 6 percent salary increase as a 6 percent *merit* increase. In effect, we have a truth-in-labeling issue. And second, it is not only employees who can be confused. By spending 6 percent on salary increases and calling this money a merit fund, the company's own CEO can be fooled into thinking that he is being munificent. Indeed, the CEO may decide he is being so munificent that he cuts the "merit" fund to 4 percent!

FORGETTING TO PUT THE MERIT INTO MERIT INCREASES

Many companies talk a good game about base salary administration. They claim they carefully review each employee's performance and then tailor an appropriate salary increase based on true merit.

Sadly, however, there is little truth in most of these claims. A dispassionate analysis performed by a computer using a multiple regression program generally shows that the single most important factor in predicting where a person will sit in his salary range—and sometimes, the *only* factor—is the length of time the person has held the position. Indeed, those with considerable talent typically are promoted frequently and thereby end up, not at the top of their salary range, but near the bottom.

If a company is serious about relating pay to employee performance, then it needs to do so explicitly. The most success seems to have occurred through use of so-called salary increase matrices. Under such an approach, the company constructs a two-way table, or matrix, where one of the dimensions is the employee's current position within his salary range and the second dimension is the employee's performance rating. The matrix consists of a number of cells, each showing the appropriate salary increase to be given for that combination of position-within-range and employee performance.

Exhibit 9–1 is an example of a salary increase matrix. As can be seen, it goes a bit further than usual in not only specifying a particular increase for a given level of employee performance but also specifying the timing of the increase, i.e., the number of months the employee must wait between one salary increase and the next.

If a company constructs such a matrix properly and then goes on to follow what it has designed, it has a reasonably good chance of injecting some pay-for-performance into its base salaries.

USING OUTMODED SHORT-TERM INCENTIVE FORMULAS

A typical approach to regulating short-term incentives is to adopt a so-called funding formula. A company generally specifies an incentive "threshold" and an incentive "multiplier." The threshold represents the lowest level of performance at which any incentives at all will be paid, while the multiplier speaks to the portion of above-threshold profits that will be diverted to executives. For example, a company may declare that it will contribute to an incentive fund 10 percent of all after-tax profits after first deducting from such profits an amount equal to a 6 percent after-tax return on its beginning shareholders' equity.

EXHIBIT 9-1

1988 Exempt Pay-for-Performance Matrix (Merit Increase Guide)

Performance Appraisal (Summaries)		Minimum 1st Qtr	1st Qtr-Mid Pt	Mid Pt-3rd Qtr	3rd Qtr-Maximum
(1) Performance Far Exceeds Overall Expectations Performance results consistently exceed expectations for virtually all standards and goal attainment.	% Inc.	8.5 – 10.5%			
	INTERVAL	6 – 8 Months	8 – 10 Months	10 – 12 Months	12 – 14 Months
(2) Performance Exceeds Overall Expectations Consistently meets or exceeds virtually all standards and established goals.	% Inc.	5.5 – 7.5%			
	INTERVAL	8 – 10 Months	10 – 12 Months	12 – 14 Months	14 – 16 Months
(3) Performance Meets Overall Expectations Consistently attains most established goals and meets most standards.	% Inc.	2.5 – 4.5%			
	INTERVAL	9 – 11 Months	11 – 12 Months	12 – 15 Months	15 – 18 Months
(4) Performance Needs Improvement Accomplishment in some key areas of the job are below the established goal and performance standards.	% Inc.	0.0 – 1.5%			
	INTERVAL	12 – 14 Months	14 – 16 Months	16 – 18 Months	No Increase
(5) Performance Unacceptable Performance results and goal accomplishment are consistently below an acceptable level.	% Inc.	No Increase			
	INTERVAL	—	—	—	—

Using a funding formula is essentially a sound idea, because it forges a compact between the executive group and the shareholders about the division of the spoils, as it were. For example, the shareholders understand that they are entitled to all of the first dollars of profits until the company has achieved a 6 percent after-tax ROE level. Then, they are entitled to 90 cents out of each additional dollar of profit.

The problem here lies not in the notion of using a funding formula but rather in the fact that such formulas generally become outdated.

Assume that our hypothetical company adopted its funding formula, say, in 1950 when a bondholder earned a 4 percent interest and when the median after-tax return on equity for companies generally was about 9 percent. Given those facts, the company's threshold could be seen as 50 percent higher than the return an investor could make on bonds and two-thirds as high as the typical company's ROE level.

Now move the calendar forward to 1987. At this point, the bond investor may be earning close to a 10 percent return. And the typical after-tax return on equity may be more nearly 14 percent. By leaving its incentive threshold at 6 percent, the company is obviously generating incentive funds much earlier in the profit stream than it originally contemplated—and, probably, much earlier in the profit stream than it should.

At the same time, the incentive multiplier of 10 percent may also have become outdated. As the business grows and profits increase, a company may increase the number of employees eligible for its incentive plan, but at a much slower rate than it did initially. There is, after all, still only one CEO in the company, and one chief legal officer.

Furthermore, if the majority of eligible employees consists of new entrants to the incentive plan, the amount required to make incentive payments will be lower (in relation to company size and profitability) than if the group consists largely of long-time members at a higher salary and incentive level. This is because "normal award opportunities" (the percentages of base salary or salary-range midpoint paid to members of the plan) almost always increase as the base salary increases. A person earning a base salary of, say, $80,000 per year might receive a normal award opportunity of 20 percent, while a person earning a base salary of $200,000 per year might receive a normal award opportunity of 40 percent, and so forth. Because most new incentive plan eligibles get there by crossing the border from noneligible status for the first time, it follows that their normal award opportunities are going to be smaller than those assigned to long-standing participants.

Finally, the simple fact that sales have increased over the years can swell an incentive fund. If 10 percent was a correct multiplier in 1950, when the company had $1 billion in sales, it is almost assuredly going to be too high a multiplier in 1987, when the company has $7 billion in sales.

Think about what happens when a flabby incentive threshold is combined with a fat incentive multiplier. Depending on performance, a fund appears where one should not have been, or a fund grows too big. Because of this, the discipline that the funding formula used to impose has disappeared. As a result, the compact forged between the executives and the shareholders has been sundered, weakening significantly, if not destroying altogether, the linkage between performance and pay.

An incentive funding formula is not for all seasons, but only for one season. It needs to be reviewed regularly and, where necessary, changed. Over the past thirty years or so, any such changes would have tightened the formula, given the effects of long-term inflation. But it does not follow automatically that change means tightening. There could be time when change means loosening, too.

PERMITTING TOO MUCH INCENTIVE DISCRETION

Formularized approaches to incentive compensation are often criticized for being too inflexible and for creating funds that are too large under some circumstances and too small under others. The alternative, so the critics claim, is to put the disbursement of incentive funds entirely in the hands of the CEO and board compensation committees. Thus, there is no incentive threshold; there is no incentive multiplier; there is only what the firm wants to spend, and it does not have to decide that until the year is over and it can reap the benefits of hindsight.

On its surface, the discretionary approach would seem to have a lot going for it. But underneath the surface, there is a hard reality, and that involves the relative spinelessness of most CEOs and board compensation committees, coupled with their almost unlimited ability to rationalize.

Consider that if the company performs abysmally in a given year and there is no funding formula, you, the CEO, are going to have to face your subordinates and give them nothing. They will know that it was you, and not some institutionalized formula, that did the dirty deed. So, wanting to be loved (a desire shared by people other than the CEO!), you start rationalizing. "Sure, we earned only a 2 percent ROE last year, but our entire industry was down (although the median ROE only dropped from

14 percent to 12 percent). And our raw material costs went up through no fault of our own. And the government raised taxes. So though I won't ask the board for 100 percent of a normal bonus fund, I will ask them for 90 percent."

In a subsequent year, when the company hits the profit jackpot, you will remember how you overspent in the last bad year—or the board will remind you. And you will decide that perhaps a fund that is only 110 percent of normal will be good enough.

Then you read an article about how few companies vary their short-term incentives in relation to underlying company performance. You will congratulate yourself on the fact that your company does indeed vary its bonuses. After all, didn't you make your executives take a 10 percent haircut the last time the company fell on its face? And didn't you give them 10 percent more than normal when the company performed magnificently?

Some discretion may well be needed in any bonus plan, because the formulas can, and do, go awry. But total discretion can be even worse than a totally formularized approach

WORRYING OBSESSIVELY ABOUT ACCOUNTING AND TAX CONSIDERATIONS

Attend any conference of executive compensation practitioners, and you will hear much talk about accounting and taxation.

Is this wrong? Shouldn't practitioners be concerned about accounting and tax issues?

Yes, there should be some concern—but, at least for now, not very much concern. Except for stock options, virtually all of what an executive receives in cash or in-kind payments is charged to a company's pre-tax earnings. It is essentially only with stock options that the accounting treatment differs.

As this book is being written, the Financial Accounting Standards Board (FASB) is still holding a sale on stock option grants. The reason: though options have value (otherwise, why would executives want them?), there is no charge to earnings required as long as the price the executive must pay to exercise the option (the strike price) is at least equal to the market price of the stock on the date of the option grant. But that sale is likely to come to an end sometime in the next few years, after the FASB adopts a new regulation requiring companies to charge their earnings with an option's approximate true value. So if there is an accounting advantage to using stock options in place of other forms of compensation, the advantage is likely to be ephemeral.

In fact, there may be no advantage at all. Studies conducted by accounting and finance scholars have suggested that financial analysts have the ability to look through a company's income statement and balance sheet and spot such anomalies as LIFO versus FIFO inventory accounting, accelerated versus straight line depreciation, *and* the true financial impact of stock option grants. To the extent that the research is correct, the imposition of new FASB regulations concerning stock option accounting will be greeted with cries of anguish by CEOs and compensation experts and with a huge yawn by the people who have the all-important task of determining what companies' stock, and hence stock options, are worth.

Turning to taxation, at the moment there is no difference in the taxation of ordinary income and long-term capital gains income. That being the case, virtually every economic benefit an executive receives is taxed the same way, thereby neutralizing the whole subject of taxation.

But suppose the current environment changes? Suppose that, one day, real accounting and tax issues do arise. Are companies supposed to ignore them?

Decidedly not. But they should not become obsessed with them either. Sadly, there have been cases when companies have sacrificed true motivation on the altars of accounting and taxation. So the company that really should have "divisionalized" its long-term incentive plan so that the pay of division managers reflected the performance of their particular segments of the company instead granted across-the-board incentive stock options. These purportedly have "good" accounting and, in the past, gave the executive a tax advantage. But in the process, the company destroyed the linkage between performance and pay, given that its divisional executives have little impact on overall corporate performance. It hurt the shareholders as well, because, though executives received a tax advantage, shareholders lost their entire tax deduction.

Accounting and taxation do play a role in executive compensation design. But their role should be limited and subordinate to the greater role of motivation.

UNWITTINGLY REWARDING PROFIT VOLATILITY

Consider a company that rewards profit growth, a factor that many companies stress heavily. Executives understand that, say, 10 percent profit growth brings them, on average, their normal short-term incentive awards. They also know that they will receive nothing if there is no profit growth. Finally, they know that if profit growth is greater than 10 percent, their bonus opportunities will rise proportionately and without limit.

Does not such a plan correctly provide an incentive for something the shareholders hold dear—profit growth? What is wrong is that the plan rewards not only profit growth but also, and unwittingly, extreme profit volatility. Assume you are the CEO and that your normal bonus is equal to 50 percent of your salary. Hence, under the aforementioned plan, you will receive 50 percent of salary for 10 percent profit growth, nothing for no profit, 100 percent of salary for 20 percent profit growth, 150 percent of salary for 30 percent profit growth, and so forth.

You could aim for a nice smooth earnings progression, such as 10 percent per year, and you would receive a bonus equal to 50 percent of salary, year-in and year-out. But how about a different strategy?

- In year one, you decrease profits by 20 percent, say, from $100 million to $80 million, and you therefore receive no bonus.
- In year two, you increase profits by 25 percent, from $80 million to $100 million. Per the terms of the plan, you receive a bonus of 125 percent of salary.

What happened? Over the course of two years, profits went from $100 million to $80 million to $100 million. Hence, profits for the two years averaged $90 million or $10 million less than the base profit level of $100 million. Meanwhile, your bonus dropped to 0 percent of salary and then rose to 125 percent of salary. For the two-year period, it averaged 62.5 percent of salary, or 25 percent more than the normal level of 50 percent of salary.

In contrast, had you increased the profits at a steady rate of 10 percent per year, profits would have averaged $110 million per year over the two-year period, and you would have received an average bonus of only 50 percent of salary.

Do you really want steady growth? Won't you make more money if you throw in a bad year every so often (but not so many bad years as to risk your job) and then, like Lazarus, exhibit a rise-from-the-dead recovery? You bet you will!

In the design of incentive plans, careful attention should be given to the issue of profit volatility and its impact on incentive payouts.

UNDEREMPHASIZING RETURN ON CAPITAL

Too many companies reward executives for increasing net income and/ or EPS, and too few companies reward them for maximizing return on capital.

Suppose you are the CEO of a company that emphasizes growth in raw profits. There are, of course, many ways to increase profits, but one way is to sell more shares to the shareholders and raise additional capital on an interest-free basis. Any return you can earn on that capital, no matter how minuscule, turns into more raw profits and hence more incentive pay. Indeed, if you cannot think of anything better to do with the extra money you received from the shareholders, invest it in a passbook savings account. Of course, if you do that, your overall return on equity may decline, but that is someone else's problem, because you are being paid to increase profits and not necessarily to earn a good return on equity.

Of course, if your company is rewarding you on the basis of EPS growth and not raw profit growth, the strategy of selling more shares to the public to raise capital may backfire. You'll get the additional capital, but you'll also get an increase in the number of shares outstanding and hence a potential diminution in EPS. But you still have one source of "free" capital left, and that is the current profits. Instead of paying some of those profits out in dividends, why not plow all the profits back into the business? Once again, you have created interest-free additional capital, and you did not have to issue more shares to do it. That interest-free capital can be dumped into the passbook savings account, if need be, creating higher EPS and lower ROE.

Any financial analyst will tell you that if you had to choose one measure of performance by which to guide your destiny, you had better choose return on capital (which can be expressed in many ways, such as return on equity, return on assets, and so forth). Yet too few companies embed that thinking in their incentive plans. As a result, their executives receive the wrong incentive signals.

FAILING TO PLACE PERFORMANCE IN A PROPER PERSPECTIVE

In the 1970s, most CEOs thought the stock market was crazy. They were increasing their companies' earnings; they were even increasing their companies' ROE levels. Yet their price/earnings multiples were falling and so was the price of their stock. These CEOs failed to understand that measuring performance involves relativities, not absolutes.

When he attained the age of seventy, the late Maurice Chevalier was asked by a reporter how he felt. His reply: "Old isn't so bad when you consider the alternative!"[1] By the same token, financial performance cannot be gauged in a vacuum. One must always consider what the shareholders could have earned from an alternative investment.

One way to understand this issue is to look at so-called risk-free returns. For want of anything better, an investor can always place his money in ninety-day Treasury bills. The interest earned may not be great, but there is virtually no risk because the obligation is guaranteed by the U.S. government and because inflation, which wreaks havoc with fixed-income investments, does not make much impact in a period as short as ninety days.

Over the past sixty years, someone who invested his money in a portfolio of stocks made up of the entire market (e.g., the Standard & Poor's 500) would have earned a compounded annual total return that averaged about six percentage points higher than the return on ninety-day T-bills. To put it another way, an investor in a stock with average risk characteristics demands a return that is about six percentage points higher than he could receive by investing in ninety-day T-bills. If he doesn't get it through appropriate company ROE levels, the investor will get it by discounting the stock's value.

It follows, therefore, that when inflation kicks up and consequently causes interest rates to rise, companies need to increase their performance goals to produce those extra six percentage points of return the shareholders demand. In other words, increasing earnings 10 percent a year when inflation is 0 percent may be indicative of magnificent performance. But increasing earnings 10 percent a year when inflation is 20 percent may be indicative of terrible performance.

In evaluating performance, therefore, one must always "consider the alternative," as Maurice Chevalier so aptly put it. One cannot assume that one season's relevant performance standard is every season's relevant performance standard.

FAILING TO TAKE ACCOUNT OF BUSINESS RISK

A moment ago, I said that on average an investor who buys a portfolio consisting of the entire stock market can earn a total return about six percentage points higher than he can by investing in ninety-day T-bills.

But a specific company may not have the same risk characteristics as the entire market. It may, for example, be involved in the securities business, a business that is notoriously volatile, as demonstrated by the events of an October Monday in 1987. Or, it may be involved in the electric utility business, a business that carries relatively low risk, since the local utility commission will generally grant rate relief even when business decisions turn out to have been wrong.

Studies of returns available to investors prove the adage "the greater the risk, the greater the return." If the entire market produces a return that is six percentage points above the ninety-day T-bill level, and your company is judged to have half again as much business risk as the typical company, then the investor will demand, not six percentage points of premium, but nine points of premium. Hence, if the T-bill rate is 6 percent, he will be looking to the company to earn about 9 percent plus 6 percent, or 15 percent on its equity. Alternatively, if the company is judged to have only half the normal amount of business risk, then the investor will demand, not six percentage points of premium, but only three points of premium. The total return demanded will be 3 percent plus 6 percent, or only 9 percent.

Too many CEOs try to increase shareholder returns by taking on more and more business risk. That by itself is not abhorrent. What is abhorrent is that these same CEOs do not increase their performance targets for incentive purposes by a commensurate amount. Hence, they transfer *all* the increased risk from the executive group to the shareholders.

FAILING TO UNDERSTAND THAT STOCK OPTIONS COST MONEY

I have mentioned the FASB's current no-charge-to-earnings posture for most stock option grants. It is regrettable but true that many CEOs have come to believe that because there is no charge to earnings for stock option grants, there is no cost to the shareholders either. The accountants can play any number of games with stock options. But at the end of the day, the true economic costs remain the same.

All you need do is keep in mind that anytime you sell something to someone at a price that is lower than what you could have received by selling that same something to someone else, you have incurred a cost. The cost is equal to the discount you gave the first buyer. That, in a nutshell, is how you should figure the true cost of a stock option. Ultimately, the cost of increasing compensation is reflected in lower EPS regardless of whether it appears as a direct charge to earnings.

Years ago, a shrewd observer of economic life remarked that there is no such thing as a free lunch. He knew much more than many CEOs and most accountants.

FAILING TO PRUNE INCENTIVE ELIGIBILITY LISTS

Too often, once an executive makes the cut and is added to the company's incentive eligibility list, that executive will be on the list year after year, no matter what happens. Indeed, the executive's career may describe the same trajectory as a jet whose engines have flamed out, but he or she will stay on the list.

That's good for the executive but a pity for everyone else. First, keeping the person on the list increases the costs to the shareholders or, alternatively, erodes the average incentive award for the others who are eligible. Second, it fosters disrespect for the manner in which a company chooses people to be eligible in the first place. Remember that most of the other executives eligible for incentives may not be able to recall the lofty position our executive used to hold, for the simple reason that they had not even been born when he or she held it! All they can see is that someone is in the incentive plan who logically should not be.

It is a good idea to review incentive eligibility every year and, where necessary, to remove certain people from the list.

IGNORING INCENTIVE PAYOUT SENSITIVITIES

Not all incentive devices operate in the same way. Assume that you, as the plan designer, are considering using either restricted stock grants or regular stock option grants. Also assume that your company has not paid a dividend and does not expect to pay one in the near future.

Operating on the premise that your company's stock price is likely to double in the next five years (from $50 to $100 per share) and knowing that for performance of this level you need to give an executive a reward of $100,000, you conclude that you will need to grant the executive either 1,000 shares of restricted stock or 2,000 option shares carrying a strike price of $50 each. With restricted stock, the executive pays nothing for the shares and if the share price is indeed $100 five years from now, he or she will then be holding shares with a value of $100,000. In the case of stock options, a payment of $50 per share must be made to exercise the option, thereby reducing the profit per share (assuming an increase in share price to $100) to $50, compared to the $100-per-share profit from the restricted shares. But by granting twice as many option shares as restricted shares (2,000 versus 1,000) you can compensate for the difference.

What you have done so far makes good sense. But the acid test of your competence as an executive compensation designer will lie in whether you are willing to go further and consider how the two plans will behave if the stock price does something other than double. After all, there are literally an infinite number of possibilities concerning what the share price will be five years from now, that it will double to $100 per share is only one possibility.

For example, suppose you adopt a Doomsday scenario and conclude that the stock price, rather than rise from $50 to $100, might instead drop from $50 to $40. In that case, you will quickly discover that the executive will not be indifferent about which kind of grant he receives. The restricted stock will still have a value of $40,000 five years from now. But the options, if they go underwater, will be worthless (although if the term of the option is longer than five years, a market resurgence might yet give them worth).

Or suppose you look at your optimal scenario, one where the stock price advances not merely from $50 to $100, but from $50 to $200. In this case, the executive again will not be indifferent. In the case of the restricted stock grant, he or she will be holding shares having a value of $200,000. But with a 2,000-share option grant and a $150 per share increase in stock price, the economic benefit will be not $200,000, but $300,000.

By valuing both restricted stock and stock options under a variety of scenarios, you will see that they behave very differently. Stock options carry more downside risk than restricted shares do, but they also carry more upside reward. Once you know that, you can make more intelligent recommendations about what sort of plan your company ought to adopt.

SETTING TARGETS TOO LOW

Unfortunately, some plan designers forget that they are supposed to be developing plans that are in the shareholders' interests and that reward true performance accomplishments. Instead, they view a plan that does not pay out as a plan that has somehow failed. As a result, they embed laughably low performance targets in the plan.

If the world's record for the high jump is say, ten feet, the crowd will sit still when the bar starts at six feet, because they know that the bar will be raised until only one person can clear it. But how is the crowd going to react when the bar is started at six feet and then *lowered* the first time a player cannot clear it? How is the crowd going to react if a trench is dug and the bar is buried in the ground to make sure that the player can finally clear it? That crowd will head for the nearest exit!

CONCENTRATING ON THE EASY PERFORMANCE MEASURES

A corollary to the problem just discussed involves using certain performance measures in incentive plans, not because they are the right measures, but because they are the measures that are most likely to pay off.

Thus, if a company is only earning $1 million on $1 billion of equity, stay away from ROE as a performance measure, because you will be mandating a sure incentive goose egg. Instead, concentrate on earnings growth. After all, doubling the profits to $2 million will not be too difficult, given your starting point. And 100 percent profit growth sounds like it ought to deserve some hefty incentive payouts. That ROE has not advanced even to 1 percent may be conveniently overlooked.

As I mentioned earlier, the prime test of whether an incentive plan is a good one should have nothing to do with whether it pays out regularly and lusciously.

REWARDING FOR OUTRIGHT FAILURE

Sadly, a disquieting number of companies, far from setting incentive targets too low or even choosing the easy performance measures, simply offer huge rewards for what can only be seen as outright failure.

Take the case of golden parachutes. Some companies offer senior executives literally tens of millions of dollars when the company is taken over. It may not always be the case that a company that is taken over is badly managed, but it is certainly usually the case. After all, if a company is well managed, the premium that a takeover artist will have to pay to buy it is likely to be excessive. Moreover, in how many companies that are taken over do the new owners retain the services of the former managers and, indeed, instruct them to continue doing exactly as they have been? More likely, there is a total housecleaning, with layers of excessive fat being liposuctioned off and whole divisions sold.

It is interesting to observe how the American public and its agents, the Congress, reacted to the millions of dollars in option profits that Lee Iacocca earned when he turned Chrysler around versus the millions of dollars paid in golden parachute money to executives of companies that were taken over. In the first case, there was universal acclaim, and some even mused that Iacocca did not make enough money. In the second, we witnessed the unlimbering of two of the three potent weapons that the government can bring into play when it smells excessive compensation: the imposition of a confiscatory tax rate on the executive and the denial of the company's tax deduction on the compensation being paid. (The third weapon involves the imposition of outright pay controls, of the type used by President Nixon in the early 1970s.)

Unlike some CEOs, the American public seems to have little trouble distinguishing between pay-for-performance and pay-for-failure.

APING OTHERS

I was a compensation director for a large corporation on the tragic day when John Kennedy was assassinated. Not five minutes after the news hit the wire, I received a call from my superior, the vice president of personnel, who ordered me to call twenty other companies in the immediate geographic area and find out if they were going to give their employees time off with pay to go to church.

This regrettable episode demonstrates what I see as "the personnel mentality." Do not do something because it may be desirable, but do something because 80 percent of comparable companies are doing it. That sort of reasoning can get a company into big trouble. If everyone else is spending 9 percent on salary increases, then you do the same, even though your performance cannot sustain such a large expenditure. Or if everyone else is granting stock options, you grant stock options, even though another incentive design would be far more effective.

Looking at what others do is important. But it is secondary to deciding what *your* company ought to do.

FAILING TO COMMUNICATE PLANS ADEQUATELY

It is interesting to see what happens after some companies have gone to the trouble to design an intelligent incentive plan. In some cases, the company tells its executives virtually nothing about the new plan. One day, a check turns up in the mail, and other than that, the executive is in the dark about what he or she is supposed to do to earn more money. It is hard to see how such a company received any return from its efforts to motivate its executives.

Some companies make the opposite mistake and assume that all of their executives are not only lawyers but also financial scholars. Why send all executives a forty-seven page legal text and an accompanying twelve pages of esoteric equations? Since few of the company's executives are lawyers, even fewer are financial scholars, and, most likely, none are both, the company again shoots itself in the foot.

The old saw about the chain being only as strong as its weakest link applies to the design of incentive plans. Without effective communication, incentive plans lose their power to motivate. It is the rare company that takes the time to communicate its plans in an adequate and comprehensible manner.

Plan communications are too important to leave to the compensation experts. Most compensation experts love numbers, and they love detail almost as much as numbers. There is a danger, ironically, of telling a plan participant too much about a new incentive plan. To be sure, the chief financial officer has to understand the twelve pages of equations underlying the new incentive plan, and even the CEO must have a nodding acquaintance with them. But the average participant needs to know only in general what the plan is designed to accomplish and what or she must do to achieve various levels of remuneration. Perhaps only two or three of the equations on those twelve pages need be given to the typical participant.

A well-designed incentive plan beautifully communicated is indeed a joy to behold.

KEEPING DIRECTORS IN THE DARK

Most large corporations have a so-called compensation committee of the board of directors. This committee, which is composed of a number of outside directors (i.e., directors who are not also officers of the company), is charged with riding herd on executive compensation plans and pay levels.

Unfortunately, a number of CEOs treat their compensation committees as adversaries. Instead of capitalizing on the experience of outside directors, they try to keep them in the dark as much as possible. To be sure they go through the motions of seeking the approval of the compensation committee for changes in policy. But the reasons underlying the recommended action often are not exposed to the degree they should be; alternative courses of action that were considered but rejected are not presented; and simulations of how a plan would pay out under many possible performance scenarios, rather than the one scenario the CEO wants the committee to examine, are never offered.

It is not at all clear to me why an audit committee of a board of directors should have its own independent counsel (that is, the company's outside auditors), while a compensation committee should be left to its own devices. Executive compensation plans are growing increasingly complex and diverse, and new ways of paying executives are being invented almost monthly. It seems reasonable, therefore, that compensation committees ought to have outside professional help so that they can properly evaluate management's proposals and so that they can properly represent the shareholders' best interests.

There are doubtless many more mistakes in the world of executive compensation that I could discuss. But the ones I have mentioned are certainly the main ones. If companies can avoid them they will have gone a long way toward having viable, and maximally motivating, executive compensation programs.

NOTE

1. *New York Times*, October 9, 1960.

10

CHOOSING APPROPRIATE PERFORMANCE MEASURES

Seymour Burchman

INTRODUCTION

A crucial issue in incentive plan design is choosing the appropriate performance measures. Historically, executive incentive plans have focused on company stock performance and/or traditional accounting measures. The use of stock performance has been criticized often because of its remoteness from executive control. On the other hand, plans based on traditional accounting measures paid out handsomely when annual earnings met or exceeded budget projections, often as stock prices declined.

Today, the focus is changing. While current stock performance remains an important measurement of executive performance, companies are also turning to financial performance measures that are more predictive of future stock performance and using nonfinancial measures that help promote and reward the execution of business-unit strategies. In addition, companies are adopting qualitative measures that reflect executives' individual performance as leaders and managers. In selecting performance measures, companies are trying to ensure consistency with their specific organizational and management environments and compensation philosophies.

This chapter explores the new performance emphasis and its impact on incentive plan measures. It discusses the key criteria companies should consider when selecting performance measures and examines the types of measures being used to evaluate executives' actions and successes.

CRITERIA FOR SELECTING PERFORMANCE MEASURES

In selecting performance measures for executive compensation programs, three criteria must be satisfied.

Shareholder Wealth Creation

Performance measures must be highly correlated with shareholder wealth creation—the ultimate mission of U.S. corporations. Although a company has obligations to its other stakeholders, including employees, suppliers, and the general public, its overall success or failure is gauged by its long-range ability to create wealth for its shareholders through stock price appreciation and dividends. Given this premise, the principal role of executive compensation programs is to motivate executives, through appropriate rewards, to make decisions, and take actions that contribute to the creation of shareholder wealth.

High correlations of executive performance with shareholder wealth creation can be achieved in two ways. First, executive awards can be linked directly to changes in shareholder wealth through stock options, restricted stock, and dividend equivalent programs. Second, internal business performance measures that lead to shareholder wealth creation can be used. These measures include *financial measures*, which predict future stock price movements and dividend payouts, and *nonfinancial measures*, which measure the company's success in gaining and maintaining a competitive advantage in the marketplace.

Environmental Consistency

Performance measures must be consistent with the company's organizational and management environment, taking into consideration strategic/financial management, executive ability to control results, and the company's culture and management style.

In assessing strategic/financial management, it must be determined whether management understands the proposed performance measures and the actions they demand, whether performance can be measured reliably and in good time, and whether the measures are consistent with the criteria used to make other important business decisions in such areas as operations, capital expenditures, and so forth. A company that has not achieved an acceptable level of strategic/financial management can adopt performance measures that are more appropriate to its current situation or use its compensation program to help improve the quality of strategic/financial management. Many companies use incentive programs, together with other educational vehicles, to introduce and reinforce concepts such as return on investment, cash flow-based management, or other key performance issues in the company. Other companies base incentive payouts on the attainment of business plan targets to "put teeth" into the planning process.

Compensation programs will only motivate executives effectively if participants are able to influence the results for which they are held accountable. An executive's ability to control results is determined by both internal and external factors. Internal factors include:

1. Organizational interdependence: Executives tend to rely more on others in functionally organized businesses and in business units that are interdependent because of shared resources or integrative strategies. In cases where the need to rely on others is great, companies can use the same performance measures for all executives, which may diminish the motivational value of the pay program but encourage collaboration and teamwork, or develop individual targets for executives, which may maximize the motivational value of the compensation program but lessen the impetus for collaboration.

2. Executive authority: Measures should focus on performance areas that executives can control. For example, a retail company's compensation program measures business-unit executives on margins (i.e., the earnings realized on a given level of sales) and asset utilization (i.e., the level of sales generated by a given level of assets). These are factors that executives at this level can control, since corporate management retains authority over the investment decisions needed to increase revenues and profits.

External factors affecting executive control include the economy, the regulatory environment, exchange rates, and the specific competitive circumstances of an industry. The importance of external factors varies depending on the industry and a business's position in the industry (for example, a firm that is an industry leader has more control over what goes on within that industry than a minor player who must often respond to the leader's actions).

Companies may take several approaches to address the uncertainty caused by external factors. Management can be given greater discretion in evaluating performance and rely less on formulas. Performance can be measured against the performance of competitors or other units in the company. The performance measurement period can be lengthened to reduce the impact of unexpected events. Or the leverage in payout formulas can be reduced to lessen the impact of uncertainty (payouts should vary less with changes in the performance measure). Care should be taken, however, to avoid a plan that does not reward executives who anticipate or respond quickly and effectively to unforeseen circumstances.

A number of issues should be considered in assessing a company's culture and management style. Performance measures should be consistent with the level of entrepreneurial behavior and autonomy the company wants to encourage. For instance, measures can focus on how things get done by rewarding the accomplishment of specific short-term projects, or on ultimate bottom-line results by rewarding executives for what they achieve, not how they get there.

The measures should be consistent with the degree of openness/information-sharing in the organization. For example, in one privately held organization where senior executives are unwilling to share actual profit data with managers, profits are expressed as a percentage of planned performance.

The measures should be consistent with the level of trust in the organization. In a health care company, employees mistrusted senior management because the prior incentive plans were perceived as unfair. As a solution, the new plan incorporated carefully defined quantitative measures and strict, formula-based awards.

The measures should be consistent with the level of teamwork and collaboration the company wants to encourage. Companies that want to promote collaboration among departments or business units should use more shared measures than individual measures.

The measures should be consistent with the strategic and qualitative focus of the company. If companies believe that managers overemphasize short-term and financial concerns, they should introduce measures that address important strategic and qualitative concerns and consider measuring financial performance over several years.

The measures should be consistent with executive movement within the organization. If executives frequently transfer among units within a larger business group, group performance may be a better measure, especially for long-term plans. Plans based on specific business-unit measures may hinder executive transfers to poorer performing units and make it more difficult to match executive rewards to their contributions.

Consistency with Compensation Philosophy

Performance measures must be consistent with the company's compensation philosophy and objectives, which determine the role of compensation in influencing behavior.

At one extreme, compensation can be neutral and culture, management style, communications, hands-on management, and so forth, are the preferred tools for directing behavior. If this is the case, the compensation program must not conflict with these determinants of management behavior. Performance measures will likely stress the bottom line, with the intent of sharing part of the earnings or value created with the management team.

At the other extreme, compensation can be a significant tool in driving executive behavior. In this case, the company must first decide what behaviors it wishes to reinforce and then identify specific performance measures for those behaviors. As an example, a service company historically focused on earnings growth and the executive compensation program reinforced this emphasis: Incentives were based strictly on earnings growth. Although the company was growing rapidly, its stock price was falling because return on incremental investments (i.e., new accounts) was below the cost of capital. The company changed both the measures it used to make business decisions and its incentive plan measures in order to emphasize return on net assets (RONA). In fact, RONA was given more weight than earnings because of the need to change executive behavior. As a result, marginal accounts were trimmed and new accounts were accepted only if pro formas indicated adequate returns. Eventually, returns and the stock price improved.

TYPES OF PERFORMANCE MEASURES

Three broad categories of performance measures may be used in executive compensation programs. *Market-based measures*, address shareholder wealth directly. They reflect the stock market's assessment of company performance through stock price appreciation and/or dividend payments. Stock-based compensation programs such as stock options, restricted stock, and performance shares rely on market-based measures. Many companies also use *internal business performance measures* to offset the limitations of market-based measures. These measures focus on internal organizational performance measured at the company, business-unit, profit center, and/or department levels. *Individual leadership and management measures* address executives' performance as leaders and managers. These measures focus on individual contributions (providing strategic direction or building a management team, for example) as distinct from the performance of the organization for which the executive is responsible.

Market-Based Measures

Market-based measures are the most prevalent measures in long-term incentive plans. Over 95 percent of the *Fortune* 200 and over 70 percent of a broader cross-section of U.S. companies use long-term incentive plans based on market performance.[1]

Market-based measures have four advantages: First, there is a one-to-one relationship between executive gains and shareholder gains. Second, stock price is determined independently; that is, it is based on arm's-length trading by parties who do not have a vested interest in selecting performance measures, setting performance goals, evaluating performance at year end, and so forth. Third, stock price reflects a long-term assessment of the company's performance. Rappaport studied the proportion of current stock price assignable to dividends beyond five years. He found that over 80 percent of current stock price was attributable to dividend payments five or more years in the future.[2] And fourth, market-based measures are simple, easy to compute, and readily verifiable.

Market-based measures also have several shortcomings. First, stock prices are subject to the vagaries of the overall economy and of the stock market. Although company performance is the primary driver of long-term stock price movements, macroeconomic forces can cause stock price to rise or fall in the short and intermediate term, as demonstrated by such events as the Arab oil embargo and the 1987 market crash. And while the most common complaint regarding the vagaries of the economy is that executives realize no gains when macroeconomic forces drive stock prices down, there are cases where macroeconomic forces have enabled executives to realize large gains independent of company performance. One example was the person who was CEO of a freight company during a five-year period of plummeting market share, return on investment, and stock price. This CEO received a 60,000-share stock option grant shortly before the market recovery and realized a $500,000 gain, even though the company's performance had not noticeably improved.

Second, market imperfections may cause a stock to be under- or over-valued. For example, the market may not have information that affects the value of the firm, information such as planned divestitures, new strategies, new investments, new technologies, and so forth. To the extent that such market imperfections exist, management may not receive full credit for its contributions to the firm.

Third, executives below the uppermost levels in a large corporation have relatively little control over company stock price and dividends. This limitation of market-based measures has grown in importance as business units increase in number and autonomy. Traditional market-based measures are particularly ineffective at rewarding business-unit heads for the success (or failure) of their units.

Fourth, market-based measures do not motivate executives to implement specific company strategies or attain specific financial goals.

Fifth, tying executive compensation to stock price alone increases executives' exposure to risks, potentially making them more conservative. Shareholders are able to balance risky investments with other investments in their portfolios. Since executives have less ability to diversify risk, and because they derive substantial portions of their income and net worth from their company's executive compensation programs, their decision making may be more conservative than shareholders would desire.

Sixth, a growing number of companies are either privately held or subsidiaries of larger companies.

Several approaches can be used to circumvent some of these disadvantages. For example, to address economic and market vagaries, some companies base executive compensation programs on "indexed" market performance. These programs pay out when the company's stock price and dividend performance achieve specific targets relative to overall market performance or the performance of peer companies (often after adjustment for relative volatility, or beta). However, an indexed approach presents potential problems. First, the link between executive and shareholder gains is weakened. Second, executives in structurally unattractive industries may be motivated to make improper strategic decisions. For example, an executive in a steel company whose stock price is falling more slowly than that of other steel companies will be rewarded for staying in the steel business, even though the appropriate strategy might be to reallocate resources into businesses that have greater growth opportunities and returns.

The more common approach to addressing the shortcomings of market-based measures is to use internal business performance measures, either alone or in conjunction with market-based measures. For example, Sibson & Company's 1987 *Executive Long-Term Incentive Survey* indicates that over half of the companies with long-term incentive plans base all or a portion of their awards on internal business performance measures.[3]

Internal business performance measures can be used in conjunction with market-based measures in a variety of ways. Combination plans can be devised (e.g., stock options plus a long-term bonus), so that part of an executive's compensation is based on market performance and part on internal business performance. Tandem plans can be structured to pay out under either a market-based plan or a performance-based plan. Single plans, which use both types of measures, can be used. The most common of these is a performance share plan. Other examples include stock option and restricted stock plans that base vesting of the option or the stock on company and/or business-unit performance.

Internal Business Performance Measures

Market-based measures may not fully satisfy the needs of a company's executive compensation program. In these cases, internal business performance measures can be used in conjunction with or in place of market-based measures.

Internal business performance measures in well-designed programs fall into two categories: *financial measures*, which address the key financial determinants of shareholder wealth, and *nonfinancial measures*, which address the key factors contributing to sustainable competitive advantage.

Financial Measures. According to Sibson & Company's annual *Management Compensation Survey,* measures of earnings, including pre-tax earnings, net income, and earnings per share growth, are the most common financial performance measures in annual and long-term incentive plans.[4] However, numerous studies have demonstrated that earnings measures are, at best, weakly correlated with shareholder wealth creation. For example, Rappaport studied the Standard & Poor's 500 Index from 1973 to 1978. During this period, while EPS grew at an annual rate of 8.6 percent, total returns to shareholders from stock price appreciation and dividends were less than 1 percent. Another Rappaport study of the Standard & Poor's 400 industrial companies during the 1970s showed similar results. Of the 400 companies, 172 achieved compound EPS growth rates of 15 percent or better from 1974 to 1979. His study found that shareholders in 16 percent of these firms realized negative nominal rates of return and shareholders in more than one-third of the firms had negative real returns (i.e., returns adequate to compensate for inflation).[5] In another study of 276 New York Stock Exchange firms, Beaver, Clarke, and Wright found that the average correlation between annual percentage changes in earnings and in stock price was only 0.38.[6] A similar study conducted by Beaver, Lambert, and Morse found a correlation of 0.49 for data from 1958 to 1976.[7]

There are four primary reasons why annual earnings are poor predictors of shareholder returns. First, annual earnings do not reflect the amount of investment needed to achieve a particular growth in earnings. Earnings growth adds value to a business only if the rate of return realized on additional investment exceeds the return required by investors, i.e., their cost of capital.

Second, annual earnings do not reflect changes in the cost of capital needed to finance the investment in the business. Inflation and/or higher investor risk can both drive up a firm's cost of capital. Unless additional earnings are sufficient to offset the increased cost of capital (from either equity or debt), the value of the firm will decline even though earnings have increased. The past two decades have shown the significant impact that inflation-induced changes in the cost of capital can have on firm value. During the late 1970s and early 1980s, the cost of capital was increasing as fast, if not faster, than earnings. In 1970, inflation was at 5 percent and an average company with a 15-percent return could cover the modest 11-percent after-tax cost of equity. By 1981, however, the cost of equity had soared to 19 percent and the average company was providing a return well below its equity costs. Rappaport's results, cited above, are largely attributable to these significant changes in the cost of capital. Slowing inflation rates after 1981 contributed to lower capital costs and companies' returns again exceeded their cost of capital. This helped contribute to the healthy performance of the stock market from 1982 to 1987.

Third, annual earnings do not capture the future impact of current decisions on earnings. For example, while major investments in advertising and research and development may have an immediate depressing effect on earnings, they may have a significant long-term positive effect on future earnings.

Fourth, the use of annual earnings assumes that accounting numbers adequately measure the true economic realities of the business. There are, however, situations in which this assumption is not true. In periods of rapid inflation, for example, earnings can significantly overstate profitability because depreciation and inventory costs are based on historic, not current, cost levels. Also, earnings generally do not address changes in the market value of significant company assets (e.g., oil resources, real estate holdings, film libraries, and so forth), which are carried on a company's balance sheet at depreciated cost.

Given the shortcomings of earnings measures, companies have searched for alternative measures of corporate performance that correlate more highly with shareholder wealth creation. Most experts agree that the

measure, both theoretically and empirically, that best meets this requirement is shareholder value. Under this concept, the value of a company is
determined by discounting the expected *future cash flows* of a company
using an appropriate cost (i.e., discount rate) for the capital at risk. Although shareholder value is a relatively new approach for evaluating a
firm's overall performance, it closely parallels concepts used by most firms
in evaluating capital expenditures, major projects, and acquisitions.

Studies of the Standard & Poor's 400 conducted by Callard, Madden
and Associates have shown that alternative shareholder value models can
explain 50 percent to 75 percent of the variance in stock prices.

Several shareholder value models have been developed, most of which
(including that developed by Callard, Madden and Associates) attribute
the creation of shareholder value to the difference, or "spread," between
the company's return on investment and its cost of capital, which measures the quality of a company's earnings; company growth, typically measured by the change in the amount of investment in the business; and the
period of time the company is able to maintain a positive spread and
growth. Exhibit 10-1 illustrates this model.

A company's value increases the longer it is able to increase the spread
between its return on investment and its cost of capital and/or increase its
investment base (provided it can do so at a positive spread).

The Alcar Group, which also bases its model on discounted cash flows,
employs a somewhat different approach to determining shareholder
value. The Alcar model consists of three "valuation components," which
are in turn influenced by a series of value drivers. The first valuation
component, *cash flow from operations*, is the product of value drivers
based on operating decisions (the sales growth rate, operating profit margin, and the income tax rate); value drivers reflecting investment decisions
(working capital investment and fixed capital investment); and value
growth duration, or the number of years that investment can be expected
to yield rates of return greater than the cost of capital.

The second valuation component, the *discount rate*, is determined by
the company's cost of capital, which is in turn influenced by business risk
and management's financing decisions. Corporate value is determined by
discounting the cash flows from operations at the cost of capital. Shareholder value is determined by deducting the third valuation component,
debt, from corporate value.[8] For example, a retailer developed a long-
term incentive plan for its division presidents based on the key Alcar value
drivers for each division. Using the Alcar software, an analysis indicated

EXHIBIT 10-1
Determinants of Shareholder Value

Spread = Difference

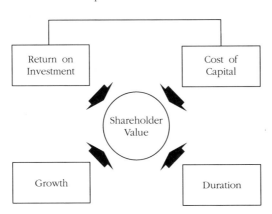

that operating profit margins and sales growth were the primary determinants of shareholder value in each division, while incremental working capital had a lesser, but material, impact. Payout matrices were designed under which competitive target awards were adjusted based on performance against three-year plan targets for each value driver. The payout matrix for one division is illustrated in Exhibit 10-2.

An alternative to using financial models is to rely on periodic outside appraisals of a firm's value. This approach is particularly useful if a significant proportion of a firm's value is based on its portfolio of assets or if a firm wants independent judgments regarding key assumptions. Such an approach was used in a "phantom stock" plan developed for the head of a company's real estate subsidiary. Under this plan, the subsidiary president was given a 5 percent ownership interest in the subsidiary. The value of the subsidiary was determined by independent appraisals of its real estate holdings conducted every three years. The drawbacks of this approach are that it is costly and does not clearly communicate how executives can affect value.

Shareholder value models can be utilized in executive compensation programs differently. For instance, as described above, a phantom stock plan can be developed in which changes in the value of the phantom shares are related to changes in the firm's shareholder value. This approach can be used to simulate equity in business units. Alternatively, if a

EXHIBIT 10-2

Divisional Payout Matrix
(percentage of target award)

Operating Profit Margin	Sales Growth				
	Plan −4	Plan −2	Plan	Plan +2	Plan +4
Plan −1.0	50.0	57.1	64.5	72.1	80.0
Plan −0.5	66.0	74.0	82.2	90.8	99.6
Plan	82.0	90.9	100.0	116.2	132.9
Plan +0.5	98.1	113.2	130.4	148.1	166.4
Plan +1.0	124.1	142.1	160.7	180.0	200.0

Adjust for Incremental Working Capital/Sales Performance

>9% Above Plan	4 – 8% Above Plan	0 – 3% Above/ Below Plan	4 – 8% Below Plan	>9% Below Plan
−15%	−5%	0%	+5%	+15%

EXHIBIT 10-3
Factors Affecting Return on Investment

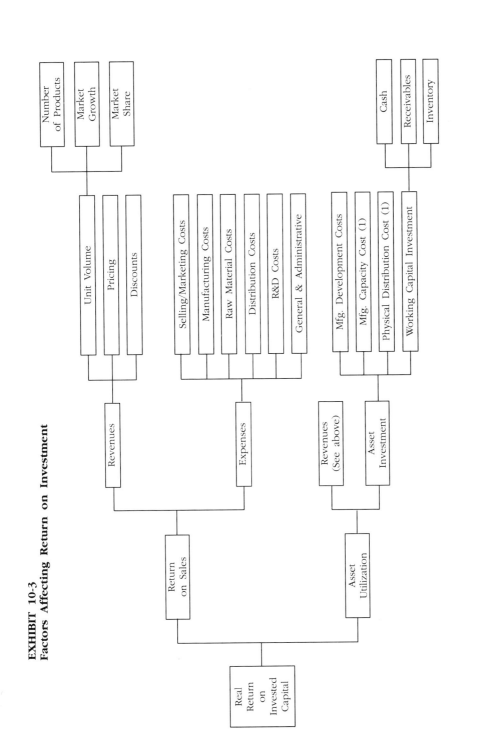

company wants its executive compensation program to be more directive, the key value drivers and their relative importance can be identified using a shareholder value model and then incorporated in a performance unit plan. The payout schedule can be developed by calculating the amount of shareholder value created at various levels of the value drivers.

Shareholder value and its principal drivers can be used to measure corporate performance or the performance of a business unit. A second issue is motivating individual executives, particularly those further down in an organization, to create shareholder value. This can be accomplished, in part, by breaking down the determinants of shareholder value into components that individual executives can influence. Exhibit 10-3 identifies some of the principal components of return on investment. These component performance measures can be incorporated into executive incentive plans to help link individual incentives to desired overall corporate results. A manufacturing firm incorporated this approach into the design of its annual incentive plan as shown below:

Position	Performance Measures	Weighting
Chief Executive Officer	—Company earnings growth and return on equity	100%
Vice President	—Company earnings growth and return on equity	50
Sales/Marketing	—Sales volume weighted for profit margin	30
	—Selling/marketing costs	10
	—Account retention*	10
Vice President	—Company earnings growth and return on equity	50
Manufacturing	—Manufacturing cost per unit	30
	—Defect rate*	20

*Nonfinancial goal

Nonfinancial Measures.   It is not always appropriate to base executive compensation programs solely on financial performance. Nonfinancial measures can be used to help balance longer-term strategic needs with short-term financial results; reinforce key elements of a company's strategy that will contribute to future improvements in growth and spread; and link incentive payments more closely to individual contributions.

Harvard's Michael Porter provides a useful framework for analyzing competitive advantage and identifying various areas in which nonfinancial measures may be developed.[9] He describes two basic types of competitive advantage:

1. *Cost leadership:* A firm sets out to become the low-cost producer in its industry. Sources of cost advantage may include economies of scale, proprietary technology, and preferential access to new materials, among other factors.

2. *Differentiation*: A firm seeks to be unique by being valued by its customers. Differentiation can be based on the product itself, the delivery system by which it is sold, the marketing approach, the support services that are provided, and so forth. A company that can successfully differentiate itself can command a premium price for its products or services.

A firm can focus either on a broad or narrow range of industry segments in achieving cost leadership or differentiation advantages.

Porter also identifies nine "value activities," which he describes as the "discrete building blocks of competitive advantage."[10] How each value activity is performed will determine whether a firm is a high- or low-cost producer relative to competitors and whether it can differentiate its products or services. The nine generic categories of value activities include five *primary* activities—inbound logistics, operations, outbound logistics, marketing and sales, and service—and four *support* activities—procurement, technology development, human resource management, and firm infrastructure.

Nonfinancial measures can be used to reinforce a business unit's strategy for achieving competitive advantage by focusing management attention on its key value activities. For example, an automotive importer's strategy is to achieve competitive advantage by differentiating itself through superior customer service. To reinforce this strategy, the incentive plan measures overall company performance according to its rating on the J.D. Powers "Customer Satisfaction Index" (a measure of customer satisfaction with after-sales service). Supporting measures in each major functional area also address service:

1. Service Department—objectives for developing superior dealer service technicians.
2. Customer Relations Department—objectives for developing a "customer service hotline" and reducing the response time to customer complaints.
3. Parts Department—objectives for improving the "parts fill rate."
4. MIS Department—objectives for developing a quality control system to track dealer service and customer satisfaction ratings in each service district.

The identification of nonfinancial measures should be closely tied to a business's planning and management systems to help reinforce key accountabilities. Unfortunately, they are often developed as independent activities with little resultant impact on the business.

After selecting appropriate performance measures, three related issues need to be addressed: First, at what level should performance be measured? Second, what is the appropriate time frame for measuring performance? And third, what focus should be used for evaluating performance?

The first issue addresses the level at which performance should be measured—company, business unit, profit center, department, and/or individual. The choice should be based on the specific characteristics of the business. Some key factors affecting the choice of organizational level for business-unit heads are shown in Exhibit 10-4.

Sibson & Company's 1987 *Management Compensation Survey* indicates that the levels companies use for annual incentive plans generally correspond to this model.[11] However, few companies have successfully incorporated business-unit performance into their long-term incentive plans. The increase in both the numbers and autonomy of business units suggests that this will be a crucial issue in future compensation program design.

In choosing the appropriate time period for measuring performance, companies generally use either their fiscal years or a longer period. A fiscal year is appropriate for measuring the attainment of annual business plan results and key strategic milestones. For longer-term incentives, the time frame can be a fixed period of time determined by the company's

EXHIBIT 10-4
Factors Affecting the Level at which Business-Unit Head Performance Should Be Measured

Characteristics Favoring the Use of Corporate Measures	*Characteristics Favoring the Use of Business-Unit Measures*
• Significant corporate management/control of business units	• Autonomous business units
• Business units interdependent because of shared resources/integrative strategies	• Significant differences in business-unit strategies/key success factors
• Need to encourage collaboration among business units	• Little interdependence of business units
• Significant mobility of talent across business units	• Little mobility of talent across business units
• Need to support strong company cultures/values	• Need to support strong business-unit cultures/values
• Pay not needed to motivate executive behavior	• Pay needed to play important role in motivating executive behavior (e.g., by basing incentive awards on specific results executives can control)

planning horizon, which in turn is affected by the sophistication of the business's planning systems and the level of uncertainty regarding business results; the company's decision-results cycle, that is, the time lapse between making decisions and the results; the extent to which the company wants to tie awards to results, as opposed to the intermediate actions taken to achieve those results; and the desired motivational impact of the incentive program (the further in the future awards are made, the less motivational impact they have).

Alternatively, long-term incentives can use a variable time frame, with payouts being triggered by specific events (e.g., reaching break-even, attaining revenue milestones, or going public in a startup). As a practical matter, almost 90 percent of all companies use performance periods of three or four years.

To determine the focus or frame of reference to use in evaluating performance, companies generally use one or more of the following standards:

1. A *goal from the business plan:* This type of goal reinforces management's commitment to the plan. Incentives can drive performance in desired directions.
2. A *fixed standard:* For example, a goal might be established to generate a certain level of profitability above the company's cost of capital. This type of goal is useful when a primary company objective is to share a portion of good company results with management.
3. *Comparative goals:* This type of goal is also useful in rewarding management for good performance. It helps to factor out external influences over which management has little control because the external influences will presumably affect peer company results as well.
4. *Comparison with historical performance:* This type of goal can be useful if the intention is to make incremental improvements in areas where baseline performance norms have already been established.

Survey results indicate that business plan forecasts are the most common standard. They are used by over 80 percent of companies in annual incentive plans and by 70 percent in long-term incentive plans.[12]

Compensation committee members favor the use of business plan targets, although there is also considerable support for the use of comparative standards as shown below:

Standard	Annual Plans	Long-Term Plans
From Business Plan	52%	80%
Fixed Standard	37	0
Comparative Goals	26	43
Historical Results	8	13

Source: *Boards, Company Performance and Executive Pay,* Sibson & Company, 1985.

Individual Leadership/Management Performance Measures

In its 1985 survey of board compensation committee members, Sibson & Company asked committee members to indicate the relative importance of various quantitative and qualitative aspects of performance.[13] Interestingly, the four highest-ranked measures—establishing strategic direction (86 percent), building a management team (84 percent), exhibiting leadership qualities (79 percent), and providing for succession (75 percent)—were qualitative measures that addressed the CEO's individual leadership and management performance.

This suggests that many important areas of performance assessment have been largely ignored in executive compensation programs and that businesses need better ways to assess the intangible qualities of corporate performance. The emphasis placed by committee members on qualitative aspects of performance suggests that the pendulum is swinging the other way after years of quantitative decision making and dispassionate portfolio management.

Based on the responses of board members, companies should consider seven broad areas when assessing executive leadership/management:

1. *Providing strategic direction,* which includes:
   - determining where the company is headed in the context of anticipated opportunities, vulnerabilities, and capabilities within a global perspective;
   - adapting corporate direction when conditions change;
   - assessing the organizational capabilities and resources required to successfully carry out strategy:
   - establishing priorities and allocating resources accordingly, including the investigation and negotiation of acquisitions and divestitures with the advice and consent of the board of directors.
2. *Providing leadership,* which includes:
   - promulgating corporate values;
   - communicating and gaining commitment to corporate values, di-

rection, and priorities among board, management, and employees;

- creating a "winning spirit" and "making things happen."

3. *Proactively managing change*, which includes:
   - analyzing and determining when change is needed or imminent;
   - maximizing the opportunities resulting from change without creating organizational chaos or deleterious short-term financial and/or nonfinancial effects;
   - promoting innovation throughout the organization in products, technology, customer service, marketing, and how work is done.

4. *Organizing, developing, and utilizing the management team*, which includes:
   - establishing, evaluating, and changing the management structure to improve organizational effectiveness and efficiency;
   - attracting, selecting, nurturing, and keeping the best available management talent;
   - ensuring continuity in the management team through appropriate succession plans;
   - successfully utilizing the management team to assist in the planning, control, and execution of corporate strategy;
   - setting clear performance standards for the management team and providing appropriate feedback.

5. *Creating an appropriate organizational environment*, which includes establishing and maintaining an organizational environment—through appropriate management style, culture, organizational structure, and systems—that enables and encourages all employees to work up to their potential (e.g., maximized morale, productivity, contribution, and so forth).

6. *Providing effective external representation*, which includes:
   - setting, maintaining, and improving the image of the company;
   - acting proactively to ensure optimum company relationships with stockholders, customers, suppliers, the financial community, the government, the press, and the general public.

7. *Monitoring and evaluating company performance and taking corrective action*, which includes:
   - checking and appraising individual and company performance to ensure that strategy is being implemented effectively and efficiently, that annual operating results are being attained, and that shareholders' interests are protected;
   - Taking necessary corrective actions on a timely basis.

EXHIBIT 10-5
Illustration of Performance Indicators
Performance Assessment Area: "Proactively Manages Change"

Element of Accountability	Performance Indicators
Analyzes and determines when change is needed or imminent	• CEO provides the board at the start of the year (e.g., as part of the business planning process) and subsequently, as appropriate, with: —An analysis of significant impending competitive, economic, technological, and regulatory changes —The implications of these changes for the company —How the company will respond to protect or further strengthen its competitive advantage in the face of these changes • Quality of the analysis is judged, in part, retrospectively by the extent to which projected and unanticipated changes occur
Maximizes opportunities resulting from change without creating organizational chaos or deleterious short-term financial and/or nonfinancial effects	• CEO implements organizational, operational, strategic, and other changes proposed for the year (e.g., see above) according to schedule and within budget • Effectiveness of the changes and the change process is judged along several dimensions, including: —Extent to which desired outcomes have been achieved (e.g., are the key milestones for implementing a new technology met; has organizational restructuring occurred) —Whether deleterious side effects have been minimized (e.g., has short-term financial performance been adversely affected; has employee morale decreased or employee turnover increased; have customer satisfaction ratings fallen, and so forth.)
Promotes innovation through the organization in products, technology, customer service, marketing, and how work is done	• CEO and the management team achieve innovation record that surpasses that of competitors and other companies in similar industries (e.g., company is first with significant new technologies, new products, new marketing strategies, new ways of performing work, and so forth)

Although considerable judgment is involved in evaluating performance in these areas, companies can take steps to prevent the process from becoming arbitrary. For example, they can identify specific leadership/management areas relevant to their needs and establish specific "indicators" to measure performance. Indicators (either quantitative measures or observable qualitative evidence) can help to clearly define performance expectations up front and to objectively appraise performance at year-end. In addition to identifying indicators, companies can also define the desired and optimum levels of performance with respect to each indicator. Illustrative indicators for "proactively managing change" are presented in Exhibit 10-5.

The cornerstone of any incentive plan is the measurement of company, business-unit, and individual performance. Our experience indicates that the vast majority of problems with incentives can be traced to performance measurement issues. One-half to three-quarters of the time spent consulting on incentive plan design is typically devoted to performance measurement.

Performance measures, if chosen correctly, can effectively reinforce and reward those factors that will lead to longer-term stockholder wealth creation. Conversely, improper measures can motivate executives to act in ways that are counter to a company's long-term well-being. There are all too many cases of shareholder wealth being diminished and/or long-term strategies being scuttled by incentive plans that used the wrong performance measures.

NOTES

1. Sibson & Company, Inc., *Executive Compensation Annual Report* (Princeton, NJ, 1988).

2. Alfred Rappaport, *Creating Shareholder Value* (New York: Free Press, 1986), p. 40.

3. Sibson & Company, Inc., *Executive Long-Term Incentive Survey* (Princeton, NJ, 1987).

4. Sibson & Company, Inc., *Management Compensation Survey* (Princeton, NJ, 1987).

5. Rappaport, *Creating Shareholder Value*, pp. 29–31.

6. William H. Beaver, Roger Clarke, and William F. Wright, "The Association Between Unsystematic Security Returns and the Magnitude of Earnings Forecast Errors," *Journal of Accounting Research* (Autumn 1979), pp. 316–340.

7. William H. Beaver, Richard Lambert, and Dale Morse, "The Information Content of Security Prices," *Journal of Accounting and Economics* (March 1980), pp. 3–28.

8. Rappaport, *Creating Shareholder Value*, pp. 50–65.

9. Michael E. Porter, *Competitive Advantage* (New York: Free Press, 1985), pp. 11–16.

10. Ibid., pp. 36–52.

11. Sibson, *Management Compensation Survey.*

12. Ibid.

13. Sibson & Company, Inc., *Boards, Company Performance and Executive Pay* (Princeton, NJ, 1985).

BIBLIOGRAPHY

Avzac, Enrique. "Do Your Business Units Create Shareholder Value?" *Harvard Business Review* (January–February 1986), pp. 121–126.

Ball, Ben C. "The Mysterious Disappearance of Retained Earnings." *Harvard Business Review* (July–August 1987), pp. 56–63.

Beaver, William H., Clarke, Roger, and Wright, William F. "The Association Between Unsystematic Security Returns and the Magnitude of Earnings Forecast Errors." *Journal of Accounting Research* (Autumn 1979), pp. 316–340.

Beaver, William H., Lambert, Richard, and Morse, Dale. "The Information Content of Security Prices." *Journal of Accounting and Economics* (March 1980), pp. 3–28.

Brindisi, Louis J. "Creating Shareholder Value: A New Mission for Executive Compensation." *Midland Corporate Finance Journal* (Winter 1985), pp. 56–66.

Chakrauarthy, Balaji S. "Measuring Strategic Performance." *Strategic Management Journal* 7 (1986), pp. 437–458.

Drucker, Peter F. "If Earnings Aren't the Dial to Read." *The Wall Street Journal*, October 30, 1986.

Fruhan, William E. *Financial Strategy.* Homewood, IL: Richard D. Irwin, 1979.

Haegele, Monroe J. "A Framework for Top Management Performance Standards." *Topics in Total Compensation* 1 (Fall 1986), pp. 23–35.

Lambert, Richard A., and Larcker, David F. "Executive Compensation, Corporate Decision-Making and Shareholder Wealth: A Review of the Evidence." *Midland Corporate Finance Journal* (Winter 1985), pp. 6–21.

Larcker, David F. "Choosing a Performance Measure: An Analysis of Alternatives." *Topics in Total Compensation* 1 (Fall 1986), pp. 57–71.

Lupton, Daniel E., and Lorda, Robin. "Performance Management in Staff Units: Putting 'Bottom Line' Measures Back into the Picture." *Compensation and Benefits Management* 4 (Winter 1988), pp. 152–157.

Merchant, Kenneth A., and Bruns, William J. "Measurements to Cure Management Myopia." *Business Horizons* (May–June 1986), pp. 56–64.

Porter, Michael E. *Competitive Advantage.* New York: Free Press, 1985.

Rappaport, Alfred. *Creating Shareholder Value.* New York: Free Press, 1986.

Reimann, Bernard C. "Strategy Valuation in Portfolio Planning: Combining Q and VROI Ratios." *Planning Review* (January 1986), pp. 18–23.

———. "Implementing Value-Based Strategic Management." *Planning Review* (July 1986), pp. 6–9, 45–46.

———. "Does Your Business Create Real Shareholder Value?" *Business Horizons* (September–October 1986), pp. 44–51.

Rich, Jude, and Bergsma, Ennius. "Pay Executives to Create Wealth." *Chief Executive*, November 21, 1982, pp. 16–19.

Sethi, Prakash S., and Namiki, Nobuaki. "Factoring Innovation into Top Management's Compensation." *Directors & Boards* (Winter 1986), pp. 21–25.

Sibson & Company, Inc. *Boards, Company Performance and Executive Pay.* Princeton, NJ, 1985.

———. *Executive Long-Term Incentive Survey.* Princeton, NJ, 1987.

———. *Management Compensation Survey.* Princeton, NJ, 1987.

———. *Executive Compensation Annual Report.* Princeton, NJ, 1988.

Solomons, David. *Divisional Performance: Measurement and Control.* Homewood, IL: Richard D. Irwin, 1965.

Stewart, Bennett. "Performance Measurement and Management Incentive Compensation." *Midland Corporate Finance Journal* (Winter 1985), pp. 76–81.

Ubelhart, Mark C. "Business Strategy, Performance Measurement and Compensation." *Midland Corporate Finance Journal* (Winter 1985), pp. 67–75.

11

SELECTING AND VALUING SHORT- AND LONG-TERM COMPENSATION

Graef S. Crystal

A PRINCIPAL OBJECTIVE in executive pay design is to ensure a proper balance between short- and long-term motivation. Place too much emphasis on the short term, and you breed executives who cut R&D, shave product quality, use obsolete equipment, and employ strategies that maximize short-term earnings and set the stage for the company's long-term demise. Place too much emphasis on the long term, and you get huge R&D budgets, gold-plated product quality, and the shiniest new equipment. But before nirvana arrives, the company may well go bankrupt.

In years past, the task of balancing short- and long-term compensation was relatively simple. Since most companies used an annual bonus plan as a short-term incentive and stock options as a long-term incentive, all you had to do to be competitive was find out what various companies paid in annual bonuses and how many option shares they granted their executives.

Today the task is much more difficult for three reasons:

First, companies now do not employ a single form of long-term incentive compensation, but a wide variety of forms. In addition to stock options, they use restricted stock, performance shares, performance units, and divisional long-term incentives, to name just the more frequently employed plans.

Second, finding out what someone received as an annual bonus or a long-term incentive payout, while useful, does not tell the whole story, especially given the proliferation of long-term incentive devices. Although you may know what an executive received for a given performance, you do not know what that person might have received had the performance been materially different.

Third, executive compensation planners are realizing that there is no God-given law that requires every company to achieve a median blending of short- and long-term incentives. It is entirely possible—and, indeed, there may be a good business reason—to place less emphasis on short-term incentives and more emphasis on long-term incentives. At another stage of the company's business cycle, it may make good sense to do exactly the opposite.

With the above as background, I will review some of the problems in valuing both short- and long-term incentives. Then I will discuss the principal long-term incentive devices, citing the advantages and disadvantages of each.

PROBLEMS IN VALUING SHORT-TERM INCENTIVES

Compensation surveys typically reveal what a person received as an annual bonus for performance during a particular fiscal year. They do not reveal what the bonus might have been had company performance, divisional performance, or the individual executive's performance been different.

To gain insight into how a company's short-term incentive plan works, a useful place to start is with the company's so-called funding formula, if it has one. A funding formula represents a compact between management and the shareholders concerning the portion of the spoils that will go to management and the portion that will go to shareholders. It typically contains two elements: a threshold and a multiplier.

The threshold represents the point in the performance spectrum below which bonuses will not be paid. Typically, bonus thresholds are measured in return-on-investment terms. The company may have to earn, for example, a 6 percent after-tax return on its shareholders' equity before any bonus payments are generated. Another company may have to earn a 10 percent pre-tax return on its total capital, where total capital means the sum of shareholders' equity and long-term debt.

The multiplier represents the portion of above-threshold profits that will be diverted to the management group. For example, a company may employ a multiplier of 10 percent of the profits over a threshold of a 6 percent after-tax return on equity (ROE). In this case, no executive will receive a bonus if the ROE is less than 6 percent; if it is more than 6 percent, then ten cents out of each incremental dollar of profit will be reserved for executive bonuses. To put it another way, shareholders will receive all the first dollars of profits, until the ROE level reaches 6 percent. After that, shareholders will receive 90 percent of all further profits.

Working with a personal computer spreadsheet program, one can analyze quickly a funding formula in terms of its sensitivities to various levels of corporate performance. Indeed, if companies paid bonuses solely in line with their funding formulas, the task of valuing short-term incentive plans would be relatively simple.

But a company's funding formula is only a starting point. It is a reasonably good bet that if the company's performance is below-threshold, there will not be any bonuses. But if the size of the bonus fund doubles, it is *not* necessarily a good bet that the size of executive bonuses will also double. The fact is that most companies do not follow their own funding formulas.

The reason is that funding formulas become outdated. The typical formula was introduced around 1950, using a multiplier and threshold that made sense in relation to the corporate bond rate and median after-tax ROE level at that time. However, inflation (as well as real growth in earnings) has caused bonus formulas to generate excess amounts of money and rewards to accrue that are out of proportion to real improvements in performance. (For a full discussion of outmoded funding formulas, see "Common Mistakes in Current Practice," Chapter 9 of this volume.)

Moreover, if the company permits unused incentive funds to be added to the granary in order to cover an incentive famine in a future year, the formula is very likely to become a joke. It may actually allow the payment of bonuses in years when the company is losing huge amounts of money.

There are two more ways to gain some insight into how a company's bonus plan operates. The first is to talk to the company itself. Short-term incentive plans typically operate with considerable management discretion. An excellent method for understanding how a plan works is to ask knowledgeable people at the company what would happen with various levels of future performance. For example, you may say: "I see that your CEO received a bonus equal to 65 percent of salary last year. Suppose your profits had been only 80 percent as high as they were. In that case, what do you think the CEO might have received as a bonus?"

The only problem with this approach is that the person you are talking to may not know what would happen under alternative performance scenarios. After all, the plan is largely discretionary, and it is the CEO who exercises the discretion. You may have to talk to the CEO to get a valid answer. But even if you do that, you still may not be getting at the truth. Some CEOs talk a better game than they play: They may tell you how macho they are going to be in cutting bonuses if profits drop, but let the profits drop, and the lion becomes a pussycat.

You can also look for past patterns. If you have information on a company's bonus payouts for several years, you can apply statistical techniques to measure the association between various types of performance and bonuses. A careful analysis of the way in which most companies' short-term incentive plans actually operate would reveal that there is very little relationship between financial performance and bonus payouts. For example, one study I conducted of thirty companies and five years of bonus history showed that it took a 20 percent change in profits to move the typical company's bonus levels a scant 4 percent. Funding formulas have lost their discipline, and CEOs have not stepped up to their obligation to relate bonuses to performance. The result is that the largest portion of what is called a bonus is in reality an additional base-salary payment in disguise.

Suppose that an analysis of bonuses paid out by a group of companies comparable to your company reveals a lack of relationship between pay and performance. Should you structure your bonus plan the way the comparators do? Or should you opt for a different, and more gutsy, approach? From a competitive standpoint, you would not be wrong to do the former. From a shareholder's standpoint, you would be right to do the latter. But whatever you decide, you need to work through the problems I have just discussed.

PROBLEMS IN VALUING LONG-TERM INCENTIVES

When we turn to long-term incentives, the task becomes at once easier and more difficult. Long-term incentives are easier to put a value on because, unlike short-term plans, they generally operate in a formularized fashion. But long-term incentives are more difficult to value because there are so many different types in use.

Stripped to its essence, a long-term incentive is nothing more than a promise to pay an executive a sum of money (or to confer property rights) provided a certain future event comes to pass. The future event, in turn, can be one as simple as the executive still being on the payroll in five years or as complicated as the company achieving a 10 percent annual growth in net income coupled with a 16.5 percent after-tax return on equity.

There are two basic techniques that can be employed to value long-term incentives:

- Constructing scenarios of future performance, and
- Placing a value on the incentive at the time of the grant.

Under the first approach, the plan designer chooses a realistic level of future performance. For example, the designer might assume that every company in a comparator group will increase its earnings per share (EPS) and its stock price at the rate of 10 percent per year. He then determines what each company in the comparator group would pay various executives in long-term incentive compensation.

The future scenario approach involves two special assumptions. The first has to do with determining an exercise date for stock options. Most long-term incentive plans specify when a person earns a payout. A performance unit plan, for example, may call for compensation to be delivered at the end of a five-year period (assuming, of course, that long-term performance warrants a payout at all). But there is one form of long-term incentive compensation—the one most frequently used—where the timing of receipt of income is left up to the executive: the stock option.

A typical stock option, for example, may become fully exercisable at the end of the fourth year after its grant, and it may continue to be exercisable for an additional six years. The question, then, is when in that six-year period is the executive likely to exercise the options? If we posit a 10-percent annual increase in the stock price, an assumption that exercise of the option will occur on the tenth anniversary of the grant will produce a much higher option value than an assumption that exercise will occur on the fourth anniversary of the grant. Valuations performed under the future scenario approach require designers to make a reasonable guess about when the executive will exercise the option grant.

The future scenario approach also requires that long-term incentives be discounted before they can be compared to base salary and short-term incentives. That is, for the year 1988, base salary is paid in 1988. The short-term incentive award for 1988 performance also is paid within a few months of the year's end. But long-term incentive grants made in 1988 may not pay out for years and years. Thus, a $100,000 long-term incentive to be paid in 1998 cannot be as valuable as a $100,000 short-term incentive to be paid in March 1989. Because of this, it becomes necessary to introduce the concept of present value. The plan designer must assume a discount factor (e.g., 10 percent per year) and use it to discount the long-term incentive payouts that are scheduled to occur at various future times. The resulting present values can then be compared properly to base salary and short-term payouts.

The scenario approach can be quite useful, *but only if the results of multiple scenarios are examined.* Accordingly, the designer will want to see not only what happens when both EPS and stock price growth are 10 percent per year, but also what happens when both are 5 percent per year, when both are 15 percent per year, when EPS growth is 15 percent per year but stock price growth is 5 percent per year, when EPS growth is 5 percent per year but stock price growth is 15 percent per year, and so forth.

Analyzing multiple future scenarios permits the designer to understand how sensitive to performance various long-term incentive vehicles are and to decide which are the most appropriate for the company.

But even the use of multiple scenarios does not help the designer to shift the emphasis of executive compensation. For example, suppose a survey reveals that, on average, a CEO earns a base salary of $500,000, receives a short-term incentive bonus of $300,000, and also receives an annual option grant on $750,000 of stock. Suppose further that the designer wishes to introduce a higher-risk, higher-reward package for this CEO, one consisting of a salary of only $400,000, the same $300,000 short-term incentive opportunity, and a greater number of option shares. How many more option shares should be offered in lieu of $100,000 of base salary? In other words, how much is an option share worth?

The value of an option share, assuming 10 percent annual growth in stock price, may be, say, $25 per share. On that basis, the CEO ought to be given 4,000 more option shares as a replacement for $100,000 less base salary. But the value of an option share, assuming only 5 percent annual growth in stock price, may be only $10 per share. In that case, the trade-off for $100,000 in base salary is not 4,000 option shares, but 10,000 option shares. Indeed, if the stock price does not rise at all, or if it falls, an option share is worthless. You would have to grant the CEO an infinite number of option shares to offset the $100,000 reduction in base salary.

So what is the true value of an option share? Multiple future performance scenarios, unfortunately, give multiple answers.

Enter the second method of long-term incentive valuation. Rather than trying to predict what a long-term incentive will be worth at various levels of future performance, this method attempts to determine what the incentive might be sold for today, if in fact the executive could sell it. To illustrate, assume that an executive has been granted the following stock option:

- 10,000 shares;
- Strike price of $50 per share;
- Term of ten years; and
- Exercisable, cumulatively, at the rate of 25 percent per year, commencing with the first anniversary of the grant.

Normally, of course, an executive stock option is not transferable. But let us pretend for a moment that it is. If our hypothetical executive could sell the options, what might an investor, operating at arm's-length, pay for them?

We know two things:

1. The investor will pay more than $0 per share. An option, after all, is a valuable right, conferring on the investor the privilege of receiving all appreciation on the stock over $50 per share during a long period of time (i.e., ten years).
2. The investor will pay less than $50 per share. For $50 per share, he can buy the stock outright and receive dividends on it (a privilege not granted to the usual option holder). The investor would receive future appreciation forever, not merely for ten years, and would lose less money should the stock decline below $50 per share. (A decline to $40 per share wipes out the entire value of the option, assuming that it has expired. But the outright shareholder has lost only $10 and still has the chance to recoup the loss at some future time.)

We know, therefore, that the option will be worth between $0 and $50 per share.

At this point, more sophisticated reasoning can be applied. Various elaborate methods can be introduced, such as the Black-Scholes option pricing model.[1] It is beyond the scope of this chapter to dwell at length on the arcana of option valuation, but the reader should be aware that it is possible to obtain a rational answer to the question of how much an option is worth.

Or, at least a preliminarily rational answer, for an executive stock option is not quite the same as an ordinary option on the Chicago Board Options Exchange (CBOE). If the CBOE were offering a ten-year stock option, an investor would have a full ten years in which to exercise the option. Yet an executive who is granted a ten-year option may find that the term is shortened due to premature termination of employment (retirement, disability, or discharge). Moreover, an investor in the CBOE would be able to exercise his option on any day during its term, but an executive who is offered a stock option generally finds that the option is not exercisable at all during the early years of the term. A huge run-up in the stock price (such as what happened between January and October 1987) may be lost if the option is not exercisable then. At another time, the stock price may demonstrate the aerodynamic characteristics of an anvil, as happened on October 19, 1987, just when the executive's option becomes exercisable.

Because of these differences, the compensation designer will have to modify some of the values obtaining from the traditional option pricing models. But at the end of the process, he or she will have a reasonably accurate idea of what an option is worth and can then offer an intelligent opinion about how many additional option shares it will take at different performance levels to offset the loss of $100,000 in base salary.

Valuing other forms of long-term incentive compensation under this second method may involve exercises in probabilistic reasoning. If an executive has been promised $100,000 four years from now provided after-tax ROE for the four years averages 14 percent or more, the designer will have to gauge the probability that the executive will still be on the payroll in four years and that the company can achieve an average ROE of 14 percent or more. Once those probabilities are applied, the designer will have to use some sort of discount rate to determine the present value of the estimated future long-term incentive payout.

Placing a price tag on long-term incentives (or short-term incentives, for that matter) is not an easy job, but it is a crucial one. Without doing so, a company will never know whether it is overpaying or underpaying because it will be unable to total all forms of compensation. And it will not be able to turn down the volume control knob on one form of compensation and turn it up on another in a rational fashion.

LONG-TERM INCENTIVE DEVICES

Let us now turn to a discussion of the major types of long-term incentive devices currently in use.

Tax-Favored Stock Options

Congress has been ambivalent over the years about conferring tax-favored status on stock option grants:

- In 1950, Congress introduced the restricted stock option, the earliest form of tax-favored option and the most beautiful of all.
- In 1964, Congress had second thoughts. It killed the restricted stock option and introduced the qualified stock option. The son was not as handsome as the father.
- In 1976, Congress terminated the qualified stock option. For the next five years, no new tax-favored option grants could be made (except from plans that had been adopted before 1976).
- In 1981, Congress introduced the incentive stock option (ISO). ISOs are still with us.

In addition to playing around with various types of tax-favored stock options, Congress has also altered the underlying tax laws that cause an option to become tax-favored in the first place.

The advantage of a tax-favored option lies in the difference between the tax rate on ordinary income and that on long-term capital gains income. The wider the gap, the more lustrous a tax-favored option appears. The gap, which was as high as 66 percentage points before 1964 (the difference between the maximum marginal ordinary tax rate of 91 percent and the long-term capital gains tax rate of 25 percent), fell to almost zero by 1970, then rose to 30 percentage points in the early 1980s and, as of this writing, has again fallen to zero. Although a tax-favored option is still on the books (the ISO), there is hardly any reason to consider using it; the maximum tax rate on ordinary income and the tax rate on long-term capital gains income is the same 28 percent.

Nonqualified Stock Options

A nonqualified stock option (NQSO) is simply an option that by its terms cannot be considered a tax-favored grant. NQSOs offer a designer more flexibility than ISOs because there is no law mandating the terms the option must have. Moreover, NQSOs are more cost-effective than ISOs. The proof underlying this last statement is as follows:

- Given a certain gain in stock price, the pre-tax spread an executive yields from an NQSO of X shares will be the same as the pre-tax spread from an ISO of the same X shares. (The term *spread* refers to the product of the number of shares exercised plus the amount by which the market value per share on the date of exercise exceeds the option's strike price per share.)
- The after-tax spread, given that the maximum tax rate is 28 percent with either option, will also be the same.
- In the case of an ISO, the company is not permitted to deduct the option spread. Hence, a dollar of spread costs the company $1.00 in after-tax terms.
- In the case of an NQSO, however, the company is permitted to deduct the option spread. Hence, if the corporate marginal tax rate is 34 percent, then a dollar of spread costs the company only $1.00 \times (1 - .34)$, or $0.66.

NQSOs come in different flavors. Though it is possible to vary the length of the option term, most companies do not, with the result that the ten-year term has become a de facto standard. But some companies do vary the ratio of the strike price to the market value per share on the grant date. Although the majority maintain the ratio at 1.00, a few companies employ lower ratios (e.g., 0.50). Once in a great while, a company employs a ratio greater than 1.00.

The popularity of stock options has, in the past, rested on three pillars: taxation, accounting, and simplicity. As already noted, the taxation pillar has been dynamited by Congress. But, for the moment, the remaining two pillars are intact.

In the case of accounting, the Financial Accounting Standards Board (FASB) and its predecessor, the Accounting Principles Board (APB), have been holding a sale on stock options since just about the time they were first introduced as an executive compensation device. The costs of all other forms of compensation are charged to earnings, thereby reducing pre-tax profits by the amount of the charge and after-tax profits by the amount of the charge times the complement of the company's marginal tax rate. With stock options, however, no charge to earnings is required, provided the ratio of the strike price to the fair market value at grant is equal to or greater than 1.00. To be sure, options do carry a cost to the extent they are exercised, because the company is required to issue more shares and has not, obviously, received full value from the executive. But dilution, like dental plaque, takes quite a while to build up. (Also, like dental plaque it is hard to remove!) If you are going to be the CEO for only another five years, the problem will be someone else's. (A careful longitudinal study of option-granting practices since options came into vogue in 1950 would doubtless show that 20 percent or more of the currently outstanding shares of quite a few companies derive from stock option grants.) In the meantime, EPS are higher than they would have been had the economic benefits conferred on the executive (i.e., the aggregate spread) been charged directly to earnings.

There is even an accounting advantage involved with options carrying strike price ratios of less than 1.00. The dollar amount by which the strike price is less than 1.00 must be charged to earnings. Thus, if an executive is granted a 10,000-share stock option with a strike price of $25 at a time when the fair market value per share is $50, the company will have to charge its pre-tax earnings with the $25 strike price discount, or $250,000 in all. But it will not have to charge its earnings with an aggregate spread that might materialize later (i.e., appreciation above $50 per share).

In recent years, the FASB has come under criticism for permitting options to enjoy a more favorable accounting treatment than other forms of compensation. A few years ago, it finally responded to this criticism by beginning a serious study of option accounting issues. It concluded that there ought to be some charge to earnings required in connection with option grants and that the charge ought to be measured by the true value of the option, either at the time it is first granted to the executive or, alternatively, at the time the option first becomes exercisable. (At this writing, the latter approach seems to be favored by the FASB.) As its study continued, the FASB came to understand that there are many problems in trying to decide what an option is worth. Executive stock options, although similar to publicly traded options, do contain some significant differences (restrictions on exercisability in the early years after the grant is made, as well as the possibility that the executive, because of resignation, discharge, retirement, death, or disability, may not enjoy the ten-year option term nominally promised). But despite these problems, the agency seems to be persisting in its objective of imposing a charge to earnings.

I think the FASB's objective is clearly laudable, provided the ultimate charge to earnings is reasonable. The accounting for stock options has created a nonlevel playing field in the area of long-term incentives for years. The result has been that some companies have stuck with stock options, not because they motivate executives more effectively than other forms of long-term incentive, but because the company sees them as the cheapest form of long-term incentive compensation.

The third advantage of stock options lies in their simplicity. An executive has no trouble remembering how many shares he or she has been granted and that an economic benefit is tied to an increase in the stock price. There are no arcane formulas to remember and no intimate knowledge of accounting or finance is required. Finally, over the years, the stock option has become an executive status symbol.

The advantage of simplicity also accrues to shareholder relations. Companies routinely market new stock option plans to shareholders on the grounds that executive interest is being tied to shareholder interest. That argument is obviously appealing to shareholders, but there is a deception here. Note that executive interest is tied to shareholder interest when the share price is rising. But the linkage ends when the share price is dropping. A shareholder who buys at $50 and sees the stock drop to $25 has sustained, at least on paper, a loss of $25 per share. But an executive whose option strike price is $50 has lost nothing.

Moreover, the loss of linkage between performance and reward in down markets has become exacerbated by the practice adopted by many companies of "swapping options." If the market price drops from $50 to $25, the company simply calls in all the old option shares and issues new ones carrying a lower strike price of $25. Without an option swap, the executive is in the position of making no money when the shareholder is losing money. With an option swap, the executive can make good money when the shareholder is losing money. For example, consider what happens if the market price drops from $50 to $25 and then rises to $35. An option whose strike price was originally $50 is swapped for an option whose strike price is $25. When the price rises, the executive makes $10 per share (the gain from $25 per share to $35 per share), while the shareholder loses $15 per share (the drop in value from $50 per share to $35 per share).

As if this were not bad enough, companies making swaps usually offer the same number of new shares as original shares. If an executive was originally granted 10,000 shares with a strike price of $50, he or she now receives 10,000 swapped shares with a strike price of $25. Suppose that there were a public market for executive stock option shares; which of the following options is more valuable: a 10,000-share option carrying a strike price of $50 per share at a time when the market price is $25 per share, or a 10,000-share option carrying a strike price of $25 per share at a time when the market price is $25 per share?

If your answer is the first option, perhaps you should consider an alternative career—something in the art world, perhaps!

The second option is clearly much more valuable than the first. The company that swaps with the executive on a share-for-share basis has, wittingly or unwittingly, *increased* the executive's total compensation as a direct function of a market price decrease. How that is supposed to tie together the interests of executives and shareholders is baffling.

There is one final item concerning stock options that should be mentioned: restrictions on exercise.

Remember that there are really two objectives underlying any long-term incentive plan: to motivate the executive for long-term performance and to keep the executive with the company. To achieve the second objective, companies almost always attach some strings to their long-term incentive grants. In the case of stock options, the grant may not be exercisable for a specified period. A common practice is to prohibit the executive from exercising any of the shares in the grant during the first year following the award, and then to allow only partial exercisability until, say, the end of the fourth year following the grant. With such restrictions in place, the executive forfeits unexercisable option shares should he or she quit the company or be discharged for cause during the restriction period.

Whether such "golden handcuffs" really work has been the subject of considerable debate. Clearly, if a company really wants someone, it can offer the person an extra payment on hire to compensate for the loss of stock option profits from the previous employer. In such a case, therefore, the exercise restrictions will fail in their objective. But just as clearly, no company can afford to offer such extra payments to every person it wants to hire; therefore, exercise restrictions actually do work in the labor market as a whole.

Stock Appreciation Rights

Officers (and outside directors) of a company with a publicly traded stock are subject to the so-called insider trading rules (the provisions of Section 16(b) of the Securities Exchange Act of 1934). These rules prevent the officer from profiting through the purchase of company shares at one price and their subsequent sale at a higher price within six months of their purchase (or, conversely, the sale of shares at one price and their subsequent repurchase at a lower price within six months of their sale). Nonofficers, on the other hand, are free to buy and sell at will, provided the shares are registered with the SEC.

To remedy this imbalance between the rights of officers and nonofficers, many companies grant officers so-called stock appreciation rights (SARs). In its most common form, an SAR permits an officer to receive in cash the aggregate option spread without having to exercise the option. An officer with a 10,000-share option and a gain per share of $25 can avoid actually exercising the option and then having to hold the shares for six months. Instead, the company gives the officer a check for $250,000 in return for cancellation of the 10,000 underlying option shares.

SARs, then, permit the officer to legally sidestep the insider trading provisions. But because cash is involved, SARs are charges to earnings, charges which are potentially quite volatile. Because of this, most companies granting SARs restrict them to officers. As for nonofficers, they look the other way when option shares are exercised on one day and then sold on the open market before the close of the very same day. (In a sense, the nonofficer is working with a do-it-yourself SAR, but his or her cash proceeds, unlike the officer's, are not charged to earnings.)

Restricted Stock Grants

Earlier, I talked about a discounted stock option, where the ratio of the strike price to the fair market value per share on the date of grant was, for example, 0.50. A restricted stock grant is the ultimate in discounted stock options, for the strike price ratio is 0.00!

An executive who receives a restricted stock grant typically pays nothing for the shares. But he or she is prohibited from selling them for a specified period. If the executive should quit the company or be discharged during this period, the shares are forfeited. Once the restriction period is over, the executive is free to do with the shares what he or she wants. During the restriction period, the executive receives the same dividend and voting rights as an ordinary shareholder.

To summarize, a restricted stock grant is, for all practical purposes, a stock option with a strike price ratio of 0.00 that yields dividends. It is, on a share-for-share basis, much more valuable than an ordinary, nondiscounted (strike price ratio of 1.00) stock option share. And it is also more costly to the company, since the entire value of the shares at the time they are granted as well as the subsequent dividends paid during the restriction period must be charged to earnings.

Executives like restricted stock grants, because they promise a payout under all circumstances except the bankruptcy of the company. Companies like them because they believe they offer more executive holding power than other forms of long-term incentive compensation. (Because there is a higher probability that the executive will actually earn something if he remains with the company, restricted stock grants probably do offer more holding power.)

Shareholders, if they took the time to think about the matter, would probably not want to sit with companies and executives in the same rooting section. The reason, of course, is that an executive can profit from a restricted stock grant at the same time other shareholders are losing their shirts.

Deferred Stock Grants

A deferred stock grant is, in many ways, the mirror image of a restricted stock grant. In the case of restricted stocks, an executive is given some free shares and is required to turn them over to the company if he or she quits or is discharged during the restriction period. In the case of deferred stocks, the executive is promised some free shares at the end of a period of time, provided he or she is still around. Because deferred stock grants are simply restricted stock grants under a different name, they carry the same advantages and disadvantages.

Performance Share Grants

A performance share grant is a deferred stock grant with teeth. To earn the free shares, it is not sufficient for the executive merely to breathe in and out on the company's payroll for, say, five years. He has to breathe in and out productively.

One company, for example, gives executives at one level 1,000-share performance share grants at a time when the market price is $50 per share and tells them:

- No matter what happens, you must remain with the company for the next five years, or else you lose all your performance shares;
- If our EPS growth over the five-year period is at least 12 percent per year, you will receive the 1,000 performance shares;
- If our EPS growth over the five-year period is 10 percent per year, you will receive 750 performance shares;
- If our EPS growth over the five-year period is 8 percent per year, you will receive 500 performance shares;
- If our EPS growth over the five-year period is 6 percent per year, you will receive 250 performance shares;
- If our EPS growth over the five-year period is less than 6 percent per year, you will receive no performance shares, even if you remain on the payroll for the entire five-year period.

Thus, performance shares offer the executive a dual incentive. The number of shares that can be earned becomes a function of company financial performance (in our example, EPS growth). The value of each share becomes a function of whatever the New York Stock Exchange assigns it.

From a shareholder perspective, performance shares are clearly preferable to deferred grants or restricted stock grants. The executive has to do something to earn them. But performance shares are obviously not as appealing to an executive as an identically sized deferred or restricted stock grant that carries no strings except that the executive remain with the company.

Moreover, performance shares carry a nastier accounting sting than deferred or restricted shares. In the case of the two latter devices, the value of the shares *at the time of original grant* must be charged to earnings. But in the case of performance shares, the value of the shares *at the time they are earned* must be charged to earnings. This change introduces accounting volatility; moreover, if the stock price rises between the date of grant and the end of the performance period, charges to earnings will be higher than those that would have occurred had a grant of deferred or restricted stock been made.

Performance shares enjoyed considerable popularity until the Accounting Principles Board introduced the special accounting treatment mentioned earlier (before that, they were treated the same as deferred or restricted stock grants). After the change, many companies abandoned them in favor of a combination of stock options and performance units.

Performance Units

A performance unit is simply an offer to pay an executive a sum of cash at the end of a long-term performance period, the amount depending on achievement of certain pre-established financial objectives. Earlier, I illustrated a performance share grant based on achieving EPS growth. To convert that grant to a performance unit grant, only one thing is necessary: assign an arbitrary value to each performance unit (e.g., $50).

With a performance unit, the executive is insulated entirely from the vagaries of the stock market. If long-term performance is excellent, the unit grant disgorges a sum of cash. The sum of cash is the same whether the stock price has gone up, down, or sideways in the intervening period.

Since cash is involved, a payment made as a performance unit grant is charged to earnings. But at least the maximum potential cost is known at the time of original grant (in contrast to a performance share grant, where the cost is not known until the end of the performance period).

Few companies grant performance units as their sole form of long-term incentive compensation. Indeed, most companies employing performance unit plans also make stock option grants. The combination of a performance unit grant with a stock option grant offers the executive, when the stock price is rising, the same payout he or she would have received from a performance share grant, but without the higher charges to earnings that would have resulted from the latter. When the stock price is falling, this combination pays out more than the executive would have received from a performance unit grant, although at a somewhat higher charge to earnings.

Performance unit payouts, like performance share payouts, can be predicated on whatever measures of long-term performance the company wishes to use. A popular measure is EPS growth, as illustrated in the discussion of performance share grants. Other measures include return on equity, return on assets, or performance vis-à-vis preselected comparator groups. It is also possible to predicate performance share or performance unit payouts on nonfinancial goals such as achieving a 10 percent increase in market share over a four-year performance period.

Ideally, a company ought to choose a performance period that reflects the typical time span between the date major long-term decisions are made and the date when those decisions come to fruition. Accordingly, a retailer engaged in a short-term business would adopt a performance period that was shorter than that of, say, a pharmaceutical manufacturer engaged in a much longer-term business.

In practice, however, there is little correlation between the type of business in which a company is involved and the length of its long-term incentive performance period. Most companies seem to have adopted a performance period of four years, with a scattering of companies employing three- and five-year performance periods.

Divisional Long-Term Incentives

There is no legal requirement that a performance share grant or a performance unit grant be linked to the achievement of *corporate* performance goals. A company could, if it wished, offer an executive working in a division or subsidiary a long-term incentive grant whose payouts would be partially or even wholly dependent on division or subsidiary performance. (Incentives of this type will be discussed at length in Chapter 12, "Recognizing Divisional Differences.")

SUMMARY

Valuing short- and long-term incentives is a dirty job, but a vital one. Determining what various types of incentives are worth may involve myriad assumptions and a lot of math, but the task cannot be sidestepped easily. The only alternative a company has is to pick the peer it most admires and ape whatever that firm does.

If a company takes the time to do its homework, however, it can design a combination of short- and long-term incentive plans that optimally balances short-term motivation with long-term motivation, helps to hold key executives, and serves vital shareholder interests.

NOTE

1. Fischer Black and Myron Scholes, "The Pricing of Options and Corporate Liabilities," *Journal of Political Economy*, vol. 81 (1973), pp. 637–659.

12

RECOGNIZING DIVISIONAL
DIFFERENCES

Graef S. Crystal

CONSIDER THIS CASE: A giant company in the telecommunications business owned 60 percent of a small computer software firm. The five principals who founded the software company owned 20 percent of its stock; the remaining 20 percent was traded publicly in the over-the-counter market. The software company was very successful. Indeed, it was so successful that the telecommunications company decided to buy the 40 percent of shares it did not already possess, on the assumption that owning 100 percent of a gold mine is better than owning 60 percent. Realizing that the senior executives of its new subsidiary no longer had a stock incentive, the parent company granted them options in its own stock. During the first year, all the senior executives quit and formed a new software firm. Within two years, the parent company had to write off its entire investment in the subsidiary.

Why was this outcome foreordained? For one thing, the senior executives of the subsidiary were well on the way to becoming millionaires in their own stock when they were bought out. For another thing, the appreciation prospects of the telecommunications company's stock were not nearly as bright as those of the software company. But perhaps most important of all, there was no relationship whatever between the performance of the software subsidiary and that of the parent company. The subsidiary commanded less than 1 percent of the revenues of the parent firm. To make matters worse, it was in an entirely different business.

Maybe owning 100 percent of a gold mine is not necessarily a better idea than owning 60 percent!

THE EVOLUTION OF EXECUTIVE
INCENTIVE COMPENSATION

Short-term incentives first came into vogue in the 1920s, before long-term incentives were used. At that time, payouts were predicated essentially on overall corporate performance, with little or no regard for divisional differences. (Here the terms "division" and "divisional" are equivalent to "group" or "subsidiary.")

One of the consequences of employing only short-term incentives was the encouragement of behavior that sought immediate results. Some management theorists trace the near-demise of the American automobile industry to the extensive use of short-term incentives in the 1950s. At General Motors, for example, the largest portion of the CEO's pay consisted of his bonus award, which reached 300 percent of salary in a decent year. During those years, GM, Ford, and Chrysler lost their footing, thereby setting the stage for the Japanese car invasion. Perhaps the imbalance between short- and long-term incentives in the car industry stimulated senior executives to pay less attention than they should have to such important matters as innovative design, product quality, and market share.

Because of the corrosive effects of employing only short-term incentives, most companies decided to introduce a second, long-term incentive. At first, this form of compensation consisted solely of stock options. Now if a manager "short-termed" it by cutting back on R&D and product quality, for example, he or she would, at least in theory, pay a price in the form of low, or no, stock option profits.

At this point—the early to mid-1950s—companies had both short- and long-term incentive devices in place. But both types of incentive rewarded only overall corporate performance.

By the early 1960s, however, American industry had begun to undergo some significant organizational transformations centered around the phenomenon of "divisionalization," in which profit centers were created. (Before this time, it was common for all production workers in a company to report through a corporate head of production and for all sales and marketing workers to report through a corporate head of sales and marketing. There was only one profit center in the company.) With multiple profit centers, it became possible to measure the performance of subunits of a company as well as the performance of the company as a whole.

Not much time passed before some insightful people noted a disparity between the way companies were reorganizing and the way they were rewarding their managers. Did it make sense, they asked, to establish a divisional organizational structure and to set performance goals in terms of divisional profits and then pay divisional managers not on the basis of their own performance but on the basis of overall corporate performance? The contradiction became more acute as the conglomerate movement got under way. The absurdity of rewarding divisional managers on the basis of overall corporate performance became more apparent when one manager headed a unit that made mattresses and another a unit that made jet engines.

Because of the disparity between organizational and reward structures, some companies divisionalized their short-term incentive plans. At first, they accomplished this feat not by redesigning the basic plan itself but by introducing divisional performance as a determinant of reward, so that the head of a division had, say, half of his or her incentive opportunity determined by the division's accomplishments (at least in theory) and the remainder determined by overall corporate performance.

This approach worked until two problems cropped up. First, some companies began to lose their nerve. If Division A performed magnificently and Division B performed abysmally, the CEO gave the managers in Division A smaller bonuses and the managers in Division B larger bonuses than the plan said they ought to get. Although there were divisional differences in reward, they were much smaller than planned.

The second problem was that most incentive plans were governed by an overall funding formula that divided the profits between management and shareholders, a formula that, in most cases, had been approved by shareholders. Plan designers had forgotten that if the overall funding formula produced no funds, then the managers of even magnificently performing divisions would receive no bonuses, even though they had been promised bonuses based on divisional performance.

Ford Aerospace, a subsidiary of Ford Motor Company, is a case in point. Ford had been paying bonuses on a divisional basis under the authority of an overall, shareholder-approved funding formula. Everything went well until the entire American automobile industry began hemorrhaging red ink (at one point, Ford lost $1 billion in a single year).

Suddenly, the Ford bonus plan ran dry. There were no funds with which to reward *any* managers, not even the managers at Ford Aerospace, a unit that continued to perform well and that was not connected to the automobile industry except through Ford's ownership. Nevertheless, the managers of the Aerospace subsidiary shared the depression in the automotive industry and received no bonuses.

What some companies did at this point was to redesign their bonus plans to permit the payment of bonuses to high-performing divisional managers in years when overall corporate performance was terrible. Ford itself took this step by obtaining its shareholders' approval to establish a separately funded short-term incentive plan for Ford Aerospace.

Let us review for a moment. Short-term incentive plans were now based on divisional performance, but divisional managers were still being given long-term incentives based solely on corporate performance.

I am reminded of a time when I met with Donald Burnham, then CEO of Westinghouse and a highly regarded manager of his day. In lamenting the inconsistency between *divisional* short-term incentives and *corporate* long-term incentives, he said:

> At Westinghouse, we are organized into four super-groups, divided into nineteen subgroups, which in turn are made up of eighty-three different divisions. Now you take one of those divisional managers. He's milking his business by cutting back on R&D, shaving product quality, reducing the advertising budget, eliminating management development programs, and deferring plant maintenance and the purchase of new and more productive machinery. Obviously, the profits boom and he receives huge rewards under our short-term incentive plan. The profits boom so much that we promote him to head a group. If he has timed it right, his former division falls apart the very next year, enhancing his legend. For years after, you hear about how Joe was a miracleworker when he was running the XYZ division and how, when Joe left the division, it just fell apart. We now have Joe working his miracles at a higher level of management. And pretty soon, unless we're awfully careful, he may engineer yet another promotion for himself.

Good old Joe was only following the signals sent out by his company's incentive plans. One plan told him to maximize his division's short-term earnings. And he did! The second plan was the Westinghouse stock option plan. But did this long-term incentive plan really motivate Joe to improve his performance over the long term? It clearly did not, because, as the manager of one of eighty-three different divisions, Joe's influence over Westinghouse's stock price was negligible. So Joe did what many people do at church: he shifted his gaze when the collection plate went by, figuring that some other parishioner would take up the slack. To put it another way, Joe reasoned, "I can maximize my short-term earnings, but if the rest of my fellow division managers take a more prudent long-term view of the world, then I can get the best of both: super-large, short-term incentive awards, as well as decent stock option profits."

In the meantime, some far-reaching changes were occurring in American business. In 1967, John Kenneth Galbraith charged in *The New Industrial State* that American managers were obsessed with making their companies larger and larger. In those days, compensation surveys revealed a fairly close association between company size (as measured by sales volume, for example) and executive pay. Accordingly, if the CEO wanted to make more money, one prescription was to increase the size of the company.

At the same time, there was commensurately less emphasis on optimizing long-term profitability. If a division was a dog, the CEO did not move too quickly. After all, if the division had $1 billion in sales, that extra $1 billion was helping prop up the CEO's high salary and annual bonus. The doggy division might have a depressing effect on the company's stock price, but with so many other divisions involved and with the usual "noise" in the stock market, could anyone say for sure that holding on to the division was costing the company $3 per share? An individual executive's stock option shares did not amount to much anyway, at least in comparison to his lofty salary and bonus.

Those good times did not last very long. Enter the Japanese, followed by the raiders. They quickly reminded American managers that doing nothing about a poorly performing division was doing no one, especially the company's shareholders, any good.

People like Raymond Miles, the dean of the Berkeley Business School, began talking about the "disaggregation of American business." In the past, companies grew from within; if they did acquire new units, the marriage was for life. Divestiture was rare. In today's business world, however, marriage is not for life, and divorce is frequent. A sense of impermanence has taken hold as companies rapidly acquire and resell new units. The management theorist Robert Waterman observed recently that today's corporate staff acts as the cold-blooded manager of a portfolio of businesses, any of which are always for sale. Corporate staffs have shrunk dramatically in this new role.

At the same time, we began to hear about shareholder value. Managers were exhorted to forget about size and concentrate on maximizing shareholder value, i.e., to take actions that, over the long term, had the effect of offering shareholders maximum appreciation of their stock and maximum dividends.

By the mid-1980s, where were executive incentives? Short-term incentives in many companies had evolved from a 100 percent corporate performance orientation to one that was part corporate and part divisional. Long-term incentives were still predicated on corporate performance. Companies had established profit centers and had reduced the role of corporate overseers. In many respects, the profit centers were on their own. There continued to be a disparity between the new forms of organization and incentive plans: long-term incentives were still based on overall corporate results.

Enter (finally!) the divisional long-term incentive plan, a device that would reward the managers of a division for their long-term efforts to maximize shareholder value. For the first time, the disparity could be removed. The disaggregated divisions would be fueled with disaggregated incentive plans.

SOME CAVEATS ABOUT DIVISIONAL
LONG-TERM INCENTIVES

Before discussing the design of divisional long-term incentives, let me first mention some caveats concerning the introduction of such plans. Before a company takes the plunge, it ought to be able to answer all of the following questions in the affirmative.

Do you have true, stand-alone profit centers? There are CEOs who, like Dr. Frankenstein, enter their laboratories and spawn creatures that are not quite human. They devise profit centers that look and feel like profit centers but really are not. For example, such a center might sell virtually all its output to another profit center of the same company at a price that is dreamed up by someone at corporate headquarters who seems to be smoking a controlled substance. Or, it might buy virtually all its raw materials from another profit center of the same company, again at weird prices.

For a divisional long-term incentive plan to be successful, the division must be a viable economic enterprise. One test of whether this is so is to ask: Could the division, as it is, be spun off to the shareholders and survive? Does it, in effect, have a heart, kidneys, and brain? Or is it missing a vital organ?

Are you willing to destroy what you think of as your corporate culture? In the 1950s, IBMers used to greet the day by singing a rousing chorus or two of "Ever Onward IBM." If you go the divisional route, you had better hire a platoon of songwriters, because at the beginning of each day, you are going to hear such new ditties as "Ever Onward IBM Entry Systems" and "Ever Onward IBM Federal Systems." Not only will these new songs drown out the traditional hymn, they will not even be in the same key! Indeed, the introduction of divisional long-term incentives may cause divisional managers to forget that their parent company owns assets other than theirs.

Are you willing to restrict personnel mobility to single divisions? Companies such as IBM and General Electric often have operated like the U.S. Army: People are transferred every two years whether or not there is an apparent reason for the move. With divisional long-term incentives in place, you may have trouble convincing a manager to leave a highly profitable division to move to a marginal one. You can try to persuade the manager that experience in the poorly performing division will prepare him or her for even greater responsibilities in the future. But the manager is unlikely to move if he or she faces a substantial cut in pay as the price for precious experience. Some special deals can be cut, but they are by definition special and cannot be offered to all comers. The result: diminished personnel mobility.

Are you willing to tolerate complexity in plan design? If you are running an airline, you can train your pilots in one of two ways. You can develop a rudimentary flight simulator that contains only a stick, an altimeter, and a compass. Using this approach, you save money and your pilot-trainees need not be confronted with very complex challenges. In the long run, however, you have an awful lot of accidents. Or you can develop an elaborate flight simulator that replicates, to the maximum degree possible, the experience of piloting an aircraft. Using this approach, you have more up-front costs and your pilot-trainees are plunged into complex situations. Those complex situations represent the real world. Because they do, your accident rate is very low.

If they are going to do the job for which they are designed, divisional long-term incentive plans sometimes have to be fairly complex.

Are you willing to tolerate pay chaos? Corporate compensation directors are fond of carrying a little card in their wallets. On one side is printed the company's corporate salary structure. On the other is the company's short-term incentive formula and its option-granting guidelines. With divisional long-term incentives, the corporate compensation director may have to stuff fifty cards in his wallet in order to remember what every division does!

Are you willing to pay an employee more than his or her boss? Most CEOs are like the queen in *Snow White*. Before retiring to bed, they ask a mirror: "Mirror, mirror on the wall, who's the highest paid of all?" If the mirror replies that the higest paid of all is the person who runs a division the CEO has trouble remembering he owns, there is going to be real trouble at corporate headquarters the next day. That corporate compensation director with the fifty cards will be out the door sans the cards. And perhaps, too, will be that brilliant compensation consultant who helped the corporate compensation director design those wonderful divisional long-term incentive plans!

In 1930, Babe Ruth was asked by a reporter how he could justify being paid more than Herbert Hoover, the president of the United States. His reply: "I had a better year than he did." By the same token, the best performer in a company may not always be the CEO or the person at the top of the hierarchy.

Are you willing to spend the money and take the time to communicate the new plans in an adequate fashion? Executive compensation plans are often communicated in curious ways. Sometimes the executive is handed a forty-seven-page legal document. Since the odds are that he or she is not a lawyer, the document goes unread. Or it is read only until the executive falls asleep. In other cases, the employee is handed sheets of equations that prove that the divisional long-term incentive plan is really encouraging an increase in shareholder value. Since the odds are that the employee is not a finance expert or a mathematician, the result is the same as that for the forty-seven-page legal document.

It is sad, but true, that most compensation experts communicate poorly. What they try to do is to impress their audience with the elegance of their design, as well as their general level of erudition. The result is hardly good communication, if good communication means having the audience understand what the plan is all about and what they have to do to earn more money.

If you have answered all the above questions in the affirmative, you now can discuss some major divisional long-term incentive plan design issues. If not, you might want to reconsider the suitability of such a plan for your company.

DESIGN OF DIVISIONAL LONG-TERM INCENTIVES

If you want to maximize shareholder value, there are only two ways to design a divisional long-term incentive plan: use actual shares or use phantom shares.

How can you use actual shares in a divisional long-term incentive plan when the division has no shares? The answer is deceptively simple: transform the division into an independent corporation.

In the 1960s, James Ling, who put together LTV Corporation (the "L" stands for Ling), was first celebrated as a visionary manager and then excoriated as a failure. But Ling did come up with at least one useful idea: he said that a conglomerate ought to sell 20 percent of the equity in each of its divisions to a combination of public shareholders and the division's own managers. That way, the managers would have a piece of the action of their own enterprises, and the parent company could still consolidate the division's results for accounting purposes.

Ling's idea languished for many years but it was revived in the late 1980s. The Coca-Cola Company, for example, gathered together most of its U.S. soft-drink bottling activities and spun them off into a separate corporation called Coca-Cola Enterprises (CCE) in 1986. Coca-Cola continued to own 49 percent of the shares; the remaining 51 percent were owned by the public and CCE's managers, who received their own stock options and restricted shares. In 1987, Coke announced that it would do the same thing with its entertainment businesses. A second set of long-term incentives involving the issue of real stock accompanied the spinoff of these businesses.

Spinning off a company or selling a small portion of its equity to the public makes the design of long-term incentives relatively simple. There is no need to figure out what the business is worth, because the market figures it out for you every trading day.

What if your company does not want to go that far but still wants viable divisional long-term incentives? In that case, you should use phantom shares and establish your own, in-house mechanism for valuing the division at any point in time.

In the early days of divisional long-term incentive design, companies fell into one of two traps: they based rewards either on the division's long-term net income or on its book value. When net income was the measure, managers responded by maximizing their division's earnings over the long term, as they were supposed to do. They paid not one whit of attention to conserving capital. Indeed, they were lined up outside the chief financial officer's door like derelicts outside a soup kitchen. When phantom shares were set to equal the book value of the division, once again incentives for the rampant use of capital had unwittingly been emplaced.

Today a compensation planner seeking to put a value on a division in order to create phantom shares ought to ask first why the stocks of companies in a particular industry trade at different multiples of their book value. One company, whose book value is $25 per share (the reported shareholders' equity divided by the shares outstanding), has a stock price of $50 per share. Another company, whose book value is also $25 per share, has a stock price that is equal to its book price, $25 per share. And a third company, whose book value is again $25 per share, has a stock price of only $12.50 per share. Are these differences simply the effect of noise in the stock market? Or are they traceable to significant economic differences in company performance?

In 1964, the major tenets of the so-called capital asset pricing model (CAPM), which explains why stock prices vary among companies with equal book value, were first laid before an ignorant public.[1] Some knowledge of the CAPM is vital for any compensation planner, since all current approaches to divisional long-term incentives that are being hawked by various consultants and financial experts rest heavily on the CAPM.

The Capital Asset Pricing Model

An investor chooses among a number of alternatives. For want of a better investment, he can place funds in U.S. ninety-day Treasury bills (T-bills). The interest is guaranteed by the government, which is about as good a guarantee as an investor is likely to find. Moreover, the short maturity of the T-bill makes it highly unlikely that the principal sum will be ravaged by inflation. For the sake of discussion, let us assume that the current T-bill rate is 6.5 percent.

If an investor places his money in anything more risky than T-bills, he wants to earn a greater return to compensate for the greater risk involved. The returns over sixty years from the S&P 500 are about six percentage points higher, on average, than the returns over the same period from T-bills. (I stress "on average" because returns on the S&P 500 relative to T-bills have actually varied widely over the years.) This 6 percent advantage represents the premium for the relative riskiness of equities. Indeed, a working definition of the term "risk" involves the probability of volatility. If the probability of always getting a 6.5 percent return is 100 percent, then we can think of that investment as carrying no risk. However, if the return is going to vary all over the map (including being negative at some points), but still average 6.5 percent, we have a different, more risky, ball game.

If the T-bill rate is 6.5 percent and the normal percentage premium for investing in equities is six percentage points, the typical investor is going to demand a 12.5 percent return for investing in equities.

But there are equities and there are equities. Investors want a 14.5 percent return on average, but are they going to settle for a 14.5 percent return for investing in Lodestar Uranium? Or, are they going to demand a return higher than 14.5 percent to compensate for the greater risk involved? Similarly, are investors going to demand a 14.5 percent return for investing in Consolidated Edison, a regulated utility that is not permitted to go bankrupt? Or are they going to settle for a return lower than 14.5 percent to reflect the lower risk involved?

In measuring risk, economists have devised the concept of beta. Compensation planners are intimately familiar with the single regression analyses that underlie studies of the relationship of sales volume to pay. There, sales volume is the *x* variable on the horizontal axis of the regression plot, and pay is the *y* variable on the vertical axis. The same concepts are involved in measuring beta. Here, the *x* variable on the horizontal axis is returns to investors from the entire stock market (or some sampling thereof, like the S&P 500) over a period of time (usually three to five years), and the *y* variable on the vertical axis is returns to investors from a particular stock over the same period of time. The result is a scatter diagram with many dots, each representing the intersection at a point in time of the returns available from the entire market and the returns available from the particular company under study. Once the scatter diagram is complete, we can draw a trendline through it.

Students of regression know that the typical regression formula is *a* plus *b* times *x*, where *a* is a constant, *b* is the slope of the regression line, and *x* is the value of the variable being tested from the horizontal axis (*b* is shorthand for beta).

The least squares trendline shows us the beta, or the relationship between the returns from the overall market and the returns from the particular company. If the beta is 1.00, then, on average, a 10 percent increase in stock prices generally is associated with a 10 percent increase in the stock price of the particular company. A 10 percent decrease in stock prices generally is associated with a 10 percent decrease in the stock price of the particular company.

If the beta is 2.00 (as it might be for Lodestar Uranium), then, on average, a 10 percent increase in stock prices generally is associated with a 20 percent increase in the stock price of the particular company. A 10 percent decrease in stock prices generally is associated with a 20 percent decrease in the stock price of the particular company.

If the beta is 0.5 (as it might be for Consolidated Edison), then, on average, a 10 percent increase in stock prices generally is associated with a 5 percent increase in the stock price of the particular company. A 10 percent decrease in stock prices generally is associated with a 5 percent decrease in the stock price of the particular company.

Knowing about beta, we can complete our discussion of the capital asset pricing model. The CAPM says that an investor will demand a total return equal to the risk-free rate of return plus the normal risk premium for investing in equities generally after first multiplying this normal risk premium by the beta of the particular stock. For example:

- With a T-bill rate of 6.5 percent and a beta of 1.00, the return demanded will be 6.5 percent + (6 percent normal risk premium times beta of 1.00, or 6 percent) = 12.5 percent.
- With a T-bill rate of 6.5 percent and a beta of 2.00, the return demanded will be 6.5 percent + (6 percent normal risk premium times beta of 2.00, or 12 percent) = 18.5 percent.
- With a T-bill rate of 6.5 percent and a beta of 0.5, the return demanded will be 6.5 percent + (6 percent normal risk premium times beta of 0.5, or 3 percent) = 9.5 percent.

Let us concentrate for a moment on a company with a beta of 1.00. We know that investors want a return of 12.5 percent, given a T-bill rate of 6.5 percent. Consider three situations:

- Suppose the company earns a consistent 12.5 percent after-tax return on its book equity, which we will assume is currently $25 per share. In this case, an investor will want to pay $25 per share for the stock. By doing so, he receives the desired 12.5 percent return. The ratio of the market price of the stock to its book value is 1.00.
- Suppose the company earns a consistent 7.25 percent after-tax return on its equity, which we will also assume is currently $25 per share. An investor will not want to pay $25 per share for the stock because if he did, his return would be only 7.25 percent.

  How is the investor going to get the 12.5 percent return that he demands? Simple! By paying only $15 for the stock. Although the company is earning only 7.25 percent on its equity, the shareholder can earn 12.5 percent on *his* equity. In this case, the ratio of the market price of the stock to its book value is 0.60.
- Suppose the company earns a consistent 29 percent after-tax return on its equity, which we will again assume is currently $25 per share. Every investor will *want* to pay $25 per share for the stock, since a $25 purchase price yields a 29 percent return. But, since every investor will be clamoring to buy the stock at $25, the price will rise. Indeed, under CAPM theory, it will rise to $58 per share, i.e., to the point where investors will be earning a 14.5 percent return on their investment. In this case, the ratio of the market price of the stock to its book value is 2.32.

Now we know why some companies' stocks sell at twice their book value, while others sell at exactly their book value and still others sell at only half their book value. Studies using the CAPM have demonstrated that the theory can, and does, explain a significant percentage of the movement in company stock prices over time.

Before proceeding further, let me summarize what the CAPM is saying:

- Investors want, not raw profits, but returns on their investment. It is not going to amuse the average shareholder if the company doubles its net income, but in doing so quadruples its investment.
- Investors want, not just any return on investment, but an ROI that is adjusted for risk. It is not going to amuse the average Consolidated Edison shareholder if the company doubles its net income by selling off half its electric-generating capacity and investing the proceeds in pork belly futures.
- Investors want, not just a risk-adjusted ROI, but one that is adjusted for inflation as well. It is not going to amuse your average shareholder if the company doubles its ROI in the face of a tripling in inflation. Recall the CAPM formula: risk-free rate plus (normal risk premium times beta). The one thing that raises the risk-free rate is inflation. Over time, the higher the rate of inflation, the higher the risk-free rate of interest demanded by investors. The higher the risk-free rate of interest being demanded, the higher the CAPM return rate will be.

In summary, the CAPM can aid the compensation planner in deciding whether a division, at a point in time, is worth its stated book value, more than its stated book value, or less than its stated book value. To put it another way, the CAPM can aid the compensation planner in determining approximately how much the division would be valued by the New York Stock Exchange if it were spun off from the company and publicly listed.

Phantom Share Plans

Using CAPM concepts, a compensation planner can design a viable divisional long-term incentive plan. There are three types of phantom share plans, distinguished by the measure of performance used. First, a phantom share plan can reward the creation of what has come to be called EVA, for economic value-added or extra shareholder value. One of the tenets of the CAPM is that, in a perfectly competitive world, no company can earn a return greater or less than its CAPM rate of return. However, at any point in time, the market is never perfectly competitive, so some companies can earn a return that is greater than their CAPM return. It is this above-CAPM return that is labeled EVA in this first type of long-term incentive.

One problem with such a plan occurs when a division is improving a below-CAPM return. A strict application of the EVA formula would produce no incentive payouts at all, even though the division is improving its performance.

Economic theory suggests that such an approach is unfair. Recall the shareholder who paid only 60 percent of book value, or $15 per share, for the stock of a company that was earning only a 7.25 percent return. Consider what happens if the rate of return begins to improve. Suppose the company succeeds in raising its return to 10 percent. It is still earning a below-CAPM return, to be sure. But if the new consistent return rate is 10 percent, wouldn't a shareholder want to pay more than 60 percent of book value for the company's stock? The answer, of course, is yes, because shareholder value has been created compared to the days when the return rate was only 7.25 percent and the stock was trading at only half its book value.

One company with this form of incentive plan modified its design to reward not only an above-CAPM rate of return but also improvements in the rate of return. Hence, the division that was falling below its CAPM rate of return but that was improving its return had an opportunity to earn long-term incentive money.

The second type of divisional phantom share incentive plan rewards both growth in net income and conservation of capital. Plans of this type typically are packaged in matrix form (see Exhibit 12-1). The vertical axis of the matrix might depict a range of increases (decreases) in net income, while the horizontal axis shows a range of investments in capital. Each cell of the matrix contains a payout figure. An examination of the cells reveals that, other things being equal, if net income growth increases, the payout increases. If capital growth increases, the payout decreases (because the return on capital is lower). An advantage of the matrix approach is that the executive knows at a glance what he or she is supposed to be doing, i.e., maximizing long-term net income growth while minimizing long-term capital usage.

A disadvantage of the matrix approach is that the vital inflation factor is difficult to incorporate into the plan design. Since three-dimensional

EXHIBIT 12-1
Example of Divisional Long-Term Incentive Matrix

Average Annual Increase in Pre-Tax Net Income Over 1987 Net Income (millions)	Increase in Average Annual Investment* Over 1987 Investment						
	($2)	$0	$2	$4	$6	$8	$10
	(Payout Dollars in Thousands)						
($1.0)	$0	$0	$0	$0	$0	$0	$0
($0.5)	$0	$0	$0	$0	$0	$0	$0
$0.0	$13	$7	$2	$0	$0	$0	$0
$0.5	$29	$20	$14	$9	$5	$3	$0
$1.0	$46	$34	$26	$19	$15	$11	$8
$1.5	$62	$48	$38	$30	$24	$19	$15
$2.0	$78	$62	$50	$41	$34.	$28	$23

*Total assets less current liabilities

matrices are still on most compensation planners' drawing boards, it is impossible to have a single matrix reflect changes in net income, capital usage, *and* inflation.

One company solved this problem by giving its division managers several matrices, each applicable to a different inflation rate. At the end of the five-year performance period, all the matrices but one were thrown away. The one kept was the one whose inflation factor was closest to the actual inflation rate over the performance period.

Finally, a long-term divisional plan can be made to look like a stock option plan. Such a plan follows the principles outlined for EVA and matrix plans, but the executive who receives a grant sees only a beginning stock price. This beginning stock price becomes the strike price, which will move up or down in future years in response to net income growth, capital usage, and inflation. Possible stock prices can be computed on a disc that permits the executive to enter any quantities for the three variables.

The executive is given a number of phantom option shares at the beginning of the performance period and is permitted to "exercise" the grant under the same terms stipulated in a conventional stock option plan. For example, during the second year the executive may be permitted to exercise 25 percent of the phantom shares or let them ride forward to another year. If the shares are exercised, the executive receives a payment equal to the number of shares being exercised times the amount by which the "intrinsic" stock price at the end of the first year exceeds the strike price.

Whatever the shape of the final plan, two major issues must be addressed. The first concerns internal equity. A child from a middle-class family may be jealous of her friend whose wealthy family drives around in a Mercedes, but her jealousy will be minuscule compared to her reaction if her brother or sister gets more favorable treatment from her parents. So it is with divisional long-term incentives.

But what, in this context, is "more favorable treatment"? If one division outperforms another, isn't that division properly entitled to more long-term incentive pay? Answering that question may be just as difficult as answering this question: Should your brother receive an extra allowance for getting higher grades than you, even though he works less hard in school than you? Some divisions, after all, are incapable of doing "A" work.

One can, of course, be tough and insist that it is only output that matters, not input. But one can also soften the terms. The poorer-performing division manager could be granted some phantom option shares in the better-performing division, for example. That way, he or she can share, at least to some degree, in the latter's success. And the manager of the better-performing division can be granted some phantom shares in the poorer-performing division. This approach will still leave the manager of the less profitable division earning somewhat less than the manager of the more successful division.

Of course, one can go to the other end of the spectrum and grant both managers the same rewards. But if that is the objective, why bother with separate divisional long-term incentive plans? Why not simply give both managers stock options in the parent company's stock? The reason you divisionalized in the first place was to provide for differential rewards based on divisional rather than overall corporate performance. Remember that in the very long run it really is output, and not input, that counts. Were the reverse true, then pay plans would offer every manager in every company the same pay, in which case, incentives would be totally destroyed.

The second major issue to be addressed is how to mix the various elements in a pay package. A compensation package ought to be adapted as the company's business environment changes. In the early days of Apple Computer, for example, it may have made eminent sense to pay people small salaries and offer them gargantuan stock options. At a later stage in the company's evolution, it may make better sense to turn up the volume on salaries and turn down the volume on stock option grants.

So, too, with divisional long-term incentives. If a company is trying to put each division on its own footing, it should not lose sight of the fact that pay packages may need to be blended differently from one division to another. The small entrepreneurial division may need to offer a mixture of low base salaries, low cash incentives, and huge phantom stock option grants. The large division in a more mature phase of its life cycle may need to offer much higher base salaries, greater short-term incentive opportunities, and relatively smaller divisional phantom stock option grants.

With different package blending, one can even solve the problem of getting a manager in a high-performing division to transfer to a low-performing one. The potential transferee may be told to anticipate several years of low, or no, short-term incentive awards and perhaps an outright salary cut as well. But the quid pro quo is a piece of the action in the form of a "mega-grant" of phantom stock options.

An investor faced with greater risk demands a greater return. The same is true for managers: The manager who leaves a division that is performing well and where the pay is good and relatively certain in order to head a less profitable division where the pay is low and nothing is very certain, is willing to take the cut because of the opportunity offered by the long-term incentive grant. If the manager turns the division around and becomes successful, he or she can look forward to earning perhaps ten times what was earned at the good old safe division. And if not, that's what risk is all about.

There is an additional advantage to rewarding risk. At any point in time, an investor has myriad alternatives, some offering no risk at all, some offering moderate risk, and some offering high risk. What happens, of course, is that investors tend to sort themselves out according to their appetites for taking chances. The high rollers will gravitate to high-risk stocks, while the widows and orphans will seek the safety of low-risk stocks.

In the same way, the company that implements divisional long-term incentive plans and then blends its pay packages differently offers its "executive investors" a menu of choices involving varying degrees of risk. Because it does, there's a high probability that the executives will seek positions that reflect their personal taste for risk. Getting the right people in the right job at the right stage in a division's life cycle is the stuff of which success, and increased shareholder value, is made. Clearly, viable divisional long-term incentive plans, coupled with different pay package blending, can help to accomplish this crucial objective.

NOTE

1. The CAPM was formulated by economists William Sharpe and John Lintner, working independently. See William Sharpe, "Capital Asset Prices: A Theory of Market Equilibrium Under Conditions of Risk," *Journal of Finance* 19(4) (September 1964), pp. 425–442; and John Lintner, "The Valuation of Risky Assets and the Selection of Risky Investments in Stock Portfolios and Capital Budgets," *Review of Economic Statistics* 47(1) (February 1965), pp. 13–37.

13

MANAGING BENEFITS AND PERQUISITES FOR EXECUTIVES

Gerald W. Bush and Robert D. Paul

LATE ONE NIGHT, Charlie Goodfellow was feeling confused and frustrated. He had to decide whether to accept WMB Motors' offer to hire him as president and chief operating officer. Charlie's progress in the fast-track world of automotive executives had been steady. After graduating from the College of Engineering at the University of Michigan, Charlie had become an assistant to the plant manager of a Superb Motors assembly factory. He was quickly promoted to plant manager at a smaller facility and continued to rise until he became, twenty-five years later at the age of forty-seven, the head of worldwide manufacturing for Superb Motors.

Now he had this tantalizing offer from WMB Motors. The base salary of $500,000 was attractive. Bonus plans would give him an opportunity to add another $250,000 if he met what seemed to be achievable business objectives. He liked the restricted stock and the stock options he was offered. But Charlie was concerned about his benefits at WMB, particularly the level of his retirement income.

Charlie realized that if he changed jobs in midcareer, the part of his pension earned at Superb Motors would be based on his salary at age forty-seven. Only the part of his pension provided by WMB Motors would be based on his much higher salary near retirement. Furthermore, if there were another period of high inflation, only the portion of the pension earned at WMB would keep up because of the relatively large salary increase he would earn in an inflationary environment. He was not sure, however, that his pension would be higher ultimately if he stayed at Superb. In the back of his mind was the thought that he might retire early, at age sixty-two, and he could not figure out how much this might hurt him.

Charlie was also concerned about disability protection. A good friend of his had been badly injured in an automobile accident when he was fifty and had received very little disability income from his employer. The entire family was suffering. Charlie was unhappy about the fact that WMB would not provide as much disability protection as Superb Motors did.

He also knew that his present employer offered a form of postemployment health insurance, but he was not sure what WMB did in this regard, or how important it might be. Realizing that he was too tired to continue the analysis, Charlie decided that he would sit down the next day and make a list of all his current benefits and compare them with what WMB was offering. His family needed financial protection and he wanted to be sure he could get it before deciding to accept this exciting and demanding new job.

HOW COMPANIES USE BENEFITS

Charlie's deliberations demonstrate that benefits can be a make-or-break part of an executive compensation package. From the company's point of view, creative benefit offers can attract and help hold talented executives. For this reason, companies must be as market-oriented in the design of benefits as they are in other aspects of their business.

Benefits and perquisites play a number of other roles. They can give an executive a sense of security and well-being. They serve as a message to the executive that he or she is well regarded and effective. They reinforce the message that the employer wants the executive to focus primarily, if not exclusively, on the problems and opportunities of the business. And they can serve as "golden handcuffs."

However, because of the amount of "chemistry" in senior executive relationships and the speed with which different kinds of demands are placed upon executives, they are at considerably greater risk than upper- and middle-level managers. Increasingly, benefits have been designed to ease the decision to terminate and to aid the terminated executive in the transition.

Finally, benefits can be used by a board of directors to reward good performance.

HOW EXECUTIVES PERCEIVE BENEFITS

For recipients like Charlie, a benefit package can determine career path as much as other forms of compensation. But, just as a company must know both the costs and benefits of various programs, executives must know how to determine the relative and absolute value of what they are offered.

First, executives expect benefits to serve as insurance, to protect them from large unanticipated expenses. The company must decide how much protection against what kinds of calamity is appropriate.

Executives also expect benefits to replace income when they stop working. The level of replacement is often expressed as a ratio such as the percentage of preretirement income that the pension plus savings plus Social Security provide. Will the ratio enable the former executive to continue an appropriate standard of living in retirement? If a company is unable to finance what it regards as an appropriate replacement level at first, it can gradually improve the plan(s) over the years.

In addition to their use as protection and replacement, benefits can be an investment vehicle for highly paid employees, who often have little time or insufficient interest to manage their own large and complex personal estates. Executives look to benefit programs to provide balance to their personal portfolios. Of course, it is in the employer's interest to have the executive feel secure and not distracted by concerns about benefits or personal finances.

Finally, benefits serve as part of the "score card" by which the executive compares his or her position to others in the company and in the industry.

QUALIFICATION AND RESTRICTIONS

Companies sponsoring benefit programs may have their purposes partially frustrated by government restrictions on plans that are qualified under the Internal Revenue Code. Despite this, qualification has two major advantages. First, employer contributions are not taxable to the covered employees at the time they are made. Second, the investment earnings of funds put aside in advance to pay the benefit are not taxed either to the corporation sponsoring the plan or to the covered employees. When the benefits are paid, the employees are taxed on what they receive. The exception is health insurance, which is never taxed, even when benefits are paid.

The IRS limits the amount of compensation upon which qualified benefits can be paid to $200,000 (indexed for inflation beginning in 1990). The effect of this limit is to prevent executives who make over $200,000 a year from collecting the amount to which they are entitled under the provisions of self-insured company pension, thrift and savings, and disability programs. For example, if a company has a pension plan that replaces 50 percent of pay, an executive who earns $400,000 a year cannot get the full $200,000 pension that the qualified plan promises. Company contributions and salary reduction contributions to a 401(k) plan can only be made on salaries up to $200,000.

Law and regulation not only restrict the amount of compensation that can be counted for a qualified plan, they also restrict the amount that can be paid from qualified funds. Under current regulations, the largest pension that can be paid from a qualified pension plan is $90,000 annually, indexed for inflation after 1987. For an executive earning $400,000, this means that his replacement ratio is not the 50 percent that the qualified plan calls for, but 22.5 percent.

Similarly, the tax code restricts the amount that an executive may contribute through pretax salary reduction to a 401(k) plan, although the typical corporate 401(k) allows employees to contribute up to six percent of salary. These restrictions reduce the allowable contribution of a $400,000-a-year executive from $24,000 to $7,000, indexed for inflation. In a typical 401(k) plan, the company may add 50 percent of the employee contribution, or, in this case, another $3,500 to the $7,000 that the executive may contribute. Although the highly paid employee may contribute an additional $19,500 after taxes to bring the total up to the maximum of $30,000 allowed to be allocated to an executive's account in any one year, more rules covering after-tax contributions discourage these additional executive contributions.

Although the law allows a maximum pension of $90,000 a year or a maximum annual addition to a 401(k) balance of $30,000 a year, it does not allow an executive to have both. Executives who work for companies that sponsor both types of plans will have their benefits cut back further. If the full $30,000 were contributed to a 401(k) plan over an entire career, the pension benefit would have to be cut back to 25 percent of $90,000, because the limit for two plans is 125 percent of the limit for one plan. This means that complicated calculations must be made to determine whether a particular executive will exceed the combined limit of 125 percent.

ERISA EXCESS PLANS

The bewildering and arcane regulations governing benefits have given rise to a type of executive benefit plan known as an ERISA Excess Plan. (ERISA stands for the Employee Retirement Income Security Act, under which complicated restrictions and regulations were first introduced in

1974.) The purpose of an ERISA Excess Plan is to restore the executive's entitlement to benefits and allow the company to make up the difference between the $90,000 ceiling and what the executive would be eligible for under the company's pension plan.

Although this approach gives back the executive's pension, it does not provide as much security as a qualified plan, since the amount required to fund the additional benefit must be paid out of annual company earnings each year after the executive has retired. The fulfillment of the pension promise thus depends on the continued existence of the company and the willingness of future managements to honor the promise or of the courts to enforce it. Although attempts can be made to guarantee the benefit, nothing is as secure as the segregation of assets in a qualified fund. For this reason, these plans are usually referred to as nonqualified or unfunded plans to distinguish them from plans that are funded in advance with segregated, dedicated assets.

ERISA Excess Plans are used to replace pension benefits that have to be reduced because of the $90,000 limit on the amount of annual pension benefit that could be paid by a qualified pension plan. Most companies reduce the pension plan amount in their qualified plans rather than the 401(k) contribution in order to meet the overall 125 percent limit. This allows executives to contribute to the 401(k) plan specified amounts to be matched by the company (defined contribution plan) up to an annual total maximum contribution by the executive and the company of $30,000.

From the executive's point of view, contributions to the individual account are more tangible than a promise of a pension to be paid many years in the future. Also, the recipient has some discretion over how at least part of the money contributed to his or her account is invested. On the other hand, establishing and maintaining an unfunded defined contribution or individual account plan is neither simple nor inexpensive for the company. An administrator has to track investment returns as though the money were invested in a qualified defined contribution plan.

Until the Tax Reform Act of 1986, it was uncommon to use ERISA Excess Plans to make up for benefits not available to executives under 401(k)s or other qualified defined contribution plans. The 1986 act's stiffer restriction on the amount of compensation ($200,000) that can count for qualified plan purposes and the $7,000 limit on salary reduction contributions to 401(k) plans, however, are changing that.

Companies that adopt a combination of ERISA excess and defined contribution plans will be able to reinstate the level of benefit expectations that executives had before the law required them to be treated differently from the rest of the employee population.

SUPPLEMENTARY EXECUTIVE RETIREMENT PLANS

Today's executives often do not work for one employer long enough to earn a pension based on a full career. If an executive has earned portions of a pension at several companies during the course of a career, those portions combined will not provide as large a pension as the person would have earned by staying at one company for the full career. The reason for this is that most pension plans are based on the average of the final three to five years' salary. If an executive has changed employers, he or she might have three pensions on retirement: one based on salary twenty years earlier, another based on salary ten years earlier, and only the third pension based on salary immediately prior to retirement. The three pieces will obviously fall short of a pension calculated entirely on the final, presumably highest, salary.

The problem is even worse if the executive wants to retire before age sixty-five. The actuarial reduction that most plans require in such cases will discourage early retirement, even if the company wants to encourage it. In other cases, professionals such as lawyers and accountants who join the executive ranks of a client may not have had any previous pension plan coverage.

Supplementary executive retirement plans (SERPs) can be used to improve all these situations. Some SERPs grant an extra year of service for each year the executive spends with the company. If a lawyer who has never had a pension plan is recruited at age fifty and works until sixty-five, a SERP will grant credit for thirty years of service instead of the fifteen years actually attained at retirement. Other plans define a level of benefits (for example, 50 percent of final five-year average salary) that is payable to all executives of a specified rank who retire with at least fifteen years of service. There are usually deductions or offsets for whatever the qualified company pension plan provides and for Social Security; sometimes there are offsets for pension benefits earned at previous jobs. In other words, a SERP is an envelope containing other pension benefits but guaranteeing a retirement income that is equivalent to that earned by executives who spend all their working years under a single plan.

One company, however, found itself in difficulty because of a SERP that offered two years of pension credit for each year of service and that began paying immediately after the executive left the company. A number of younger employees with ten to fifteen years of service who were promoted into the plan found that they would be better off financially if they left the company. In one case, a forty-eight-year-old executive with thirty years of pension credit felt that he had to quit, take the pension, and look for another six-figure job. A plan sponsor must be careful to think through unanticipated consequences and make sure that a benefit program achieves its intended goals.

Frequently, regular retirement plans do not include short-term incentive awards or bonuses as part of the compensation in the calculation of pensions. If bonuses are an important part of compensation, leaving those payments out of retirement income can defeat their purpose as incentives. On the other hand, the cost of counting bonuses in the pension formula in addition to counting overtime (which is required by IRS rules) could be prohibitive. Therefore, many companies include bonuses in their SERP formula only, and restrict the qualified pension plan to base salary.

Other arrangements can be made to supplement benefits lost when an executive changes jobs. To entice an executive to accept a position, a company might offer a nonqualified defined contribution account of, say, $100,000. That account balance then can be assumed to earn interest at the prime rate or the long-term U.S. Treasury bond rate. If the executive stays to retirement or is asked to retire early by the company, the account balance is paid out over a fifteen-year period.

Most SERPs begin as individual employment contracts designed to help recruit specific people. In time, companies develop more general policy in the form of a SERP that applies to all similarly situated executives.

Individual contracts may continue to be used to take care of special situations that cannot be included in a general policy. However, most companies try to keep such contracts to a minimum to avoid administrative hassle, allegation of favoritism, and the risk of negotiating a contract that turns out to be more expensive than anticipated because it was not designed as carefully as a general policy would have been.

The role SERPs should play in executive compensation depends heavily on a company's overall compensation and business strategy. Startup companies do not favor SERPs, but mature businesses that have trouble recruiting good executives may. Fitting SERPs and other executive benefits into a company's overall strategy will be discussed more fully later in this chapter.

DEFERRED COMPENSATION

Executives like to be able to defer some of their compensation, particularly all or part of their incentive pay, which can vary widely from year to year. The ability to defer serves a number of purposes:

- It smooths the level of current income by spreading the high earnings of some years across lower-income years;
- It allows executives to wait for a year of lower tax rates;
- It provides an orderly way to accumulate a fund to pay for extraordinary items such as a vacation home or college tuition, or to enlarge savings for retirement;
- It provides the convenience of having the company manage the money;
- It shelters the earnings on the deferred compensation from taxes; and
- It may provide a higher return than other investments, if they are pre-tax dollars and the company guarantees an attractive rate (such as 1 percent or 2 percent above the U.S. thirty-year bond rate).

Deferral brings with it certain risks for the executive. First, the tax rate when the money is paid could be higher than anticipated. Second, the fact that the deferred money remains a corporate asset means that it might never be paid to the executive if the corporation gets into serious financial trouble or is taken over by a company whose management chooses not to honor past promises. To reduce this risk, various methods have been devised to increase the security of deferred pay.

The most common of these is to segregate the deferred compensation and its investment earnings in a trust fund. Such a trust fund has come to be called a rabbi trust because it was first used as a way to provide deferred compensation for a rabbi. Usually the trust is revocable by the company so that the recipient cannot be taxed on the amount being held for him or her. If the company has financial difficulty or is about to be taken over, the trust becomes irrevocable. Once the company gives up the right to recall the money, the executive must pay taxes on what is in the trust fund for his or her benefit. A bank, acting as trustee for the benefit of the executive, will be required by the terms of the trust to distribute the money. Receipt of deferred compensation can also help an executive who is temporarily unemployed as a result of a takeover or a company's financial problems.

Another way to protect deferred compensation is to deposit it in an escrow account during a takeover or financial crisis. The escrow agent is obligated to pay the money to the executive.

Sometimes companies decide to fund their deferred compensation obligations by buying life insurance policies on the lives of the executives who have deferred some of their bonuses. Because the proceeds of a life insurance contract are not taxable, the company can recover the money it will ultimately pay the executive, including the interest it guarantees. Even though the purchase of corporate-owned life insurance does not directly improve the executive's chances of receiving deferred compensation in the event of a corporate takeover, many life insurance sales people try to convince corporate purchasers that it does because so much money would be wasted if the contract were surrendered for cash. If the company instead gave the contract to the executive, he or she would have to pay taxes on its value, which might be less than the accumulated value of the deferred compensation but would certainly be better than nothing.

A final way to secure deferred compensation is to use a secular trust, so called to distinguish it from a rabbi trust. Contributions to a secular trust and their earnings are taxable to the executive as they accumulate. Payout from the trust to the executive, however, is made only on the executive's retirement. As long as corporate tax rates are higher than personal rates, the company can afford to gross up its contributions to cover the executive's taxes and still be at least as well off as if it had used a rabbi trust. The executive is more secure because he or she is always fully vested in the amount that has been deferred. In other words, the trust fund owes the money, not the company. The trustee, usually a bank, can be expected to distribute the fund properly.

Deferral of compensation may affect other benefit programs. Life insurance, for example, is reduced if it is based on an executive's salary and part of that salary has been deferred.

Similar rules apply to pension plans and 401(k) plans. That is, deferred compensation is excluded from the calculation of final average salary on which pension is based. However, because there is already a $200,000 limit on the amount of compensation that can be counted in determining a pension and because it is easy to stop deferring income during the three- or five-year period before retirement if that limit has not been reached, income deferral will probably continue to appeal to highly paid executives. In any case, an executive whose deferral might have cut back the pension can have it restored through a nonqualified SERP.

The effect of deferral on long-term disability plans, contributions to 401(k) plans, and profit-sharing plans or ESOPs also might be considered.

ADDITIONAL BENEFITS

The limits on the level of salary that can be counted for pension, 401(k), profit sharing, ESOPs, and similar plans means that most companies should consider providing make-up benefits in some or all of these areas.

These make-up benefits will be taxable to the recipient. Companies can gross up to cover the extra income tax the executive will be required to pay. The following are some examples of supplementary benefits.

Health insurance. In the past, many companies provided full protection against all medical costs for key executives and their families without taxation to the executive. The Tax Reform Act of 1986 has changed that. Imputed income required for plans that discriminate in favor of the highly paid will apply, if companies continue this benefit.

Postretirement life insurance. Retired executives often need relatively large amounts of life insurance so that when they die there is ready cash to pay estate taxes and to keep their families going until their affairs have been settled. However, major companies usually do not provide large amounts of postretirement life insurance. Accordingly, special programs are sometimes introduced to cover key executives. Because of rules designed to prevent companies from discriminating in favor of highly paid executives, these programs can cost more than they promise. For example, the executive would be taxed for the cost of a postretirement life insurance program and the estate would be taxed for a self-insured program. In either case, benefits would have to be raised to make up for the extra taxes.

Financial planning. In the increasingly complex world of tax laws that are so arcane that even professionals have trouble understanding them, it is not surprising that financial planning services are an important part of most executive benefit programs. These plans typically provide each executive with an allowance for professional advice. The company sometimes contracts with one or more services for the convenience of executives. However, even when that is done, employees usually are free to choose their own advisers. Executive are liable for the taxes on the financial planning allowance.

Legal assistance. Executives engage in a variety of transactions (home purchases, estate planning, and divorce settlements) in which legal advice is necessary. Some companies allow executives to use the financial planning allowance to pay for such services. Others provide access to their own legal departments. At the least, companies can help executives locate professional advisers.

Perquisites. A perquisite is something the company buys an executive. Examples are many: country club or luncheon club memberships; cars, with or without drivers; travel on corporate jets; entertainment; vacations; and tuition assistance. All of these were once used as tax-free ways of compensating executives. Although perquisites are now taxable, the convenience and prestige such privileges confer appeal to many executives.

Loans. Companies also lend executives money. Although such loans are no different from loans obtained from a bank, the convenience makes them appealing.

DESIGNING AN EFFECTIVE PROGRAM

Executive benefit programs are costly, sometimes unexpectedly so. Company benefit planners should get professional help to determine the cost of any program they are thinking of offering.

WMB Motors may be tempted, for example, to offer Charlie Goodfellow a supplementary annuity of $50,000 a year to entice him to join the firm. When Charlie reaches age sixty-five that will have cost the company $500,000. Although the company never intend to cover anyone else so generously, word gets around. Before long, ten or fifteen similarly placed executives will be asking for the same supplementary annuity.

How do you decide what executive benefits to offer and when? Some of the issues to consider are:

- Cost in absolute terms, as a proportion of revenue and as a percentage of salary;
- Your company's position in its growth cycle;
- Competitive pressures in your industry;
- Your company's culture;
- The value of a potential employee who is asking for certain benefits;
- The level within the organization at which such programs should be available; and
- The probability that a benefit will help achieve strategic purpose.

Some priorities seem pretty clear. When statutory benefit ceilings restrict the amount of protection executives get, that protection probably ought to be restored as quickly as the company can afford it. In addition, companies should try to do what pleases executives the most. It makes little sense to spend money on what are essentially tailor-made benefits and then expect every executive to be happy with the "one size fits all" program that may not in fact fit. Finally, companies should design benefit programs that will not involve executives, their lawyers, and the plan sponsors in lengthy and costly disputes. After all, the purpose is to help, not to hassle.

Increasingly, companies are beginning to realize that a dollar allowance may be the ideal supplementary benefit. The company contributes $5,000 to $10,000 per executive (or 5 percent of base salary) and leaves custom design up to the recipient with the help of the benefits department. The executive understands that, beyond replacing the benefit cutbacks required by statute, the company's only obligation is to provide this taxable allowance to be used for any other benefits he or she feels are needed.

When Charlie Goodfellow analyzes what WMB Motors is offering, he should be able to modify the benefit package to his liking. As the next president of WMB Motors, he deserves nothing less.

PART II-B

The Role
of Stock
and
Ownership

14

FOUR WAYS TO OVERPAY
YOURSELF ENOUGH

Kenneth Mason

THE FIGURES ARE OUT. Amid the blossoming of the spring's proxy statements came news of the annual salaries of the country's top executives. True, many people have found the numbers unconscionably high. Are they too high? Think of the pressure the CEO must withstand and the talent he or she must possess.

Maybe they're too low. But some companies have lost money under such well-paid helmsmanship.

How fortunate that we live in a scientific age. We don't have to ponder whether top executives are being compensated fairly. We can simply choose one of four approaches that have dominated executive remuneration planning for most of this century. Each school of thought, of course, has airtight logic and guarantees that shareholder value will be protected.

The Iron Law School. This school's central tenet is the Iron Law of Wages, according to which executives' compensation should be exactly equal to the amount that they require to subsist and reproduce, so as to perpetuate the executive population. Because of the remarkable biological diversity of executives, descended as they are from vastly different genetic pools, proponents of this theory have had to develop an enormous data base in its support. According to the 1987 figures, in manufacturing concerns with $1 billion to $5 billion annual sales, entry-level accountants joining the controller's department require $24,000 per year to subsist. Beginning-level MBAs joining the marketing department require $37,500 to subsist.

Managers of midwestern food plants employing approximately 1,000 workers can subsist on $80,000 per year plus a modest bonus, but New York advertising agency account executives supervising three people cannot. Just a few years ago, most *Fortune* 500 CEOs could feed and clothe themselves and their families on less than $1 million per year. Today, perhaps as a result of ozone depletion and acid rain, a rapidly increasing number need more.

The School of Supply and Demand. Followers of this school hold that executives' salaries are determined by the relationship between how many executives there are and how many are wanted. Lee Iacocca was happy to go to work for Chrysler at a salary of only $1 a year because he knew that while there was a vast supply of automobile executives clamoring for the job, there was demand for only one.

The forces of supply and demand also account for the enormous incomes earned by stockbrokers and investment bankers. Most Wall Street firms will not even interview a candidate who does not have a postgraduate degree in moral philosophy, and it is a Street rule that all new employees serve a five-year apprenticeship before being permitted to contact clients directly. In view of these rigorous educational and training requirements, it is hardly surprising that few young people are attracted to a career on Wall Street these days, and that those who are can command exceptionally high salaries.

The Hay Entitlement School. It was at Camp Maxey, Texas, in 1941 that an obscure master sergeant solved the problem of getting 60,000 southern draftees to salute the one black officer on the post. He simply announced that in the military you salute the uniform, not the person.

This theory's most important postwar extrapolation is the Hay Entitlement System, which posits that there is a salary range for every job title, and you pay the job title, not the job holder. One attractive feature of the Hay system is that the salary ranges allow wide discretion in determining the wages actually to be paid the executive. If performance is clearly unsatisfactory, for instance, the incumbent's pay can be held within the high-middle and low-high part of the range.

The flexibility of the Hay system also has great appeal to management: the Hay team stands ready at all times to add points to any job title whose salary maximum is preventing an increase for an incumbent who does not merit promotion to a higher-rated position but who is the kind of decent chap one hates to disappoint.

The Pay-for-Performance School. This school's highly controversial compensation theory originated in the world of professional sports. It first attracted general attention when Babe Ruth, on being asked how he could justify making more money than President Hoover, replied, "I had a better year than he did." Compensation theorists immediately recognized that the concept of linking compensation to such clear criteria as runs batted in or goals scored or sales quotas met or profit plans achieved had some real advantages over the compensation systems generally in use at that time.

The greatest advantage of the Pay-for-Performance approach is that, unlike the Iron Law theory, the Supply-Demand method, and the Hay Entitlement system, it enables the compensatee to play a role in the compensation process. It also allows participants to relate compensation not just to the past or present but also to the future—not just to the kind of job the executive used to do, not just to the kind of job the executive is doing now, but also to the kind of job you wish the executive would do.

This novel and powerful idea of compensation as incentive caused the emergence of a faction group, whose leaders have dominated pay-for-performance thinking throughout the post-Ruthian era. Their contributions to the discipline include such incentive devices as phantom stock, stock appreciation rights, the golden handcuff, the golden parachute, and, most recently, the golden walking stick and the golden rocking chair.

The test of any managerial tool, compensation policy included, is its effectiveness in helping achieve management's operating goals. The goal most frequently proclaimed number one by America's 1,000 largest corporations in 1987 was to increase shareholder value. Do any of the four schools of compensation support that goal?

Does the Iron Law, a school whose central thesis derives from the discredited ideas of Malthus and whose followers ignore important contemporary shibboleths like quarterly earnings and P-E ratios? Obviously not. Which is not to say the Iron Law is totally without merit in regard to shareholder value. By ensuring that each executive is paid no more than what is needed to subsist and send one child through business school, the Iron Law curbs the lavish salaries, bonuses, pensions, and postretirement consulting contracts that have reduced the earnings and, by extension, the shareholder value of more than a few American corporations in recent years. Unfortunately, restraining executives' compensation, as opposed to controlling the conditions under which it is paid, has never been shown to improve shareholder value over the long term.

According to the School of Supply and Demand, strong demand for executives committed to increasing shareholder value will create a supply of those executives, and as these executives are hired, shareholder value will creep up. While this a highly plausible theory, in real life things are different. The demand for executives committed to shareholder value does not create a supply of executives committed to shareholder value; it creates a supply of candidates committed to being interviewed for a high-paying job. While some of these candidates may indeed have the capability of increasing shareholder value, a correlation between use of the Law of Supply and Demand for compensation and a rise in shareholder value has never been established.

It is surprising, but unfortunately true, that the Hay Entitlement system, despite its modern genesis, also has proved unhelpful to corporations whose goal is to increase shareholder value. By rating jobs instead of executives, the Hay system produces a corporate environment in which managers compete with each other for the best jobs instead of the best results. With rare exceptions, shareholder value is an objective in name only when the Hay team has been at work. Although more than 90 percent of companies using the Hay system increased shareholder value significantly during the 1980s, they did so by virtue of policies and conditions unrelated to compensation.

Of all the approaches to executive compensation, one would expect Pay-for-Performance to be the best for boosting shareholder value. A plan that ties compensation to results surely must produce those results, at least over the long term. Yet in practice, Pay-for-Performance works no better than the other compensation theories. The problem is that management tends to introduce a new incentive plan the moment it appears that disappointing operating results are going to produce disappointing executive bonuses. When profits are rising, compensation is tied to profits. When they begin to sink, the plan switches. Suddenly compensation is tied to achieving a corporate ROI equal to industry ROI. If results fall short of industry ROI, the compensation plan is again revised to link pay to improving ROE by a point or two.

In the 1975–1983 period, the compensation incentive plans of the 200 largest industrial companies in the United States had an average life span of less than eighteen months. The Pay-for-Performance school seems to have evolved into the KCR school, whose theory is Keep Compensation Rising no matter what.

A familiar example of KCR at work is the underwater stock option. What better executive incentive than the stock option for a corporation whose objective is to augment shareholder value? The executive does not benefit unless the shareholder does. No tickee, no washee, right? Wrong, says KCR. No tickee, we give you new tickee. Within days after 1987's Black Monday stock market crash, the business press was reporting that several major corporations planned to replace their executives' newly drowned options.

This is exactly what many corporations did after the market decline of 1973. The experience of one high-level executive in the food industry is typical of that era. In 1973, he was granted an option for 2,500 shares of his corporation's stock at $40. Just after that, profits slumped. Two years later, the company replaced his stock option award with one for 7,000 shares at $15. He was not penalized by the company's decline in shareholder value; indeed, his financial future was actually enhanced as a result of it.

It is questionable whether stock options are effective incentives even in normal times because they seldom constitute a meaningful percentage of an executive's anticipated long-term compensation. True, options often turn out to be worth a lot, but for most executives they are just extra icing on an already well-frosted cake. A refreshing exception was Lee Iacocca's $1-a-year salary buttressed by a huge stock option award. His eventual payoff was enormous, but so was the risk of Chrysler going under, in which case he would have received very little.

It is a sad commentary on the intellectual vigor and financial discipline of the U.S. business community that so many corporate executives are receiving entrepreneurs' rewards for doing bureaucrats' jobs. The important decision-making jobs in American corporations today hardly ever entail financial risk to anyone except the shareholders. If my compensation package awards me $1.5 million when I meet the corporate profit plan and $1 million when I don't, where's my risk? Succeed or fail, the twenty top executives in most large corporations are almost certain to become wealthy.

Even getting fired is generally no financial blow to these executives. Personnel experts delight in figuring out a generous severance package for an executive who has been sacked after running a profitable division into the ground or making a fantastically dumb acquisition or launching five consecutive new product failures. They may not condone the executive's disastrous business decisions, but they will defend with their lives his or her right to be paid almost as much as if those decisions had been good ones. A typical severance package for an executive who has done a really bad job consists of a couple years' salary, a consulting contract, and a pension supplement giving the executive the same pension payments in early retirement that he would have gotten had he been sufficiently competent to stay the course. One executive's early retirement package included the merit increase he would have received at his annual review a few months hence had he not been fired for poor performance!

Executives' financial rewards must be linked more clearly and more emphatically to shareholders' if increasing shareholder value continues to be the first priority of U.S. corporations, and if compensation strategies are expected to play a role in achieving that objective. The Shareholder-Executive Linkage Formula (SHELF), a new incentive compensation strategy, tightens that link by introducing three long-overdue financial and ethical constraints into the corporate compensation process:

1. The annual cash compensation paid to executives of publicly held companies is limited to either 250 percent of the salary of the president of the United States or 25 percent of the compensation of the prior year's most valuable player in the National Basketball Association, whichever a corporation feels better fits its image. Are your executives more like President Reagan or Larry Bird? Strict observance of the limit by all publicly held corporations is enforced by the SEC.
2. Compensation in excess of the cash limit may be paid only in the publicly traded stock of the company. This stock must be purchased by the company on the open market and must be held by the executive for a minimum of five years. The company provides an annual interest-free loan to cover the annual income taxes due on this compensation. The executives repay the loans when they sell the shares or when they leave the company, whichever comes first.
3. The executive stock option is declared illegal and replaced by the Simultaneous Call and Put. A SCAP gives an executive a three-year call on one share of stock at a strike price of 130 percent of market price on the day of grant less dividends paid during the three-year period. At the same time, the executive commits to a three-year put on identical terms.

While some critics have dismissed SHELF as overly complicated, too risky, even radical, the plan is in no way at odds with the conventional compensation theories American industry is now following. The proposed presidential or Birdian limit on cash compensation, for instance, is entirely consistent with the Iron Law's subsistence requirement. Since the president of the United States pays no rent, it is not surprising that a CEO should require two-and-a-half times the president's wage to subsist and reproduce. Conversely, the sports star's shortened career span justifies his 4 to 1 advantage over CEOs, who often persuade their boards to let them keep playing into their dotage.

Nor does an upper limit on cash compensation violate the Law of Supply and Demand. There never has been a demand for high-salaried executives, only a large supply. The demand is for high-*performance* executives. Here there is also a large supply, but current compensation is not always a reliable clue to their identity. Many corporate executives now brazenly pay themselves annual salaries and bonuses that bear no correlation whatsoever to what any manager or company can accomplish in a single year. A corporation's paying $1 million a year for a run-of-the-mill CEO is not unlike the Pentagon's paying $150 for an ashtray: in both cases you know one just as good can be had for much less. The SEC has scores of regulations on its books designed to protect investors' interests in publicly held companies, yet under present regulations there is nothing to prevent a corporation from paying its CEO $1 million a week if it so decides. Shouldn't the shareholder be protected from such a move?

The requirement that all compensation over the cash limit be in the form of company stock and that this stock be purchased by the company on the open market serves a two-fold purpose. One is to make executives more appreciative of shareholder concerns by replacing no-risk stock options with normal-risk shares purchased at the price everyone else pays. The second is to provide a trickle-down benefit to the shareholders: the more executives are paid, the more stock the company must buy on the open market. This puts upward pressure on the stock price, boosting shareholder value.

Replacing stock options with SCAPs would put an end to a form of insider self-dealing that is extremely unfair to shareholders. Why should insiders be allowed to purchase shares at what is often a fraction of the price the public must pay? How is it fair to shareholders to dilute their ownership positions by issuing new shares for this purpose?

A call makes much more sense for executives and shareholders alike. Basing its strike price on a 10 percent annual growth premium makes it fair to the shareholder, while the automatic expiration date eliminates executive risk in timing the exercising of an option as well as any concern about trading on insider information. And pairing a company put with an executive call corrects a serious weakness of stock options as incentive compensation: options are a pleasant incentive when the stock is going up, but managers tend to lose interest when it is not. With the call-put combination, managers never lose interest, no matter which direction the stock is going in.

How might a typical well-paid corporate executive expect to fare under SHELF? Consider the pretax compensation of a top executive in a large information systems company over a six-year period in the 1980s. Under a conventional compensation plan, her salary and bonus were $550,000 in year one, $600,000 in year two, $750,000 when profits surged in year three, and $700,000 for each of years four, five, and six, when profits fell and then flattened. She also received an annual stock option grant equivalent to one-fifth of compensation. The option prices and quantities for years one through six are as follows:

3,667 shares at $30   2,000 shares at $70
1,600 shares at $75   2,154 shares at $65
1,500 shares at $100   2,333 shares at $60

Annual dividend payout during the period was $1.80, $2.00, $2.25, and, for each of the last three years, $2.50. For the whole six-year period, this executive received $4 million in cash compensation and had a paper profit of $110,000 in options for 3,667 shares of stock.

Now look at the pretax compensation history of the same executive under SHELF. Assuming the company had chosen the presidential cash cap, her cash compensation would have been $500,000 for each of the six years. Her compensation in excess of the cap would have been paid over the six years in the form of 14,766 shares of the company's stock with a current value of $885,960. In addition, the 3,667 call options received the first year would have to be exercised in year four. The strike price is calculated like this:

$$($30 \text{ stock price} \times 130\%) -$$
$$($1.80 + $2.00 + $2.25) = $32.95$$

Since the market price of the stock in year four is $70, the executive makes a profit of:

$$($70 - $32.95) \times 3,667 \text{ shares} = $135,862$$

In year five, however, she has to pay the company $41,200 for the shareholders' year-two put and in year six, $93,750 for the year-three put. At $912, her call-put net for the period almost breaks even, making her total compensation for the period $3,886,872, 5 percent less than she would have received under the conventional method.

Now consider the future. The company's objective is to increase shareholder value. It did well at the beginning of the period, but shareholder value has declined for three straight years. Which executive has the stronger incentive to turn the company around? The executive under the conventional plan, who currently has a paper profit of $110,000 in her options and stands to make an additional paper profit of $268,710 if the stock gets back to $100 before the options expire? Or the executive under SHELF, who owns 14,766 shares of the company's stock, the value of which will increase by $590,640 if the price goes back up to $100, who stands to make $151,366 on her current calls if the stock gets back to $100 next year, and who could lose $108,115 if the stock stays where it is for another three years?

Radical though it appears to some, the Shareholder-Executive Linkage

Formula proposes only two quite modest refinements to present methods of executive compensation. The first requires compensation at the highest levels to be in the form of company stock. It affects only the handful of corporate executives who make the kinds of decisions the original owners of the business made before they took the company public. As owner surrogates, shouldn't these managers share some of the risks of ownership as well as the rewards? And mightn't this dramatically improve their decision making?

The second refinement replaces stock options with simultaneous calls and puts. The call portion of SCAPs corrects the basic unfairness to shareholders of selling stock to corporate insiders at lower than market prices. The put portion does something even more important: it prevents top corporate executives from walking away from a losing game for shareholders without losing something themselves.

Too radical? Too tough? Or high time?

15

EXECUTIVE COMPENSATION LINKS TO SHAREHOLDER VALUE CREATION

Louis J. Brindisi, Jr.

IN 1982, I directed a study of corporate performance, the market valuation process, and executive compensation practices for the previous twenty-year period. This study of the linkage between shareholder value creation and executive rewards resulted in the publication of *Creating Shareholder Value—A New Mission for Executive Compensation.*[1]

The study had five major conclusions that were at the time at odds with conventional wisdom:

- The market rewards superior long-term performance in the form of higher market-to-book multiples as well as total returns to shareholders. In essence, the study refuted the "vagaries of the market" viewpoint so prevalent at the time.
- For most industries, the primary corporate performance measure that drove stock price was not earnings per share growth—then the basic foundation of corporate budgeting and compensation systems—but sustained return on equity. While the market also rewarded earnings growth, it did so only when return on equity exceeded the cost of equity.
- Compensation paid to corporate officers was, for the most part, not related to the amount of value being created for shareholders. Throughout the 1970s, management was being paid handsomely through misguided pay delivery systems while shareholder value was being destroyed.
- The mix of pay elements in most executive compensation packages was weighted too heavily toward annual compensation (salary and bonus) relative to long-term incentives. This contributed significantly to the short-term orientation for which American management was so severely criticized.

- Corporate "winners" were not sufficiently differentiated in compensation from lackluster performers or "losers"—those who were destroying shareholder value.

Executive compensation programs adopted during the 1970s were mainly pay delivery systems; in the 1980s, consultants led the effort to restructure executive compensation programs to be drivers of shareholder value creation.

As a result, in many American corporations:

- Return on equity replaced earnings per share growth as the financial performance measure upon which annual and long-term incentives were based.
- Stock options were issued in greater magnitude and frequency than they had been during the 1970s.
- Stock options, combined with three- to five-year leveraged cash incentives (such as performance units or long-term cash bonuses), constituted a larger part of total compensation packages, counterbalancing short-term performance plans.
- Relative performance measures replaced absolute measures, thereby reducing the effect of exogenous factors on the performance evaluation and reward system.
- Long-term incentive plans were "unbundled," i.e., incentives were provided for business-unit performance as well as overall corporate performance.
- Strategic performance measures were integrated in both annual and long-term incentive plans.[2]

In sum, many companies have fundamentally restructured their executive compensation programs to reward the creation of shareholder value. This restructuring has been based on valuation analyses that addressed four major questions:

- What performance measures drive shareholder value (as measured by market-to-book multiples, stock price appreciation, and total returns to shareholders)?
- Over what time frame does the market value performance for the company's industry?
- What performance levels are required for the company to create shareholder value?
- What are the potential shareholder value-creation opportunities at dif-

ferent levels of performance, and what is the reasonable amount of that value to share with management?

SHAREHOLDER VALUE CREATION AND EXECUTIVE COMPENSATION

Managements and compensation committees of boards of directors must continually ask these questions about value creation as the economy and operating environments evolve, and as dynamic financial markets respond in various ways to these changes. Analyzing the performance factors that drive shareholder value is the first step in developing an executive compensation program that rewards the creation of value.

Regression analysis is a useful means for identifying relationships between financial performance and measures of shareholder value creation. The types of performance and shareholder value measures that we frequently test can be seen in Exhibit 15-1.

In most industries, return on equity is the performance measure that correlates most strongly with measures of shareholder value (see Exhibit 15-2). In others, particularly those in the rapid growth phase of their product life cycles, growth in sales or earnings may be the primary driver of market value (see Exhibit 15-3).

Valuation analysis also shows the amount of "value leverage" that exists in an industry. Value leverage is the increase in market value that comes from a given performance improvement. It is represented by the slope of the regression line representing the relationship between performance and

EXHIBIT 15-1
Selected Measures of Performance and Shareholder Value

Performance Measures		
Growth in	Return on	Shareholder Value Measures
Revenues	Sales	Stock Appreciation
Net Income	Total Assets	Market to Book
Operating Income	Total Capital	Total Return (Appreciation
Earnings per Share	Total Equity	Plus Reinvested
Total Assets	Common Equity	Dividends)
Total Capital		Price/Earnings Ratio
Total Equity		
Common Equity		
Cash Flow		
Cash Flow from Operations		
Cash Flow per Share		

Note: Variables based on earnings and cash flows may be measured before or after interest, taxes, unusual or extraordinary items, or any combination thereof.

EXHIBIT 15-2

ROE vs. Market-to-Book in the Chemical Industry

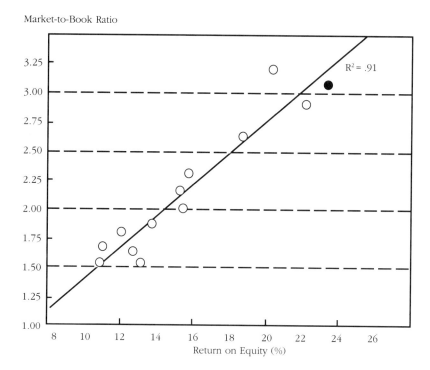

Market-to-Book Ratio

$R^2 = .91$

Return on Equity (%)

market value (see Exhibit 15-4). Value leverage is an important consideration in formulating an appropriate executive compensation strategy and in designing long-term incentive plans.

Although the valuation analyses form an essential foundation for developing a company's compensation strategy and program, they must be supplemented by a thorough understanding of the company's competitive positioning, past financial performance, and future financial and strategic plans. These inputs help frame the magnitude of the management challenge. The development of the compensation strategy also requires a detailed review of the organization structure, major management processes and style, and roles and responsibilities of key executives.

The goal is to develop a strategy attuned to the company's unique strategic, financial, competitive, and organizational situation. This approach results in programs that can be implemented smoothly and that serve both management and shareholders well.

EXHIBIT 15-3
EPS Growth vs. Total Return in Information Industry

Three-Year Average Annual Total Return (%)

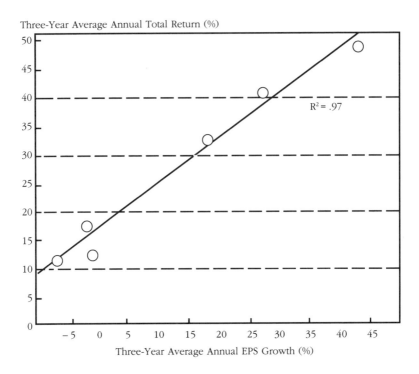

Three-Year Average Annual EPS Growth (%)

The executive compensation strategy should address the following key elements:

- The total pay opportunity
- The leverage in the incentive plans; that is, the degree to which incentive awards vary with performance below and above target levels
- The time periods over which performance is measured for determining incentive awards
- The most strategic equity vehicle(s)—stock options, restricted stock, value shares, and others—and the mix of equity to cash incentives
- Performance measures for use in incentive plans
- Specific performance goals that trigger minimum, target, and superior payouts

The total pay opportunity.   Pay opportunity should not be simply a function of competitive pay practices, but should reflect the degree of difficulty of the management task, the risk to shareholders of a failed strat-

EXHIBIT 15-4
Hypothetical Relationship between Performance and Stock Price

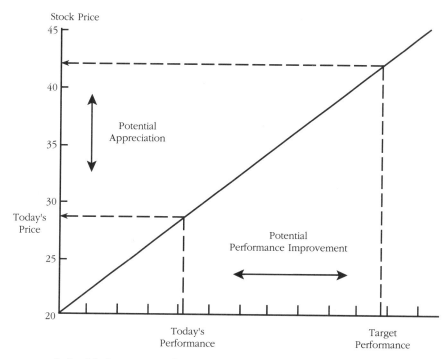

egy, and the likely magnitude of the shareholder value-creation opportunity. In certain situations, it may be appropriate to provide total compensation opportunities that exceed industry practices. In turnaround or restructuring situations, for example, "competitive" levels of total compensation may not provide adequate reward for tasks such as major acquisitions and divestitures, asset redeployment, organizational integration, and facilities rationalization.

For example, in the mid-1980s, a major communications company brought a new management team into a turnaround situation. Because of the substantial management task involved, unusually large stock option grants were awarded to a small group of key executives. The opportunities provided were well outside the parameters of "competitive" practice, but they were commensurate with the challenge presented to the new team. Within three years, the turnaround was essentially complete, and over $6 billion of shareholder value was created. The management team's rewards were well beyond what was typical for executives at peer companies, but the rewards were a fraction of the value created for the shareholders.

The leverage in the incentive plans.   "Leverage" refers to the relationship between increases in pay and increases in performance. As described above, valuation analyses reveal the degree to which improvements in performance have been associated with increases in shareholder value (value leverage) for a given industry. The greater impact performance improvements have on stock prices, the more incentive the management team should have to achieve incremental improvements in performance. Exhibit 15-5 depicts the relationship between performance and incentive payouts for one company with a high leverage plan and another with a low leverage plan.

Strategic imperatives may warrant higher levels of incentive plan leverage. In cases where accelerated achievement of performance goals is critical, e.g., in a turnaround situation, or where major debt repayments are required, the additional incentive of a highly leveraged plan design can be a powerful management tool.

Further, certain firm- or industry-specific characteristics may affect the choice of leverage. The degree to which management is able to control variations in performance influences the proper plan leverage. The more performance is influenced by exogenous factors (such as industry cyclicality), the less leverage should be in the plan.

The performance measurement time frame.   The time frame over which the market values performance will help determine the appropriate mix of short-, medium-, and long-term incentives, as well as optimum performance measurement periods. Some industries, such as the food industry, are typically valued based on annual performance. Others such as the information industry are valued over an intermediate time frame—approximately three years. Still others, including multiline insurance companies, are valued over at least a five-year time frame. The degree to which an underperforming company is in danger of becoming a takeover target may also determine the optimum time frame for measuring and rewarding performance. The more urgent the tasks, the more emphasis is needed on short-term incentives, if a company's goal is independence.

For example, in a recent study of the banking industry, valuation analyses supported the use of a five-year performance measurement cycle. However, the board of a client bank believed that performance had to improve dramatically within a shorter period to avoid being forced into a merger. Three-year performance goals were established for the bank's new long-term incentive plan. That plan had a unique triggering device,

EXHIBIT 15-5
Hypothetical Long-Term Incentive Plan Leverage

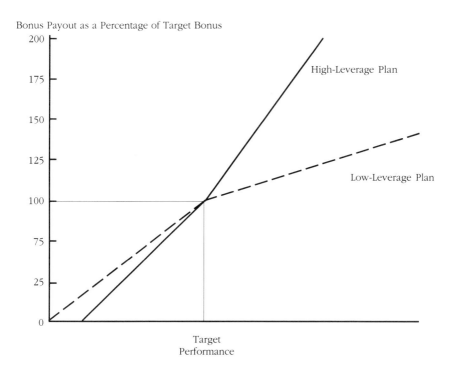

Bonus Payout as a Percentage of Target Bonus

High-Leverage Plan

Low-Leverage Plan

Target
Performance

which allowed executives to achieve full payment at the end of two years
if performance goals were achieved at that time. The additional pay opportunity contributed to the accelerated achievement of long-term goals.

*The choice of equity vehicle(s) and the mix of equity and cash incen-
tives.*   Where substantial value-creation opportunity exists, large stock
option grants are appropriate. Where appreciation potential is not substantial, option grants should be smaller, and the other elements of the
long-term incentive plan—restricted stock and cash incentives—should
be larger.

A communications company provides an example where the incentive
power of options was low. Valuation analyses revealed that the company
was overvalued relative to its 13 percent return on equity. Its market-to-
book multiple implied that the market expected a future return on equity
of 18 percent following anticipated restructuring. Thus, significant im-

provement in performance was required simply to maintain the current market-to-book level.

Given the limited near-term appreciation potential of the stock, extremely large option grants would have been required to meet target long-term compensation levels. Therefore, a long-term restricted stock and cash-based incentive plan was introduced, with significant rewards payable for return on equity at 18 percent and above. These incentive opportunities served to "light the fire" under management, and the value-preserving restructurings were undertaken.

In addition, if dilution of outstanding shares is a major concern, restricted stock may be preferable to options as an equity vehicle. This is because fewer shares are required to achieve the same target compensation with grants of stock (where the executive receives the full value of a share) than with options (where the executive receives the appreciation only). However, the desired level of risk to the executive should also be considered. Exhibit 15-6 demonstrates that the value to the executive changes more with options than with restricted stock, as the stock appreciates more slowly or more rapidly than expected.

At a diversified food company, a new CEO faced a major task of portfolio restructuring and performance improvement. ROE was 8 percent in the year he took over. In addition, because the businesses in the portfolio were unrelated—not all in core food businesses—the market discounted their total value by 20 percent.

The major feature of the compensation strategy for this company was what we called "super" options—unusually large option grants to a relatively small group of key executives with the most impact on corporate performance. Two percent of the shares outstanding were granted to nine people with exercise restrictions that extended over a seven-year period. As a result of massive restructuring and subsequent investment strategy, ROE rose in a few years to among the highest in the industry, and the shareholders' investment increased fourfold.

Once the company's ROE and market-to-book ratio were at industry highs, further increases in value were expected to come mainly from steady growth in equity coupled with sustained superior returns. With a more limited appreciation potential, options became a less powerful incentive vehicle. At this stage, retaining the management group was a key imperative. Therefore, the option program was replaced with an ongoing series of restricted stock awards.

Without an understanding of the valuation process for the company's stock, a poor equity-based compensation strategy could have been imple-

EXHIBIT 15-6
Hypothetical Incentive Value of Options and Restricted Stock

Value as a Percentage of Target Value

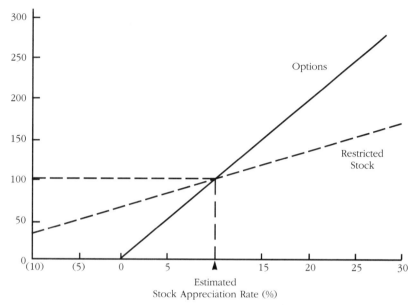

Estimated
Stock Appreciation Rate (%)

mented, particularly if the plan design were driven solely by competitive practices in the food industry.

Performance measures. The choice of corporate performance measures for an executive compensation program should be driven by the results of the valuation analyses described above. Business-unit executives should also be rewarded for their units' contributions to the primary drivers of shareholder value (see below).

The achievement of strategic goals that are not immediately reflected in financial results is often of crucial importance to the company's long-term success. To emphasize their importance, strategic performance measures can supplement financial performance measures in annual as well as long-term incentive plans.

A leading consumer goods company that had lost its dominant position to a relatively new entrant is an example of the value of using performance against strategic goals as a basis for incentive awards. Since new product development and a revamped customer service function were crucial to regaining share and profitability, incentive plans were redesigned to include measures of new product entries and improved customers service. Within two years competitive positioning was restored.

Performance goals.   Performance goals must be set in a competitive context. The market values a company's performance relative to industry performance. Once an investor decides to invest in a particular industry, he or she chooses the company that has the best opportunity to create shareholder value. A company could be chosen because it has the best opportunity to improve returns, or is capable of sustaining an already high-return position and has significant growth opportunities, or is undervalued relative to the true earning potential of its assets. Thus, goals under incentive plans must reflect improved competitive positioning in growth and/or returns.

Companies that are satisfied with achieving internally set goals that result in sustained mediocre relative performance not only fail to create shareholder value, but also become candidates for raid or acquisition. Competitive financial and valuation analyses provide the data base required for informed goal setting under incentive plans.

Take the case of a financial institution that had a long-term incentive plan based on earnings-per-share growth. It had set goals that were relatively modest compared with competitors' performance. In addition, the earnings-per-share growth goals encouraged investment in low-return projects and discouraged asset redeployment. Returns, which were the true drivers of value in the industry, actually decreased, dragging down the stock price—even though executives were rewarded for achieving the EPS goals set under the plan.

The long-term incentive plan was redesigned to reward for return on equity. In addition, relative performance goals were established, with awards based on ROE relative to a carefully selected group of peers. Payouts under the plan started at median performance and reached maximum levels at top quartile performance.

By establishing goals that reflected competitive and valuation realities, the company signaled to the market that management was focused on the true drives of shareholder value, and executive rewards could be fully justified based on performance—a major concern of the board of directors.

OPTIMIZING BUSINESS-UNIT PERFORMANCE

The value of a corporation reflects the values the market attaches to each of the businesses in its portfolio. The more value created in the business units, the more value will be created in the corporation.

A key issue in developing an executive compensation strategy for a corporation with multiple business units is the extent to which unit executives' incentive awards should be based on unit versus overall corporate performance. Under a fully "unbundled" compensation strategy, executives in each business unit have awards based solely on the performance of their unit.

A study of organizational interdependencies is necessary to determine if an unbundled incentive program will help a corporation maximize shareholder value creation. If key interdependencies exist among units—making individual growth and/or profitability difficult to control or measure—it may be desirable to link some or all of business-unit executives' incentive awards to corporate-level performance. Such linkage ensures interdivisional cooperation and protects against business units seeking gain at each other's expense.

If business units function independently, a very powerful approach is to allow business-unit executives to share in the value the unit creates for its parent shareholder. Executives can be granted surrogate stock or stock options in their units. The goal is to make them behave like owners of the business and do whatever is required—restructuring, rationalization, maximization of growth and returns—to drive value higher. The model is the LBO, where management usually has a significant ownership position.

A business-unit, value creation-oriented compensation program requires a methodology for estimating the shareholder value and value-creation potential of the unit. The ideal approach is to base value estimates on actual market data for publicly traded companies in the unit's industry. For example, a corporation may have a division that operates a chain of supermarkets, which tends to sell at a straight multiple of earnings. Although the division has no actual market value, the earnings stream *implies* a market value, and can be capitalized.

For subsidiaries in other industries with many "pure play" publicly traded competitors, the valuation analyses can be used to determine the primary drivers of shareholder value and the relationship between performance and market-to-book ratio. These analyses can then be used to estimate a market-to-book ratio based on the subsidiary's performance, and the ratio in turn can be applied to the subsidiary's equity to estimate its market value. Exhibit 15-7 illustrates this approach.

While market-based approaches provide the most accurate estimation of a business unit's market value, they are not always feasible. Many business units do not have an easily defined group of publicly traded peers; in other cases, it is difficult to develop acceptable methodologies for allocating equity to business units. The alternative to market-based approaches is a theoretical economic valuation model, which estimates the value of a business using economic theory rather than the realities of the marketplace. To be effective, theoretical models must be simple and easy to communicate to incentive plan participants. The most common theoretical valuation model is the discounted cash flow approach, in which the anticipated future cash flows are discounted to the present by a risk-adjusted discount rate. The resulting present value is, theoretically, the amount an investor would be willing to pay for the business unit.

Although such a methodology provides an estimate of market value for those businesses that cannot utilize market-based approaches, it has drawbacks. Uncertainty surrounding future cash flows may be so great as to render the model unreliable. Selecting the discount rate, which should reflect the business unit's cost of capital, is also difficult and assumption-based. In addition, the correlation between theoretical and actual values has to be demonstrated empirically.

A compensation program that allows business-unit executives to share in the value created by their unit is an extremely exciting one and can help a corporation maximize the potential of its various businesses.

SHAREHOLDER VALUE, EXECUTIVE COMPENSATION, AND RAIDERS

An executive compensation program driven by shareholder value-creation objectives, thoughtfully conceived and successfully implemented, has obvious advantages to all corporate constituencies. The greatest advantage from management's perspective is that strong shareholder value creation is the best defense against raiders—both individual and corporate. As Carl Icahn said in a newspaper interview, "I look for disparity between the stock price and the true value. The companies I won't go near are the ones where the stock is close to the true value. That's a company's best defense."[3]

EXHIBIT 15-7
Example of How Performance Implies Market Value

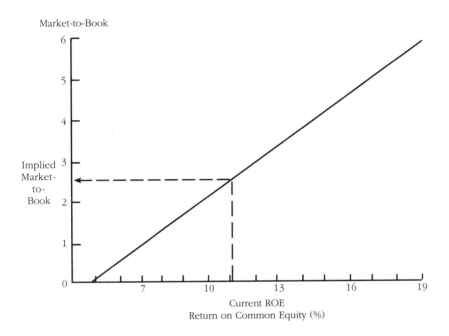

Individual and corporate raiders seek to buy embedded value. That is, they want to buy assets with the potential to generate cash flow beyond the level that has been capitalized in the stock price. Since the raider pays an acquisition premium above the market value of the stock, he must improve performance to justify the price paid (see Exhibit 15-8). In the case of leveraged buyouts, such performance improvements must come quickly as the acquirer struggles to pay down debt. This required performance improvement will come through the divestiture of unrelated or unprofitable businesses, organizational integration, facilities rationalization, product line pruning, distribution system combination, and improved management of cash flows.

A fundamental question is why chief executive officers do not perform the same value-enhancing tasks a raider does, *before* the company is subjected to a buyout or leveraged cashout. The ultimate irony of the leveraged cashout is that management assumes all the performance enhancement burden of the raider, but receives none of the raider's rewards.

One of the major reasons they do not may be the executive compensa-

EXHIBIT 15-8
Hypothetical Acquisition Premium and Performance Needed to Justify It

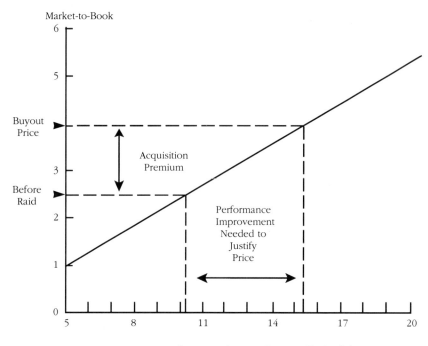

Return on Average Common Equity (%)

tion program, which usually does not motivate CEOs to get at embedded value, and may actually discourage them from doing so. The flaws include salaries tied to size (sales), bonuses tied to earnings rather than profitability, and management's small ownership stake in the business.

After a leveraged buyout, management typically owns about 15 percent of the stock, around 5 percent of which is in the hands of the CEO. It is little wonder that going private is increasingly popular. Commonly the initial reasons given for going private are to have owner boards, less reporting, and streamlined management processes; however, the major, often-unmentioned, reason is the magnitude of the management compensation opportunity.

If directors want ownership behavior from management, they must insist on highly leveraged executive compensation programs with significant upside potential for significant shareholder value creation. Characteristics of these programs include:

- Uncapped annual and long-term incentive opportunities;
- Performance measures that drive value;
- Performance goals that reflect competitive performance; and
- Most important, large stock ownership opportunities for a small group of executives who have a major impact on performance.

Much of present corporate stock option strategy is ineffective because a significant portion of available options is diverted from key senior executives to middle-level managers. This practice is inimical to the organizational realities of shareholder value creation, as there are only a handful of corporate executives who can influence stock price—those making business portfolio and financing decisions and those who drive the performance of major operating units.

Other managers should participate in performance-enhancing long-term incentive plans that reward them for controllable performance, without diluting the pool of options available for grant. This does not mean that former stock option holders would have reduced compensation opportunities; rather, future rewards would simply be tied to performance on which they can have an impact.

Another effective tool for avoiding corporate raiders is the total return to shareholders index. This approach rewards senior executives directly for the stock appreciation and dividends received by their shareholders relative to those at competitor companies. Thus, executives are strongly motivated to get at embedded value and increase returns to shareholders while being protected from market- and industrywide downturns.

A diversified packaging company serves as an example of successful implementation of a value-building compensation strategy. Stock options were granted in the amount of 2 ½ percent of outstanding shares to ten corporate executives. These were what we refer to as "premium-priced options"—the exercise price was above market price at time of grant. In this case the price was 15 percent above market (see Exhibit 15-9). Thus, the first 15 percent of appreciation would go to shareholders, signaling the market that management would be rewarded handsomely only if it exceeded the market's expectations. Over the next three-year period, a business unit that had been a major drag on the company's valuation was spun off, and major new investments were made in core businesses. The stock price more than doubled. The rewards to management were significant, but were only a small fraction of the total value created for the shareholders. The interests of the shareholders and management were one and the same.

EXHIBIT 15-9
Hypothetical Incentive Value of Regular and Premium-Priced Options

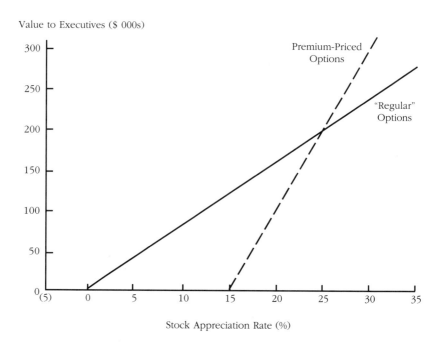

Value to Executives ($ 000s)

Stock Appreciation Rate (%)

REQUIREMENTS FOR SUCCESSFUL PROGRAM DEVELOPMENT AND IMPLEMENTATION

Most *Fortune* 500 corporations have management compensation programs with at least some linkage to the shareholder value-creation process. Only a minority of these companies have programs that are fully value-driven.

We have found that there are five factors necessary for successful linkage:

- A senior management group that understands the market valuation process and encourages the use of executive compensation as a tool to realize potential value.
- A compensation committee and board of directors that endorse strategic levels of financial reward for performance and value creation. They eschew surveys of competitive practices and instead seek innovative programs aimed at value sharing.

- Organizational structures and management processes that integrate the strategic planning, financial planning and reporting, and compensation functions. Each process has to be linked to ensure that the value-driven compensation program is properly designed, maintained, and given appropriate visibility.
- Use of the program as a signaling device. Design features like premium-priced options, relative performance measures, and uncapped bonus plans are unique signaling devices and should be made known to shareholders and the investment community. Similarly, rewards linked to value creation are important signals to employees of what constitutes valued contribution in the organization.
- Vision of the program as a tool to achieve competitive advantage. Like strategic planning, compensation is a process that has to be monitored continuously as a mechanism for achieving competitive advantage.

NOTES

1. Louis J. Brindisi, Jr., "Creating Shareholder Value—A New Mission for Executive Compensation," *Midland Corporate Finance Journal* (Winter 1985), pp. 56–66.

2. Louis J. Brindisi, Jr., "Paying for Strategic Performance," in Robert Boyden Lamb, ed., *Competitive Strategic Management* (Englewood Cliffs, NJ: Prentice-Hall, 1984), pp. 333–343.

3. "Too Much Gold in the Parachute," *New York Times*, January 26, 1986.

16

THE PAST, PRESENT, AND POSSIBLE FUTURE ROLE OF EXECUTIVE STOCK COMPENSATION

Theodore R. Buyniski, Jr.

INTRODUCTION

Over the past twenty years, long-term incentive plans have become increasingly important, both in absolute dollar terms and in percentage of total compensation. Whereas long-term incentives were only 15 percent of compensation in 1970, they could easily be more than 60 percent of a chief executive officer's total compensation in 1988[1] and, in some cases, exceed 80 percent of total compensation, as was the case of Lee Iacocca's compensation at Chrysler in the mid- to late 1980s.[2] This growth increases the importance of long-term incentives and focuses attention on their components, particularly on stock compensation.

Stock compensation forms an integral part of the incentive package offered to senior executives today. In 1988, more than 80 percent of the largest companies ($1.5 billion and larger) used stock compensation as their primary long-term incentive vehicle.[3]

The primary rationale for stock compensation is a simple one. Executive rewards should be linked to shareholder return—stock price appreciation and dividends. Stock compensation links the interests and rewards of managers directly to those of the shareholders by making stock price the primary performance measure. If executive performance improves the value of the company, both shareholders and executives gain; if there is no improvement, there is little or, in the case of stock options, no executive reward. Cash plans, which generally have one or a series of financial measures, may provide incentives to improve particular aspects of a company's performance, but they will only indirectly link the fates of the shareholder and the executive. For example, a plan that rewards execu-

I would like to thank Henry Rothschild for his kind help and advice in the preparation of this chapter.

tives based on a common accounting measure such as cumulative earn-ings per share could promote expansion for its own sake without regard for the rate of return those expanded operations would generate for the shareholder.

Periodically, this straightforward tool comes under renewed scrutiny because of stock market action or changes in the tax or securities laws or accounting rules. In 1988, all three factors caused a reexamination of the place of stock compensation: the stock market dropped precipitously in October 1987, the tax laws changed in 1986, and the Financial Account-ing Standards Board (FASB) proposed changing the accounting treatment of stock compensation. Although the stock market recovered to some ex-tent and the FASB eventually tabled the accounting change, the attention provided the opportunity to revalidate the central place of stock compen-sation in executive compensation packages.

WHAT IS STOCK COMPENSATION?

When we speak of "stock compensation" we are actually referring to a variety of tools that provide compensation to executives based on the in-creasing value of company equity, e.g., stock options, restricted stock and performance shares, dividend equivalents, and stock grants in all their variations.

Stock Options

Stock options, the form of stock compensation used by 81 percent of those companies that use stock compensation, represent the right to pur-chase stock at a fixed price for a period of time, regardless of subsequent stock price movement.[4] The compensation element is provided by the difference between the option price and the market price of the stock at the time of exercise (the "spread"). The executive is rewarded solely on the growth of the company over a base line represented by the option price.

Stock options come in several forms, including incentive stock options (ISOs), which still provide limited tax benefits to executives, and dis-counted stock options (DSOs), which are issued below market price as a form of deferred compensation.

Stock options reward the executive only for increases in the value of the stock of the company. Generally, there is no reward tied to dividends. This situation is changing among companies with high-dividend stocks such as NYNEX and many electric utilities, which have instituted plans that accrue dividends until an option is exercised. This enables companies to tie executive return to total shareholder return rather than to stock price appreciation only.

A potential drawback to the use of options is that their value is strongly influenced by the volatility of the stock. The options of a company with a high beta will, on similar performance, be worth more than those issued by a company whose stock is less volatile. Consequently, options tend to be most effective in high-growth, low-dividend companies. For example, whereas 81 percent of general industry long-term incentive plans use stock options, only 56 percent of plans sponsored by utilities do, reflecting the lower volatility and higher yield of utility stocks.[5]

Stock Appreciation Rights

Stock appreciation rights (SARs) are the right to receive the spread between the market price and the grant price of the SAR in either cash or stock or a combination of the two. Generally, SARs are granted solely to corporate "insiders" who are subject to the six-month holding period imposed by Section 16(b) of the Securities Exchange Act of 1934. SARs allow these individuals to exercise options and sell the underlying stock at the same time. The use of SARs is generally limited to insiders because of the accounting costs. Whereas stock options generally do not cause a charge to corporate earnings, SARs will require that the spread be accrued from year to year.

This need may disappear, however, due to changes in Section 16(b) proposed by the Securities and Exchange Commission. Under these proposed changes, the exercise of a stock option will not be considered a "purchase." Therefore, insiders may exercise an option and sell the underlying stock without the need for SARs. As of this writing in July 1990, these rule changes have not yet been finalized.

One area where SARs are extended to a broader group of executives is in closely held businesses. It is possible to give executives the right to share in the appreciation of the value of the company's stock (as measured by an objective standard) without actually granting them equity. SARs (or, as they are more commonly called in this situation, cash appreciation rights) can be issued without requiring a dilution of the owner's control or the creation of a nonvoting class of stock.

Restricted Stock and Performance Shares

Restricted stock, used by 35 percent of companies,[6] is granted to executives without a cash commitment on their part, subject to vesting based on remaining with the company for a specified time, and sometimes on attaining certain performance goals as well. Performance shares are structured in the same manner, with payment conditional on the achievement of performance goals and with the value of the shares paid either in cash or in shares at a fixed point in the future.

Whereas the compensation value of options is based solely on the appreciation of the stock after the grant, restricted stock and performance shares provide compensation based on the total value of the stock at the time of payment and, generally, the dividends earned between the award date and the time the restrictions lapse. Consequently, fewer shares of restricted stock are needed to provide a given level of compensation than is the case with stock options.

Performance shares are, therefore, more appropriate in those situations where dividends constitute a significant part of the shareholder return and the stock is less volatile, as in the utility industry. Alternatively, if shares carry long-term restrictions, they can serve as a retention device for key executives as in the program at Coca-Cola under which shares are forfeited if the executive terminates employment before retirement.

Stock Grants/Purchases

Under a stock grant, the company issues shares to the executive without restrictions or conditions. Grants are not commonly used in ongoing compensation programs; they occur in fewer than 5 percent of companies.[7] However, they are frequently used in special situations such as turnarounds or startup companies, where there is a need to provide key executives with an immediate stake in the company, or where there may be cash flow constraints on more traditional forms of direct compensation. Examples of this approach include the Henley Group or the stock purchase (with loan forgiveness) made by John Cunningham when he joined Computer Consoles.

It should be noted that in these situations, the share price is usually very low, either in absolute terms, as in the startup, or relative to the company's industry, as in the turnaround. Therefore, stock is perceived by the company as an inexpensive form of compensation. It provides an opportunity for significant gain to the executive if the turnaround/startup succeeds. In effect, it can provide key managers with an LBO simulation without an actual LBO occurring.

As with restricted stock, the entire value of the grant represents compensation as well as future dividends. Consequently, fewer shares are needed to deliver a predetermined level of compensation.

Book Value Plans

The foregoing approaches can be based on book value as well as market value. Some companies, such as Digital Equipment Corporation, offer book value stock options. Others, such as Citibank, provide book value stock purchase plans.

These plans enable the company to insulate its performance (and executive reward) from the vagaries of the stock market, but at a price: under current accounting rules, publicly traded companies that offer book value plans must accrue accounting charges to earnings based on the increase in market value. As a result, the cost will generally exceed that of market-only-based plans.

Other forms of stock compensation represent variations or combinations of these approaches: junior stock, for example, is a form of discounted restricted stock or performance shares; convertible debentures represent an option once the share price exceeds the conversion price; a stock purchase plan with loan forgiveness is a cross between a stock grant and restricted stock. A complete review of the characteristics of the various types of stock plans in common use today is shown in Exhibits 16-1 and 16-2.

THE TRACK RECORD: STOCK PLANS IN THE 1970s AND 1980s

Stock compensation is not used in a vacuum. In examining the historic use and value of stock compensation, it is necessary to focus on three outside factors: the stock market, tax laws, and accounting principles. Although none of these factors affect the link between shareholder return and executive compensation, companies have historically modified their compensation plans in reaction to these factors.[8]

Stock Plans in the 1970s

Between 1970 and 1980, the stock market, as measured by Standard & Poor's 500 index, increased by less than 2 percent annually.[9] In that

EXHIBIT 16-1
Types of Long-Term Plans

	Incentive Stock Options	Nonqualified Stock Option Plans	Stock Appreciation Rights	Performance Share/Unit Plans	Restricted Stock Plans	Phantom Stock Plans
Description	A right granted by employer to an employee to purchase stock at a stipulated price during a specified period of time in accord with Section 422A of Internal Revenue Code.	A right granted by employer to purchase stock at stipulated price over a specific period of time.	Employee realizes appreciation in value of specified number of shares of stock. No employee investment required. Time of exercise of rights is at employee's discretion.	Awards of contingent shares or units are granted, without cost to the employee, at beginning of specified period. Awards are earned out during the period that certain specified company performance goals are attained. Price of company stock at end of performance period (or other valuation criteria) determines value of payout.	Shares of stock are subject to restrictions on transferability with a substantial risk of forfeiture, and are granted to employee without cost (or at a bargain price).	Employee is awarded units (not representing any ownership interest) corresponding in number and value to a specified number of shares of stock. When units mature, they are revalued to reflect the current value of the stock.
Characteristics	• Option price is not less than fair market value on date of grant. • Option must be granted within ten years of adoption or shareholder approval, whichever is earlier, and granted options must be exercised within ten years of grant.	• May be granted at price below fair market value. • Option period is typically ten years. • Vesting restrictions are typical. • Previously acquired company stock may be used as full or partial payment for the	• May be granted alone or in conjunction with stock options. • A specified maximum value may be placed on amount of appreciation that may be received. • Distribution may be made in cash or stock or both in amount equal to the growth in	• Awards earned are directly related to achievement during performance period. • Performance periods are typically from three to five years. • Grants usually are made every one to two years as continuing incentive device.	• Shares become available to employee as restrictions lapse—generally upon completion of a period of continuous employment. • Individual has contingent ownership until restrictions lapse. • Dividend equivalents	• Award may be equal to value of shares of phantom stock or just the appreciation portion. • Dividend equivalents may be credited to account or paid currently. • Benefit can be paid in cash or stock or both.

EXHIBIT 16-1
(continued)

Incentive Stock Options	Nonqualified Stock Option Plans	Stock Appreciation Rights	Performance Share/Unit Plans	Restricted Stock Plans	Phantom Stock Plans
• $100,000 limitation on total amount that first becomes exercisable in a given year (measured on date of grant). • Pre-1987 options must be exercised in the order given. • Previously acquired stock may be used as payment medium for the exercise of incentive stock options. • Written approval of shareholders (within 12 months before or after adoption).	exercise of nonqualified stock options. • Shareholder approval is generally required by SEC and stock exchanges. (Note: pending SEC rule change.)	value of the underlying stock. • Shareholder approval is generally required by SEC and stock exchanges. (Note: pending SEC rule change.)	• Payments are made in cash or stock or combination. • Shareholder approval is required by SEC if paid in stock. (Note: pending SEC rule change.)	can be paid or credited to the employee's account. • Shareholder approval is generally required by SEC and stock exchanges. (Note: pending SEC rule change.)	• Generally, shareholder approval is required by SEC if value paid in stock. (Note: pending SEC rule change.)

Federal Income Tax Considerations
Employee

Incentive Stock Options	Nonqualified Stock Option Plans	Stock Appreciation Rights	Performance Share/Unit Plans	Restricted Stock Plans	Phantom Stock Plans
• Employee does not recognize income upon grant or exercise. • Any appreciation in value from grant to date of sale is long-term capital gains if the stock is held for at least one year from date of exercise and two years from	• No tax consequences at time of grant. • The excess of stock's market value at exercise over option price is taxable as ordinary income. • Any appreciation in value from exercise date to date of sale is	• No taxable income when stock appreciation rights granted. • Upon exercise, the amount received is taxable as ordinary income. • For a stand-alone right with an apprciation	• No taxable income on date performance shares/units are awarded. • Taxable income recognized on the date the award is paid.	• No taxable income at time of award if stock is subject to substantial risk of forfeiture (unless employee election described below). • Excess of fair market value of stock over employee cost is taxable as ordinary income	• No taxable income at time shares of phantom stock are awarded. • The value of the award paid is taxable as ordinary income. • Any dividend equivalents received are taxable as ordinary income.

date of grant. However, since 1988 capital gains have been taxed as or-dinary income.	long-term capital gains if the stock is held for more than one year.	limitation, taxable income occurs when specified maximum appreciation is attained.	when restrictions lapse. • Alternatively, employee may elect within 30 days from date of grant to be taxed on the stock value at grant over employee cost. If stock is forfeited, no deductible loss is available. • Any dividends received during period of restriction are taxed as ordinary income unless early tax payment is elected.		

Employer

• No business expense (compensation) deduc-tion allowed to em-ployer.	• Tax deduction in the amount, and at the time, the employee realizes ordinary income.	• Tax deduction in the amount, and at the time, the employee realizes ordinary income.	• Tax deduction in the amount (including dividends), and at the time, the employee realizes ordinary income.	• Tax deduction in the amount, and at the time, the employee realizes ordinary income.	• Tax deduction in the amount (including dividends), and at the time, the employee realizes ordinary income.

Accounting Considerations

• No accounting expense under current FASB rules required upon grant or exercise of in-centive stock options. • There is a possible dilu-tion as the number of outstanding stock op-tions is considered in calculating earnings per share.	• Generally, under current FASB rules, no accounting expense required if option price equals market value on date of grant. • There is a possible dilution as the number of outstanding stock options is considered in calculating earnings per share.	• Estimated expense is accrued quarterly from date of grant to date of exercise. Expense generally is equal to the amount of appreciation during each year. Restrictions on exercise may affect the amount of accrual. • For combination plans permitting choice between options or	• Estimated expense is accrued annually equal to difference between stock's market value on date of grant and price paid (if any) by employee. • If stock is forfeited, the compensation expense record in previous periods may be reversed to reflect the amount of the forfeiture.	• Estimated expense is accrued quarterly by amortizing the initial value of the awards and subsequent appreciation over the earn-out period based on performance against goal.	• Estimated expense is accrued quarterly by amortizing the initial value of the awards and/or subsequent appreciation over the maturity period. • Payment or crediting of dividend equivalents is expensed at the time of payment or credit.

EXHIBIT 16-1
(*continued*)

Incentive Stock Options	Nonqualified Stock Option Plans	Stock Appreciation Rights	Performance Share/Unit Plans	Restricted Stock Plans	Phantom Stock Plans
Comments • Payment of property or cash (stock appreciation rights) may accompany the exercise of incentive stock options.	• Can be constructed using formula-related stock (e.g., book value shares) rather than publicly traded shares. • Corporate insiders may defer taxable gain (for six months) provided the sale of optioned stock could give rise to a profit under SEC Rule 16(b). (Note: pending SEC rule change.)	rights, compensation cost is measured according to the most likely choice. • If stock appreciation right is paid in cash, special SEC rules require that exercise occur at designated times throughout fiscal year for executives subject to Rule 16(b). (Note: pending SEC rule change.)	• Occasionally used in combination with nonqualified options with performance share value designed to avoid open-ended expense liability. • Can be constructed using formula-related stock rather than publicly traded shares.	• Minimal or no employee financing required. • Timing of removal of restrictions may be related to company performance goals.	• May be used as a self-contained plan or as a deferral vehicle for annual incentive plan awards.

EXHIBIT 16-2
Effectiveness of Long-Term Plans

	Stock Options	SARs	Phantom Stock	Restricted Stock	Performance Shares	Performance Units/Long-Term Bonus
1. Align executive interests with the long-term interests of shareholders	●	●	●	●	●	◐
2. Retain executives	◐	◐	●	●	◐	◐
3. Focus on longer-term performance/reinforce long-term planning process	◐	◐	◐	◐	●	●
4. Provide means of estate-building/long-term capital accumulation	●	●	●	●	●	◐
5. Provide competitive compensation	◐	◐	●	●	●	●

Potential for Meeting Objectives

● Significant Potential ◐ Some Potential ○ Little or No Potential decade, total annual shareholder return (share price appreciation plus dividends) was less than 7 percent.[10] In the same period, companies focused on creating cash bonus plans to replace stock options.

There was a steady movement away from stock compensation as a percentage of an executive's total compensation. In 1970, a CEO could expect to receive options with a value of approximately 4.5 times his annual salary.[11] By 1980, this multiple had fallen to 1.3.[12] The rationale for this approach was that long-term incentives, particularly stock incentives, were of limited value given the lack of stock market movement. Unanswered was the question of whether added executive incentives were appropriate given the lack of shareholder return.

An additional factor was at work as well. The tax code has historically favored stock compensation: A favorable capital gains tax rate was an integral part of the code, and since 1963, there had been "qualified" stock options, which encouraged the use of stock compensation (qualified in terms of being eligible for special tax treatment under Section 421 of the Internal Revenue Code of 1954). In 1976, the qualified stock option was removed from the tax code. As a result, the only stock options that could be granted thereafter were the nonqualified options that now comprise the bulk of stock compensation. At the time, this change was perceived as a blow to stock compensation, although the actual impact on executives and their companies was minimal.

Stock Compensation in the 1980s

The 1980s saw the renaissance of stock compensation, in large measure because of the resurgence of the stock market beginning in August 1981. Whereas the performance of the Standard & Poor's 500 for the 1970s was marginally better than a passbook savings account, in the period from August 1980 through August 1988 the index increased at better than 12 percent annually, with total shareholder return exceeding 15 percent.[13] Although stock option multiples for executives have not returned to their 1970 levels, for CEOs they have increased to a median value of about 3.6 times salary.[14] Coupled with the improved stock market conditions of the 1980s, the gain opportunity available to executives through stock plans as a multiple of salary is two to six times that of the mid- to late 1970s.[15]

Additionally, the 1980s saw the growth of the ultimate stock compensation vehicle, the management-led leveraged buyout (LBO). In a classic case of the potential rewards of this ultimate form of stock compensation, the executives of Allegheny Ludlum took a lackluster company private at a cost of $178 million (of which only $20 million constituted common equity) and in the course of seven years built up the company to the point where the executive holdings were worth $412 million, resulting in a 35 percent annual return on their investment.

In addition to the resurgence of stock compensation at senior levels, the 1980s saw the expanded use of stock compensation at lower levels. This is a trend in many startup companies, particularly prevalent in high-technology industries, where it is common to give stock options to most if not all employees.[16] Further, it reflects a growing emphasis on pay-for-performance at all levels.

This resurgence of stock compensation was accompanied by the return of qualified stock options in a new form: incentive stock options (ISOs). Similar in concept to the qualified stock option, where, after an appropriate holding period, all gains are capital gains, the ISO provides for a shorter holding period (one year after exercise instead of three) at the expense of limiting the amount that could be issued to an executive in a year and the order in which they could be exercised.

The rekindled interest in stock compensation increased steadily until Black Monday—the October crash of 1987. Suddenly, in a reprise of the early 1970s, executives and their companies were rethinking the place of stock in executive compensation packages. One survey reported that approximately half of the companies surveyed anticipated deemphasizing stock compensation in the wake of the crash.[17]

Lessons of the 1970s and 1980s

As noted earlier, stock compensation is designed to tie together the interests of the shareholder and management. This would theoretically be the case in both bull and bear markets, regardless of tax and accounting treatment.

In practice, companies have tended to mold their compensation plans to reflect the opportunity for executive gain rather than corporate performance. When the stock market stagnated in the 1970s, companies turned to increased annual incentive awards and formula-based cash plans. When the market recovered in the early 1980s, stock compensation returned to prominence. Now, at the start of the 1990s, stock plans are being examined yet again. Additionally, even in the 1980s, the primary stock vehicle was options, the stock vehicle that insulates the executive from poor stock performance.[18]

THE PRESENT: STOCK COMPENSATION AT THE CROSSROADS

As we enter the 1990s, stock compensation is under renewed pressure from the usual suspects: the stock market, tax laws, and accounting rules.

The Stock Market

In the aftermath of the 1987 crash, a majority of companies surveyed were considering a change in their long-term compensation structure to deemphasize the stock component. This is the same reaction of the 1970s and early 1980s: follow the market.

What this reaction fails to address is whether there is a reason to unlink the performance of the executive from the performance of the stock. If the primary mission of the executive is to maximize shareholder wealth, there should be a direct correlation between that return and the executive's return, in both bull and bear markets; consequently, the use of stock compensation should be immune to market shifts. Historically, this has not been true.

If there are some aspects of market performance that are not affected by management actions and from which executives should be insulated (on the theory that you should not reward or penalize on the basis of actions beyond the control of the individual), stock compensation is still appropriate and can be, to some extent, protected from nonmanagement market shifts through the use of peer comparisons. For instance, if the stock of Company A performs no better or worse than that of other companies in the same sector, have the managers provided shareholder value? To the extent that they have successfully insulated their firm from market downturns or are better positioned for general economic improvements, an argument can be made to reward the managers even in a generally falling market. This approach is currently receiving significant attention in the savings and loan and utility industries, where outside factors (interest rates and weather, for example) can have a significant impact on company performance.

An example of an effective peer group plan is the performance stock plan used at United Illuminating: if the company cannot achieve median performance in a group of its peers, no award is paid; for employees to earn a full award, the company must perform at least at the 90th percentile.

A peer group measure, however, must be a two-edged sword: if performance is below peer performance in a bull market, rewards should be adjusted downward. This approach is, however, the exception rather than the rule. The interest in peer company comparison tends to be highest among those companies in a suffering industry such as the thrifts, where a company outperforms its peers in "damage control," not gain maximization.

Tax Law Changes

The Tax Reform Act of 1986 supposedly dealt a serious blow to stock compensation by eliminating the favorable taxation of long-term capital gains. In practical terms, the act eliminated what had been a tacit federal subsidy for stock compensation. In its most extreme case (ISOs), the change created an additional tax of up to 13 percent on stock compensation.[19]

This "added" tax cost has merely served to make the playing field level for all forms of compensation: cash, stock, or perquisite. Equalization has not made stock compensation a *less* efficient compensation vehicle than cash, it is simply no longer *more* efficient. The underlying argument that stock compensation serves to bind the shareholder and the manager together remains intact.

Accounting Concerns

The Financial Accounting Standards Board has made changes (and is considering others) that reduce the attractiveness of stock compensation from an accounting standpoint. Currently, there is no accounting charge for market value stock options and the accounting charge for other forms of market value stock compensation (e.g., restricted stock or stock grants) is generally lower than the actual value of the compensation delivered to the executive.[20]

In 1988, the Emerging Issues Task Force (EITF) of the FASB ruled that book value plans of publicly traded companies would create a charge to earnings in a manner similar to SARs.[21] As a result, there is now disparate treatment of market-based and formula-based stock plans, a disparity that is difficult to explain in a manner that makes economic sense.

The FASB has also been reconsidering the treatment of market-based stock compensation since the early 1980s. Based on the 1988 FASB deliberations, there would be both a current compensation charge to earnings, based on a formula, and an ongoing dilution of earnings, based on the shares represented by the stock compensation. By September 1988, the proposal to create a charge based on a "fair value" of the compensation at the time of vesting had been tabled, pending a broader review of general equity versus debt issues.[22] By January 1990, the FASB had moved no closer to resolving this issue, although from past experience it may resurface as early as 1991.

In theory, the tax law changes and the proposed FASB revisions remove the previous subsidies provided to stock compensation and place all types of compensation on the same level. Some analysts have suggested that these changes will, in fact, signal a permanent reduction in the use of, or even the elimination of, stock compensation.[23] This claim is an overstatement of the situation, as the economic cost of the compensation does not change.

Competitive Pressures

A principle of stock compensation is to reward executives for increasing shareholder wealth. One question left unresolved in the 1970s and 1980s is what is the appropriate level of reward? There is probably no single or simple answer to the question. By providing long-term compensation opportunities, companies encounter competing pressures: Competitive practice, the specific needs of the company, and executive retention needs must be balanced against what the shareholder surrenders in terms of equity. Each year various publications compile tables of executives who generate the most shareholder return per dollar of compensation. The highest-paid executives are not necessarily those who provide the greatest shareholder return.[24] Does this mean that their compensation structure is inappropriate? Not necessarily.

Executive talent across industries is not necessarily fungible. Although executives such as John Sculley can move from comestibles to computers, these moves are not common. Executives are more likely to remain in their broadly defined industry and incentive targets will vary depending on that industry. For example, executives in more mature or more stable sectors such as insurance or utilities will generally have lower incentive levels than their counterparts in mortgage banking or high-technology firms.[25]

THE FUTURE FOR STOCK COMPENSATION

The stock market does not move in one direction only; tax laws are not as favorable as they once were; proposed accounting changes would increase the accounting cost of stock compensation. These elements would suggest that the future of stock compensation is at best limited, at worst finished. This is not, in fact, the case.

Stock market swings and tax and accounting changes do not affect the underlying rationale of stock compensation, for several reasons.

Market Movement

Historically, the use of stock compensation has followed the stock market, supposedly because in a bad investment environment it is not possible to provide adequate incentives to executives. To the extent that executives are not creating shareholder wealth, it is questionable whether there is performance that should be rewarded.

This short-term market focus tends to ignore the fact that stock compensation focuses on the longer term. Stock options, for example, generally have a ten-year exercise period. Many of the executives currently bemoaning the "worthlessness" of their options are the same ones who saw their "worthless" options of the late 1970s become their 1980s' nest egg.

Tax and Accounting "Subsidies"

The tax benefits of stock compensation have been reduced for the time being. In bemoaning this lost subsidy, executives and companies are overlooking three points.

First, stock compensation is treated no more harshly than other compensation. To the extent that stock compensation still provides for executive timing of the recognition of income (as is the case with stock options and stock appreciation rights), there is a valuable tax benefit that is not available for most nonstock compensation.

Second, under current tax law, nonqualified stock options are *more* cost efficient than ISOs under the "old" tax law, as shown in Exhibit 16-3.

Third, we have been through this before: Tax laws are constantly changing as government places more emphasis on revenue sources. For example, there are proposals to restore capital gains preference, which would theoretically make stock more attractive again. Tax change, however, should be viewed in the same way as New England weather: Since it changes constantly and nothing can be done about it, plan for the worst, hope for the best, and do not let it be the deciding factor in your plans.

The same is true of the accounting issues. Recent proposals would create a book charge to earnings. It is not certain at this time whether the

EXHIBIT 16-3
Stock Option Efficiency

Assumptions:
1. $50,000 of executive gain
2. Executive is always in highest marginal tax bracket
3. Corporation is always in highest marginal tax bracket

Return to Executive

	Pretax Reform		Post-Tax Reform	
	ISO	*NQSO*	*ISO*	*NQSO*
Gain	$50,000	$50,000	$50,000	$50,000
Taxes	(10,000)	(25,000)	(14,000)	(14,000)
Net Cost to Company	$40,000	$25,000	$36,000	$36,000

	ISO	*NQSO*	*ISO*	*NQSO*
Pretax Cost	$50,000	$50,000	$50,000	$50,000
Tax Benefit	(0)	(23,000)	(0)	(17,000)
Net Cost	$50,000	$27,000	$50,000	$33,000
Efficiency				
Benefit to Executive	$40,000	$25,000	$36,000	$36,000
Cost to Company	$50,000	$27,000	$50,000	$33,000
Efficiency (benefit divided by cost)	0.80	0.93	0.72	1.09

charge will be greater than that associated with cash compensation; however, it must be noted that regardless of the charge, it will be an accounting charge only. The FASB proposals will have no impact whatsoever on the cash flow and shareholder value associated with stock compensation. As a result, it is an issue to be aware of in plan design, but it should not be a prime factor in plan choice.

Shortcomings of Nonequity Alternatives

Perhaps the prime reason why stock compensation is still appropriate is that none of the alternatives provide the same or similar benefits in an efficient manner. Specifically, nonstock vehicles cannot directly tie executive returns to shareholder wealth, and provide the potential for tax benefits (capital gains if reinstated and executive timing flexibility) in a manner that is cash efficient.

Since stock compensation remains a viable compensation vehicle, even if it is under repeated siege, what then does the future hold for it? If the future creates a level playing field for all forms of compensation, we can stop trying to fit plans into regulatory straitjackets in order to maximize the benefits associated with specific tax and accounting rules and refocus attention on the true value of stock compensation: rewarding executives for creating shareholder wealth. The elimination of subsidies gives us the opportunity to reexamine useful tools that have been ignored because they did not take advantage of the former subsidies. Specifically, we need to look at:

1. *Performance-based plans*. Current accounting rules create a charge to earnings for plans that only vest based on performance. In a subsidy-free environment, the relative cost of performance-based plans is reduced, so there will be more opportunity to link pay and performance.

   Few companies now tie stock option vesting to corporate financial performance. Thus, the plan ensures that the executive will not reap a windfall if stock prices rise without underlying corporate economic improvement. Conversely, if economic performance exists without shareholder return, options will vest quickly, but the executive's reward is deferred until the shareholders benefit from price rises. For example, Texas Instruments, a company with a broad distribution of stock options among employees, has a form of performance-based vesting tied to cumulative earnings per share over a ten-year period. If performance is exceptional, all options could mature in several years. Alternatively, poor performance would result in the options being unexercisable until just before expiration. Under the Texas Instruments plan, all options will eventually vest, to avoid the accounting charge. In a neutral environment, if performance were poor enough, no options would vest, and therefore there would be no reward for below-threshold performance.

   The same reasoning holds true for performance shares. Currently, the use of performance-based restricted stock is limited because of accounting considerations. In a nonsubsidized environment, the performance-based plans become more attractive.

2. *Peer group plans*. Another form of performance evaluation is the measurement of the performance of a corporation against that of its competitors. One complaint about stock compensation plans is that they react more to market trends than to corporate performance. This concern can be addressed by tying vesting to the performance of a company versus that of its peers. The approach may be especially valid in the case of companies where short-term stock price performance is, in large measure, beyond the control of corporate executives.

This approach must be used with care, however, to ensure that the peer group is legitimate: If the peer group is selected by the participants, it is possible to "stack the deck" with poorly performing companies. To maintain objectivity, selection should be made by the compensation committee of the company's board of directors. By choosing the highest-quality peer group, it ensures that the performance goals represent truly outstanding performance.

3. *Discounted stock options (DSOs)*. Options issued at less than fair market value are becoming more common, primarily as a deferred compensation device for directors, as at Hewlett-Packard. Currently, only a few companies, such as Hospital Corporation of America, provide discounted stock options to executives as well as directors. Their use on a broader basis has been limited by accounting costs, by the reduced opportunity for capital gains, and, to some extent, by concern that the IRS will determine that some forms of DSOs result in immediate recognition of income. As the first two concerns become less important, DSOs should become increasingly popular, because they are the only deferred compensation device that gives the executive complete control over the timing of compensation without constructive receipt problems. The third concern can be addressed by properly pricing the DSOs to avoid the possibility of their being considered substantially equal to grants of the stock itself.

4. *Tandem plans*. Accounting costs currently may limit the use of "tandem" long-term incentive compensation plans that provide a payment in either cash or stock at the discretion of the board of directors, since there may be an accounting charge created if it appears likely that the cash component of a plan will be paid. To the extent that accounting charges are leveled, tandem plans that provide stock or cash compensation become more viable.

5. *Stock appreciation rights*. Current wisdom and accounting rules limit the use of SARs to those executives subject to the limits of Section 16(b) of the Securities and Exchange Commission Act of 1934. This is another area where the accounting subsidy may distort the compensation market. To the extent that a company wishes to reward executives for stock price movement (as opposed to specifically encouraging executive stock ownership), SARs are the ideal vehicle: they require no cash commitment, are fully deductible to the company when paid, and require no actual stock transfers, resulting in administrative efficiency. Their only current drawback is their accounting cost. If all stock compensation generates similar accounting

costs, then the SAR will come into its own at all management levels, not just at the corporate officer level.

CONCLUSIONS

Stock compensation is not a thing of the past. Potentially, it is more useful than ever. In a subsidy-free environment, more attention can be focused on achieving the company's compensation objectives.

The stock market crash should not have a major impact on compensation planning. Stock market movement is not a reason to adopt or reject stock compensation plans; rather, it is the measure of performance, the scoring mechanism. The market measures whether executives have improved shareholder wealth.

In the 1990s, we should see an increase in the variety of forms of stock compensation. What remains to be determined is the degree to which corporations will retain a commitment to shareholder value as the corporate goal worthy of long-term measurement and reward. If companies abandon stock compensation and return to accounting-based, long-term cash compensation plans, where the rewards are not linked directly to shareholder return, we will have a replay of the 1970s, when the tracking of executive compensation and shareholder return was more coincidence than compensation.

NOTES

1. Comparison based on computation of data from sources compiled in the Sibson & Co., Inc., "15th Annual Study Executive Compensation," 1981, and Sibson & Co., Inc., "Executive Compensation, 23rd Edition," 1988.

2. Proxy analysis 1985–1988, performed by the author.

3. Sibson, "Executive Compensation, 23rd Edition," p. 95.

4. Sibson & Co., Inc., "1987 Executive Long-Term Incentive Survey," pp. 2–8.

5. Edison Electric Institute, "1988 Executive Compensation Study."

6. Sibson, "Executive Long-Term Incentive Survey."

7. Ibid.

8. For example, based on a telephone survey of ninety-eight large manufacturing, service, financial, and utility companies conducted in April and May of 1988, 50 percent have eliminated the use of incentive stock options in response to the elimination of favorable income tax treatment for long-term capital gains by the Tax Reform Act of 1986.

9. Standard & Poor, *The Outlook*, weekly publication, various dates.

10. Ibid.

11. Sibson & Co., Inc., "Sixth Annual Management Compensation Study," 1971.

12. Sibson, "15th Annual Study Executive Compensation."

13. Standard & Poor, *The Outlook*, various dates.

14. Sibson, "Executive Compensation, 23rd Edition," p. 109.

15. Ibid.

16. In high-technology companies, 32 percent include all nonexempt employees, 73 percent include select nontechnical staff, 85 percent include select technical staff, and 98 percent include middle management. By contrast, in general industry, only 4 percent of companies provide options to more than 50 percent of employees, while 44 percent limit them to less than 6 percent of employees. Radford Associates, "Radford Associates Executive Compensation Survey—Spring 1987," and Sibson & Co., Inc., "1988 Management Compensation Survey."

17. Sibson & Co., Inc., telephone survey conducted April–May 1988 of ninety-eight large manufacturing, service, financial, and utility companies. Reported in Sibson, "Executive Compensation, 23rd Edition."

18. Sixty-one percent of all stock-based plans are stock option plans. Sibson & Co., Inc., "Executive Compensation, 24th edition," 1989.

19. For individuals subject to the phase-out of the 15 percent bracket.

20. The FASB has for some time considered creating a charge to earnings for stock compensation, through a revision of APB Opinion 25. Under the current APB Opinion 25 rules, stock compensation is valued for accounting charge purposes at the time the number of shares becomes fixed. The charge is the value of the compensation element at that time. For stock options, this will be zero (unless the options are issued at a discount from market price); for restricted stock, the price at grant will (hopefully) be less than the price when the restrictions lapse.

21. EITF Issue #87-23 issued April 21, 1988, and EITF Issue #88-6 issued June 2, 1988.

22. Announced at FASB meeting, September 14, 1988.

23. Frederic W. Cook & Co., Inc., "The High Cost of Stock Options," August 3, 1988.

24. See, for example, "Who Made the Most—and Why," *BusinessWeek*, May 2, 1988.

25. Radford Associates, "Executive Compensation Survey;" Edison Electric Institute, "1988 Executive Compensation Survey;" and Sibson, "Executive Compensation, 24th Edition."

PART II-C

The Administration of Compensation

17

COMMUNICATING EXECUTIVE COMPENSATION PLANS

Evan B. Dean and Fred W. Meuter, Jr.

INTRODUCTION

A successful executive compensation process is participatory. Its ultimate value is determined by the level of understanding, involvement, and support of the executives participating in it. Because participants must believe that the opportunities offered by the program are real and based on factors they can influence, the success of the plan depends on effective communication.

This need for understanding, involvement, and commitment from the participants argues strongly that a chief executive should veto an executive compensation plan that may be a designer's dream but is so complicated and confusing that few participants would fully understand it. Rather, management should favor a plan that may contain only 80 percent of the design features possible, but lends itself easily to communication and understanding.

Over the past thirty years, we have been involved with a large number of executive compensation plans and planners. We are convinced that the establishment of an effective communications program and the process for developing that program are as essential to a compensation plan's success as are its design features.

COMMUNICATIONS: WORTH THE EFFORT

It is true that a well-designed executive compensation plan can help an organization focus effort and attention on specific goals **and** exert some holding leverage on key executives. Because of this fact, companies allocate a significant part of an executive's total compensation to incentive plans tailored to meet a variety of needs. A great deal of time and money is spent on developing new compensation approaches to meet competitive pressures, address business problems, or support new strategic directions.

Unfortunately, in too many cases the communication of the objectives and mechanics of the plan does not receive the same degree of management attention. Often the result is the implementation of a plan that fails to deliver the intended results because the executives do not understand the objectives or are unable to identify the actions they can take to support the organization's goals.

For example, one large high-tech company implemented a performance unit plan designed to increase the firm's return on assets only to discover, after the completion of a full payout cycle, that the majority of the participants did not understand what they could do to make an impact on return on assets. Had the company followed a process that solicited input from executives before the plan was finalized (as it does today), a communications program that included training in asset management would have been a key component of the implementation process for the long-term incentive plan.

This kind of faulty communication leads many executives to view their total compensation program as a "Pandora's box," full of sometimes unpleasant and unexpected surprises. Thus, it is hardly surprising that they read other companies' proxies with more than a passing interest, or accept the headhunter's call. These executives understand neither the strategic concepts and objectives that serve as the foundation of their program, nor the potential payouts available for taking the appropriate actions encouraged by the plan.

For example, several years ago an executive came to us to exercise a nonqualified option that was about to expire. The option had been granted in recognition of his promotion to executive status. The grant had been accompanied by a strong message about the value the company placed on an executive's eligibility to participate in the stock option program, the company's desire to have its executives own stock, and the executive's obligations to treat the option as long-term investment.

Although the option had been granted at the market price of the stock on the date of the grant, the stock price had subsequently declined and at the time the executive was going to exercise, the option price was higher than the market price of the stock. Even though the option was "underwater" and should have been allowed to expire, the executive believed, based on the earlier communications, that the company expected him to exercise and hold the stock for future gain. Clearly, only a part of what should have been communicated came through.

Fortunately, there is an increasing awareness of the necessity for the effective communication of total compensation. Although there is still a wide disparity in the level of communication expertise, CEOs are beginning to hold their compensation professionals responsible for not only good plan design, but also the communication effort required to ensure that plans will be effectively implemented and understood so an incident such as we have cited above will not occur.

Why should a corporation launch a communication effort? Why not limit the data provided to the participants and thereby avoid difficult questions that might arise? After all, compensation programs are "confidential." Why risk letting nonparticipants learn the details? There are still many executives who believe that the "closed book" approach is valid and that a formal communication program means a loss of personal privacy and the beginning of restrictions on a company's discretion to act.

We, however, believe that when people know little, they tend to expect the worst. Experience has convinced us that a well-conceived and correctly implemented communication effort will provide the dialogue that offers positive results both for the company and the executive. Good communication provides immediate returns by clarifying the compensation program's objectives, by involving the executive as a member of the team, and by helping to create positive values that will have a lasting impact on an organization's culture.

From the Company's Perspective

The company stands to gain the most if an effective communication program is put in place. Companies that avoid telling the plan's "story" are losing the maximum impact for the dollars and time spent in designing, implementing, and operating executive compensation plans.

An effective communication process serves management objectives in several ways.

First, the CEO can define what he or she wants done. In an environment driven by increasing competition and fast-paced technological change, executive compensation can be an important factor in establishing a competitive advantage. The communication process supporting the compensation plan offers an ongoing opportunity for the CEO to define exactly what is expected of the management team. The chief executive officer, who has the ultimate responsibility for achieving the company's stated goals, should play the key role in shaping that message in the clearest way possible.

Second, senior management can inspire executives with whom it does not have regular contact to act in ways that support the company's goals and long-term strategies. Many executive compensation plans such as stock option plans or annual incentive plans reach well down the ranks of middle management. When communication efforts are directed to these executives, they "buy into" the CEO's goals and strategies more readily and become partners in the enterprise. They can better understand how they can contribute to the organization's success and why their resistance could cause its failure.

Third, the company can motivate participants by showing them the potential value of the awards/instruments held. Many executive compensation plans are designed to motivate the participants. However, if the participant does not understand the true present or future value of a stock option or a performance unit, the leverage in an annual bonus plan, or the protection offered by a SERP, it is doubtful that much, if any, motivation will result. If participants understand all the factors that can affect payouts, the company may get a significantly higher yield from the dollars expended on the compensation plan.

Fourth, the company can demonstrate to its executives that its compensation plans are competitive. Factual information, which explains what the company offers in clear and appealing terms, can be effective in reducing executives' concern about their relative relationships to the marketplace. Although very few companies offer executive compensation programs that are positive in all aspects, most firms can build a total compensation opportunity that stands up well in their competitive environment. There is nothing wrong in admitting to what may be a shortfall in a particular plan if the total program stacks up well. Shortfalls, however, do not have to be highlighted when the compensation program is explained to the participating executives. Conversely, a company should not hesitate to emphasize in the most persuasive and attractive way those aspects of its program that compare favorably with those of its benchmark competitors.

Fifth, management can clear up possible confusion and misunderstandings, which damage the overall effectiveness of a compensation program. A well-designed communication program can eliminate many of the misunderstandings that, if not corrected, lead to the spread of inaccurate and misleading data through the informal communication network. Proliferation of bad data through the grapevine damages the overall effectiveness of a company's program.

Further, if a company has an ongoing dialogue with its executives, any future effort required to clarify or reinforce an aspect of the program or redirect efforts toward a changed goal is less likely to be viewed with suspicion.

From the Executive's Perspective

In the early 1960s, the design of executive compensation programs was straightforward and uncluttered. In most cases, the program was composed of two basic elements of direct compensation: base salary and a short-term incentive or bonus plan. The size of the salary increase often served as a substitute for any more formal attempt at an annual performance review. The actual amount of incentive or bonus payment, typically a share of the profits or an award made on a discretionary basis, also reflected management's judgment of performance. When stock options were used, the grant was often at the CEO's discretion. There were no formal published guidelines and little additional formal communication was required. The minimal approach was considered adequate at the time. Communication between the executive and superior was, at best, limited to the essentials. The company was in control.

Today, the situation is very different. Complex plans and complex laws have greatly complicated the decision-making process and created the need for better, faster, and more detailed information. Executives have more varied backgrounds and differing goals and aspirations than those of previous generations. They insist that the communication effort be tailored specifically to their individual situations.

Today's executives are a more financially sophisticated audience than they were twenty-five years ago. They are better educated and have better financial advice available to them. They want assurance that the plans offer gains that are achievable with realistic efforts. They are more likely to question the reasons for new or modified plans. They are critical of the ability of the company to meet the performance targets established and may challenge the potential values offered.

The competitive environment of the 1980s has forced many companies to take cost reduction actions resulting in manpower and salary reductions, salary freezes, and benefit plan redesigns that shift costs and require more financial participation by the executive. All of these actions, particularly those aimed at reducing manpower levels, have eroded the social contract that once existed between executive and company. Communication efforts that confront these facts and take into account the career concerns and needs of its executives are essential if a company is to compete successfully.

THE COMMUNICATION PROCESS

Effective communication is a process, not a product. The process is continuous and must take into account the opportunities and limitations that are created and constantly changing in any business environment.

An executive compensation communication process does not exist in isolation. It must be a part of, or build from, the overall communication environment in the organization. At a minimum, an executive communication process cannot conflict with the overall approach to communication in the company and the process used to explain pay and benefits programs to the general work force.

An executive compensation plan establishes a complex relationship between the participants and the company. On the one hand, the plans and programs can be powerful tools to stimulate executives to support company strategies and fulfill company goals. On the other hand, in a properly designed plan actions taken by the executive on the company's behalf will operate in his or her own interest.

Establishing a successful communication process is a major undertaking. It requires thorough analysis, considerable planning, and cooperation from senior managers, professional staff, and participants as well as other parties with a vested interest in the plan. It is a time-consuming, intensive process that, once established, becomes a valuable tool in the management and future development of a company's total compensation plans.

Step One: Develop the Strategy

The communication process should start before the plan design is complete. The company must identify what it wants to achieve with the plan and what the participants must do to make the plan successful. At a minimum, a communication effort must be targeted at these two imperatives. By involving those responsible for communication at an early stage of plan design, possible communication approaches can be identified and adjustments to the plan design could result. With a tentative communication strategy in mind, the communication specialists are in a better position to solicit input from those who will be affected by the plan.

Step Two: Identify the Audiences

After the communication strategy has been determined, a firm needs to identify the audiences and analyze their requirements. Once the audiences have been identified and their needs outlined, the program can be tailored appropriately.

Participating executives.   The most important audience is the participating executive. An effective communication program educates plan participants about the objectives and advantages of the program; explains clearly the program's objectives; and addresses the executives' concerns about the impact on and the confidentiality of their personal financial situation.

A company must consider a number of communication design issues. Among them: How do the executives want to receive information about the plan? Do they recognize and relate to the total compensation picture? Will they perceive the link between direct pay, annual incentives, long-term incentives, perquisites, and the qualified benefit plans offered to all employees? Do they know how their job objectives fit into the plan and what they can accomplish by good performance? Will they understand and take advantage of the company's nonqualified benefit or supplemental plans? These are just a sampling of the issues that designers must explore before a communication plan is developed.

The best way to identify these issues is by conducting interviews or small group meetings with a sample of the participants. Feedback can also be gathered directly from executives through a short survey.

A truly effective communication program, however, is not limited to executives. The following other audiences must be considered as well.

Specialized professional staffs.   Meetings with the specialized professionals staff such as communications, legal, tax, and accounting are required so that their technical expertise can be utilized. Their early involvement will also help speed the more formal concurrence they must provide before the program is finalized.

Senior management.   One often neglected group is senior management. If a company's executive compensation program has been properly designed, it undoubtedly has been greatly influenced by each member of the senior management team. It is essential that the members of this core group be knowledgeable about the company's total executive compensation program. They must be satisfied that the plans are linked to the company's overall strategies; that the communications ensure executive and operating-unit commitment; and that the costs and rewards under the plan make sense within the planning period utilized by the company.

Board of directors.   Today, the board has a heightened awareness of its responsibility to the shareholders. The compensation committee and the board no longer just accept the CEO's word that a new or revised plan is "good." They want to know how the plan operates and the cost and financial value of the awards to be granted. Our litigious society makes directors, especially outside ones, examine more closely what is presented to them for approval.

An effective working relationship with the board requires both formal and informal communication approaches. Compensation professionals must realize that members of boards have neither the time nor the incentive to listen to or read detailed explanations of new and continuing compensation plans and instruments. Instead, the basic concept of the pay plan and its essential working details must be given to this audience without the technical jargon used by many compensation designers.

Our experience has shown that some corporate directors do not feel comfortable asking basic questions (during a board's compensation committee meeting) about the workings of an executive compensation plan. We have found that informal one-on-one meetings with individual directors on their home turf gives them the opportunity to probe plan designs and ask questions without being placed in a potentially embarrassing situation in the presence of their peers.

This group also needs to be assured that the plan is not only consistent with the policy and strategy of the company but also realistic in the competitive environment.

Nonparticipating employees.   Most companies concentrate on the executives participating in the executive compensation plans. Unfortunately, they forget that there is a hidden audience in the company—those employees who are not participating in the plans. The need to communicate with this group cannot be ignored. Even in companies that maintain a highly confidential approach, word about the executive compensation programs gets out. (Remember the damage done to employee commitment and morale by the disclosure of golden parachutes for a select few executives in proxies? Remember, too, the resultant rush to explain and rationalize their use?)

At a minimum, nonparticipating employees should receive the same information released to the shareholders and the public.

Without a doubt, employees today receive misinformation concerning companies' executive compensation plans from external sources. One indirect but effective way to help increase this audience's general awareness of the company's posture on compensation is to establish a stronger direct communication link between senior management teams and the public. Companies' leaders should not be reluctant to speak out on issues they believe in. And they or their representatives should participate in the legislative process that shapes the laws affecting executive compensation and benefits programs. A proactive stance can help establish a climate where the general employee population is less suspicious of management's motivations.

Step Three: Decide on Methods of Communication

Whether the communication approach is formal or informal depends on the particular culture and market cycle of the company. A company that is in the early stages of a growth cycle and that has an unstructured culture may do best with informal approaches to communication. However, a medium-to-large company with a high degree of stability and structure would probably do best to use a formal approach, even though that approach may be enhanced by additional informal efforts.

Given the organizational culture and having identified the requirements of the audience and the objectives of the communication effort, the communication team can plan a program that achieves the targeted goals.

Many traditional methods that are effective for communicating the broad-based compensation and benefits story are not appropriate for the more limited executive audience. These methods include the company news magazine, bulletin boards, video tapes, operating-unit newsletters, and other vehicles designed for mass audience, nonconfidential communication.

However, the communication specialist has many different methods by which the program can reach its objectives. Obviously, some media are better than others, depending on the intended purpose. For example, the announcement of a stock option plan requires informing all participants quickly about the plan. The information must be sufficient to answer immediate questions so the plan will receive a favorable response. This can be done with a letter from the chief executive, accompanied by a brochure or booklet explaining the key features of the plan. Later, individualized projections of the current and potential value of each participant's award can be made to enable individuals to tailor the option grant to their financial situations. Further, small group meetings may be held, an executive's financial planner may be briefed, and one-on-one counseling sessions can be made available to executives.

As the use of personal computers (PCs) expands, companies are able to offer more personalized communication options. Using a PC, an executive can perform what-if calculations that show the implications of different stock prices on an outstanding option. Or the executive can model how various company or operating-unit return-on-asset or return-on-equity performances might affect a bonus or a performance unit plan.

The communication specialist can select from an increasing array of products the most appropriate method or combination of methods required to deliver the message that meets the needs of the targeted audience.

Step Four: Brief Participant's Financial Advisers

It is essential that the executives' financial advisers understand what their clients hold and how plans work. Otherwise, financial advice may be completely off the mark. The executive compensation expert must keep financial advisers current. The advisers should receive copies of plan documents and communication materials and be briefed in meetings with the compensation expert. External financial advisers can be valuable assets to the compensation manager in the positive implementation of a program. Confused financial advisers, on the other hand, can do substantial damage to executives' perceptions of the value of their compensation programs.

Step Five: Train Line Organization Personnel/ Compensation People

One trap executive compensation specialists fall into is that they become the only source of information about executive compensation plans. There are some plans (i.e., a short-term incentive plan restricted to corporate officers) that should be known only to a limited number of people. But other plans that are more broadly based (i.e., a company's long-term incentive plan) should be widely known and explained and communicated by line personnel or compensation staff.

This can be accomplished by training the compensation and personnel staff in decentralized units in the mechanics and philosophy of the company's executive compensation plans. This approach takes a significant load from the executive compensation manager: he or she will not be faced with endless questions from participants.

Step Six: Package the Communications

Packaging an executive compensation communications program is a vital ingredient in its overall success. It is important to tie together all key documents that may be related. A documentation package that organizes the materials well and that captures the attention of the executives is more likely to be retained and used as a reference source than are a series of seemingly unrelated memos and brochures. Depending on the resources available to the company, the materials can be produced internally or externally.

Step Seven: Evaluate the Program

After the materials have been delivered, and at least once a year thereafter, the compensation manager should analyze the results of the communication process to ensure that it continues to accomplish the goals for which it was designed. The evaluation process employs many of the same approaches used to solicit the initial input for the communication program. It asks executives, line management, and personnel experts through interviews, meetings, and surveys:

1. Is the company achieving or making progress toward the goals the plan was designed to support?
2. Have executives undertaken the activities needed to support the goals of the company?
3. Are the materials clear and understandable?
4. Do they increase an executive's knowledge and understanding of his or her total compensation?
5. Have the personnel specialists received positive or negative feedback from executives?
6. Have any relevant attitude survey scores been improved as a result of the communication effort?
7. Has participation in any programs increased or changed in other ways because of communications?
8. Are decentralized personnel specialists able to handle more inquiries locally?

The evaluation should also analyze the cost of the program and measure the communication cost against industry benchmarks.

SUMMARY

Many business observers have concluded that in the 1980s corporate leaders came to fully recognize the importance of a communication strategy that leads to the involvement of the human resources of the business. If increased competition and the change in the composition of the executive work force have taught us anything about productivity and competitiveness, it is that corporate strategies and corporate goals are not attainable unless and until all executives become involved and committed partners in the business.

The 1990s will be a challenging period. If organizations are to get a return on their investment in executive compensation they must make the effort to find the best communication solution to support the objectives of their executive compensation programs.

Despite the progress that has been made, companies cannot be content to stand still. The ability to direct the process of communication of executive compensation must become one of the skills demanded of today's human resource or compensation executive. This individual must assume the responsibility for planning and directing the communication of the programs in ways that allow each executive to link his or her responsibilities to the company's goals.

18

HOW TO ORGANIZE, STAFF, AND DEVELOP SKILLS WITHIN THE EXECUTIVE COMPENSATION FUNCTION

Bruce Overton

WHEN DESIGNED IN conjunction with business strategies, executive compensation plans have the potential to motivate executives and focus their energies on behavior that directly supports or fulfills organizational goals. But how do chief executive officers and other senior managers structure activities so that executive compensation plans achieve this potential? This chapter addresses the process by which companies develop the role of the executive compensation function, resources needed to support the function, alternatives for organizing and staffing, and ways in which compensation professionals can fulfill and grow within their assigned roles.

Change in business methods affects how companies organize and staff the executive compensation function. New approaches in human resources, planning, taxes, accounting, and law all affect compensation and benefit design, and executive compensation in particular. Because of constant change, the organization and staffing of the executive compensation function should be reviewed regularly.

ROLE DEVELOPMENT

For the senior executive, the process of defining the role of the executive compensation function should start with the annual and long-term strategic business plans of the organization. This analysis should focus on three key questions:

1. What is the future direction of the business (as stated in the strategic plans)?
2. What are the implications of these business goals for the human resource function?

3. What support functions are needed to assist in the achievement of human resource goals?

In companies where business plans and human resource goals require strong support from the executive compensation function, correspondingly strong roles should be established for those responsible for executive compensation. Further, in this business environment, the executive compensation function should be expected to develop strong programs in support of business objectives. All too often, senior managers tolerate executive compensation departments that simply look at what competitors do and peg programs and pay levels to competitive practice. A better approach and one frequently overlooked is to set compensation strategies and programs on the basis of a business plan analysis. Examples of how compensation programs can evolve from corporate strategy follow.

Providing Incentives for Growth

A fast-food company is expanding and projects 15 percent growth in the number of stores over the next three years. This growth, in combination with turnover in existing stores, will necessitate additional staffing (estimates of which are contained in the business plan). The human resource issues are very clear: Where will the extra manpower come from? What quality standards will be established prior to employment? Where and when will stores require new staff? Analysis of the business plan suggests a major role for the executive compensation function and a high-risk/high-reward executive compensation strategy (i.e., higher than typical incentive compensation if specified business goals are achieved).

Compensation programs that could help advance the company's growth strategy include:

1. Short- and long-term incentive plans to reward executives for achievements such as identification of new sites, completion of construction plans, maintenance of or increases in average store sales, and so forth;
2. Field incentives to reward new store openings, increases in per store sales averages, and other achievements that reflect growth; and
3. New pay programs to attract potential store managers from the college campus into company career programs.

Providing Incentives to Develop New Products

A mature durable goods manufacturing company projects a conservative 5 percent growth over the next three years. Its business plan also refers to new products that would take three to four years to develop. If these new products are developed, they could produce 15 percent growth after five years. Again, the business plan suggests a major role for the executive compensation function and a high-risk/high-reward compensation strategy that will attract and retain executives who will lead the product development activities. Such a company should consider the following:

1. Adding new performance goals to the annual bonus plan to reward executives for achieving certain milestone or interim goals in product development during the next three to four years.
2. Introducing special compensation programs to attract new employees with the special skills needed to assist in product development activities. Such programs might include up-front bonuses or restricted stock, enhanced retirement plans, one-time stock option grants at employment, and so forth.
3. Introducing special entrepreneurial incentives that would deliver long-term income to both executives and nonexecutives if the product development goals were achieved. For example, the company might offer stock ownership or substantial long-term income payments, perhaps three to four times normal salary if the product is successful.

These examples show how executive compensation can directly support business objectives. It follows that the role of an executive compensation professional should be properly aligned with corporate strategy. The executive compensation manager should focus primarily on identifying new programs and/or changing programs to support current business needs and help realize corporate objectives rather than on improving the technical aspects of compensation administration.

RESOURCES NEEDED TO SUPPORT THE EXECUTIVE COMPENSATION FUNCTION

The daily activities and planning of a compensation professional require coordination with other functions both within and outside of human resources. Those responsible for organizing the executive compensation program should recognize that at least seven other functions are involved in the establishment of executive compensation strategies.

Planning Department

Line management typically develops the annual and long-term business plans, but many organizations employ planning professionals to provide guidance on procedures, formats, growth assumptions, and so forth. Executive compensation professionals need to tap the expertise of planners so that appropriate performance goals and measures are used in executive pay plans. It is logical to base annual incentives on the objectives of the annual or operating business plan of the organization and to base long-term incentives on the company's strategic or long-term business plan. When incentive plan goals are correlated with business goals, executive pay plans can drive executive behavior in the most appropriate direction.

Accounting Department

The cost of executive compensation programs must be determined through the joint efforts of corporate accountants and compensation experts. Chief executive officers want no surprises when it comes to profit and loss or balance sheet costs, so it is essential to calculate these expenses before their accrual. When compensation program costs are included in budget cycles, they are unlikely to become roadblocks to a successful program. Both initial and ongoing costs must be accurately budgeted. For example, although a CEO or board compensation committee member may understand the grant or target cost of a performance share plan, he or she may not realize that each performance share, if earned, has a value that varies according to stock price. Such an open-ended liability could produce unanticipated costs in future years.

Tax and Legal Departments

Tax experts and lawyers can add considerable value to executive compensation strategies and programs, especially if they are involved early in the development stage. Long-term income programs in particular are subject to a number of legal requirements (i.e., registration with the Securities and Exchange Commission, shareholder approval) as well as to the provisions of the tax code. The company's legal experts not only will provide counsel about individual and company tax liability under various plans, but also will help determine the differences in the treatment of current versus deferred income. Executives are interested in a tax-effective compensation program.

I do not suggest that tax and legal aspects of executive pay should drive plan design. It is important, however, to anticipate and communicate the tax and legal ramifications of executive pay programs to all approving parties and participants. Executives should be told, for example, whether amounts earned from a long-term plan are taxed as ordinary income or capital gains. CEOs should be told before they approve an executive compensation plan whether payments must be published in proxy statements or 10K forms.

Treasury Department

Long-term executive compensation plans that involve the use of company stock can be smartly managed if the treasury department reviews them, for two reasons. First, treasury shares (i.e., shares purchased on the outside market by a company for use in executive compensation plans) are frequently utilized in stock plans. By purchasing the stock when the price is low, the treasury can lower the cost of a stock plan. Second, executive compensation plans cause periodic demands for cash, when plan payments are made. Treasury experts can anticipate such demands by reviewing compensation programs in advance.

Human Resource Department

The obvious can sometimes be overlooked: clearly, labor relations, management development, benefits, employment, and personnel data systems must be coordinated with executive compensation plans through the chief human resource officer. For example, incentive plan payments to executives should be integrated with labor negotiations and contracts. An organization can be seriously disrupted if executive plans are paying large sums of money at a time when labor contracts are not. It is also crucial to integrate benefits with compensation. For instance, if a plan combines bonus payments with salary to calculate pension benefits, proper coordination must take place with benefits and payroll personnel who calculate pensionable earnings.

Line Management

There is little hope for success with an executive compensation plan if line management has not been consulted. Line managers are responsible for implementing compensation programs, and therefore should take part in their development. Because they often are the people who communicate programs to employees, managers can assess how executive compensation plans are received and evaluate their probable success. Line managers often pick up potential flaws or problems, since they usually are not distracted by the technical aspects of a program. The support of line managers is essential to the success of any compensation program or strategy.

Having reviewed the resources that support the executive compensation function, let us now turn to how a compensation professional might establish or audit his or her responsibilities.

RESPONSIBILITIES OF THE EXECUTIVE COMPENSATION FUNCTION

The top executive compensation manager should concentrate primarily on the design and development of pay programs. This involves discussing with top management and participants the objectives and the results of pay programs (i.e., Are existing programs achieving desired behavioral changes and results? How should plan design be amended in response to changes in corporate priorities and the business environment?) The head of executive compensation must study the strategic plans to keep up to date on business goals so that he or she can design new plans or modify existing ones.

The effectiveness of executive compensation programs can be influenced significantly by communication of their provisions and intent. When participants understand what is expected, they are better positioned to achieve plan goals. Therefore, the head of executive compensation must continually monitor and evaluate communication documents, training material, and participant feedback as well as keep informed on the tax, accounting, and legal aspects of executive remuneration. The latter involves technical analysis of whether compensation plans are tax-effective for executives and cost-effective for the company. Keeping current about regulations also involves maintenance activities such as the design of deferral forms that meet IRS constructive receipt requirements, determination of format for stock exercise transactions, review of performance appraisal forms used with annual or long-term income plans, and so forth.

Once plans are introduced, the head of executive compensation must supervise record keeping, data analysis, and payment calculations. Administration of pay plans is becoming more complex and can be the

Achilles' heel of the compensation professional because the margin of error in calculating payments is zero. The job requires designing new systems from time to time to monitor as well as maintain programs.

The head of executive compensation should also prepare agendas, data, and other information for the board compensation committee. In this regard, he or she is fulfilling a key role as the CEO's representative to the committee. This task, more than any other, demands an individual who thinks and acts like a business person (not a technical expert) and who has the experience and maturity to deal with members of the board of directors.

And finally, the compensation head is responsible for developing and maintaining outside contacts. To keep policies and programs up to date, compensation directors must maintain an ongoing exchange with competitive companies, government and regulatory agencies, compensation consultants, and community, business, or professional associations.

Although the responsibilities listed here are typical for both the industrial and service sectors, in the final analysis the compensation professional's role is whatever the head of human resources or the CEO believes it should be. The nature of the job can be influenced significantly by the compensation professional, however, if he or she sees pay as directly relating to and supporting business objectives.

Organizing the Executive Compensation Function

To whom should the executive compensation manager report? What support positions does the function require? There is not, of course, only one way to organize an executive compensation department. What is right for one company is wrong for another. Areas of expertise, individual strengths and weaknesses, and personality are all considerations that should be part of the decision about how to organize the function.

Another important factor is size and type of business. Large companies typically assign executive compensation to a specially trained individual, while smaller organizations typically either assign the job to someone already performing a similar function in the organization or hire outside consultants. A medium-sized company might use one or both of these alternatives. The volume of work will determine the number of positions and the distribution of responsibilities within the executive compensation department.

Determining Reporting Relationships

Executive compensation positions typically report to a top human resource executive or a top compensation/benefits executive. There are four types of organization in common use.

1. Executive compensation under the top human resource executive. This structure is used in both large and medium-sized companies and can be charted as follows:

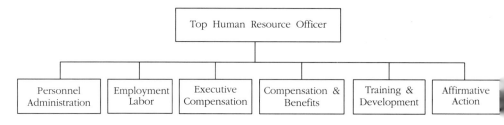

The executive compensation manager has equal status with other functional executives in the human resource department. He or she must possess strong human resource management skills and in-depth knowledge of executive pay, the organization, and its business and financial plans. In addition, that person should be a strong leader so that, along with the top human resource executive, he or she is able to interact smoothly and knowledgeably with the CEO, other corporate officers, and board members.

2. Executive compensation under a top compensation or compensation/benefits executive. This organization of the compensation function is found in large (*Fortune* 100) companies, which use one of two different approaches. The first approach divides compensation into functional areas of accountability. The second divides it into organizational areas of responsibility. An organizationally driven reporting relationship looks like this:

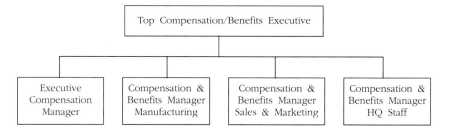

Reporting relationships based on functional accountability are organized this way:

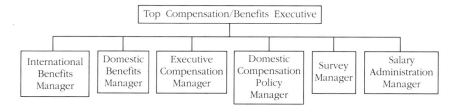

An important consideration in deciding between the two approaches is the "value-added" by the top compensation and benefits executive. If most of the design input on executive pay programs comes from the top compensation/benefits person who is coordinating domestic and international pay and benefits, then the functional alignment makes the most sense. An organizationally driven structure, on the other hand, is typically used where design is largely determined by the top executive compensation executive.

3. Executive compensation under a financial position.

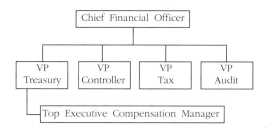

This is the most frequent reporting arrangement outside the human resource function. It is used when the human resource staff does not possess financial knowledge or when executive pay issues are more compatible with treasury, accounting, or tax accountabilities. Under this organization, the financial officer who handles executive pay must be knowledgeable about executive pay programs, incentive plan design, salary administration, and so forth. An MBA with experience in finance, salary administration, and incentive plan design would be a welcome addition to almost any organization.

4. Executive compensation under the chief executive officer.

A final organizational strategy is to have the top compensation position (with accountability for executive compensation) report to the CEO. As shown above, the executive may also have other human resource responsibilities. Such an arrangement is appropriate in a small company or in a company where the CEO is heavily involved in the design and administration of executive pay programs.

Determining Support Needs

The next important step in the organization of an executive compensation department is providing the support staff. In large companies (500 to 1,000 participants in executive pay programs), the high volume of administrative activity necessitates a support staff like this:

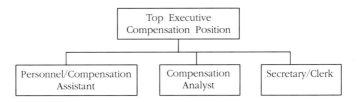

The assistant has primary responsibility for maintaining records. He or she keeps track of the following:

- Salary information
- Annual incentive award eligibility lists
- Annual incentive award goal statements and descriptions of performance measures
- Annual incentive award individual award recommendations and goal achievement forms
- Annual incentive award accounting accruals
- Stock option grant, vesting, and exercise records
- Stock option accounting accruals and shares outstanding

- International employee stock equivalent grant records, vesting records, and exercise records
- Other long-term income eligibility records, performance goals, and performance measures
- Other long-term income award recommendations
- Other long-term income accounting accruals
- Previous annual incentive and long-term income payments
- Deferred compensation records
- Individual participant executive compensation statements
- Confidential (executive) payroll

The length of the list makes it plain that a full-time employee is needed for record keeping in an organization with 1,000 or more executive participants. The data retrieval and storage requirements demand programming skills on either PC or mainframe equipment. The assistant must be articulate and detail-oriented, since the margin of error in the role should again be zero. The job requires a high level of maturity in dealing with sensitive information that cannot be discussed outside the immediate work area.

The compensation analyst helps determine appropriate levels of executive pay by surveying and analyzing the policies and levels of pay in other companies. Specific duties might include the following:

1. Analysis of company proxies and executive compensation survey data;
2. Surveys of competitive companies, so that one's own pay policies, practices, and levels can be compared and evaluated;
3. Analysis of target versus actual short- and long-term income awards paid by one's own company and by competitive companies;
4. Calculation of actual values received by executives both within the organization and in competitive companies from long-term income and stock option programs;
5. Preparation of material about executive compensation programs for participants;
6. Multiple regression analysis of the relationship of executive pay to sales, assets, income, and so forth to identify predictors of executive pay levels; and
7. Study of current tax, accounting, and SEC regulations that affect executive pay.

A person with a bachelor of science degree and one or two years' experience in salary administration, an MBA with one to two years of experience, or an in-house person with experience or a demonstrated ability to think at the college level can be trained as an analyst.

Use of Outside Consultants

Outside consultants can be a valuable extension of, or part of, the executive compensation department. A small company, in particular, often finds that outside expertise is valuable in the design or implementation of new programs.

Companies typically use consultants for three purposes.

1. *Technical resources.* Like benefits, executive pay is subject to a great deal of regulation, and, particularly in small companies, the skills of an expert are often useful. For example, a small public company may need guidance on how to follow SEC regulations that require companies to report pay levels of top people. Or, a company might use an outside consultant to provide information on the accounting costs of current or proposed executive pay programs. In small companies it is normally more cost-effective to buy these services than to employ an inside executive compensation analyst or manager.

   Outside consultants can also be a technical resource in the design of executive pay plans. In small, medium, and large companies, consultants can review current business plans, interview senior executives about key business needs and goals, and design a program appropriate for the specific company. If the firm employs its own staff to manage the executive pay plan, the staff can work with the consultant in design and implementation.

2. *Temporary staff.* An outside consultant can be hired for a specific task. For example, a small company without an executive compensation staff might use a consultant to help implement a new or modified pay plan by developing written material on the plan, briefing the participants, designing administrative forms and training company personnel on how to use or process them, and so forth. In medium and large companies, this sort of activity can be done by a consultant in conjunction with company staff.

   Outside experts hired as temporary staff can also be used to obtain an objective assessment of executive pay levels. Consultants can quickly review job accountabilities, interview jobholders, and provide internal and external data for establishing the value of individual executive jobs.

3. *Outside opinion.* In deciding about pay levels or plan design, a company can use consultants to provide a third-party opinion. This can be useful to outside directors or compensation committee members, particularly with regard to the pay level and pay programs for the chief executive officer. Even in companies that employ an executive compensation professional, the fact remains that this person reports directly or indirectly to the CEO; a third-party opinion can maintain the integrity of both parties.

Regardless of how firms organize their executive pay functions, most can benefit from having a consultant perform a "sanity check" on the purpose, design, participation rates, and levels of executive compensation. A periodic outside evaluation can be a useful indicator of whether an executive pay plan has clearly defined objectives consistent with business plans and needs, whether the plan is meeting these objectives, and whether the plan is understood by the participants.

CHOOSING A TOP EXECUTIVE COMPENSATION PROFESSIONAL

In addition to an in-depth knowledge of compensation theory, practice, and administration, what other characteristics should an executive compensation professional possess? Interviews with practicing managers indicate that a knowledge of business is essential. A person with sufficient expertise in compensation, tax, accounting, and corporate law will no doubt have some familiarity with business procedures, including the ability to read profit and loss and other financial statements. In order to design compensation programs with a clear business purpose, the professional must have a thorough knowledge of the company's operation.

A head of executive compensation must also be able to analyze and solve problems: to define them, select alternative solutions, predict results, and recommend action. This ability should be based on experience, not theory; the compensation director must be able to understand financial measures such as debt and asset ratios, earnings per share, and so forth; design a regression analysis; and draw conclusions based on the spread of linear points, standard error, coefficient or correlation, and similar statistical data.

There are very few top support positions in today's business world that do not require computer knowledge, and executive compensation is no exception. Mainframe data systems and PC-based applications are common in most companies. (The head of executive compensation must be sure that PC programs are integrated with mainframe data so that basic employee information is not duplicated.)

Many consulting firms offer excellent software that can help:

1. Maintain current and historical salary and bonus information. Such programs can store the current target bonus, last payout amount from short- and long-term incentive plans, actual payments as a percentage of targets, and so forth. In addition, the programs can keep track of performance appraisal information.
2. Maintain deferred accounts, with interest/dividend payments, by individual and by plan.
3. Record stock grants and stock option information, including vested and unvested shares, exercised shares, and previous grants, along with exercised amounts.
4. Generate individual executive compensation statements, which provide participants with information on the total compensation they have received (base salary, short-term and long-term incentives) and the amounts they will be eligible to receive in the future. An example of what can be kept on an executive compensation data base is shown in Exhibit 18-1. In this example, the total compensation for J. Doe (base salary, annual bonus, long-term income grant, and perquisites) is $440,000 plus another $330,000 "in the bank" or available in future years if he or she remains with the company. This information can be powerful for retention purposes.

An executive compensation professional must possess honesty and integrity as well as the ability to keep all compensation data strictly confidential. Both qualities can only be identified by observation or reputation.

And, finally, the finest intellectual skills are useless if a head of executive compensation is not articulate. Because of the need to communicate with corporate officers and directors on compensation committees, the manager of executive compensation must be able to pitch presentations to the level of the audience as well as "sell" his or her ideas when appropriate.

DEVELOPMENT OF THE COMPENSATION PROFESSIONAL

In today's ever-changing business world, it is crucial that the compensation professional keep current on government regulations, as well as on

EXHIBIT 18-1
Sample Executive Compensation Statement

This is a summary of your compensation. It reflects potential pay if specified performance levels are achieved by you and the company.

PREPARED FOR: J. DOE   COMPANY: ABC, INC.
TITLE: VICE PRESIDENT   DATE: 1991

Element of Compensation			Annual Value
1. Base Salary			$200,000
2. Annual Bonus (50%) (at target)			$100,000
3. Annual Long-Term Grant (55%) (at target)			$110,000
4. Previous Long-Term Grants			
Year	*No. Shares*	*Grant Value*	*Date of Full Vesting*
1988	1,000	$100,000	1991
1989	1,000	$110,000	1992
1990	1,000	$120,000	1993
	3,000	$330,000	
Annual Value of Dividends (if any)			$ 10,000
5. Annual Value of Executive Perquisites			$ 20,000
Total Annual Compensation			$440,000

economic, business, and labor market trends. The changing environment makes it necessary to hone existing technical, business, and personal skills.

Technical Skills

In order to improve technical skills, those working on executive compensation programs must be able to identify what is needed for personal development. A natural starting point is to attend intercompany meetings, outside seminars, symposiums, or conferences. These programs may be part of the employer's training and development activity, or they may be run by industry organizations, local groups, or professional societies such as the American Compensation Association.

The key to technical development is to take the time to analyze one's own abilities and weaknesses and then to discuss them with one's manager. Once a compensation professional learns how his or her skills compare to those of peers in other companies, a personal development program can be initiated.

The American Compensation Association, as well as many colleges, universities, and consulting firms, offer a variety of educational opportunities to identify or meet personal development needs. Programs include:

- Executive compensation courses covering short- and long-term incentives, tax, and accounting basics;
- Executive compensation symposiums where information is exchanged on current topics or problems; and
- Industry survey association groups and meetings.

Many observers have pointed out that the technological changes of the past twenty years outnumber those of the previous two hundred years.[1] Although urgent daily tasks can consume one's attention, a key element in successful executive compensation practice is taking the time for professional development, particularly in today's business environment where job priorities constantly change.

Business Skills

The executive compensation professional must analyze the company's business plan in order to understand where the business is targeted to go and what goals it has established. A compensation director who thinks the way a business manager does has accomplished a major step in professional development. Business skills are typically developed through an undergraduate or graduate education and five or more years of experience.

Personal Skills

The final need in professional development is to hone the skills that enable the compensation professional to implement programs. The ability to analyze data, write and speak effectively, manage time well, and promote new ideas and programs are important personal skills. Many professional associations, training institutions, and schools provide excellent opportunities to improve such skills. One aptitude that is frequently underdeveloped by people in the profession is the ability to sell new compensation programs, which requires logical organization of thoughts, crisp and to-the-point oral presentations, confidence, political sensitivity, and, finally, knowledge of one's audience. A number of organizations offer excellent training in the selling of compensation programs. One of them, The Connellan Group, of Chicago, suggests that communicators create a listener profile, or outline of the personality, background, opinions, and "hot buttons" of various listeners, and know what kind of presentation each prefers.

The essential first step in selling a program is to establish a need for it. If the people who must approve a new plan do not perceive its necessity, they will not be likely to endorse it. The compensation professional must use his or her knowledge of business plans, goals, and the individual objectives of the audience to prove a clear need. In addition, establishing the need is also important when selling ongoing compensation plan changes such as salary range adjustments, annual merit budgets, new target bonus levels, and so forth.

Once the compensation professional has promoted the need for a change, he or she should produce facts to show expertise in the subject. The presentation and interpretation of facts are essential for building credibility. Compensation planners should seek the same kind of training that salesmen receive. As a personal development exercise, they should learn how to "close the sale" of a compensation program. This requires the ability to clearly summarize the benefits of the recommended change and then "ask for the order" or approval of the plan.

Selling a program is much more difficult than it sounds. Political sensitivity and preparation are essential. By political sensitivity, I mean knowing the priorities of the decision maker. Will a CEO view a new proposal from a cost perspective or from a personal perspective? Will the CEO seek the opinions of others? (If so, the head of compensation should solicit other opinions before asking for a decision.) If the CEO serves on another company's board of directors, the compensation head should find out what executive pay plans the other company uses in order to know what the CEO has been exposed to. "Selling" also refers to what is commonly called "water dripping" the decision maker. Drop clues directly or indirectly so that the proposal is not a surprise. With training, knowledge, and preparation, the compensation professional can succeed in selling his or her ideas.

Managing Daily Activities

Many compensation professionals neglect to audit their own effectiveness. They should periodically analyze how time is *actually spent* versus where time *should be spent*, based on the company's definition of their role. It is easy to be sidetracked from primary areas of responsibility by daily phone calls, questions, and requests. Many people find themselves "putting out fires" rather than focusing on how to prevent them. To avoid this, the compensation professional ought to review, on a monthly basis, his or her own management of time. At the beginning of each month, list projects and activities that must be accomplished. Include time for special requests, phone calls, and other unplanned activities. At the end of each month, review how time was actually spent. This exercise can expose mismanagement of time or neglect of key responsibilities.

The effectiveness of compensation managers also can be monitored via statistical and verbal feedback. Reports can provide information on whether executive compensation programs are accomplishing their defined objectives. Verbal assessments from senior executives and other users can reveal whether programs are succeeding, identify problems that may require creative solutions, and help those who are accountable for executive pay to fulfill their objectives by exposing conceptual deficiencies in existing practices as well as problems in administration, implementation, and communication.

Meeting Expectations of the CEO and Board Compensation Committee

Some consultants advise that instead of reporting to the CEO or head of human resources, the executive compensation professional report directly to the board compensation committee so that the board can have better access to information used to establish pay levels for the CEO. The duties of the compensation committee typically include the following:

1. To approve the compensation for the CEO and other corporate officers or executives who report to the CEO;
2. To approve the purposes and design of executive pay plans;
3. To monitor the results and costs of executive pay plans; and
4. To represent shareholder interests by ensuring that performance is the basis for executive pay levels.

Regardless of the reporting relationship, it is essential that the head of executive compensation understand the roles of the board compensation committee and the CEO in setting executive pay. If a review of existing documents does not provide this understanding, then an interview with the top HR executive, CEO, or chairman of the board compensation committee might help.

Another issue is whether the executive compensation professional is involved in setting the pay for members of the board of directors. If so, he or she would present recommendations on remuneration to the CEO, since the CEO is an employee and directors are often nonemployees. Discussions with the CEO and chairman of the board (if he or she is not also the CEO) are essential in order to identify the expectations for directors' pay in the organization.

In summary, with a full understanding of the company's business plan and CEO and compensation committee expectations, the executive compensation professional can establish a clear definition of his or her role and an understanding of what is necessary to fulfill that role. The executive compensation professional is then equipped to evaluate and introduce or change compensation programs so that they motivate executives and focus them on activities that create success in the business. This is a most challenging job in any organization.

NOTE

1. See, for example, John Naisbitt's *Megatrends* (New York: Warner Books, 1982).

PART II-D

The Role of the Compensation Committee of the Board

19

CEO AND BOARD COMPENSATION COMMITTEE CONCERNS: A PERSONAL VIEW

Samuel J. Silberman

THE MOST SENSITIVE intersection of board and management roles and responsibilities is the matter of executive compensation. How could it be different! Involved are the most basic questions of self-worth, judgments by peers, as well as fairness, equity, and evaluation of evaluators. Seldom does anyone volunteer for the compensation committee of a public corporation; one is usually "tapped" for the duty. For the chairman of the committee it is especially sensitive because it involves a one-on-one relationship with the chief executive officer, in which lines are drawn more as a matter of human relationships than by the authority sanctioned by their respective offices. To sort out the conflicting dynamics and to organize them into a rational framework within which it is possible to operate, requires a strong, clear, and coherent philosophy. And this cannot be developed in a vacuum, it must be forged by everyone involved in terms of what best serves the company, the organization, and the shareholders.

Before I proceed further, there are some axioms that should be stated. Regardless of the system of compensation, it is essential that every final judgment be a balance between the objective and the subjective. Both are essential. Structure provides the objective; flexibility provides the subjective. Flexibility gives the chief executive and senior management the power necessary to effectively direct an organization, to enforce discipline, and to demand loyalty and performance beyond what can be measured or weighed. No company can survive being run like a civil service. The objective component ensures a full measure of fairness and equity without which organizations will quickly become a collection of individuals without a common purpose, allowing a political culture to develop that would encourage behavior worthy of the trusties of a despot.

The role of a compensation committee is more simply stated than fulfilled. In my view it is: (1) to ensure a competitive salary structure; (2) to exercise restraint to the extent of ensuring that compensation is tied to performance; and (3) to be the external interpreter and advocate for the compensation policies of the company. These are the cornerstones for the functioning of an effective committee, which can work well with an organization and still serve the shareholder's interest. If one takes these three points seriously, it is not difficult to determine what is needed to do a creditable job.

To ensure a competitive structure is certainly in the interest of the organization, the company, and the shareholders. If one believes that people make the difference, and there are few situations in which they do not, it is not possible to prosper with the substandard staff that results from noncompetitive pay scales. Companies must pitch their compensation according to the level of talent they require. To know what is competitive requires a mass of external information, which, in turn, requires analysis and judgment, because no two situations are identical.

Ensuring restraint requires a coherent, comprehensive, and flexible compensation policy, tied to performance, with limits preset so as to avoid open-endedness. Too often, policies are protestations of all that is good and right, and do not provide a framework for operating within them. A well-drawn policy should provide answers that minimize conflicts. Policies must be responsive to the needs of the company. And those needs will depend, in large part, on how the company is organized to meet its objectives. Unless there is frank and open discussion that allows for reality, policies will, in the end, be disregarded. Exceptions always will be necessary. For example, salaries of new hires cannot always fit neatly into the established pattern. The important point is to know how great the contemplated deviation is and to be able to evaluate the potential fallout and ripples. But in no case should exceptions be allowed to so overwhelm policy that it becomes moribund. Too many exceptions indicate a need for modification.

The compensation committee is expected to act as an independent body accountable for compensation matters, with the ability to explain and justify compensation policies and actions to the company's external constituencies. That responsibility is the keystone to a solid working relationship with the chief executive officer and senior officers of the company. It puts everyone on the same side of the table. And it establishes the most important element in the relationship—the need to know, indeed, the right to know. As with a lawyer and a client, the ability to defend depends on knowing all the facts. The entire group assumes a common responsibility—accountability.

It is clear that outside professional help is needed to establish what is competitive and what are the limits. Most companies have a full spectrum of consultants, lawyers, accountants, architects, engineers, real estate experts, and so on. The compensation consultant should serve the board through its compensation committee in much the same way the independent auditors serve the board through its audit committee. While the consultant must be able to work with management, it should be firmly established that the ultimate responsibility is to the board through the compensation committee.

With the foregoing as background, it is possible to present my own experience as chairman of the Gulf + Western Compensation Committee as a case example. I became chairman after having been a member for a few years. As is still true in many companies today, we relied on our best business judgment to make compensation decisions. I asked the committee whether the time had come to develop a more structured compensation policy, tying compensation to performance in a more formal way yet retaining the flexibility to exercise business judgment. There was sufficient consensus that this would be desirable, if possible to achieve, and that a request should be made of the board that the committee be permitted to hire a consultant with whom it could think through our many questions and dilemmas. We received permission, interviewed four candidates, and picked one.

Our original intention was for the consultant to work exclusively with the committee. After functioning on that basis for a time, the company correctly pointed out that it would make better sense if the company had access to the same expertise in making recommendations as the committee had in considering them. This is our present setup, but it is understood that our consultant's primary responsibility is still to the committee. If I had one recommendation to make to other companies, it would be to establish this relationship. Everyone agrees that in our case the arrangement has worked to the benefit of everyone.

Once we had a consultant available, we were able to address the problem of developing and establishing a compensation policy that could be recommended to the board for its approval. This process took over two years, because the deeper we got into the questions involved, the more obvious it became that a policy without plans for implementation would serve no useful purpose. Management participated throughout in developing both. There is no space here to describe the evolutionary process that strengthened everyone's commitment to the outcome, but what finally emerged was the following: We would phase in, as quickly as feasible, a total compensation approach broken into salary, annual awards, and long-term awards. Salaries would be pitched to the 75th percentile; annual awards would be based on company performance; and long-term awards would be based on company performance over time. Performance was to be based on return on investment and growth. Individual performance was to be recognized, both good and poor. A total compensation pool which could not be exceeded, would be established and based on performance.

Had we stopped there, the job would have been easily and quickly done. But it became clear during the development stage that, to be effective, plans for implementation had to be drawn and management had to be fully involved in the design. Executives were placed into salary grades tied to their positions' potential to make contributions to the company's performance. The percentage of salary, which was to be available for each of the annual and long-term awards, was set to vary with grade on an ascending scale. Company performance was to be measured by both external and internal criteria. A midpoint target for performance was to be established, which would pay out the percentage set for each grade. This figure would then be adjusted up or down, depending on company performance compared to target. Each award was then to be further adjusted for individual performance. The total pools for annual and long-term awards were to be the dollars generated by applying and totaling all percentages assigned to individuals' salaries assuming midpoint performance. Those totals were then to be adjusted up or down, depending on actual performance. These totals are inviolate and mechanisms were put in place to adjust all awards downward proportionally if required to stay within the total. The committee reserved the right to withhold grants or to reward outstanding individual performance outside the plan on a recommendation from management. Looking back, it is small wonder that it took two years to establish the compensation policy.

It is approaching a decade that the plan has been in effect. Minor adjustments have been made from time to time but, overall, it has worked well. I attribute this to the process by which the plans were developed. The point to be made is that even in a complex organization such as ours, which at one point had over eighty profit centers, it was possible to establish workable policies and plans to implement them.

Philosophy, policy, and plans are meaningless without the ability and desire to implement them. The extent to which agreement on broad principles has been achieved is the extent to which opportunity for conflict has been minimized. As we approach the end of each year, when it is possible to project with reasonable accuracy the year's results, management starts the computations and evaluations that will form the basis for its recommendations for annual and long-term awards. Since the overall pool has been established, there is little to discuss except what consultation the chief executive officer might wish to have with the committee. When recommendations are made, they are interpreted and explained so that the committee has a complete understanding of the background and logic for the recommendation. By the time recommendations come to the committee, there is rarely need for modifications. To those who criticize compensation committees generally as merely rubber stamps, I would answer that the ultimate objective of the committee should be to serve the company and its shareholders without conflict. A well-designed policy with means for implementation should, by its very nature, virtually eliminate conflict. The evidence of a good policy, supported by a good plan, is effectiveness without conflict, not the opposite. Companies do not prosper long term in turmoil.

Shortly after making recommendations for awards in the current year, management starts its internal process to develop objectives for the next. Management draws up a business plan, which is then evaluated in terms of comparisons with previous years, objectives for growth, and return on investment. This part of the process requires considerably more discussion than the specifics of year-end awards. Whatever evolves is then further evaluated, using external comparisons for similar companies and similar industries. Only then are targets for compensation set, after reconciling them with the targets for operations. Finally, the figures for the corporate group must be consistent with the sum of the component parts. All this is done in the most frank and open fashion.

The title of this chapter is: "CEO and Board Compensation Committee Concerns." The single greatest concern must be the harmonious handling of this most sensitive area of corporate life, consistent with the best interests of the shareholders, the company and its constituents, and the organization itself. In summary, my view is that this is best achieved if:

1. The role of the committee is clearly defined to ensure that the salary structure is competitive, that restraint is exercised in order to tie compensation to performance, and that the committee act as advocate and interpreter for the compensation policies of the company;
2. There are clear comprehensive compensation policies with appropriate plans to implement them, which can be easily understood and explained both internally and externally;

3.   There is available to the compensation committee a qualified consultant, who can act as educator for the committee, bringing to it expertise concerning salary ranges, returns on investment, and so forth of comparator groups, the latest in what is transpiring in the field, and independent judgment about compensation proposals. The consultant should be available to work with management, but should be responsible to the board through its compensation committee;

4.   There is a process for developing policies and plans for implementation that involves management, the committee, and the consultant;

5.   The relationship between management and the committee is collegial, with neither trying to control or manipulate the other; and

6.   There is continuing open and frank dialogue concerning compensation matters so that when decisions need to be made or approvals given, all parties have been privy to the background for recommendations, which eliminates last-minute pressures.

Finally, a word needs to be said about the imponderables. When does a refusal to approve create even more problems than an inadvisable approval? Who says the consultant is always right? In the 1930s, I was working in Seattle when the Tacoma Bridge collapsed; it was designed by experts. What does it mean to be lean? Should the compensation committee be concerned with the numbers of executives (too few or too many) as well as their compensation levels? To what extent should the nonmonetary reward system be a concern of the committee? These questions can go on and on.

By the time issues such as these start to surface, you may be sure that the major concerns of the compensation committee and the chief executive have been resolved. Addressing these will require the same collegial process that dealt successfully with the basics.

20

CEO COMPENSATION: THE CASE OF MICHAEL EISNER

Graef S. Crystal

IN MORE ROMANTIC TIMES, a dispute between two lands was sometimes settled mano a mano, that is to say, by two warriors pitted one against the other. The hopes and dreams of all the people were represented by these two men, and the winner was given recognition and rewards almost beyond contemplation. The loser, sadly, and in the vernacular of today, bought it.

Competitive struggles might no longer be resolved in such romantic fashion, but the image of the brave warrior who fights and, if necessary, dies for his people is alive and well and, if not living in Pasadena, dwells in the heart of every modern-day CEO. It is because today's CEO symbolizes the warrior of old that what he does—and how he is paid—takes on such significance.

To understand, if only in microcosm, the importance of how, and how much, CEOs are paid, let us concentrate in this chapter on a single CEO, Michael Eisner, the chairman and chief executive officer of The Walt Disney Company.

Eisner was the president and second-ranking executive of Paramount Pictures, a subsidiary of Paramount Communications (formerly called Gulf + Western Industries), when he was approached by the Disney board of directors and asked to take the helm of a troubled company and turn it around. Disney, once a great name in entertainment, had been living on its reputation since the founder's death and that reputation had just about run out. Revenues were sluggish and the company's after-tax return on equity (ROE) was running well below average—at about 9 percent.

Eisner had been compensated handsomely at Paramount, in large part because under his leadership (and that of his superior, Barry Diller) the studio had had nine years of unbroken success. His cash compensation package was into seven figures.

Eisner negotiated with Disney's board and came away with a six-year employment agreement that contained much more risk—and much more reward—than the one he was giving up at Paramount. The major pay elements in Eisner's original deal with Disney were:

- A base salary of $750,000 per year that would be frozen during the six-year period,
- An annual bonus equal to 2 percent of all after-tax profits in excess of a 9-percent ROE level, and
- An option on approximately two million Disney common shares, with a ten-year period of exercise and a strike price equal to the then fair-market value of approximately $14 per share.

Let us first look at Eisner's compensation risk:

- He agreed to have his salary frozen for six years. It may be difficult to work up special sympathy for someone whose pay, even if cryogenic, is $750,000 per year. But that level of pay was about what Eisner had been receiving at Paramount and was par for senior entertainment industry executives in 1984, the year he joined Disney.
- His bonus formula essentially required him to improve Disney's profits beyond their current level before he would receive even a dollar of incentive award. By contrast, the CEOs of most companies have most of their bonuses locked in once the company is in the black, even to a small extent. Moreover, at about the time Eisner joined Disney, I was studying the bonus-funding formulas of the top 100 industrial companies in America and determined that the median company required only about a 6-percent after-tax ROE level before the bonus spigot was opened.
- At first glance, the use of stock options as a long-term incentive device at Disney does not seem unusual. However, in the entertainment industry, where low risk and high reward are every executive's idea of a sound employment contract, the long-term incentive device of choice is not options but restricted stock. With the latter, the executive does not have to sweat out an increase in the company's share price. Rather, he or she gets the entire value per share as well as the dividends. Hence, there is relatively little risk in restricted stock compared to stock options.

Now let us consider Eisner's potential rewards:

- He had a personal bonus-funding formula that called for 2 percent of the after-tax profits of the company once the threshold level of performance (9-percent ROE) had been reached. Therefore, his bonus potential was huge and unlimited. More important, he didn't have to agonize over whether the board would lose heart and refuse to pay him what he deserved if he really did turn the company around.
- Though his stock option was risky, it was also massive. With two million shares, he stood to earn $2 million for each point the stock price rose above $14 per share.

In the process of negotiating Eisner's agreement, the board used an independent consultant and spent a good deal of time considering the pros and cons of each element in the agreement. Among other things, the board was well aware that the proposed agreement contained more than the usual amount of risk and reward.

With the agreement in place, Eisner signed on and in what seems like short order wrought a magnificent turnaround. For the year prior to his joining the company, profits had been less than $100 million; for fiscal 1988 they rose to close to $550 million. And where the stock had been languishing at $14 per share when he joined Disney, at the beginning of 1989 the share price was $66.

Eisner, of course, was paid magnificently. His annual bonus rose to the $7-million range. On paper, profits on his two million option shares reached $104 million. Indeed, no other CEO of a major company in the United States appeared to earn as much as Eisner did during the period of 1984 through 1988.

Though Eisner was likely the highest-paid corporate executive in the United States, there did not seem to be any complaints from shareholders, and for good reason. If one calculates the stock appreciation Disney should have had under normal circumstances (about 14.5 percent per year for a company with its risk characteristics) and then subtracts the result from the appreciation that Disney did have, there remained *an extra $5 billion for the shareholders*. Alternatively, if one subtracts the appreciation one could have obtained by investing in the S&P 500 from Disney's actual appreciation, the excess would have been over $6 billion. So who was to complain that Eisner was way overpaid?

Or, at least, who among the shareholders would complain? There were, however, other parties at the table, including employees, independent producers, actors, writers, and the like. It is curious that that dry document called the proxy statement is read by quite a few people nowadays. Many advocates in the gainsharing camp wax eloquent about the virtues of giving ordinary employees stock. But the dark side of the practice—at least as it is viewed in some circles—is that those same employees receive proxy statements and actually read them. There is also, of course, the press, and when a CEO receives what Michael Eisner receives, you can be sure that it will make all the newspapers.

Apparently, there were few Disney employees, independent producers, actors, and writers who begrudged Eisner his millions. Indeed, they admired him greatly, probably thought he deserved every cent he got, and assuredly thought they ought to share in Disney's newfound wealth. Hence, in collective bargaining negotiations with Disney's hourly employees, Eisner's pay package began to be mentioned, and not by those on the company's side of the bargaining table.

Compensation experts are taught that before they make pay comparisons they must be sure that they are comparing apples and apples—that the duties and responsibilities of the positions being compared are substantially the same. But ordinary employees, independent producers, actors, and writers are not compensation experts. Seemingly they are unaware that it is considered theoretically improper to compare the job of an hourly ticket taker at Disneyland with that of the chairman of the company.

Many other people fall into the same theoretical trap. Schoolteachers argue that they should be paid more than policeofficers. Nurses argue that they should be paid more than truck drivers. Professional football players argue that they should be paid at least the same as professional baseball players. Although these comparisons are simply not valid, they are constantly made.

At the same time that Eisner's pay arrangements became a sort of homing beacon for anyone who thought they should earn more money, Disney's board undertook to persuade Eisner to extend the time he would stay with the company. After all, maybe he had another rabbit (that is, another $5–6 billion of excess appreciation) in his seemingly bottomless hat. In early 1989, Eisner and the board reached agreement that he would extend his commitment to run the company from late 1990 to late 1998. In return, he received options on a further two million shares. However, he also agreed to increase substantially the risk in his current compensation arrangements—arrangements that were already more risky than normal:

- He agreed to have his $750,000 salary frozen all the way to late 1998. Assuming that executive salaries will generally rise around 7 percent per year in future years, then the present value of a constant $750,000 salary is a much lower $500,000 per year.

- He agreed to have the threshold in his bonus raised from a 9-percent ROE level to an 11-percent ROE level. (He would still be entitled to 2 percent of all profits in excess of the threshold amount.) Had this new formula been operative for fiscal 1989 (it will not take effect until fiscal 1991), the dollar amount of after-tax profits represented by the threshold would have been close to $300 million. In effect, before he received a single dollar of incentive compensation, Eisner would have to produce three times the amount of profits that Disney produced in the year prior to the year he joined the company.

- He agreed to have any "excess" annual bonus delivered to him in the form of restricted shares of Disney common stock. The term "excess" here refers to the amount by which Eisner's actual bonus for a given year exceeds the bonus he would have been paid had Disney achieved, not its actual return on average equity for the year, but a return on average equity of 17.5 percent. Paying Eisner in shares rather than cash increases his compensation risk in two ways. First, he cannot have the degree of financial portfolio diversification he otherwise might wish to have. Second, and more important, he is being required to "invest" some more of his own money in Disney. If the company's future results should turn south and thereby depress the stock price, Eisner will not only take a hit on his existing option shares, but the value of his restricted shares will also decline.

- He agreed to accept an "out-of-the-money" strike price (i.e., the price per share he would have to pay to exercise his stock option shares) on 500,000 of his two million new option shares. At the time the shares were granted, Disney's stock was selling for $69 per share. Although the strike price on 1.5 million of the two million option shares was set to equal the $69 price, the strike price on the remaining 500,000 shares was set $10 higher, at $79 per share. Normally, an executive begins to benefit from a stock option grant the moment the stock price rises above the market price prevailing on the date of grant. But in this case, Eisner would not begin to benefit from those 500,000 shares until Disney's stock price climbed $10 per share.

- He agreed to accept "back-loaded" option exercise restrictions. In the large majority of companies making stock option grants, the entire option becomes exercisable in no more than four years from the date of grant; indeed, in some cases, the entire option becomes exercisable in a year or two after grant. In Eisner's case, however, the new option shares will not become fully exercisable until a few months before the end of their ten-year term.

There is no question that Eisner, despite the extra risk he has assumed, will earn another fortune if he performs as he has in the past and can deliver for his shareholders during the years until 1998.

In these negotiations, Disney's board once more employed the services of an independent consultant—the same consultant who advised the board in 1984. Before approving Eisner's agreement, the board wanted to be thoroughly knowledgeable about the extra risks Eisner would take and, more important, the enormous extra reward potential he would receive. Although the board knew full well that Eisner would likely continue to be the highest-paid American CEO, it did not flinch; rather, it tried to inject sufficient risk into Eisner's pay package to justify his being paid as high as they come.

One has to assume that the other constituencies mentioned above— the ordinary employees of Disney, independent producers, actors, and writers—will be following Michael Eisner's pay progress in future years with the same sort of rapt attention they have given him in the past. One has to assume too that the pressures on Eisner to assent to more compensation for these constituencies will intensity. How will he respond? It seems to me that he can opt for one of three strategies:

First, he can resist the pressures. This is the "Marie Antoinette School of Management" strategy. Eisner, if he is Economic Man, should head in this direction. After all, he keeps his costs down, his profits up, and his bonus and stock values soaring. But if the above-mentioned constituencies become restive enough, he may face lowered productivity, strikes, the inability to sign on key independent producers, actors, and writers, and so on. If those unhappy events materialize, Eisner may earn less, not more, compensation for himself.

Second, he can accede to the pressures and pay the constituencies more compensation. Eisner could roll over and grant large salary increases, for example, or he could pay an actor $5 million to make a movie instead of only (!) $3 million. Eisner stands to earn less money with this strategy because his costs will be higher. Moreover, higher salaries and higher actors' fees increase Disney's fixed costs and thus the volatility of its earnings. With more volatility, the probability increases that Disney will experience years when ROE is lower than 11 percent. In those years, of course, Eisner will see his bonus evaporate.

Third, he can accede to the pressures but do so by introducing the same sort of contingent compensation concepts that are built into his own pay package. Raises for workers could be tied to accomplishing key company financial goals. And the famous actor might be persuaded to accept, not a $5 million or even a $3 million fee, but rather a puny (!) $1.5 million fee along with a percentage of the adjusted gross income the picture produces. Indeed, the percentage might even accelerate as the results improve, e.g., 5 percent of the adjusted gross until adjusted gross reaches, say, $20 million and then 7.5 percent of all further adjusted gross. Under this strategy, costs would increase, but so might productivity. And so, paradoxically, might Eisner's total compensation.

THE CEO AS SYMBOL

Perhaps CEOs in other companies are not as visible as Michael Eisner, but in their own ways, they are symbols. And because they are, the manner in which they are paid is of interest to many beyond their boards of directors. The case of Michael Eisner and The Walt Disney Company is instructive on a number of fronts.

Injecting Risk

The Disney board faced the issue of pay risk squarely. It understood what it was doing because it had studied scenarios showing what Eisner would earn under various future assumed levels of ROE and shareholder return. If there is a failing on the part of boards of other companies, it is more apparent in this area than in any other. Discussions of pay risk in boardrooms around the land are about as rare as snow in San Francisco. Attempts to quantify pay risk, as was done in the Disney case, are even more rare, for the simple reason that, in other companies, so much of what the CEO receives is received in a discretionary (i.e., nonformulaic) manner.

But ignoring consideration of CEO pay risk, ironically, puts a board at even more risk—this time, at the hands of dissident shareholders. As mentioned above, virtually no shareholders complained about Eisner's pay level. Virtually none of Chrysler's shareholders complained about Lee Iacocca's pay level. Indeed, any complaints would have been plainly ill-mannered, given that the shareholders made millions, nay, billions. But suppose Michael Eisner and Lee Iacocca had not soared. Suppose they had fallen on their faces. What then? The probable answer in both cases is that shareholders would still not have targeted the CEOs' packages for criticism. In both cases, shareholders would have witnessed CEO pay falling at the same rate as Isaac Newton's apple. In short, if a shareholder has to experience pain, it is at least comforting to have company.

Suppose, for the sake of argument, that Eisner had received the following alternative pay package:

- A base salary of $750,000, with normal annual raises,
- A bonus equal to 1 percent of all the after-tax profits, but with no threshold, and
- One million restricted shares, instead of two million option shares.

If Eisner had been paid in the above manner and if Disney's performance had been relatively poor, he would have earned less, to be sure, but his "less" would still have ranked among the highest pay packages in the country, and one shudders to think what might have been his treatment at the hands of the shareholders.

The plain fact is that our citizenry, though seemingly unsophisticated, well understands at least one fundamental principle of economics: the greater the risk, the greater the return. They understood the risk Babe Ruth assumed one day years ago when he pointed to centerfield. When he delivered, they began a long celebration that continues to this day.

Deciding on the Level of Reward

The ancient question, How high is high? applies in spades to the world of executive compensation. Moses did not descend from Mount Sinai with an eleventh commandment: Pay the median. Moses may have been a stern lawgiver, but, on the evidence, he was a statistical sophisticate: He knew a median is predicated on a series of numbers, some of which must, inescapably, be higher or lower than the resulting median. Yet too many boards act as though "Pay the median" is the Eleventh Commandment. They pay it for good performance; they pay it for bad performance. And then they wonder why they are criticized.

Since deciding on the level of compensation is always a relative matter, boards first must consider the basis of comparison. In the case of Disney, is the measure the Hollywood studios? Should CBS, ABC, and NBC be thrown in for good measure? Or should the comparator group also include *any* major company that produces goods and services for individuals and that is heavily dependent on consumer taste? Having selected the comparator group, boards must then decide where to target CEO compensation within the range of pay levels found in the comparator group.

If the majority of boards, by default, selects the median of the market as the pay target, there is a minority that, by design, selects the 75th percentile of the market. Among other things, it makes them feel good to be generous. It probably makes them feel even better if they can be generous without parting with any of their own money. There is nothing wrong per se with targeting to the 75th percentile of the market—*as long as you are willing to inject a commensurate amount of pay risk into the package.* Unhappily, matching reward with risk is not a speciality of most boards.

Choosing a Time Frame

In addition to risk and reward, boards must also consider how much of the CEO's pay package should ride on short-term results and how much on long-term results.

Once again, most boards are guilty of thoughtlessness on this subject. A consultant comes to a board meeting and presents a neat pie chart showing, say, that 40 percent of the median CEO's pay package consists of base salary, 25 percent consists of short-term incentive awards, and 35 percent consists of long-term incentive awards. The board promptly alters its CEO's pay package to conform to this hypothetical median.

In the process, the board has lost sight of two minor items:

- The median is a hypothetical construct. If the consultant had taken the time to examine the pay package blend (of base salary, short-term incentives, and long-term incentives) of each company in the comparator group, he or she would likely have found that not one company had a blend that precisely matched the median.
- The blend changes depending on the assumptions that are made about both short- and long-term future performance. Hence, if you want to assume long-term results on a par with Disney's, then perhaps the value of long-term incentives will comprise 75 percent, not 35 percent, of the CEO's pay package.

Once again, boards need to confront each issue squarely, rather than by default.

Considering Other Constituencies

As suggested by the Eisner case, there are a lot of proxy readers out there, and they continue to make those theoretically improper comparisons. In this matter, boards do not act so much by default. They simply turn a blind eye to these other constituencies. In that sense, they are just like the compensation experts. And in that sense, they are plain wrong.

Cruel as it sounds, there is nothing fundamentally wrong with the Marie Antoinette School of Management. But if you are going to subscribe to it, do it with full malice and forethought, not by accident. Viewed from this perspective, it is really impossible to design a CEO's pay package by looking only at the pay packages of other CEOs. One must, finally, give at least passing recognition to those theoretically improper comparisons everyone else is making and consider the CEO's pay in relation to the pay of other constituencies.

Considering Other Senior Executives

In discussing other constituencies, we have, until now, focused on lower-level employees. What about the chief operating officer (COO), the chief financial officer (CFO), the division presidents, and so forth? For example, studies of the relationship of the pay of the COO to that of the CEO suggest that the median COO ought to earn about 70 percent of the total compensation (including both short- and long-term incentives) of his or her CEO. If a CEO like Michael Eisner is going to be offered a munificent pay package, should the board offer the COO a pay package that is fully 70 percent as rich? And if not, why not?

Some historians assert that great historical trends are triggered by great personalities—Churchill, Roosevelt, and MacArthur, for example. Others assert that history is a long process and great personalities are, in retrospect, bit players on a vast stage. Boards implicitly buy into one or the other of those theories. If they choose the Great Person theory, they are likely to offer Michael Eisner the moon and yet feel quite comfortable in restricting their largesse to Michael Eisner. If they choose the process theory of history, they are likely to want to offer the company's COO a substantial share of the largesse and to share the wealth with the other senior executives in the organization as well.

Of course, there are middle-ground answers to the question of how to compensate top-level management. But whatever the answer, it surely would be useful if boards would pose the question as a matter of routine.

Dealing with the Media

Boards must recognize that what they do will be reported on, and not necessarily accurately. Years ago, when I was more naive, I approached the public relations head of the consulting firm of which I was an officer and director and suggested that the firm ought to sponsor an annual seminar for members of the media so that they might know how to read proxy statements and interpret fairly the way CEOs are paid. Her reply: No one would attend the seminar, because newspapers and magazines typically assign a new writer to write the annual round-up on CEO compensation. Apparently, this assignment is considered not a high honor but a rite of passage—passage to more interesting, and career-enhancing, topics.

Boards could sit back and let the media say what it will. Or they can be proactive and try to guide the media to a more informed level of reporting. Boards ought to adopt the latter strategy, but once again, inertia seems to prevent them from doing so.

Dealing with Shareholders

Perhaps because they pay too much attention to counsel, most boards communicate with shareholders on matters of executive compensation only to the degree legally required. They tell the shareholders what they have done for the CEO, but not why. They tell the shareholders what the CEO actually received in the way of pay, but not what he or she would have received had the company's performance been other than what it was. Shareholder relations would be much improved if boards took the time to communicate with shareholders in these additional ways.

Although many lawyers take the narrow view concerning shareholder disclosure, at least one, Joe Shapiro, the general counsel of The Walt Disney Company, is of the opposite opinion. He figures that if you make a less than honest and full disclosure, and if you bury what you do tell shareholders in three-point type, the financial analysts, who have much to do with what your share price will be, probably will mark down your stock. In Shapiro's view, honest and full disclosure is a strategy that can enhance shareholder value.

Using Internal Compensation Resources

In structuring the pay package of a CEO, a board can turn for advice, if it wishes, to the company's head of human resources and/or its head of compensation. These two executives have knowledge in the subject, but they may also have grave conflicts of interest should the CEO happen to be more avaricious than the norm. If they offer honest opinions, their careers are likely to be stunted—or even curtailed. Nevertheless, internal resources can be invaluable in providing insight as to how the company's internal constituencies are likely to react to a given CEO pay package design. They should be heeded.

Using External Compensation Resources

In theory, a board can retain an independent executive compensation consultant and be assured that it is receiving impartial advice. But theory is one thing and practice is another! If a consultant confronts a covetous CEO head-on and recommends that the board not approve whatever it is the CEO is pushing that day, will he or she be called back for another assignment? If the consultant is part of a firm that offers more than executive compensation consulting services, will the firm continue to provide actuarial services, to consult on benefit plan design, to restructure the organization of Division X, and/or to help the corporation write a sound long-term business plan?

Perhaps there is no sure way to guarantee that a consultant will be conflict-free, but companies can make substantial progress in this area if they:

- Require that the consultant be hired by the board or its compensation committee. If independence is the objective, the consultant should not feel that the client is the CEO. Rather, the consultant should feel that the client is the board of directors or its compensation committee.
- Prohibit the consultant from performing any work for the company other than advising the board. If the organization needs help in establishing a new salary structure or designing a new incentive plan for a particular subsidiary, let it hire another consultant. Hiring the board's consultant might expose him or her to a perhaps irresistible degree of temptation.
- Prohibit the consultant's firm from performing *any* work for the company. If the consultant is a member of a firm that offers actuarial services, make sure that the company hires an actuary from another firm.
- Have the board set forth in writing just what it expects from the consultant. One hopes the charter will contain the words "we want honest advice."
- Make the consultant offer his or her views not only verbally but also in writing. A paper trail helps to ensure that the board will not dismiss lightly a consultant's recommendations. Establishing a paper trail also

helps to underscore to the consultant that his or her recommendations are not merely academic.

These suggestions are not likely to be greeted with enthusiasm by either CEOs or compensation consultants. But if objectivity is the objective, it is folly to do less.

In summary, how a CEO is paid and how much he or she is paid are matters of critical importance, not merely to the CEO and the board of directors, but to the company's shareholders, to its other senior executives, to its ordinary employees, to the media, and to the general public.

21

THE ROLE OF THE COMPENSATION COMMITTEE*

James W. Fisher, Jr.

ACCORDING TO RECENT SURVEYS, between 84 percent and 99 percent (depending on the sample) of large, publicly held firms assign the supervision of executive compensation to a special committee of the board of directors.[1] Members of the committee establish and maintain a marketplace within companies to encourage and reward particular patterns of decisions, actions, and results. Cumulatively, these patterns shape and change the company, hopefully in accord with the goals and strategies agreed to by the board of directors.

The compensation committee of a major company is often a focal point of corporate governance and a lightning rod for the discontent of shareholders or the public. The most frequent criticism of compensation committees is that they lack independence and objectivity and are too willing to rubber-stamp greedy management proposals. Symptoms of this, critics say, include low performance targets for incentive plans, ready forgiveness and virtually unreduced payouts when those low targets are not met, and executive rewards that seem exorbitant compared to the pay levels of hourly workers or the executives of overseas competitors. According to William M. Batten, former chief executive of J.C. Penney and former chairman of the New York Stock Exchange, "Boards have been too complacent in going along with management. Too many corporations are being managed for the benefit of the managers."[2]

The suspicion that committee members lack independence extends even to outside directors. Critics accuse directors of being overconcerned about retaining their seats on the board, or, because they are usually executives of other companies, of being inherently sympathetic to manage-

---

*This chapter includes material drawn from my article "Crafting Policy for Performance and Rewards: A Model for a More Effective Compensation Committee," which appeared in *Directors & Boards* (Winter 1986).

ment. Even some of the people who generally support corporations and boards view perceptions that boards lack independence as damaging to effective corporate governance.

Unions protest when favorable executive compensation actions seem inconsistent with a company's posture during labor negotiations. Laid-off as well as active employees are also sensitive to perceived or actual differences in treatment of executives and hourly workers. Hostile acquirers may attempt to refuse to honor commitments they claim were made inappropriately.

Some of the charges against compensation committee practices are technical: that committees misuse survey data, allow an excessive ratio of short-term to long-term compensation (said to lead to behavior that worsens the U.S. competitive position), or set an excessive ratio of fixed to variable compensation. Some feel that compensation committees should tie executives' rewards more closely to the performance of company stock, while others feel that volatile stock markets give executives a "free ride" often unmerited by the company's performance.

Critics assail incentive payouts that appear more generous than called for by the latest quarterly results (even though the payments may have been established for performance over a previous or long-term period), or that compensate executives for taking necessary strategic steps that depress current earnings. Skeptics also ask whether the incremental compensation at present levels really pays off in increased motivation. The basic question underlying these technical issues is an important one: Is compensation contributing effectively and efficiently to strategic advantage for the corporation?

In order to judge whether the charges against compensation committees are justified, it is necessary to understand why the task of setting executive pay is delegated to a handful of people from outside a company. It is to this that I now turn.

WHY DO COMPANIES USE COMPENSATION COMMITTEES?

Most of the functions of the compensation committee fit within the general responsibilities of the entire board of directors. However, there are good reasons for delegating these duties to a small group. Practically all boards include members of company management; giving responsibility for setting executive pay to a committee composed entirely of outside directors offers at least some degree of protection from self-serving decisions. This can be important in maintaining good relations with shareholders and the public, in defending against potential legal challenges, and in winning the confidence of the general employee population.

Serving on the compensation committee is recognized as an important and sensitive responsibility; it is also hard work. Committee members must be able to handle the complexities of strategy and integrate overall compensation and benefits approaches with organizational structure, management succession, and the like. They also must take into account the shareholder and public scrutiny brought to bear on compensation matters, and the intentional or unintentional messages that may be sent by particular actions. And finally, compensation committees must be able to work with increasingly complex types of compensation and benefits vehicles, survey information, legal and regulatory constraints, and so forth. This not only generates significant work for the members of the committee, but also calls for abilities and knowledge that often only a few members of the typical board possess. In 1985, consultant Lance Berger commented that the "Amateur Hour" is over in the selection of members for compensation committees."[3]

Committee members must have knowledge of the company's strategies, organization, and key management as well as personal abilities and objectivity that will be credible inside and outside the company. The other members of the board should hold committee members responsible for studying situations, doing what is right, and defending their decisions. Because of the crucial role of compensation in controlling the overall direction of human activities within the company, all corporate governance is in peril if the committee does not function properly.

PURPOSE OF THE COMMITTEE: POLICY RATHER THAN PARTICULARS

If it is functioning properly, the compensation committee can contribute objectivity to pay design. Its members bring a sense of responsibility to shareholders, awareness of public opinion, and knowledge of compensation gained from their collective experience. All of these perspectives are helpful for setting compensation *policy* (coordinating plan design with corporate strategy) and for setting the remuneration of top management. These are the most visible functions of the committee and the ones for which it is uniquely suited.

The perspectives of outsiders are of less use, however, in considering the compensation *particulars* of individuals more than three or four layers below the CEO level. The sheer number of details can swamp the time of the committee and actually decrease its effectiveness in forming policy. Compensation decisions at lower levels are best made by management according to agreed-upon guidelines and philosophies.

More and more companies acknowledge the interdependence of executive staffing (including management succession and development), structure, and pay in achieving organizational goals. Because of this, the compensation committee today often has a broader charter than formerly, and might be designated the "organization and compensation committee" or the "management development and compensation committee." Even in those companies that retain the traditional title, the committee generally is responsible for executives' total compensation (salary and bonus, stock options or other long-term compensation, benefits, perquisites, employment contracts, golden parachutes, and so forth).

In some companies, compensation tasks are divided among several committees. For example, there may be stock option, benefits, and/or pension committees as well as a compensation committee. This approach, which requires a great deal of coordination for an integrated compensation strategy, raises several questions. Why should short- and long-term incentives that help implement related strategies be dealt with by separate groups? Why should the policy for pensions be considered separately from the policy for base salaries when most pension schemes are calculated on base salaries? Can special hiring or termination packages for major executives be handled effectively by numerous committees when such packages typically contain trade-offs among different compensation elements?

Companies that split up the compensation responsibility should have plans for handling these problems; for example, they might arrange substantial overlap in committee membership. "Nonoverlapped" members who are tapped for their special skills on specific committees must understand that coordination is required.

ELEMENTS OF A SMOOTHLY FUNCTIONING COMMITTEE

Committee Charters

A well-designed charter assists not only in the internal functioning of the committee but also in defining the nature of communications with management. Without a charter that establishes general responsibilities, no one knows what the committee is expected to oversee and accomplish. In the absence of this understanding, any of the following could occur:

- Management could act unilaterally on issues on which committee members feel they should be consulted.
- Other directors could expect the committee to be maintaining surveillance over areas it is not covering.
- Management could swamp the committee with routine information and proposals on matters best handled internally. Frequently, neither side has specific standards for clearly identifying items that do not require committee attention.

The charter must be reviewed and updated as the company changes. A charter that concentrates the committee's attention on the top positions in the company as defined by a grade or salary cutoff could result in the committee's reviewing several times as many positions as it did originally as the company grows and salary levels change.

Although the content of the charter varies substantially from company to company, the following activities are typical. (Representative charters are included in the appendices at the end of the chapter.)

- Approval or endorsement of short- and long-term incentive plans, particularly those for which corporate officers are eligible.
- Annual establishment of executive salary ranges, grant eligibility, and amount guidelines. Increasingly, guidelines are being treated as administrative matters that are delegated to the committee and not specified in plans, except perhaps for "fail-safe" limits (such as three times salary).
- Establishment of specific pay for key officers (particularly if they are members of the board). This includes base salary, bonus, and grants under long-term plans. The rules about which levels of management receive specific individual-by-individual attention should be reviewed from time to time. Typical definitions are "all officers," "all corporate officers," "all executives in grade X and above," or "all executives with salaries of at least Y."
- Review of payouts under various plans. The committee addresses questions such as the following: What percentage of the long-term performance unit is to be paid? If an executive terminates before restricted stock is vested, do the circumstances of the termination call for lifting the restriction? What is the total amount of money available for corporate officers' bonuses? What bonus pool is available to be allocated to nonofficers at management discretion, and should the amounts vary by divisional performance? What will be the proportion

of stock to cash disbursements? What, if any, adjustments are required or permissible (and if permissible, merited) to reflect changes in the tax law, massive recapitalization, or restructuring of the firm? And so forth.

- Approval or endorsement of executive employment contracts, golden parachutes, or individual retirement packages.
- Approval of executive benefit and perquisite packages (supplemental executive retirement, life insurance, or health programs; rabbi trusts for nonqualified deferred compensation; company-paid financial counseling and/or income tax preparation; cars, country clubs, luncheon clubs, and so forth).
- Approval of broadly offered benefit programs (in the United States, this includes ERISA-covered pension and savings programs in particular) and supervision of the committee responsible for administrative functions such as pension fund management.

Presentation of Materials

Normally, the committee makes the final decision on matters presented to it. However, the committee may receive and review other materials that do not involve decision making:

- Compensation-related items that require board or shareholder approval, for which the committee is a natural arena for consideration. An example is a new or revised incentive plan. The compensation committee usually helps shape such plans, although management, staff, legal counsel, and/or outside consultants may do the actual drafting. The full board expects the compensation committee to provide leadership in the development, review, endorsement, approval, and (if necessary) defense of such plans.
- Items for which the committee has delegated decision-making authority but has requested after-the-fact notification. For instance, the committee may delegate the authority to accelerate certain incentive plan vesting for nonofficers upon company-initiated or mutually satisfactory retirement, but request periodic summaries of such actions. Or, the committee may delegate to an internal management committee the authority to hire and terminate outside managers of pension funds, but request periodic updates on how managers are performing vis-à-vis their portfolio targets and the reasons for addition or termination of specific managers.

- Material designed to inform the committee. This includes statistics on employee demographics, turnover trends by level and by performance rating, shares of stock still available for use in various incentive plans, or the implications of accounting rules changes for various compensation and benefits plans.

Of course, management is expected to provide well-substantiated recommendations on virtually any item calling for committee action. The initiative on CEO compensation may be shared by management and the committee or be in the hands of the committee alone (or its chair); the company (sometimes the compensation executive) provides an additional perspective in private conversations.

Communications

The task of the compensation committee is complex even when communication with management is excellent. Poor communication can easily result in confusion and misunderstanding. Directors deserve to know from management why various materials are being presented and what action, if any, is expected of the committee. Similarly, formal committee resolutions may be so complicated that it is helpful to deliver them with a written or oral explanation of why they are required and what they are designed to accomplish.

Normally, the chairperson is the focal point of the committee. (He or she is often paid either an extra retainer fee and/or a higher attendance fee than other members of the committee.) The leader not only conducts the meetings and generally spends more time than other members in reviewing proposals and preparing for meetings, but also keeps in touch with management. The dialogue between the chairperson and management can cover a range of subjects from ideas that management is considering to requests from the committee for information.

The committee chairperson should see that appropriate records of all meetings are kept, report results of discussions from which management members are excused (e.g., the setting of CEO compensation), and deliver a summary of key committee actions to the full board. The chairperson also may be designated to review and approve the CEO's expense reports.

On especially delicate matters, the CEO and/or another member of top management may serve as the liaison with the committee and its chairperson. In some companies, this may be the only contact between management and the committee. However, in large companies, the chair of the committee may have regular discussions with a staff member, such as the executive in charge of compensation.

It is important to acquaint new committee members with the company's compensation philosophy and to summarize its programs. This task often falls to the compensation executive and can be accomplished through one or more briefings, possibly supplemented by standard or specially prepared written material on incentive plans and the like. (The committee chairperson should be informed of the meetings and be allowed to participate.) During the briefings, compensation programs should be described in the context of the corporation's organizational structure and human resource approach. The charter and functions of the compensation committee should be covered fully with incoming members. Selected statistics on total salaries, bonus funds, and shares allocated to incentive plans may be presented, although the meeting is of greatest lasting value if it concentrates on philosophy rather than numbers.

Scheduling

Most compensation activity falls into a natural cycle that can be accommodated by a fairly stable meeting schedule. Executive salary plans, bonus determinations, long-term grants, and contributions required by qualified benefit plans all come under consideration at predictable times, and usually can be handled in one meeting per quarter. Care should be taken to avoid conflicts with the meetings of other committees on which members of the compensation committee may serve.

Naturally, ad hoc or unprogrammed items arise (for example, the hiring of a major executive). Sometimes such matters come up at times that fit into the regular schedule. Otherwise, companies use various procedures. Special items can be brought to the committee as they occur if extra meetings are scheduled around board meeting time. Particularly urgent matters can be handled by circulating materials for written consent; the compensation executive or committee chairperson can telephone individual members to ensure that concerns are resolved.

With respect to unscheduled salary actions, the committee may prefer meeting more frequently, postponing salary adjustments until regularly scheduled meetings, approving actions with retroactive effective dates, or (with a prior understanding that management may proceed with certain types of transactions) simply ratifying management decisions.

LEGAL RESPONSIBILITIES OF THE COMMITTEE

During a National Association of Corporate Directors (NACD) conference on compensation issues, attorney Robert Salwen outlined the duties of directors:

- to act within the scope of their authority, and in accordance with the law;
- to exercise board/committee authority in good faith and with undivided loyalty to the corporation and its shareholders; and
- to exercise board/committee authority with rational, independent, and informed business judgment, and with the care that an ordinarily prudent person in a similar position would exercise in the same circumstances.

Salwen also pointed out that directors in the United States are responsible for ensuring that there is a " 'rational' or 'reasonable' relationship between the value of compensation paid to officers and the value of the services rendered." Furthermore, under ERISA, a fiduciary (generally defined as anyone who has discretionary authority or control over the administration of an employee benefit plan) must discharge his or her duties with respect to benefit plans

> solely in the interest of the participants and beneficiaries; for the exclusive purpose of providing benefits and defraying expenses with the care and skill that a prudent man familiar with such matters would use in the conduct of similar enterprise, by diversifying the investments of the plan so as to minimize the risk of large losses; and in accordance with the plan documents, provided they are consistent with ERISA.[4]

ESTABLISHING COMPENSATION LEVELS

The evolution of compensation programs should be an interactive process between management and the committee. Committee members should share their philosophies with management in order to influence the development of programs and specifics at an early stage. Management should make compensation proposals that reflect an integrated approach to the use of compensation, organizational structure, and staffing to support overall corporate strategies. Compensation surveys and advice from consultants also contribute to program development.

Survey Data: Handle with Care

In developing compensation proposals, management is certain to consider survey data. Survey material today is vast and complex; large companies spend more than the equivalent of one full-time person on compensation survey work. It is usually more helpful for management to inform the committee regularly about the types of surveys available, the corporation's philosophy of market positioning, and the company's situation rather than to display all the detail. Management should flag and explain proposals that go against survey trends.

Committee members do need detail on the competitive situation of the CEO, however. Committees are sometimes accused of following peers' pay practices too closely when setting CEOs' salaries, and at other times accused of paying too much relative to their peers. Paying "too much" is probably more spectacular than paying too little, but paying too little or paying for the wrong thing can be damaging to the motivation and commitment of the most talented executives, people whose operating impact, particularly in the long run, far outweighs their total costs to the organization. Compensation should be driven by a clear strategy; therefore, a simple "parallel the market" approach is usually superficial, particularly at top levels. Extraordinary actions, well considered within the overall situation, can be more defensible than allegiance to survey percentiles.

Use of Consultants

Even very large organizations with highly sophisticated internal resources use compensation consultants. Much of the vast amount of survey data is available only through consultants, who offer expertise, can take advantage of economies of scale, and guarantee confidentiality to respondents. Good consultants can offer perspective—including a degree of independence—as well as information. In addition to supplying information, they can help client organizations create effective programs with up-to-date or, in some cases, entirely new approaches. Committee members should know the compensation consultants employed by the company and may welcome them at selected committee meetings. However, the committee should remember that, just as it should not take over management's responsibility to propose compensation programs, it should not turn over those responsibilities to consultants whose role is even more differentiable than directors' from that of company management.

CONCLUSION

The board committee responsible for compensation has an extremely powerful role to play, whether viewed from the top down (corporate governance), the outside in (the critical public), or the bottom up (management). If it fails to do its job, there are potentially serious consequences to shareholder and public interests, as well as to the concerted strategic thrust of the corporation.

The criticism of compensation committees—some of it justified, some of it contradictory—has led to change in companies and their boardrooms. Directors today have a heightened awareness of the responsibilities (and occasional hazards) of board membership, and are increasingly serious about their duties as compensation committee members. They are more active in identifying, considering, and discussing information outside the committee materials. They consider proposals from a wider perspective, and aggressively subject new incentive formulas to "what-if" scenarios and sophisticated sensitivity analyses.

Within the NACD, board members have made it clear that they want a more thorough understanding both of the technical aspects of compensation and of the overall environment in which directors' responsibilities are performed. The NACD has responded by creating a series of conferences for directors on compensation issues.

I agree with Robert Lear, executive-in-residence at Columbia Business School, former CEO of F&M Schaefer Brewing Company, and chairperson of several compensation committees, who said,

> As long as we have a free society, we will have a few people who abuse the incentive compensation privilege and a few organizations and compensation committees who let them get by with it. On the other hand . . . 90 percent of us . . . are sincerely trying to do an effective job.[5]

NOTES

1. J. E. Richard, "Compensation Committee Issues, 1989," *Director's Monthly* (June 1989), p. 3.

2. Walter Guzzardi, "Wisdom from the Giants of Business," *Fortune*, July 3, 1989, p. 88.

3. Lance Berger, "New Initiatives for the Compensation Committee," *Directors & Boards* (Winter 1985), p. 35.

4. Remarks made by Robert Salwen, Esquire, at the National Association of Corporate Directors Conference on Compensation Issues and the Corporate Director, December 1986.

5. Remarks made by Robert W. Lear at the National Association of Corporate Directors Conference on Compensation Issues and the Corporate Director, December 1986, as published in *Director's Monthly* (January 1987), p. 4.

BIBLIOGRAPHY

Fisher, James W., Jr. "Compensation Responsibilities of Outside Directors." National Association of Corporate Directors Board Practices Monograph, vol. 2, no. 2, NACD, Washington, DC, 1985.

APPENDIX I

Updating the Compensation Committee Charter at Crane Company

Robert Lear, newly appointed chairman of the organization and compensation committee at Crane Company, has described the approach used in developing the committee's charter and procedures:

> The human resources director and I took on the task of revising our overall procedures. The human resources director personally visited six comparable companies and picked up copies of their compensation committee charter, programs, procedures, and forms. I contributed a few (including those of Air Products and Chemicals). And of course, he talked to the companies of each of our outside directors. We came up with a draft of a revised approach which included a modified charter, a change of name to the Organization and Compensation Committee, a series of new approval authorities, and a schedule with basic agenda for five committee meetings to be held each year. We also produced a completely new set of forms to be used for submission of recommendations to the Organization and Compensation Committee. . . . We then asked the CEO, COO, CFO, and legal counsel to comment on our draft and, with their changes and comments, submitted the new approach to the other committee members and thence to the board for final clearance. The whole process took three months to do, but was very worthwhile. (Extracted from remarks made by Robert W. Lear at the National Association of Corporate Directors Conference on Compensation Issues and the Corporate Director, December 1986, as published in *Director's Monthly* [January 1987], p. 4.)

As a result of these efforts, Crane Company adopted the following charter:

EXHIBIT 1
The Crane Company Compensation Committee Charter

Membership

The Organization and Compensation Committee (the "Committee") shall consist of three to five directors who are not and never have been employees of the Company, and who shall designate a Chairman among themselves.

Function

The Committee is charged with the Board responsibility for assuring that the officers and key management personnel of the corporation are effectively compensated in terms of salaries, supplemental compensation, and benefits which are internally equitable and externally competitive.

Scope

The Committee serves at the pleasure of and is subject to the control and direction of the Board of Directors.

Duties and Responsibilities

The Committee has responsibility for the compensation of Officers and Division Presidents and will review and recommend to the Board compensation for the Chief Executive Officer.

The Committee is expected to:

- Review annually the compensation and allowances for directors as recommended by Company management.
- Review and approve executive payroll salary policy, systems for distribution of inventive compensation or bonuses, and the design of any new supplemental compensation program applicable to the executive payroll.
- Upon recommendation of Company management, review and approve the number of shares, price per share, and period of duration for stock grants under any approved stock option plan.
- Review recommendations of the Chief Executive Officer for major or special changes in existing retirement and benefit plans that have application to significant numbers of total employees or that have a significant impact on Company profits.

Procedure

The Committee shall meet as scheduled by the Committee Chairman. Meetings will be with members of management and with representatives of the independent consultant at the request of the Committee.

The Committee may meet privately with the independent consultant and be free to talk directly and independently with any members of management in discharging its responsibilities.

The Chairman of the Committee will periodically report the Committee's findings and conclusions to the Board of Directors.

The Committee will be assisted by the Secretary who will serve as Executive Secretary to the Committee.

EXHIBIT 2
Regular Meeting Schedule Organization and Compensation Committee of Crane Company

---

(All meetings to be held at 9:00 a.m., prior to Board meetings, except when otherwise noted)

January: Annual bonus payments. (May be subject to minor modification after final earnings are determined.) Annual salary review of top group. (Increases to be effective as of January 1.)

March: Annual stock option review including SARs and other long-term incentives. (Official grants to be approved by Board at April meeting.) Annual Human Resource review of organizational structure, management needs analysis, management development programs, and performance appraisal procedures.

September: Annual review and appraisal of corporate employee benefit programs and specific benefits of top group.

November: Appraisal of annual bonus plan format and application. Appraisal of long-term incentive plans for top group.

Whenever appropriate, additional items will be added to the regularly scheduled agenda.

(Charter and schedule provided courtesy of Richard B. Phillips, Human Resource Director at the time of the study and now Vice President, Human Resources, Crane Company.)

APPENDIX II

The Charter of the Management Development and Compensation Committee, Air Products and Chemicals, Inc.

The Management Development and Compensation Committee shall:

a. review the Company's management resources, its executive manpower selection and development processes, and the performance of key executives;

b. review long-range planning for orderly succession of senior executives, including adopting emergency procedures for management succession in the event of the unexpected disabilities of senior executives;

c. review significant organization changes;

d. review the Chairman of the Board's recommendations of candidates for corporate officers of the Company and monitor appointments of divisional operating officers and assistance officers;

e. review and monitor the Company's policies established to provide equal employment opportunity;

f. establish for and on behalf of the Board the salary rates for all employees who are members of the Board of Directors and for all corporate officers of the Company who are elected by the Board of Directors;

g. take any final action on the salary rates of divisional operating officers and all other executive personnel of the Company and its subsidiaries whose base compensation is, or by reason of any proposed change will be, in Company salary grade "x" or above;

h. take any final action with respect to any matters as to which the Board of Directors or a committee thereof is or shall be empowered to act in relation to the Performance Share Plan, the Long-Term Incentive Plan, the Annual Incentive Plan and the Deferred Stock Plan of the Company (together, the "Incentive Plans") and take all action required or deemed desirable to be taken in relation to said Incentive Plans, including, without limitation, amending each Plan from time to time to the extent only that such authority has been heretofore granted to the Board by the provisions of the Plan provided by the shareholders of the Company;

i. periodically examine the compensation structure of the Company and its subsidiaries insofar as employees in salary grade "x" and above are concerned, to determine that the Company and its subsidiaries are rewarding its executive personnel in a manner consistent with sound industrial practices;

j. take any final action required or deemed desirable with respect to any agreement between the Company and any member of the Board of Directors or other executive personnel of the Company relating to the services of any such person;

k. take any final actions with respect to lending any money to, or guaranteeing any obligation of, or rendering financial assistance to, any officer or other employee of the Company or its subsidiaries, including adoption of any plan or program for rendering financial assistance to such persons whenever the same may be expected by the Committee to benefit the Company;

l. take any final action with respect to any matters as to which the Board of Directors or a committee thereof is or shall be empowered to act in relation to the Retirement Plan for Salaried Employees, the Supplementary Retirement Plan, the Pension Plan for Hourly Rated Employees, the Savings and Stock Ownership Plan and the Employees' Shareholder Plan (together, the "Benefit Plans"), including without limitation:

(1) amending each Benefit Plan from time to time upon recommendation of and consultation with the Employee Benefit Plans Committee constituted by the Board;

(2) appointing members of the Employee Benefit Plans Committee; and

(3) reviewing actions taken by the Employee Benefit Plans Committee, including periodic reports submitted by the Employee Benefit Plans Committee, with respect to its administration of each Benefit Plan; but excepting such matters with respect to which the Board delegates authority and responsibility to the Employee Benefit Plans Committee or may reserve to itself exclusive authority or where delegation of the Board's authority may, in the opinion of the General Counsel of the Company, be in contravention of law. The Management Development and Compensation Committee shall have oversight responsibility with respect to each of the Benefit Plans, and when acting in such capacity, shall be a named Fiduciary (as defined in the Employee Retirement Income Security Act of 1974) with respect to each Plan (except the Supplementary Retirement Plan). The Employee Benefit Plans Committee shall be responsible for the control and administration of each such Benefit Plan and its Plan assets to the extent set forth in the Benefit Plans, and when acting in such capacity, shall be a Named Fiduciary with respect to each Plan (except the Supplementary Retirement Plan);

m. present to the Board of Directors an annual report pertaining to the Management Development and Compensation Committee's actions and to the administration of each Benefit Plan by the Employee Benefit Plans Committee and, except in the case of the Supplementary Retirement Plan, pertaining to the management of the assets of the Benefit Plans.

22

REMUNERATION OF OUTSIDE DIRECTORS

Bruce Overton

THE DESIGN AND ADMINISTRATION of compensation, benefits, and perquisites for executives are most difficult managerial challenges. Managing the remuneration of nonemployee members of a company's board of directors is even more difficult. A person does not apply for a board seat; he or she "explores" such an opportunity. In many cases, it is not compensation that attracts top people to boards, because most outside directors already hold high-paying jobs and/or are successful in their occupations. People often want to be on boards for the challenge, prestige, and contacts.

A corporation does not employ a director; he or she is elected by the stockholders. The amount of time that an outside director spends on company matters is considerably less than that spent by any member of top management. Evaluating the individual performance of directors is difficult because of the strategic (rather than tactical) nature of their role and because of the time horizon necessary to judge their contributions.

For these reasons, compensation and benefits for directors are arrived at differently than they are for executives within a firm. The process for establishing appropriate remuneration requires unusual thinking and the development of new and different approaches.

In this chapter I will discuss the role of the outside director and the goals of outside director remuneration. I will identify the forms of outside director compensation and give advice on how to select the appropriate one. The chapter concludes with recommendations for reviewing and evaluating the performance of outside directors.

ROLE OF THE OUTSIDE DIRECTOR

Outside director compensation must reflect the ever-changing role of directors. In 1979, *BusinessWeek* reported that outside directors were becoming more independent, assertive, and willing to exercise initiative.[1]

They proved so in the 1980s. In that decade, examples of aggressive boards included those of Allegheny International, Mellon Bank, Pillsbury, RJR Nabisco, and United Air Lines. In all of these companies, a vote of the board of directors replaced the CEO. The role of outside directors will continue to expand throughout the 1990s.

Indeed, today's outside director is no longer a rubber stamp, or someone a CEO keeps in the dark. Outside directors have and will continue to fulfill responsibilities well beyond those legally established by state laws on corporate governance and by SEC regulations. Moreover, in my opinion, the current focus of most outside directors on representing *shareholders* will in the 1990s expand to a focus on representing *shareholders and employees*. As corporations continue restructuring, downsizing, merging, acquiring, and recapitalizing, outside directors will continue to adopt broader roles in helping management fulfill the original purpose of the corporation as "an instrument for creating products, services and jobs . . . by which members of society can improve their lives."[2] The outside director cannot be responsible only to shareholders and/or Wall Street deal makers, but must also consider employees who are affected by restructuring and similar events.

There are already signs that this is occurring. More than 60 percent of all public companies have adopted some form of takeover defense,[3] including:

- Requiring a staggered reelection of board members so that a new majority owner cannot attempt to unseat all board members at one time;
- Establishing special shareholder rights plans that create additional ownership opportunities for current shareholders whenever a takeover begins. This can be extremely effective whenever ESOPs have been implemented;
- Instituting poison pill provisions that make it hard to "swallow" a company because of costs or financial obligations; and
- Enacting special employee protection plans such as golden, silver, and tin parachutes (enhanced severance plans) for executives and mid- and lower-level employees who are subject to termination after a takeover.

These examples are a mix of shareholder and employee protection efforts. Therefore, one can conclude that outside directors, as policy creators and strategic planners for corporations, will lead companies in representing shareholders and employees in the 1990s.

They will, however, continue to perform their present responsibilities, which include:

- Providing advice and counsel to the CEO and other senior executives on the strategic direction of the organization;
- Reviewing the performance of the company to ensure that it is achieving its strategic goals;
- Evaluating financial systems and financial reports; and
- Approving remuneration and management succession plans of the organization.

With respect to the last two items, most boards have audit, compensation/benefit, and nominating committees that represent significant areas of accountability. Nominating committees approve CEO succession plans, while compensation/benefit committees approve pay levels of the CEO and other officers.

The compensation levels of the CEO position continue to receive more media coverage and subsequent public reaction every year. Outside directors must apply the "prudent man" rule to compensation judgments, and this is prompting increased use of third-party, outside consultants to help review executive pay levels and design performance-driven pay programs.

Board audit committees review and validate the financial reporting processes and internal controls of the company. In accomplishing this responsibility, they need internal and external company resources to make such validations of company financial systems. In the late 1980s, former SEC commissioner James C. Treadway led a special group composed primarily of senior company executives in identifying guidelines on how board audit committees should fulfill their role and thus prevent fraudulent financial reporting.

A similar need exists today in the area of board oversight of executive compensation, one that is likely to be addressed during the 1990s. Commissions like Treadway's are a means of addressing the issue of outside director accountability. Guidelines from such groups can become accountability charters for board committees and provide a basis for evaluating the performance of outside directors. Moreover, such guidelines can ensure that outside directors avoid interlocking board memberships (i.e., when similar board members serve in different companies, or more seriously, when CEOs serve on one another's boards, or worse still, when CEOs serve as one another's chairman of the compensation committee), for which companies have been strongly criticized. Whatever the board composition, committee guidelines and charters are excellent tools for identifying accountability for the current and expanding roles of outside directors.

The remuneration of outside directors will increase because of the continued expansion of their role. In 1985, U.S. companies paid outside directors an average annual retainer of $15,000.[4] Gardner Heidrick, then president of the executive search firm Heidrick & Struggles, had been predicting for years that corporations would make more use of outside directors and that directors' pay would rise considerably. Both of his predictions proved accurate. During the past five years, annual director compensation in the nation's largest corporations and financial institutions has risen 27 percent, from $19,544 to $24,729, according to a recent study by Korn/Ferry International. The $24,729 average total annual compensation includes an annual fee of $17,824 and a per meeting fee of $986, up from the $13,629 annual fee and $834 per meeting fee reported five years ago. As would be expected, the larger the company, the higher the compensation. Directors of billion-dollar industrial and service corporations earn an average of $27,862, while directors of $5-billion-and-over companies earn an average of $32,512.[5]

GOALS OF OUTSIDE DIRECTOR REMUNERATION

Remuneration is not what attracts a person to a board of directors. Although the average outside director of a large company now earns close to $40,000,[6] the average CEO in a large company earns over $400,000.[7] Cash compensation and other forms of pay do indicate to directors, however, the value put on the time they spend on company business. Therefore, the first purpose of outside director remuneration is *proper pay for the value of time provided*.

Companies typically set outside director pay levels based on competitive data about other companies' practices. This approach frequently leads to constant adjustments in order to keep up with the competition, rather than productivity or performance improvement. This situation needs to be changed. The remuneration of outside directors should be increased only when there is a change in their roles that necessitates a greater time commitment to the company. Companies should not increase directors' pay simply because a survey concludes that average outside directors' compensation increased 5 percent from one year to another. In addition, survey organizations should identify the role and responsibility changes associated with increases in directors' remuneration. Efforts in this direction will provide a better correlation of directors' pay with their specific duties and the time allocated to them.

Another approach to the issue of paying properly for directors' time is to compare the hourly rate of directors to that of the CEO. A comparison of the hourly rate for board activities with that for nonboard activities also can be meaningful, and may influence how directors allocate their time commitments. This allocation, in turn, is of interest to the company searching for board directors.

If a director is paid $30,000 per year and spends twenty hours per month on board activities, that translates to $125 per hour. If the CEO of the company earns $300,000 in base salary per year and works 200 hours per month, that also translates to $125 per hour. This is *not* to say that if a CEO makes $300,000 in base salary, then directors should make $30,000, but comparisons of rates of pay for outside directors and CEOs are relevant if pay is to be representative of value-added to the business. Conclusions about the appropriate relationship will vary, depending on specific roles and responsibilities. Typically, a CEO has a higher hourly rate than the outside directors because his or her accountabilities and impact on the organization are greater. For example, RJR Nabisco, prior to its LBO in 1989, paid its CEO $900,000 annually, or approximately $350 per hour. Its outside directors were paid $50,000 a year, or about $200 per hour.

The second purpose of outside director remuneration is *to reward good performance*. Historically, this has been done primarily by increasing pay levels. But better methods are needed and variable incentive pay is one alternative. To reward board members with variable incentive pay, however, has always been difficult because the performance of directors is hard to evaluate. Furthermore, few companies currently believe that the annual incentives commonly offered to executives could have a significant impact on directors' performance. Nevertheless, rewarding boards for the achievement of goals is a challenge that must be met by companies in the future.

Incentive pay is rarely what attracts an outside director to board service, but it can be used successfully as a way to encourage more active involvement in board activities. Paying fees for *attendance* at board and committee meetings is one example, as is giving stock to directors. The use of stock grants is one of the most significant current trends in the area of variable incentive pay for board members. Stock grants can attract people to serve as outside directors, retain high-quality directors, ensure that directors focus on employee and shareholder interests, and reward directors for making decisions that protect those interests. One-third of the *Fortune* 100 companies now give stock-based compensation to outside directors.[8] But how many do so as a reward for positive contributions to the company, and tell the director that? I suspect few companies do, and I believe they should! (I will discuss this in more detail later.)

Another significant development is an increase in the number of companies offering directors retirement benefits. Such benefits can reward good performance and help keep outside directors on a board. But unlike stock-based compensation, where share price provides a built-in performance indicator, retirement benefits, once granted, cannot be readily utilized to correlate pay and performance. A direct relationship between pay and performance is difficult to demonstrate with retirement benefits, but if an outside director is not performing his or her stated job, that director can be removed from the board before retirement.

The third primary purpose of outside director compensation is *to reward board members for their role in representing shareholder (and employee) interests.* The dual constituency is particularly important when acquisitions, divestitures, LBOs, mergers, and restructurings occur. A classic example is RJR Nabisco, which was acquired in 1989 by Kohlberg Kravis Roberts & Co. (KKR) in a $25-billion leveraged buyout. At that time, the pay of RJR Nabisco's outside directors was clearly among the highest for directors in American industry.[9]

However, in light of the tremendous responsibilities they had in guiding the company through the LBO and in protecting the interests of shareholders and employees, one could argue that the directors were conservatively rewarded (or even inadequately rewarded in individual cases). Five of the board members served on a special committee, whose purpose was to evaluate all offers, including those of the management and various outsiders. The committee (as well as all outside directors) decided the major issues, which included whose offer should be accepted, and for what price; how equity in the firm should be distributed; whether existing businesses should be sold to service the new debt structure of the company; what employee protection programs (e.g., severance) were appropriate; and so forth. The directors were dealing with the future of a company with $17 billion in sales and over 100,000 employees; it is obvious that they earned every dollar of their compensation. The same is true of outside directors involved in almost every type of merger, buyout, or major change in management.

The fourth purpose of outside director remuneration is *to reward board members for advising management.* Board members can bring advice, counsel, judgment, and perspective to the CEO and contribute to the company on such substantive matters as business purpose, business planning, evaluation of products/services, appointment and compensation of key personnel, investments, dividends, utilization of financial resources, and public and social policy.

By assisting the CEO and other key executives, outside directors contribute to the organization's strategic and tactical planning. Directors play increasingly important roles in business organizations in this country as they help to change business focus, products and services, organizational structure, and financial and human resource management in response to competitive need and ever-changing business conditions.

FORMS OF OUTSIDE DIRECTOR REMUNERATION

Outside directors are paid in a variety of ways. The first and most common method of remuneration is cash in the form of fees and/or retainers for both committee service and nonmeeting activities that support the roles and responsibilities of the board. Outside directors normally serve on one or more of the following committees: audit, investment, compensation and benefits, finance, public issues, or nominating. Committee work normally is compensated separately, although some companies do provide an overall retainer or fee to outside directors. The other form of direct compensation is stock, a vehicle whose popularity is growing. Let us look more closely at the forms of direct remuneration.

Direct/Cash Compensation

Annual retainer.   A direct payment typically given monthly or quarterly, the retainer ranges from $5,000 per year in small companies to $50,000 per year in larger ones. It is normally intended to reward directors for service and performance. Time spent at board and committee meetings is usually compensated for separately. Large companies that pay retainers plus meeting fees include General Electric, Exxon, Sears, Roebuck, and Merck. Companies such as American Express, Du Pont, Johnson & Johnson, and Xerox provide only one annual retainer with no meeting fees.

Board and committee meeting fees.   When used, fees are in the form of a retainer (ranging from $1,000 to $5,000 per year) or of a payment per meeting (ranging from $250 to $1,000). Those firms that pay meeting fees separately from the annual retainer do so to encourage and reward attendance.

Stock awards. Stock options or stock grants (sometimes with a time lapse or other restrictions) are occasionally paid in addition to or in lieu of annual retainers and committee fees. One purpose of stock compensation is to align directors' interests directly with those of shareholders. Most outside directors do not own a great deal of company stock; providing shares instead of increasing fees is one way to augment directors' stock ownership.

General Electric uses a stock option plan that provides nonemployee directors with annual grants, permitting them to buy up to 1,500 shares of GE's common stock from the company at the fair market value of the shares on the date the option is granted. The options expire ten years after the date they are granted. The plan is administered by a committee of nonparticipating directors who have authority to interpret the plan but no discretion with respect to the selection of directors who are to receive the options, the number of shares subject to the plan or to each grant, or the purchase price. As another example, Exxon recently provided 1,500 restricted shares to each of its nonemployee directors. (The restriction lasts until the director is no longer eligible for reelection.)

One simple way for a company to structure direct cash compensation for outside directors is to establish a target or desired total amount, then "back into" amounts of retainers, fees, or stock. For example, a company may decide that the appropriate total cash compensation for each outside director is $20,000 per year, to be paid as follows:

Annual Retainer	$15,000
Committee/Meeting Fee	
($500 × 10 meetings)	5,000
Total	$20,000

At times, companies give added compensation to committee chairpeople, who must devote more time to committee activities. If a general member of the audit committee is paid $500 per meeting, then the chairperson may receive $1,000 for each meeting or perhaps $2,000 to $5,000 added to the annual retainer to recognize the additional service.

Deferral of Cash Compensation

Annual retainers and meeting or committee fees are typically provided to outside directors as current income, which is taxed as wages/salaries. Alternatively, such compensation can be deferred. If payment is deferred, the company usually offers the same investment alternatives that are available to company employees. For example, if a company offers top management the prime interest rate on deferred compensation, it gives the same interest rate to outside directors.

Indirect Compensation

Retirement benefits.　Organizations can provide payments to retiring board members after they have met specific tenure requirements. As mentioned, providing retirement benefits is a growing trend in outside director remuneration and an important tool in attracting and retaining high-quality people, particularly those from a noncorporate background where significant retirement benefits are not common. The typical benefit is a percentage of the annual retainer. For example, 50 percent of the annual retainer might be paid if retirement occurred at age seventy after five or more years of board service, for a period equal to the total number of years of board service, or ten years, whichever was less. A representative outside directors' retirement plan is summarized below:

> The Directors Retirement Plan provides each eligible director with a monthly allowance equal to the director's fee payable on the date the director's service terminates. The maximum benefits payable under the Directors Retirement Plan are (a) for those directors with ten or more years' service, 180 monthly payments; (b) for those directors with less than ten but more than five years' service, monthly payments equal to 180 multiplied by a fraction, the numerator of which is equal to the years of service of such director and the denominator of which is 10; (c) for directors with less than five years' service, 48 monthly payments. For the purpose of computing years of service, partial years of service count as a full year.[10]

Medical/life insurance.　Some companies provide life insurance equal to either a fixed percentage of a director's annual retainer or in a specified amount (i.e., either one times the annual retainer or $50,000), and minimum medical expense reimbursements. Medical benefits might include the use of company-sponsored clinics and/or percentage reimbursements of doctor, hospital, and dental bills after a deductible is met. These plans typically are structured in the same way as for regular employees, with appropriate offsets for coverage provided from other insurance plans. Medical insurance can be particularly valuable in recruiting directors who are self-employed. In addition, companies must always provide insurance to outside directors to protect them from personal liabilities arising from the business operation.

Meeting expenses.   Companies reimburse all expenses for board, committee, or annual stockholder meetings. They also frequently provide outside directors with special support resources such as use of company aircraft, chauffeured limousines, and so forth. It is common to offer outside directors the same travel arrangements that senior company executives receive.

Use of company products/services.   Companies often give directors use of company products and services at no or low cost, both as a means of increasing their knowledge of the firm and as a means of attracting and retaining high-quality board members. Although not all organizations can offer this benefit, consumer product companies, automobile companies, and so forth find it a most attractive way to reward outside directors.

The more experience and expertise an outside director possesses, the more important it is that he or she be adequately paid, directly and indirectly. A company or a CEO can receive significant value per hour from a qualified director. What is true about employees is true about nonemployee directors: one gets and holds what one pays for.

Charitable donations.   A new benefit that could become a major trend in the 1990s is to provide outside directors with funds for them to use as charitable donations to nonprofit organizations. With this special benefit companies can fulfill two objectives: attracting and retaining outside directors and meeting obligations to society.

SELECTING OUTSIDE DIRECTOR REMUNERATION

The compensation/benefits provided outside directors should be set in recognition of both competitive practice and the needs of the particular organization. Many business associations (e.g., The Conference Board), most major consulting firms (e.g., Ernst & Young), and some executive search firms (e.g., Korn/Ferry) publish data about directors' compensation annually. Industry norms should be compared with one's own insurance program, travel support, pay, and so forth. A designer of outside director remuneration should then review internal factors such as:

1. *The need to attract additional or new types of outside directors.* Companies may want directors with a variety of backgrounds or areas of expertise in order to serve the changing needs of the business and to complement the strengths of the CEO. Most executive search firms

employ experts in identifying and evaluating outside directors; several search firms specialize in this area (e.g., The Heidrick Partners Inc.).

2. *The competitiveness of the current executive compensation program.* Although executive pay and director pay do not have to run parallel, a comparison of the two can indicate the level of remuneration appropriate in both cases. For example, if a company pays its executives at the 50th percentile, it might want to pay outside directors at a similar level. A very aggressive company that pays its executives at the 75th percentile might want to reward its board members as generously.

3. *The focus of the chief executive officer.* What kind of message does the CEO want to give or reinforce to the members of the board? Possibilities include a focus on austerity, high quality, retention, and so forth. Knowing the CEO's priorities can help determine the types and levels of outside director compensation and benefits. For example, the CEO of a company in the midst of a major turnaround may want a very conservative outside director remuneration program. On the other hand, the CEO of a successful company who is looking to expand the business and add outside directors with experience and skills not possessed by current directors may wish to have an aggressive remuneration program that will help to attract the new board members.

One novel approach to setting outside director compensation—an approach mentioned earlier—is to determine the per diem (or hourly) income of the CEO and apply it or a percentage of it to the board members. Obviously, one needs accurate knowledge of the number of days (or hours) a year that directors spend on company business. One rule of thumb is that for each meeting day, an equal amount of time is needed to do the necessary homework and other preparation. This method of setting directors' pay focuses on one of the most precious assets that a board member has to offer: time. (In order to attract outside directors, companies should think about reducing the time required of board members by holding fewer board meetings, relying more on committees, or combining meetings. It makes good sense to schedule two or three meetings in one day whenever possible.)

In the last analysis, the remuneration for outside directors should be a function of the role they are assigned and the needs of the organization. Exhibit 22-1 depicts a representative compensation program for a *Fortune* 500 industrial or service company.

EXHIBIT 22-1
Representative Compensation Program for Outside Directors
(***Fortune*** **500 Company)**

Annual Retainer	$20,000
Annual Shareholders Meeting Fee	500
Committee Retainer	5,000
Board Meeting Fee ($500 × 10)	5,000
Total Cash Compensation	$30,500
Retirement:	50% of annual retainer after five years of service for either ten years or the number of years of service as a director, whichever is less.
Travel to Board Meetings:	Company aircraft or commercial first class plus reimbursement of all other travel expenses.
Life Insurance:	$50,000 paid by company; imputed income to director.
Liability Insurance:	Paid in full by company.

Note: Current trend is to include stock compensation as part of outside director total cash compensation, in lieu of one or more existing payments. For example, in lieu of the board meeting fee, provide 100 shares of restricted stock (with a $50 grant value = $5,000), with a three-year time lapse restriction (i.e., stock issued but held three years before delivered to director if he or she is still on board). Dividends received by director during the three-year period.

REVIEWING AND EVALUATING OUTSIDE DIRECTORS

As I have mentioned, the contribution of outside directors is difficult to evaluate, for numerous reasons. First, there are no job descriptions or annual objectives for outside directors. Second, board members' contributions are more intangible than tangible. For example, the value of verbal contributions to a board meeting are not easy to measure. Third, the strategic vision provided by outside directors takes time to evaluate, and the prestige and credibility that particular directors add to a company emerge gradually. And, finally, the world of the outside director is quite political and, as in Congress, pay-for-performance is difficult to achieve.

If a CEO does not believe that a director is "on the team," a parting of the ways can be quick regardless of the board member's performance. This is not to say that CEOs typically have or want a tractable board. In fact, most CEOs regard constructive criticism or disagreement as healthy. As John Wooten, the coach emeritus of the UCLA basketball team said, "One can disagree without being disagreeable."

Although there are few readily available or obvious performance evaluation criteria for outside directors (other than attendance), in practice the chairman of the board judges their contributions. Perhaps in no other occupation is the term "lead by example" more appropriate; outside directors must consistently demonstrate their value in strategic planning and operational analysis of the organization. Their performance is on the line at every board meeting and in most counseling sessions with the chairman of the board. The performance of outside directors is, therefore, extremely visible. When their contribution stops, their compensation also stops.

Despite the difficulty of evaluating outside directors, the following requirements can be used in reviewing their performance:

1. Attendance at and contribution to board meetings;
2. Possession and use of special skills that add value to business development, strategic planning, or operational activities in the organization;
3. Committee participation and leadership; and
4. Use of business contacts, position, or reputation on behalf of the organization.

One of the most difficult things a CEO has to do is to counsel outside directors if they are not fulfilling their board responsibilities. It is also quite difficult to fire a nonemployee director. Board members frequently are good business friends of the CEO and other board members. Often directors have close connections with management—they might be a company banker, lawyer, or even someone's in-law—so to ask for a resignation is not easy.

How can a CEO avoid firing directors? Several suggestions should be considered:

1. At the time of initial election to the board, a new director should be told that in each of the first few years, and periodically thereafter, he or she will sit down with the CEO and/or the chairman of the board (or the chairman of the nominating committee) to review board policies, procedures, and the new director's role. If such meetings occur routinely, no one is threatened by or withdraws from open and honest dialogue. In addition to reviews, letters should be sent to newly elected board members spelling out the responsibilities and authority of directors, the provisions of compensation and benefit programs, meeting dates, and other information on board policies, procedures, and established performance evaluation criteria.
2. Whenever the board, the CEO, or director is dissatisfied, the director can be discouraged from running for reelection. Because directors usually serve until the next annual shareholder meeting, the decision to run for reelection can be reviewed annually. Choosing not to run is a diplomatic alternative to resignation.
3. Companies should publish a directors' manual stating that nonem-

ployee directors may resign at any time or choose not to run for re-election. Companies might also require outside directors to resign if they change occupation or organization. Although the board does not have to accept such a resignation, requiring one forces members to consider whether the new position disqualifies the director for service. It should be understood that if a conflict of interest develops, because of an acquisition or merger, for example, then the outside director with the conflict would resign or not run for reelection.

4. A specific retirement age should be part of an agreement with an outside director, just as compensation and benefits are part of the agreement. Directors typically retire at age seventy.

While the review and evaluation of outside directors is definitely more challenging than for executives, it can be accomplished constructively and with dignity so that individual and organizational needs are fulfilled.

SPECIAL CONTRACTS FOR OUTSIDE DIRECTORS

Occasionally, board members provide special services to a business. When this occurs, a contract is drawn up for the director, as it would be for retired senior executives and outside consultants. These special contracts typically designate the remuneration for specific consulting services. Examples of special consulting services are:

1. *Serving as chairman of special committees.* Many international businesses, for example, rely on an advisory committee to develop and review global strategies. Obviously, such a supplemental board committee must be made up of select individuals with extensive international experience and, ideally, an international reputation. Usually an executive from the company serves as primary coordinator of the committee, but sometimes an outside director plays this role, in lieu of or in addition to the executive. When this occurs, a special contract and fee for the chairman is established.

2. *Providing expert advice.* Outside directors or employee directors now retired are often retained to provide strategic and/or tactical advice to company executives. The advice might be in broad areas such as legal counsel on litigations and patents, financial advice on balance sheet accounting, banking relationships, and so forth. Outside directors who provide special consulting services can be employed with a contract that outlines and details both the services to be provided and the fees to be paid. Companies must be careful that it does not appear

to the shareholders that a consulting outside director is more loyal to the management than to the shareholders.

CONCLUSION

The determination of appropriate remuneration for nonemployee outside directors requires special analysis of roles and the identification of where value can be added, based on the limited number of hours available. Direct and indirect forms of remuneration can be selected as rewards. But the structure of directors' rewards is significantly different from that of company executives because of the unique relationship between directors and CEOs. It is because of the uniqueness of the relationship that establishing appropriate rewards for outside directors is most challenging.

NOTES

1. *BusinessWeek*, September 10, 1979, p. 72.
2. The Business Roundtable, "The Role and Composition of the Board of Directors of the Large Publicly Owned Corporation" (January 1978), pp. 2–3.
3. Ernst & Young, "Report on the Organization & Composition of Boards of Directors, 1988," p. 11.
4. Towers, Perrin, Forster & Crosby, "1980 Survey of Outside Director Compensation."
5. Korn/Ferry International, *17th Annual Board of Directors Study* (NY: 1990), p. 7.
6. RJR Nabisco, "1989 Survey of Outside Director Compensation."
7. Sibson & Company, "1989 Annual Report of Executive Compensation."
8. Ernst & Young, "Survey of the Organization & Composition of Boards" (1988), p. 51.
9. RJR Nabisco, "1988 Survey of Outside Director Compensation."
10. RJR Nabisco Proxy, April 5, 1989, pp. 1–2.

BIBLIOGRAPHY

Chingos, P. T. "How Companies Are Using Stock Options for Directors." *Directors & Boards* 12(3) (1988), pp. 37–39.
Dobrzynski, J. H., Schroeder, M., Miles, G., and Weber, J. "Taking Charge." *BusinessWeek*, July 3, 1989, pp. 66–71.
Hallenbeck, G. T. "Pension Planning for Outside Directors." *Pension World* 23(11) (1987), pp. 67–68.

Meuter, F., Jr. "Questions the New Compensation Committee Member Should Ask." *Directors & Boards* 13(2) (1989), pp. 31–33.

Meyer, P. "The Rise of the Outside Director as an Equity Owner." *Directors & Boards* 10(3) (1986), pp. 41–43.

Miller, A. "A Director's Questions." *The Wall Street Journal*, August 18, 1980.

Ochsner, R. C., and Simpson, D. R. "The Pros and Cons of Incentives for Directors." *Directors & Boards* 12(3) (1988), pp. 40–41.

"Outside Directors Receive Deferred Compensation." *Employee Benefit Plan Review* 42(3) (1987), pp. 94–98.

Singh, H., and Harianto, F. "Management-Board Relationships, Takeover Risk, and the Adoption of Golden Parachutes." *Academy of Management Journal* 32(1) (1989), pp. 7–24.

Tauber, Y. D. "Trends in Compensation for Outside Directors." *Compensation and Benefits Review* 18 (January/February 1986), pp. 43–52.

Tilghman, T. S, and Wasserstrum, D. J. "Director Compensation: The Appeal of Retirement Plans and Stock Option Programs." *Directors & Boards* 11(3) (1987), pp. 38–39.

PART III

Strategic Executive Compensation at Work: Applications

PART III-A

Executive Compensation in the High-Tech Industry

23

A FRAMEWORK FOR COMPENSATION AT ANALOG DEVICES

Ray Stata

A FRAMEWORK FOR COMPENSATION grows out of what the partners in a corporation believe to be its purpose. A corporation is a voluntary association of people, primarily employees and stockholders, but also customers and suppliers, who share a common, long-term interest in the success of the firm. People enter into this association because they believe they can be more productive and successful working together toward common goals than working alone. When such partners are motivated by enlightened self-interest, they do not seek short-term gratification, but rather, guided by reason, look for an integrated plan for long-term success and happiness. The interests of the employee and the company coincide, since the individual's long-term career goals can be achieved best when the business is strong and healthy.

In a capitalist society, private corporations are the property of shareholders who have the right to establish the terms and conditions of employment and other contracts. However, the conventional wisdom that says that the purpose of the corporation is to increase shareholder wealth is a narrow and unrealistic view. Although shareholders own the assets, a corporation is really a partnership among shareholders, employees, customers, and suppliers, each of whom has the right to enter into mutually beneficial agreements.

Corporate success is measured by the degree to which the long-term goals of the partners are met. This need not be a zero-sum game where the interests of one constituency are traded off against the interests of another. In successful companies, all partners win; customer satisfaction is measured by market share, shareholder satisfaction by returns on investment, and employee satisfaction by the level of compensation.

Customers' goals are met not only by the lowest price. On-time delivery, short lead times, high product quality and reliability, dependable service and support, and innovative solutions to customers' problems are also

403

important to buyers. By the same token, employee expectations are met not only by the highest compensation. Opportunities for personal growth and career advancement, the satisfaction of challenging work, secure employment, safe working conditions, and the chance to associate with and learn from people with similar interests are all counted in the total reward received by employees. Likewise, shareholders are looking not only for above-average returns, but also security, liquidity, and, in some cases, pride of ownership.

If a partnership hinges entirely or even mostly on tangible rewards such as price, pay, or return on investment, then the corporation and its members are not likely to be successful over the long term. Values assigned to less tangible rewards are also very important.

DETERMINING VALUE-ADDED

Within this framework, what compensation policy works best? Compensation must be competitive in the labor market and it must motivate employees. It also must be fair according to an objective measure of performance.

There are two closely related ways to determine the value-added by an employee. One way is to focus on the value of the position filled, the other way on the value of the employee's personal contribution. Most corporate compensation policies give more weight to the importance of the job than to the worth of the individual's contribution because the former is much easier to measure.

The value assigned to a position often depends on its size, which can be measured by revenues. Executive pay ranges (divisional and corporate) within a given industry segment are approximately proportional to the logarithm of revenues; that is, pay is higher by a fixed percentage for each tenfold increase in revenues.

The size of a position also can be measured by the number of employees managed or by the scope of responsibility. The greater the responsibility, in terms of function, geography, product lines, markets, or other measures, the greater the value-added. For example, a management position with responsibility for the design and marketing of one product line would be assigned less value than a divisional management position with responsibility for manufacturing. Or, a divisional management position with administrative functions, including human resources and finance, would be assigned more value than one without these functions.

Determining the value of positions by their size has merit for static, slow-growing companies. In dynamic, fast-growing organizations, however, size is a less relevant measure of value-added. Starting up and nurturing a new business requires an extraordinary set of skills and the value contributed by successful achievement is very high. (The venture capital community clearly recognizes this by awarding large incentives for success.) Even in established companies, there is much debate about who adds the greatest value to the firm, the manager of a large, mature division, or the manager of a new business unit with only a handful of subordinates. The person in charge of the fast-growing product line may have greater potential impact on a company's profitability than the manager of the slow-growing division with all the bells and whistles. Just as the real value of a new business might be judged only by such intangibles as market potential and the quality of strategic plans, the value of a managerial position in a new business unit might depend on such intangibles as skill in projecting a vision of opportunity and the ability to engender commitment to ambitious goals.

Companies also must be precise about the *source* of value-added. Within an existing corporation, a relatively young, inexperienced manager may be assigned to head a new business under the close supervision of a more senior, experienced manager, while the president of a startup company must function more autonomously. The amount of supervision required should be an important factor in setting compensation for these positions. The pay range assigned to a job must be capable of reflecting the employee's dependence on the supporting infrastructure. The contribution of supervisors is often downplayed in the administration of compensation.

Emphasizing size alone in setting compensation reduces organizational flexibility and encourages empire-building. In today's business world, it is essential to be able to change back and forth from a centralized to a decentralized structure quickly, without being blocked by rules that tie compensation to one particular form. When a company bases compensation on unit size, it sacrifices the freedom to experiment with a variety of structures.

The foregoing suggests that a rapidly growing business requires more emphasis on evaluating employees' actual performance than their positions. Even in mature, slow-growing businesses, there is increasing recognition of the difference between caretakers and change agents who assume responsibility for renewal and performance improvement. In a dynamic environment, or one where managers agree to be aggressive, we must emphasize the *process* of achieving success. To evaluate performance, we must develop a set of criteria to describe and appraise the skills required to reach long-range goals.

VALUING EMPLOYEE CONTRIBUTIONS AT ANALOG

To aid us in appraising employees' contributions, at Analog Devices we recently elevated competency review to a major component of performance evaluation. We plan to give as much weight to *how* results are achieved (the process) as to what results are achieved (the goals). We have chosen the following management competencies or attributes to be evaluated: job knowledge; planning/goal-setting; execution/control; quality/method improvement; acceptance of responsibility; conceptual/strategic ability; judgment/decision making; leadership; selection/development; delegation/participation; teamwork; objectivity; and openness. Some categories such as teamwork, objectivity, and openness are included because we are making a strong effort to inculcate these qualities among our people. We also are experimenting with peer and subordinate review.

We have much work to do to reach a common understanding of how to judge these qualities in different functions and levels of responsibility. That will be a focal point of our training and development program.

We also have begun to discuss how to apply greater weight to competencies in assigning labor grades. One reason companies are reluctant to emphasize competencies in setting labor grades is the tendency of supervisors to inflate performance evaluations and overlook their subordinates' deficiencies. Managers are often more objective in evaluating positions than individuals. This problem is alleviated by working out objective criteria for judging competence. It also is alleviated by a performance review system that includes input from a broad cross-section of individuals.

These are difficult issues that we have only begun to explore. The efficacy of our compensation system will be measured by our progress in training supervisors and managers to make better judgments and evaluations, not of positions, but of people.

DETERMINING VARIABLE COMPENSATION

At Analog, we believe that there should be a good deal of bonus compensation at all levels. Variable compensation should represent a greater percentage of total pay at the top of the organization than at the bottom, because higher wage earners can cope better with fluctuations in income and because they have more impact on those fluctuations.

Variable pay has many advantages. It fosters alignment of individual and organizational goals and provides a way to focus attention on the criteria by which success is measured. Variable bonuses also help companies maintain employment security through downturns in the business cycle. During the industry slump of 1985–1987, for example, Analog's bonus play stopped paying out for six quarters. This represented a decrease of $9.6 million or 8.2 percent of a total U.S. payroll of $117 million. To equal the savings we achieved with the help of the bonus cuts, we would have had to lay off 267 people or 8 percent of our domestic work force.

Should bonuses be computed on the performance of the individual, the department, the division, the group, or the corporation? The answer depends on the situation and the firm's goals. At Analog Devices, we encouraged decentralization and divisional autonomy in the past, but now we are emphasizing teamwork, sharing of resources, cross-divisional collaboration, and flexibility in reconfiguring the organization and allocating resources to the most promising opportunities. These objectives call for a strong emphasis on corporate performance with additional recognition for extraordinary divisional performance. Historically, we have used growth and return on assets to compute bonuses, but now we are pushing hard to assimilate continuous quality improvement into our culture. We are considering how to factor customer service, product quality, and time-to-market into our bonus calculations. It is essential that performance standards be tied to criteria that take into account customer satisfaction as well as shareholder and employee expectations.

Since our bonus play is intended to reward group performance, what provisions are made to reward individual performance? Rapid promotion is one important way we recognize and reward individual performance. Another way to recognize superior achievement is to award stock options and restricted stock grants. Restricted stock grants at Analog are reserved for executives, managers, and technologists who have high impact on corporate results. Awards may be made annually, but not necessarily every year, with cliff vesting after five years in amounts ranging from 0.25 to 1.0 times base salary.

For a growth company, stock options and stock grants are the main components of the long-term compensation of key managers. With consistent growth in share price, annual stock grants can accumulate into significant assets for an employee. For the company, such incentives provide holding power, while aligning the long-term interests of management and shareholders. Stock schemes have the disadvantage of being affected by vicissitudes in share price that are unrelated to corporate performance. However, managers and shareholders are in the same boat in this respect.

ADAPTING COMPENSATION PLANS

There is no "correct" compensation policy. The reward system, however, must be designed to achieve corporate goals within the context of the changing environment.

For nearly twenty years, we grew at an average rate of 25 percent per year. After becoming a public company, our share price averages similar appreciation. The occasional recession was temporary. In such an environment, our bonus and stock option plan worked well.

However, from 1985–1987 our growth averaged only 6 percent per year. (Although disappointing, this was still very good compared to that of most other U.S. semiconductor companies.) Analog's stock price also deteriorated over this period. Our response to this prolonged slowdown was to cut all nonessential expenses and to reduce or eliminate investments in marginal businesses. Strategically, we took the long view and continued to build investments in programs that we believed were vital to our future success. The result was that profits dropped and our bonus plan, based on a combination of sales growth and return on assets, stopped paying. For the first year this did not cause a morale problem, but after the third year, following the collapse in the stock market on Black Monday, we became concerned about a loss of confidence in the future of the company and defections of our best people.

The question we faced was, should we lower our standards and start paying bonuses or stick to the principle that employees and shareholders are in the same boat and should suffer together? We decided to discard our old bonus formula and start rewarding incremental improvement. If in 1988 the company doubled earnings per share, then we would restore bonuses to a normal level, even though return on assets would be below our past standards. Furthermore, we repriced stock options that were underwater but did not make adjustments in restricted stock grants, held mostly by higher-echelon employees. We believed that shareholders would be pleased if we met this challenging goal and would endorse an incentive plan to achieve it. Three years is too long to expect even the most loyal employees to wait out a major correction in the market, especially when the response of management and the progress being made by the employees is fundamentally sound.

The investments made during the tough times paid off handsomely for shareholders and employees. Halfway into 1988 we were well on the way to doubling earnings per share and paying out a well-earned bonus. We also have seen a partial recovery of our stock price.

Compensation systems are a means to achieve the purpose and goals of the corporation. While we use compensation systems to support management decisions, we must remember which is the tail and which is the dog. We cannot become slaves to the compensation system. After all, people are real; compensation plans are abstractions. We can go only so far in attempting to force people to conform to models. We must be flexible in adapting compensation to real circumstances.

24

STRATEGIC EXECUTIVE COMPENSATION IN THE HIGH-TECH INDUSTRY

J. E. Richard

MANY COMPANIES IN THE high-tech sector have developed and implemented pay methods as creative and unique as the products they manufacture. This is primarily because high-tech companies encourage risk-taking and innovation in management techniques as well as in product development.

The untraditional compensation arrangements that complement the entrepreneurial culture in rapidly growing high-tech firms have created thousands of new millionaires (and hundred millionaires!), many in their twenties and thirties. In the five years from 1981 to 1986, for example, thirteen executives at one company, Advanced Micro Devices, realized net values from their stock options of $23 million. Wealth has been accumulated not only by top executives, but also by technical contributors, product designers, sales and marketing professionals, and other employees.

One of the most significant characteristics of compensation in the technological industry is the relatively high level of equity participation offered to employees. (Exhibit 24–1 summarizes the amount of stock held by key employees at eight high-tech firms.) Compare these figures to the average of 6-percent employee ownership in industries across the board. Companies in the technological sector are more willing than their counterparts in other businesses to experiment with such novel devices as junior common stock (pioneered by Genentech and Amdahl) and convertible debentures. (Exhibit 24–2 defines these and other methods of granting equity.) Technological firms are less likely than their peers in other industries to adopt fixed-cost benefits such as qualified retirement plans. High-growth firms with cash-flow constraints prefer to make the potentially rich rewards of their business contingent on performance.

EXHIBIT 24-1
Sampling of High-Tech Firms That Place Heavy Reliance on Equity Participation

	Total Shares Outstanding (in millions)	Shares Approved for Key Employees (in millions)	% of Total Shares Outstanding Approved for Employees
Tandem	41.4	12.2	29.5
Datapoint	17.8	5.1	28.7
National Semiconductor	90.7	23.7	26.1
Apple Computer	62.7	16.0	25.5
Mentor Graphics	15.8	3.7	23.4
Digital Equipment	128.9	29.5	22.9
Monolithic Memories	21.6	4.8	22.2
Genentech	78.9	15.0	19.0

Source: Company annual reports and legally required filings with Securities and Exchange Commission, 1987–1989.

THE HIGH-GROWTH SEGMENT OF THE INDUSTRY

It is a common mistake to stereotype the high-tech industry. In reality, significant differences in product, location, size, stage of the business cycle, ownership, competition, and company culture rule out a single high-tech profile. A small, independent software company in Bellevue, Washington, designs its compensation program differently than Boston-based Lotus does for a newly acquired firm in Nashua, New Hampshire. Large companies on Route 128 or in Silicon Valley that rely heavily on defense contracts manage their programs differently than companies engaged primarily in commercial applications. Subtle differences also can be detected when comparing the computer industry to the semiconductor or instruments industry, all of which are considered part of the high-tech sector.

Differences in pay techniques among high-tech companies are attributable mostly to the stage in the business cycle firms have reached. Large, more mature companies prefer planned, formal, and traditional compensation programs. Control Data, IBM, Hewlett-Packard, and Texas Instruments all compensate executives in ways similar to big companies in the durable goods industries. Young high-tech companies, on the other hand, avoid excessive structure and formality, preferring flexibility and special tailoring to meet current and anticipated labor needs. (Exhibit 24–3 compares executive compensation in the two types of firms.)

The tens of thousands of rapidly expanding companies in the high-growth segment of the industry are intensely competitive both in product

EXHIBIT 24-2
Innovative Capital Accumulation Techniques

Junior Stock
—Special form of restricted stock that is convertible into regular stock, usually after a specified goal is attained. Severe restrictions reduce the value of the shares at grant. Combines low price to the employee and tax-free conversion to regular shares.

—Accounting Treatment
Compensation should be measured whenever the ultimate number of shares of regular stock becomes known. The amount is the difference between the fair market value of the regular stock and the price paid for the junior shares.

—Taxation
Executive —no tax at delivery of shares, no tax at conversion. Difference between proceeds and price paid for junior stock is ordinary income when sold.

Corporation—no deduction.

Formula Value or Delta Stock
—Restricted, nonconvertible stock sold to executive at a formula price equal to fair market value less a specified dollar amount. May be subject to permanent right of first refusal (requires executive to sell back at formula price).

—Accounting Treatment
Formula price is fair market value. Appreciation charged to earnings annually.

—Taxation
Executive —no taxable income upon purchase. Ordinary income deferred until sale of shares.

Corporation—no deduction if established at fair market value.

Convertible Debenture
—Fixed-income debt securities (sometimes based in part on earnings) convertible after time or achievement of specified goal to common stock. Executive usually pays a fixed, fair-market-value price. Usually issued in $1,000 denominations, interest equal to prime, payable quarterly. Ten-year maturity.

—Accounting Treatment
Same as junior stock.

—Taxation
Executive—no tax at purchase. No tax on conversion to stock. The excess of proceeds over the original price paid for the debenture is ordinary income when the converted stock is sold.

Corporation—no deduction if executive pays fair market value. Interest paid on debenture is deductible.

Subsidiary Stock
—Corporation establishes a wholly owned subsidiary that must have its own independent operations. Executive is granted stock at fair market value. Used because of low founder-stock value. (Must be salable to third parties.)

—Accounting Treatment
No compensation is recorded (consolidation with minority interest required).

—Taxation
Executive—ordinary income when shares of parent corporation are sold.

Corporation—no deduction.

EXHIBIT 24-3
Compensation Patterns

	Smaller, Growth Companies	*Mature Companies*
Total Pay Mix	Average salaries and incentives, moderate benefits, low or no perquisites	High salaries and incentives, high benefits, high perquisites
Structure	Informal administration	Rigid administration
Annual Incentives	Wide eligibility, awards closely tied to profits	Narrow eligibility, awards less tied to profits, "management by objective" administration
Long-Term Incentives	Focus on stock ownership	Low to moderate stock ownership
Benefits	Low	High
Perquisites	Low	High
Golden Parachutes	Not prevalent	Highly prevalent
Expensive Insurance/SERPs	Cannot afford	Popular

design and service. Investment in research and development is high, and obsolescence rapid. The time it takes to develop new products (from concept to manufacture) has shortened appreciably over the years. Markets are highly segmented, as illustrated by the race among Cray, ETA Systems, and major Japanese firms to produce the best microprocessor and the fastest supercomputer. There is even more fragmentation (and opportunity) in software, where American superstars such as Lotus and Microsoft lead the pack. Large amounts of venture capital help finance the high-growth segment of the industry, whose markets and competition are increasingly global.

Most small, growing firms are managed by the founder(s), who often began the company with a technological innovation. Such leaders usually have a strong personal influence on their organizations. They place much importance on freedom, individual initiative, and creative problem solving. They see the firm as a playground in which to try new ideas. They make sure that the company shows respect for each employee and they go to great lengths to deal personally with problems. As a result of these attitudes, a high-growth technological company typically has the following attributes:

entrepreneurial management
ad hoc management process
frequent reorganizations
egalitarian culture

mobile management and professional staff

risk-taking orientation.

COMPENSATION IN THE HIGH-GROWTH SEGMENT

The high-tech firms that I have described above have unique organizational requirements. Because modern technological companies are involved constantly in product startups, they often are organized into product development teams. "Key technical contributor" groups function as self-contained units, pushing projects to completion by adhering to tightly controlled, pre-established goals and milestones. This requires strong esprit de corps, team leadership, dedication, control of turnover, and fair, specially tailored reward mechanisms that aid in retaining valuable, scarce human resources. Therefore, compensation is often dependent on team results (via key group awards tied to product sales and profitability results). The rewards frequently take the form of founders' stock, granted at pennies per share. If the company is successful, the participants can reap a considerable fortune when the firm goes public and the stock market responds positively.

Other characteristics of the rapidly growing segment of the industry affect the design of executive compensation. The fact that there are slim or no operating margins for sustained periods requires creative cost controls, efficient product development, and operational productivity. Rapidly changing staff needs call for sophisticated personnel strategies. And finally, disparities arising from mergers, especially between east- and west-coast firms, require special treatment.

These problems make it essential to position pay properly in order to attract executives of high caliber, especially for the jobs of chief executive officer and the top team. (However, direct or cash pay for the CEO may be relatively poor compared to senior executive pay levels in other industries. Within the industry, executive pay sometimes depends on the organizational structure; companies that establish a president and chief operating officer pay their number-two executives better than companies that place four executive vice presidents/group leaders in the structure.)

Exhibits 24–4 and 24–5 are planning tools that a rapidly growing high-tech firm with aggressive performance goals can use to set executive pay in relation to competitors. The starting point is to decide on a level of total compensation. Since high-tech companies seek a return on capital that exceeds the average weighted cost of capital, they should set total compen-

EXHIBIT 24-4
Tiered Compensation Positioning Model*

	Total Compensation Potential (percentile)	Total Cash Compensation (percentile)	Base Salary (percentile)		Short-Term Incentive (Target-Maximum) % of Salary	Annualized Long-Term Incentive (Multiple of Salary)
Policy-Level Executive Officers	90th	60th	40th–50th	+	30%–125%	1.0–2.0 ×
Middle Management	85th	65th	45th–55th	+	20%–70%	0.5–1.2 ×
Lower Management	80th	75th	50th–60th	+	15%–60%	0.3–1.0 ×

*For high-growth, high-performance company. High-growth, high-performance firms should compare themselves to an appropriate industry subset with a substantial representation of firms at a similar stage in their life cycle.

Source: Designed by J. Richard for clients.

EXHIBIT 24-5
Compensation Positioning Model

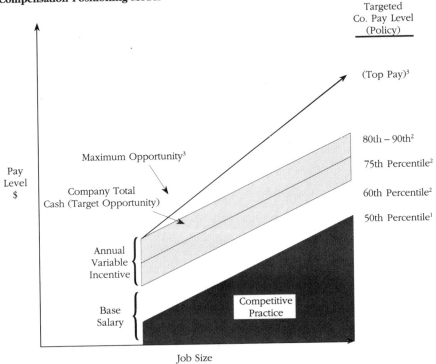

Notes:
1. For average performance relative to peer group
2. For exceeding average peer-group performance
3. With long-term incentive

Source: Designed by J. Richard for clients, including ETA
Systems, Silicon Systems, and Verbatim.

sation potential relatively high, somewhere in the 80th to 90th percentile of companies in their subset. (The composition of the comparator group is critical; the more select or high-performing the group, the higher total compensation potential will be. Another important determinant of total compensation is how aggressive the target performance goals are; generally, high-growth, high-performance firms should aim to increase revenues by 20 percent-plus annually in order to gain/maintain market share.)

Choosing appropriate performance measures is also difficult for high-tech firms. Pay systems based only on profit improvement or sales growth may lead to severe declines in longer-term productivity and failure to innovate and develop new products. The reliance on stock options in the industry is in part a way to ensure a greater correlation between long-term increases in shareholder value and executive rewards.

In practice, the determination of the right executive compensation program to reinforce corporate strategy in a technological firm is a difficult and arduous undertaking. The relatively long-term nature of high-tech corporate goals and the less-than-scientific means of measuring results make the process an art that is subject to failure and fumbling. The fact that only a fraction of new ventures succeeds guarantees that risk will be a component of an executive pay plan in the industry.

LONG-TERM INCOME: CAPITAL ACCUMULATION

Key employees of high-tech firms want and demand a piece of the action in exchange for the risk they assume. (Their positive attitude toward company ownership is quite different from the attitude of their peers in other sectors.) Boards of directors and shareholders also favor managerial ownership because the personal financial stake seems likely to motivate executives to improve a company's market value.

As previously mentioned, national surveys have proved that the industry uses a great deal more of its equity than other industries for executive compensation. (In most surveys, the median ranges from 8 percent to 18 + percent of common stock outstanding.) From the executive's point of view, stock rewards account for a substantial portion of his or her total pay package. In companies that experience fast growth (a 20-percent plus increase in revenues annually), the potential rewards from stock may far outweigh base salary and bonuses.

Executives are not the only beneficiaries of equity plans. At Mentor Graphics one of the industry's superstars, up to two-thirds of the employees hold options. At Cray, employees can elect to take bonuses in the form of discounted stock for up to 50 percent of payouts. Among the members of the American Business Conference (ABC), many of whom are high tech, more than 30 percent of company stock is held by employees.[1] The intent of these equity programs is to turn employees into entrepreneurs and to reward creativity.

Like the high-tech market itself, equity plans were varied and complex in the 1980s. Stock options, however, are still the dominant element of high-tech executive compensation packages and will continue to be until tax regulations and accounting rules change. The nonqualified option (NQSO) has been used in the same form for the past forty years.

During the past twenty years, a new generation of long-term performance plans (using performance units or performance shares) was developed by larger *Fortune*-ranked companies. Such devices are not used much in the high-growth, moderate-size company portion of the technology industry today, partly because of their accounting costs and the difficulty of setting long-term performance standards.

Stock options continue to be popular in high technology because of five characteristics, the combination of which has not been found in any other long-term pay program:

1. Options are simple to understand and relatively easy to administer.
2. Option values are determined by the market. Directors avoid the difficult and often questionable decisions about the levels of long-term profit that justify executive rewards in performance plans.
3. Option gains do not result in compensation expense.
4. Shareholders enjoy the same increase in value as key employees who hold options.
5. The executive can choose when to recognize gains. Options are only one of a few devices in general use that permit the recipient to delay the recognition of income while holding vested values.

Even if they do not continue to offer the leveraged opportunity of founders' stock, many small and expanding high-tech companies can provide stock option incentives that are attractive enough to hold key executives. These companies are willing to risk a deeper dilution of their equity. Some dilute equity by up to 15–20 percent, compared to 5–10 percent average dilution among large corporations.[2] This is possible because of shareholder tolerance, perceived potential for rapid growth, and the confidence shown by the investment community.

There are risks in stock options, however, for both the executive and the firm. Any growth industry is relatively volatile. A faltering economy will do greater damage to entrepreneurial efforts than to more firmly rooted businesses. In recent recessions, high-tech companies suffered more than their peers in other sectors. Many firms in the semiconductor industry, for instance, have been forced to cut back on production, lay off employees at all levels, and in some cases institute across-the-board pay cuts. Advanced Micro Devices, long known for its no-layoff/no-pay-cut policy, had to reverse its position after two consecutive years of red ink. Apple Computer has also cut back on its personnel in certain areas in recent years.

EVOLUTION OF EXECUTIVE COMPENSATION AS THE COMPANY MATURES

Compensation programs in high-tech companies must be refined as the business grows. As the entrepreneurial style of the young high-tech company evolves into a more complex, formalized management approach, it is necessary to standardize, document, and effectively communicate administrative systems such as pay. Over time, the number of people deemed to be "key" may change, as well as the skills and competencies required of employees. The company may decide to encourage either more or less risk taking. Or, it may decide that overall corporate results do not reflect individual performance adequately.

When the growth rate of a high-tech company slows, a firm typically alters the type of long-term compensation it offers. (Exhibit 24–6 shows how executive compensation programs change as growth rate subsides.) As the after-tax gains from options deteriorate, maturing companies often add full-value plans. Because full-value plans such as performance share, performance unit, or restricted stock programs use measures of long-term performance rather than growth in stock market value, ROI, or EPS, they provide executives with an incentive to achieve the company's long-range fundamental business strategy. Performance plans usually provide a stronger link between financial goals and executive awards than stock options do. And executives like them because they generate enough cash to fund the exercise of options and the resulting tax liability.

Maturing high-tech companies often decide to measure performance at the business unit level rather than at the corporate level. If the correlation between divisional or product performance and the performance of the company's stock is weak, then stock options will fail to motivate executives. (Exhibit 24–7 compares compensation programs in two different kinds of business units.)

As they refine their compensation programs, mature high-tech companies continue to make pay contingent on the creation of value rather than lock-step progression through a hierarchy. Such companies also make a serious effort to tailor their pay programs to the key groups in the company. (Exhibit 24–8 demonstrates a tiered pay program for an assortment of key groups.)

INNOVATIVE INCENTIVES

Many high-tech businesses (69 percent) have used recruiting bonuses to compete for scarce executive talent.[3] This practice can help to alleviate

EXHIBIT 24-6
Typical Executive Compensation Program Development

Stage of Development	Base Salary	Bonus	Benefits	Perks	Capital Accumulation
Startup period	Below market	None	Low	None	Founders' stock
Initial public offering stage	Slightly below market	Modest plan	Moderate	Low	Stock options
Growth	At market	Highly leveraged	Average	Moderate	Combination program: options, restricted stock
Threshold/Emerging	At market	Total cash concept with unit variations	Average to above average	Average	Equity/cash balance
Mature/Declining	Above market	Layered plans	Above average/costly	Many/controversial	3–5 Overlapping programs

Exhibit 24-7
Variation in Compensation by Type of Business Unit

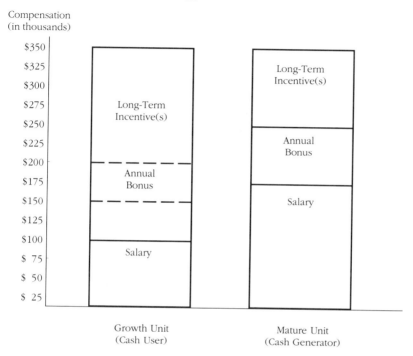

Compensation
(in thousands)

	Growth Unit (Cash User)	Mature Unit (Cash Generator)

future salary compression problems and control fixed costs. Moreover, when recruiting bonuses are awarded in the form of company stock, no cash outlay is needed. This is especially critical to the startup and emerging company.

Some high-tech companies have increased the frequency of bonus payouts. Analog Devices, a well-known leader in incentive design, is one of a few companies that pays bonuses every quarter. Awards depend on varying combinations of return on assets and revenue growth.

One long-term incentive program may be unique. At Apollo Computer, bonuses were awarded by lottery. The CEO selected a limited number of employees to receive "contingent awards." The lucky participants had to remain at the company for five years and meet certain other standards to receive payouts. The awards ranged from three to seven times average annual earnings for a specified period. The program was an addition to incentive stock options, nonqualified stock options, and a special restricted stock program.

EXHIBIT 24-8
Compensation Elements by Key Groups

Compensation Elements	Corporate Executives	Other Management	Key Technical Contributors	Top Sales/ Marketing	Board Members
Base Salary	Prevalent	Prevalent	Prevalent	Usually	Retainer
Bonus	Prevalent	Prevalent	Milestone awards	Commission	Meeting fees
Qualified Benefits	Prevalent	Prevalent	Prevalent	Prevalent	Sometimes
Special Perquisites	Prevalent	Sometimes	Sometimes	Prevalent	Prevalent
Stock Options	Prevalent	Prevalent	Prevalent	Not usually	Sometimes
Discounted Stock Purchase/401(k), Savings Plans	Prevalent	Prevalent	Prevalent	Prevalent	Not usually
Long-Term Cash Incentive (Performance Units)	Prevalent	Sometimes	Sometimes	Rarely	Never
Stock Awards (Restricted)	Prevalent	Not usually	Sometimes	Sometimes	Sometimes
Special Loans	Sometimes	Not usually	Not usually	Not usually	Not usually
Contracts	Prevalent	Not usually	Sometimes	Sometimes	Not usually
Number of Elements	1—10	5–7	4–9	3–6	2–6

RETENTION PROBLEM

Even though the compensation they offer successful executives can be very liberal, many high-tech companies, particularly in the technological hotbed, have difficulty holding on to top managers. Once the executives cash in on their stock gains, there is little chance of a similar windfall in the same firm. (Companies generally back off from a high level of equity dilution after the initial growth phase.) For those who thrive on risk and challenge, there is a great temptation to try it again. Many executives do just that, and leave to join new startups. Those who join a company too late for the first round of large-scale, low-priced stock distribution also are ripe for picking by head hunters serving new firms.

How do established firms compete with the aggressive compensation strategies of younger, high-growth companies? How do they retain executives once they have hired them? First, not all executives are motivated by risk, pressure, and astronomical pay opportunities. There is a certain amount of self-selection that distributes the more cautious executives into appropriate positions. Second, many maturing companies use performance-based restricted stock to achieve management continuity. The executive receives stock that is subject to various transfer restrictions until certain performance or time requirements are met. This device, used by CooperLasers, Silicon Systems, Tektronix (TEK), Unisys, and Varian, helps a great deal to hold key people. (Exhibit 24–9 shows how the program works.)

USE OF VENTURE UNITS BY MATURE COMPANIES

Many mature companies in the electronics industry have set up venture units alongside existing research and development functions in order to encourage the performance achieved by high-growth firms. Hoping to transfer technology from present products to new applications in electronics, alternative energy sources, and biomedicine, Bell Labs, Emerson Electric, Exxon, Genentech, General Electric, Eastman Kodak, and ITT have established venture units.

In order to staff the venture with capable professionals, companies may adopt pay programs that differ from the normal corporate plan. Companies typically offer generous salaries and benefits, cash bonuses for reaching specific financial goals, and significant equity participation. The Appendix to this chapter describes a compensation plan adopted by one corporation for a new venture.

EXHIBIT 24-9
Performance-Based Restricted Stock Plan

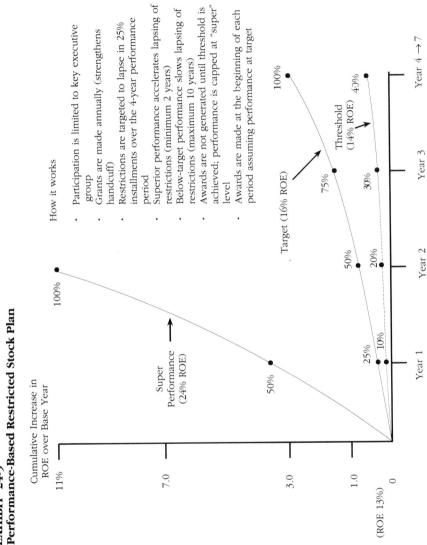

How it works

- Participation is limited to key executive group
- Grants are made annually (strengthens handcuff)
- Restrictions are targeted to lapse in 25% installments over the 4-year performance period
- Superior performance accelerates lapsing of restrictions (minimum 2 years)
- Below-target performance slows lapsing of restrictions (maximum 10 years)
- Awards are not generated until threshold is achieved; performance is capped at "super" level
- Awards are made at the beginning of each period assuming performance at target

Cumulative Increase in ROE over Base Year

Source: J. Richard Model of Variable Lapsing (Time Accelerated)
Schedules Based on Return-on-Equity Performance Attainment (operating cash flow can also be used).

Tektronix, a leading high-tech firm in the Northwest, offers a formal corporate program to assist key employees who need venture capital funds. TEK retains a percentage of ownership in the venture and actively supports its activities. AT&T has also instituted venture units to encourage entrepreneurship. Begun in 1983, the relatively small units have grown steadily. Various compensation schemes are offered to participants, ranging from continuation in the corporate plan (no added risk) to an opportunity to invest in the venture through payroll deductions. Hewlett-Packard has also begun to use progressive compensation approaches in special units.

CRITICISM OF HIGH-TECH COMPENSATION

Organized labor, the press, the courts, and shareholders[4] have attacked the executive compensation practices of many larger technological companies in recent years. The large number of high-tech business failures, takeovers, mergers, and consolidations in the industry have contributed to the condemnation. Usual targets of criticism are:

stock option repricings during prolonged down markets;

golden parachutes (with tax gross-up features) that provide rewards regardless of corporate performance;

nonqualified deferred compensation plans such as rabbi trusts/expensive insurance arrangements that generate large payments;

special executive benefits in the form of variable perquisites that cause employee morale problems;

stock appreciation rights (SARs); and

time-based (instead of performance-based) restricted stock awards.

Many critics are asking, What happened to risk?

The compensation committee of the board of directors is responsible for ensuring that executive compensation programs reinforce business goals and strategies. As the authority that establishes equitable pay for officers, determines the mix and balance of compensation elements, and administers incentive plans, the committee has a fiduciary responsibility to the owners and shareholders to set appropriate rewards for managers. Because of the public attention that has focused on the actions of board committees, the directors of high-tech companies are more deeply involved in corporate compensation matters than ever before.

CONCLUSION

The successful high-tech company uses its executive compensation program to reinforce its strategic direction. One reason so many companies in the industry have prospered in a market that is keenly competitive is because of their emphasis on plain vanilla stock option plans. This form of highly leveraged compensation offers the encouragement executives want and the results companies in other industries envy and emulate.

In all likelihood, state-of-the-art compensation practices will continue to emerge from the high-tech sector. In their experiments, high-tech companies will seek to maintain the flexibility to retool pay programs as circumstances and conditions change. And they will undoubtedly continue to rely on equity ownership as the most alluring incentive for executives.

NOTES

1. Donald K. Clifford and Richard E. Cavanagh, *The Winning Performance* (New York: Bantam Books, 1985), p. 2. ABC includes Analog Devices, Apple Computer, Ask Computer, Cray Research, Cooper Companies, EDS, Data General, Sanders, Western Digital, and Xidex, among others.

2. Matthew Ward, "How to Meet Institutional Investor Concerns in Management Compensation," *Journal of Compensation and Benefits* (February 1990), pp. 242–244.

3. Reid C. Linney, "Signing Incentives—Fad, Fancy, or Strategic Tool?" *Compensation Briefs* (New York: Peat, Marwick, Main & Co., 1987).

4. Ernst & Whinney, *Annual Meetings: Addressing the Concerns of Shareholders* (E&W Publication No. 42725, 1987), pp. 14–15; and Deloitte, Haskins & Sells, *Questions at Stockholders' Meetings—1989* (New York: DH&S Publications, 1989), p. 6.

BIBLIOGRAPHY

Abetti, Pier. *Linking Technology and Business Strategy.* New York: The Presidents Association, The Chief Executive Officers Division of the American Management Association, 1989.

Abetti, P. A., LeMaistre, C. W., and Smilor, R. W., eds. *Industrial Innovation, Productivity and Employment.* Austin, TX: IC² Institute, 1987, pp. 23–43.

Aisenbrey, Beverly. "Long-Term Incentives for Management, Part 3: Restricted Stock." *Compensation and Benefits Review* (November–December 1989), pp. 34–46.

Allan, Lionel, Carruth, Ronald, and Clair, John. *Equity Incentives for Start-Up Companies.* Berkeley, CA: California Continuing Education of the Bar, 1985.

Arthur Anderson & Co. *Accounting for Compensation Arrangements.* New York, 1987.

Balkin, David. "Compensation Strategies for R&D Staff." *Compensation Strategies for Achieving Organizational Objectives* (Winter 1987), pp. 207–215.

Betz, Frederick. *Managing Technology.* Englewood Cliffs, NJ: Prentice-Hall, 1987.

Bracotta, Louis, and Sommer, A. A. *The Essential Guide to Effective Corporate Board Committees.* Englewood Cliffs, NJ: Prentice-Hall, 1987.

Brandt, Steven C. *Strategic Planning in Emerging Companies.* Reading, MA: Addison-Wesley, 1981.

Burgelman, R. A., and Maidique, M. A. *Strategic Management of Technology and Innovation.* Homewood, IL: Irwin, 1988.

Chingos, Peter T., et al. *Financial Considerations of Executive Compensation.* New York: John Wiley, 1984.

Clifford, Donald K. *Managing the Threshold Company.* New York: McKinsey & Co., 1973.

Cohn, Theodore, and Lindberg, Roy A. *Compensating Key Executives in the Smaller Company.* New York: AMACOM, 1979.

Collard, Betsy A., and The Resource Center for Women. *The High-Tech Career Book.* Los Altos, CA: Crisp Publications, 1986.

Collier, D. W., Monz, J., and Conlin, J. "How Effective Is Technological Innovation?" *Research Management* (September–October 1984), pp. 11–16.

Cook, Frederic & Co. *CEO Views of Stock Options for Executives.* Survey Report, February 1989.

Deloitte, Haskins & Sells. *Questions at Stockholders' Meetings—1989.* New York: DH&S Publications, 1989.

Ellig, Bruce R. "Strategic Pay Planning." *Compensation and Benefits Review* (July–August 1987), pp. 28–43.

Executive Compensation Service. *Report on Executive Capital Accumulation Programs.* Fort Lee, NJ: 1987.

Foster, R. N. "Boosting the Payoff from R&D." *Research Management*, January 25, 1982, pp. 22–27.

Freedman, George. *The Pursuit of Innovation: Managing the People and Processes That Turn New Ideas into Profits.* New York: AMACOM, 1988.

Fushfeld, Herbert. *The Technical Enterprise.* Cambridge, MA: Ballinger, 1986.

Galbraith, Jay R., and Nathanson, Daniel A. *Strategy Implementation: The Role of Structure and Process.* St. Paul, MN: West Publishing, 1978 (Chapter 6 discusses research linking reward systems and career paths to the organization's strategy).

Garfield, Charles. *Peak Performers.* New York: Morrow, 1986.

Gilman, J. J. "Stock Price and Optimum Research Spending." *Research Management,* January 21, 1978, pp. 34–36.

Grove, Andrew S. *High-Output Management.* New York: Random House, 1983.

Hannan, Mack, and Haigh, Tim. *Outperformers.* New York: AMACOM, special edition prepared for The Presidents Association, 1989.

Harvard Business Review. The Management of Technological Innovation. Boston: Harvard Business School, 1982.

Henderson, Bruce. *The Concept of Strategy.* Boston: The Boston Consulting Group, 1982.

Ketteringham, J. M., and White, J. R. "Making Technology Work for Business." In R. B. Lamb, ed. *Competitive Strategic Management.* Englewood Cliffs, NJ: Prentice-Hall, 1984, pp. 498–519.

Madden, Robert E. *Tax Planning for Highly Compensated Individuals.* Boston: Warren, Gorham and Lamont, 1983.

Martin, M. J. *Managing Technological Innovation and Entrepreneurship.* Reston, VA: Reston (Prentice-Hall), 1984.

Massachusetts High Tech Council (sponsor). *MASS HIGH TECH.* April 14–27, 1986. (Study results of fifty-one New England high-tech firms.)

Miller, Roger. *The Process of Emergence of High-Technology Firms.* Cambridge, MA: Harvard University Consortium for Research on North America, 1983.

Miller, Roger, and Côté Marcel. "Growing the Next Silicon Valley." *Harvard Business Review* (July–August 1985), pp. 114–123.

Peat, Marwick, Mitchell & Co. *Shareholders' Questions 1984.* New York: 1984.

Pinchot, Gifford III. *Intrapreneuring.* New York: Harper & Row, 1985.

Porter, Michael E. *Competitive Strategy.* New York: Free Press, 1980.

Practising Law Institute. *Executive Compensation.* New York: PLI, 1989.

Ramo, Simon. *The Management of Innovative Technological Corporations.* New York: John Wiley, 1980.

Rappaport, Alfred. *Creating Shareholder Value.* New York: Free Press, 1986.

Richard, J. E. "Restricted Stock: Linking Executive Pay to Corporate Performance." *Consultants Perspectives.* Los Angeles, CA: December 1980.

———. "Pay, Perks and Promises." *Computerworld,* October 3, 1983, pp. 42–44.

———. *Board Compensation Committee Sourcebook.* Moss Beach, CA: Executive Compensation Institute, 1989.

Roberts, Edward B., ed. *Generating Technological Innovation.* New York: Oxford University Press, 1987.

Roberts, Edward B., and Fusfeld, Alan R. "Staffing the Innovative Technology-Based Organization." *Sloan Management Review* (Spring 1981), pp. 19–25.

Rosen, Corey, and Quarrey, Michael. "How Well Is Employee Ownership Working?" *Harvard Business Review* (September–October 1987), pp. 126–132.

Salter, Malcolm S. "Tailor Incentive Compensation to Strategy." *Harvard Business Review* (March–April 1973), pp. 94–102.

Schuster, Jay. *Management Compensation in High-Technology Companies.* Lexington, MA: Lexington Books, 1984.

Stata, Ray, and Maidique, Modesto A. "Bonus System for Balanced Strategy (Analog Devices)." *Harvard Business Review* (November–December 1980), pp. 156–163.

Tracman, Matthew, and Rosen, Corey. "Report to the National Venture Capital Association on the Relationship of Employee Ownership and Corporate Growth in High-tech Firms." Unpublished paper, 1985.

Tushman, M. L., and Moore, W. L. *Readings in the Management of Innovation.* 2d ed. Cambridge, MA: Ballinger, 1988.

Twiss, Brian. *Managing Technological Innovation.* 3d ed. London: Pitman, 1986.

Vesper, Karl. *New Venture Strategies.* Englewood Cliffs, NJ: Prentice-Hall, 1980.

von Hippel, Eric. *The Sources of Innovation.* New York: Oxford University Press, 1988.

Ward, Matthew. "How to Meet Institutional Investor Concerns in Management Compensation." *Journal of Compensation and Benefits* (February 1990), pp. 242–244.

Yavitz, Boris, and Newman, William H. *Strategy in Action.* New York: Free Press, 1982.

APPENDIX

Injecting Risk into a Spinoff's Compensation Plan

A pioneering, *Fortune*-ranked, diversified company in the high-tech sector decided to enter a keenly competitive arena with a new product at the high end of the market. In order to keep the project confidential, the key managerial, technical, and marketing teams were to be taken from the parent and subsidiaries. The company did not anticipate having a problem staffing the venture because it was perceived as offering excitement and prestige. However, the existing corporate compensation policies and those that were planned for the new entity were so different that the company was uncertain how to present the proposal.

On the basis of interviews with key personnel and a comprehensive review of human resource requirements, compensation histories, and ex-

TABLE 24-1
Executive Compensation Program Analysis

	Current Corporate Program	New Technical Unit	Remarks
Base Salary	75th percentile	40th–50th percentile	Below market
Bonus	20–50% targets	10–30% targets	Below market
Benefits	Average: 30% of salary	Average: 20% of salary	Below market
Perquisites	Auto, life insurance, clubs	Auto allowance	Below market
Profit Sharing	Maximum legal limits with 401(k) integrated	None	Below market
Stock Purchase	85% discount type	None	Below market
Stock Options	ISOs/SARs (5% of common shares outstanding)	ISOs at "founder" prices (15% of common shares outstanding)	Above market
Restricted Stock	Time lapsed	None	NA
Performance Units	Annual grants values based on attainment of specified EPS	None	NA

isting plans, the company prepared a comparison of executive compensation under both plans (see Table 24–1). The comparison served as a discussion tool for the board compensation committee.

The primary differences in the new unit's compensation plan were:

1. Less total cash compensation for two to three years during the development period.
2. Less guaranteed retirement plan accumulation. (Contributions would terminate as of transfer date.)
3. Few qualified benefits and perquisites.
4. No participation in corporate profit-sharing and stock purchase plans.
5. Highly leveraged long-term incentives in the form of founders' stock that might produce substantial gains (from three to ten times current salary) if performance targets were met over a three- to six-year period.

It quickly became obvious to board members that the new program was "countercultural" in that key employees would be exposed to much greater risks in the new subsidiary. The committee assumed that the programs would not be very attractive to middle-aged employees with many years of service. After several meetings and thorough discussion, the board decided to test the idea on the key management group.

Surprisingly, all management group members preferred the new, riskier compensation plan, although financial hardship could result in the near term and the chances for the long-term payoff were perceived to be no better than 50 percent.

PART III-B

Executive Compensation in Health Care

25

STRATEGIC EXECUTIVE
COMPENSATION IN HEALTH SERVICES

J. E. Richard

INTRODUCTION

The health services industry has been among the last to embrace incentive or variable compensation for its executives. Until the 1980s, health care organizations compensated key management only with fixed-pay elements, including base salary, tax-sheltered annuities, ordinary benefits, and perquisites such as autos and discounts on health care. Changes in the industry during the past decade altered traditional compensation practices. Today the risks and prospects that executives in health care face are similar to those that their peers in other sectors face. To explain how this change came about, let me begin with a review of socioeconomic issues and developments in the industry.

THE HEALTH CARE INDUSTRY

The catalyst for change in the health care industry has been public concern over alarming increases in medical costs, increases that exceeded inflation by a significant margin throughout the 1980s. Legislative mandates quickly transformed the industry from a protected, heavily regulated one to an intensely competitive one. (According to government statistics, health care now accounts for approximately 13 percent of the gross national product.)

Hospitals that formerly depended on Medicare to reimburse a high percentage of their costs had to learn to live with fixed payments for specific procedures (today classified into "diagnostic related groups"). The advantage of increasing costs under the previous reimbursement system became an extreme disadvantage in the competitive market where new third-party payors were cutting back on their expenses and charges.

Long dominated by not-for-profit, single-unit hospitals, medical associations, independent practice groups, and free-standing clinics, health care was infiltrated by "super meds," investor-owned chains that operated for profit (including Humana, Hospital Corporation of America, National Medical Enterprises, and Whittaker). The entrepreneurial attitudes of the new organizations changed priorities throughout the industry. Profitability replaced community service as the ultimate purpose of many medical organizations. Business people replaced physicians and community leaders on boards of trustees. Committees specializing in marketing, strategy, personnel, organization, and compensation began to play a major role in governing health care institutions. Not-for-profit hospitals created profit-seeking venture units. Some undertook restructure, merger, acquisition, or conversion to for-profit status activities. In short, the management of health became a business. (Exhibit 25-1 outlines the major changes in the industry during the past decade.)

Because hospitalization was the most expensive medical service, both third-party payors and hospitals turned to nonacute care services as a means of lowering costs. Many organizations began to provide services such as home health care, skilled nursing care, emergi-centers, and so forth. By venturing outside of their traditional line of business, hospitals assumed the additional risks inherent in starting a new business. Enter the entrepreneur!

Increasingly, tax-exempt hospitals were faced with competition from proprietary acute care hospitals and like ventures (such as day-surgery facilities). The strategy of the proprietary businesses often was to "skim the cream" by taking profitable segments of the business and leaving the unprofitable segments to the not-for-profit institutions. Tax-exempt organizations realized that if they were to continue to provide uncompensated care and other community services, they had to compete vigorously.

To do so, hospitals and others intensified efforts at controlling operating costs, developing and building viable revenue bases, and managing their assets and finances more effectively. In pursuit of a dominant role in their service area, organizations trying to make money and provide high-quality health care followed these kinds of strategies:

creation of a coordinated health promotion program;
targeting of business and industry for special programs;
enhancement of equipment (purchase of lasers, cat scans, and so forth);
implementation of aggressive public relations campaigns;
development of physician referral programs;

EXHIBIT 25-1
Changes in the Health Care Industry, 1980–1990

	1980	1985	1990
Government Financial Support	Strong	Moderate	Weak
Concern about Costs	Little	Some	Intense
Physician/Provider Competition	Some	Moderate	Intense
Management	Service-minded, low-risk orientation; managers called administrators; single-unit accountability	Higher-risk orentation; "presidents" and "vice presidents" created	Profit-motivated; strategic management; stronger leadership
Boards	Housewives, clergy, community leaders, volunteers, professors	Small business people; physicians, lawyers, other professionals	Business leaders
Culture	Egalitarian; guaranteed employment	Paternalistic	Challenging, competitive, risky

refinement of productivity and quality assurance plans; and adoption of a marketing-oriented personnel approach.

THE EFFECT OF CHANGE ON EXECUTIVE COMPENSATION

A more strategic approach to running health care organizations affected top managers in several ways. Job security was weakened by the number of mergers and restructurings in the industry. On the other hand, many organizations added new executive functions and titles. Managers with business and financial experience began to be recruited from outside the industry as well as from competitors within health care. Executive compensation in all areas not only increased, but became more dependent on performance than it had been.

Today, CEO base salaries in health services have risen to over $200,000 per year. Variable pay, earned only on achievement of defined goals, now represents a major portion of executive pay. There are more than twice as many annual performance incentives for executives as there were several years ago, and organizations with plans in place have increased their leveraging (raised maximums) to acknowledge increased diversification and risk. (In the not-for-profit sector, variable incentives have been used to supplement fixed compensation in a growing number of organizations.)

One reason management incentives have taken so long to become popular in the industry is that the health services "product" is considered difficult to define. The relationship between executive actions and financial results is less distinct than in other industries. However, the shift to cost and productivity as measures of financial success has created new opportunities for assessing management performance. Among health care entities operating for profit, operating margin, return on investment, cost control, service quality, growth, and market share are the primary measures of financial performance in use today. Traditional hospitals, on the other hand, still focus on service quality and the introduction of new services. (Exhibit 25-2 defines common measures of financial performance.)

Long-term deferred income and equity plans have also become more important parts of executive compensation, especially in profit-seeking venture units. Stock programs, profit sharing, and related capital accumulation plans are relatively new phenomena and have been implemented with varying degrees of success. Benefits, too, offer more after-tax compensation today. And finally, more organizations are using employment contracts for top managers. (Exhibit 25-3 compares emerging compensation practices with traditional ones.)

Let me now examine the design of executive compensation in health care in more detail.

THE DESIGN OF EXECUTIVE COMPENSATION

In order to attract people who are willing to be judged and accept the risk of a competitive environment, health care compensation must include:

EXHIBIT 25-2
Common Measures of Financial Performance

Profitability	Operating margin (OM) (total operating revenues less operating expenses divided by total operating revenues)
Capital Structure	Fixed-asset financing (FAF) (long-term liabilities divided by net fixed assets)
Liquidity	Average payment period (APP) (current liabilities divided by operating expenses less depreciation divided by 365)
Leverage	Long-term debt to equity (LTDE) (long-term liabilities divided by fund balance)
Current Asset Efficiency	Days in patient accounts receivable (DAR) (divided by net patient service revenue divided by 365)
Equity	Restricted equity (RE) (total restricted fund balances divided by unrestricted fund balance)

EXHIBIT 25-3
Total Compensation Shift Strategy

100% of Compensation Pie

vs

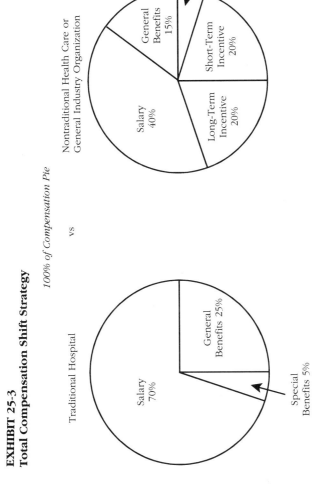

Traditional Hospital

Salary
70%

General
Benefits 25%

Special
Benefits 5%

Nontraditional Health Care or
General Industry Organization

Salary
40%

Long-Term
Incentive
20%

General
Benefits
15%

Special
Benefits
5%

Short-Term
Incentive
20%

1. A credible performance measurement system that objectively determines individual contributions to results;
2. Competitive base salary;
3. Annual variable performance incentives to reward specific short-term achievements;
4. Long-term (three to five years) capital accumulation potential to stimulate concern for future success; and
5. Benefits/perquisites that provide for security, health, and comfort.

Like any business, a health care enterprise should have short- and long-term financial, operating, developmental, and service goals. Executives must be judged according to how well they meet the budget, control costs, improve patient satisfaction, increase operational efficiency, maintain good relations with the community, succeed in new ventures, and so forth. Any number of criteria can be used:

Financial Performance

Increase in gross revenue attributable to new programs

Increase in gross revenue attributable to patient days

Improvement in surplus

Improvement in return on capital

Rise in collection rate

Improvement in results of audits

Enhancement of reserves

Reduction in unit cost of key services

Reduction in cost per patient day

Improvement in costs or prices compared to national or regional standards

Rise in percentage of income derived from direct contractual ties with insurers or purchasers.

Operating Performance

Reduction in cost of services while maintaining quality

Increase in net revenue

Increase in market share

Change in patient mix

Developmental Performance

Successful restructuring or merger
Preparation and continuous review of strategic plan
Management of plan within cost and time budgets
Acquisition of equipment within budget

Service Performance

Success in serving key population groups
Development of innovative health care programs
Review and refinement of the institution's health care mission
Contribution to development of public policy in health care

Exhibit 25-4 is a table for tracking achievement of operating objectives; Exhibit 25-5 shows sample criteria for CEO evaluation.

The amount of pay executives receive can be a function of corporate, unit, department, or individual performance. The relative importance of each can be indicated by assigning weighted values. For example, compensation might be 40 percent dependent on meeting or achieving favorable budget variance; 20 percent dependent on improving patient care; 20 percent dependent on community/medical staff relations; and 20 percent dependent on long-term project results.

At the end of each performance year, the compensation committee compares executive performance to the pre-established goals. Performance under each objective can be rated numerically to derive a total score, as illustrated in Exhibit 25-6, a sample CEO appraisal.

The ideal performance appraisal system should attract and motivate capable executives, focus their efforts on areas in which they have an impact, encourage a balance between financial results and patient care, and facilitate planning and communication. It should also be simple to understand and adaptable to changing business conditions.

INCENTIVE COMPENSATION IN
TAX-EXEMPT ORGANIZATIONS

Until 1988, the IRS viewed the use of incentive compensation by not-for-profit organizations as a prohibited distribution of the net earnings of a tax-exempt entity. Failure to adhere to this prohibition subjected an organization to possible loss of its tax-exempt status, a deliberately severe

EXHIBIT 25-4
Sample Operating Objectives

		Frequency of Review			
			Board		
	Key	Manage-	Finance	Entire	Trend
Objectives	Objectives	ment	Committee	Board	Analysis
Payor Mix The ratio of patients who have commercial insurance, Medicare, Medicaid, or Blue Cross to those who pay their own costs. Important because the reimbursement from some third-party payors covers less than the hospital's full charges. Patients who pay their own costs tend to have the highest delinquency rates.	Patient mix				
Productivity A comparison of inputs and outputs. A variety of measures can be used. Inputs per outputs Salaries per patient day Equipment costs per units of revenues Total debt costs per department measures (e.g., tests, cases, meals, visits, square footage)	Pro- duc- tivity				
Inpatient Expenses (per admission and patient day). How much does the hospital spend to care for one patient for one day? For one patient for an entire admission? This figure is a good indicator of the effectiveness of cost containment activities. Data can also be provided by diagnosis.	Inpatient expenses				
Gross Inpatient Revenues per Admission A parallel indicator to inpatient expenses, this shows how much revenue the hospital generates per patient. When broken down by types of patient and diagnosis, or by department, it shows the relative operating margins of providing different types of service.	Gross in- patient revenues per admis- sion				
Outpatient Expenses/Revenues Similar to the figures above, shows the relationship of expenses and revenues for treating outpatients.	Outpatient expenses/ revenues				

EXHIBIT 25-5
Sample Criteria for CEO Evaluation

Area of Accountability	Qualitative Measures (Examples)	Quantitative Measures (Examples)
Planning and Organizing	Implement a strategic planning process that effectively involves members of the board, medical staff, and management.	Develop a five-year strategic plan.
	Maintain good morale among hospital staff.	Recruit a vice president, finance. Develop a new organizational plan for emergency services.
Achieving Unit Objectives	Ensure minimal disruption of patient services during construction.	Open ambulatory surgery unit by July 1. Hold bad debt to 1.5% of revenues. Show bottom line profitability of at least 5%.
Compliance with Regulations	Foster a constructive rather than an adversarial relationship with regulators, wherever possible.	Achieve accreditation from • JCAH • State licensing boards
Quality of Medical Services	Keep relationships with the medical staff productive and free of needless conflict with management.	Implement quality assurance program with medical staff by January 1.
Allocation of Resources	Continually identify for the board trends with regard to resources, problems, opportunities, and strategies for the future.	Implement a program of departmental productivity reporting by June 1. Do not allow costs per admission, adjusted for case mix, to rise more than 7% this year.
Crisis Resolution	Do not surprise the board with crises. When a crisis occurs, develop a strategy and brief the board (or the appropriate committee) on developments.	Develop a plan for operating during a potential nursing strike. Resolve the issue of closing membership in several medical staff departments—and the antitrust implications of doing so—without a crisis or confrontation with the medical staff.

penalty. In its audits, the IRS focused on persons most able to influence the organization (i.e., top management). Consequently, incentive programs designed to generate the greatest benefit to the organization were the programs most highly scrutinized by the IRS.

The IRS altered its position on incentive compensation in General Counsel Memorandum 38905. The ruling involved a proposal to pay the manager of a title-holding corporation (exempt under section 501(c)(2) of the Code) in part on investment results. The IRS recognized "that benefits

EXHIBIT 25-6
Top Management Performance Appraisal
Hospital Administrator

I. Position Objectives	II. Individual Planning Goals 19___	III. Midyear Progress Review	IV. Annual Achievement Evaluation —Supporting Statements —Improvement Remarks	V. Row Total
40% WEIGHT % 1. Achieve approved Hospital budget. MEASURE(S): Net cash flow.	1. Meet budget of $2,850,000.	Midyear budget results appear on budget.	5 4 (3) 2 1 Met budget. No benefits from positive net cash flow. Considerable room for improvement next year.	1.2
40% WEIGHT % 2. Improve patient care. MEASURE(S): Review of results from available data as illustrated by reports on disallowances, quality assurance audit, nursing quality, patient complaints, incident reports, etc.	1. Ensure nursing proficiency through training programs. 2. Install new patient care checklist. 3. Install new life-saving equipment in Emergency Room.	Midyear patient care levels clearly exceed those of previous year. Emergency Room equipment credited with saving lives.	(5) 4 3 2 1 Excellent progress in improving patient care as reported by audit team, nurses, and lower incidence of patient complaints.	2.0
10% WEIGHT % 3. Design or implement improved informational and operational systems. MEASURE(S): Review of results from project reports, as illustrated by projects grid as, Hospital Information Systems, Clinical Laboratory Information, Computerization, Radiology Retreival Project, Contract Management, etc.	1. Install new HIS system for accounts receivable and payable. 2. Develop new computerized customer billing system. 3. Develop an EDP-processed payroll system that contains performance rating information.	Only a computerized billing system has been developed. EDP-processed payroll system has hit snags, as with accounts receivable and payable.	5 4 3 (2) 1 Underachieved developmental target in HIS system for accounts receivable and payable and EDP-processed payroll system.	.2

WEIGHT %			5	
10%	1. Develop objectives, accountabilities, and tasks for positions.	Performance-oriented system developed. Midyear progress looks good.	⑤	Excellent results obtained from performance-oriented pay system. Will need additional year, however, to get longer-term results in cost containment, productivity, etc.
4. Develop a performance-oriented personnel pay system.	2. Provide performance measures.		4	
	3. Determine levels of performance.		3	
MEASURE(S): Review of results achieved by work force in areas of productivity, cost containment and specific project areas in year-end performance approval.	4. Review results.		2	
			1	0
WEIGHT %			5	
5.			4	
			3	
MEASURE(S):			2	
			1	
WEIGHT %			5	
6.			4	
			3	
MEASURE(S):			2	
			1	

ANNUAL ACHIEVEMENT EVALUATION SCORE

3.9

DEFINITIONS: Achievement Levels

5 — Distinguished: Exceptional, clearly unique performance. Significantly exceeds position accountabilities, achievement which clearly exceeds performance of others at similar position levels. (Very few employees will receive this rating.)

4 — Commendable: Exceeds position accountabilities, achievement which exceeds that of most others at similar position levels.

3 — Competent: Meets position accountabilities, achievement which is expected from experienced and qualified individuals. (The performance of the majority of employees will be at this level.)

2 — Adequate: With few exceptions, meets position accountabilities, however, some improvement is desirable.

1 — Provisional: Does not meet minimum position accountabilities. Performance that is clearly below the acceptable level. (Very few employees will receive this rating.)

derived from incentive compensation plans generally accrue not only to employees, but also to charitable employers (e.g., increased productivity, cost stability)." The decision set forth a number of guidelines for the development of an acceptable compensation arrangement.

Although GCM 38905 significantly changed the IRS position, it was intended for a specific, limited situation. Moreover, the ruling contained some troubling restrictive language. It stated, "Where the interests of the employee and the organization are competitive and the compensation arrangement is not adequately safeguarded against abuse, a finding of inurement is likely." Because of these limitations, it cannot be said that the IRS established a "safe harbor" for incentive compensation in health care. Consequently, although incentives were now available to tax-exempt organizations, they had to be used with much caution.

Three types of incentive compensation plans have been used by tax-exempt hospitals: bonuses based on a percentage of gross receipts; awards based on cost savings or achievement of efficiency standards; and contingent compensation based on a percentage of net earnings (surplus). Because the IRS suspended the issue of private letter rulings for plans based on net earnings, it would be wise for the present to base awards on gross receipts or achievement of cost/efficiency standards. Even using these measures, hospitals that wish to be sure their incentive plan will not jeopardize their tax-exempt status in the future should seek a private letter ruling before implementing the plan.

The IRS uses the following criteria to determine whether an incentive compensation arrangement results in private benefit (inurement):

1. The contractual relationship between employee and hospital must be completely "arm's-length";
2. The payments must serve a real business purpose to the organization;
3. The amount of incentive must not depend principally on the exempt organization's incoming revenue, but rather on the accomplishment of the objectives of the contract;
4. There must be no evidence of abuse or unwarranted benefits (prices and operating costs should compare favorably with those of similar organizations); and
5. There must be a ceiling or reasonable maximum to prevent windfall benefits.

No single factor is determinative, but the IRS has stated that it will remove tax exemption in cases that do not meet the above standards unless there is a clear and convincing showing against operating abuses. For this reason, it is not prudent to base executive incentive compensation solely on net profit. If for some reason a not-for-profit hospital wants to make regular use of net profit as a benchmark for bonuses, it should seek a private ruling.

Incentives are customarily paid in cash, and for many institutions this is still the form of payment that meets employees' needs most effectively. If executives can afford to, it may be possible to defer the payment of incentive compensation or, in the case of a not-for-profit, to use tax-sheltered annuities as a payment medium. (See Appendix for a description of an executive incentive plan in a not-for-profit health service organization.)

DEFERRED COMPENSATION

The principal benefits of deferred compensation in health care are that plans can be tailored to the unique requirements of each position; they are exempt from the limiting requirements of legislation such as ERISA, TEFRA, DEFRA, REA, the Tax Reform Act of 1986, and so forth; the payment schedule can be varied; and rewards are based on performance.

The most prevalent form of deferred compensation offered by not-for-profit organizations was traditionally tax sheltered annuities or tax deferred annuities (TSAs or TDAs). Usually such plans were funded through executive contributions that were invested in insurance contracts.

Obviously, profit sharing and equity participation are not often feasible for not-for-profit entities. But other forms of deferred compensation are being used successfully. For instance, funded/unfunded, nonqualified supplementary executive retirement plans (SERPs) have found their way to the health care sector from general industry in recent years; this trend should continue, barring legislation prohibiting them. Not-for-profits have found SERPs are very effective ways to retain key executives. In combination with other, qualified pension plans, SERPs typically replace about two-thirds of an executive's final average pay (see Exhibits 25-7 and 25-8).

Capital accumulation plans in health care have become increasingly complex over the past several years. This is partly because of changing tax laws and increasing competition, and partly because hospitals are designing programs that support strategic goals. Like any other business, medical enterprises use equity accumulation plans to motivate those who are in a

EXHIBIT 25-7
Sample of a SERP

Executive:	James Smith	
Position:	Senior Vice President	Age: 61

Cash Compensation	
Current Annual Base Salary	$106,000
Plus Deferred Compensation	20,000[a]
* Total Direct Compensation	$126,000
Compensation Projected to Retirement in 1994 at Age 65 (Normal Retirement Age)	$168,616[b]
Total Potential Annual Retirement Benefit (Calculated at Maximum 70% of Final Pay)	$118,031[c]
Less Qualified Pension Plan Distributions, and	− 33,461
Social Security Integration	− 10,942
SERP Funding Requirement (Annual)	$ 73,628[d]

Notes: a. Used toward premium of life insurance contracts.
b. Assumes 6% increases per annum for five years.
c. Present value of annuities with life expectancy of 18.63 years.
d. Total funding required would be $898,885 (principal necessary in 1994 to permit withdrawal; modified lump-sum distributions could be considered).

position to affect long-term growth to achieve success, to attract and retain talented managers, and to control compensation expense.

Special care must be taken in structuring capital accumulation plans. if an executive is given a nonforfeitable interest in a nonqualified trust, for example, he or she will be subject to taxes immediately. It is also important to review the effects on a funded SERP of the complex and burdensome requirements of ERISA (Title 1).

Usually the top two to five executives are eligible for supplementary retirement benefits. This is especially appropriate for individuals with many years of service whose long-term contributions are worth recognition. The plan can provide for deferred payments either in a lump sum or in installments, and can be funded with life insurance.

On the face of it, a tax-exempt organization might be regarded as a poor candidate for a funded deferred compensation plan since the receipt of the face amount of the life insurance policy (and the deductibility of the payments to the recipients) do not have the same leverage they would have in a for-profit business. Bear in mind, however, that a qualified plan suffers a similar loss of leverage. And the absence of a nonqualified plan jeopardizes the ability of not-for-profit organizations to attract and retain qualified executives.

EXHIBIT 25-8
Sample Executive Retirement Benefit

Actuarially Determined Salary at Age 65	$200,000
Qualified Plan Benefit	60,000
Social Security	20,000
TSA	20,000
SERP	30,000
Replacement Income at Retirement	$130,000*

*65% of base salary for twelve years.

EMPLOYMENT CONTRACTS

As competition and risk in health care have increased, employment contracts have proliferated as a way to secure competent managers, from the company's point of view, and to hold onto a job, from the executive's point of view. The important provisions of such contracts cover:

term,
base salary,
salary adjustments,
bonuses,
disability payments,
retirement benefits,
deferred compensation,
tax-sheltered annuities,
special insurance programs,
confidential disclosure restrictions,
agreement not to compete, and
change-in-control arrangements (golden parachutes).

Executive employment agreements also usually contain provisions concerning hiring, duties and responsibilities, reimbursement of expenses, benefits, termination payments, and post-termination obligations. The agreement ought to specify what will happen if the organization merges with or is taken over by another hospital during the term of the contract. This is essential to encourage key executives to remain with the business.

Health care organizations sometimes initiate executive contracts for security reasons. Service area know-how and other trade secrets can be protected with noncompete clauses.

MANAGED CARE: A MODEL FOR OTHER HEALTH SERVICES

Although all health services have been making dramatic changes in their pay practices, the managed care segment has been the most assiduous in adopting the principle of pay-for-performance.

Effective marketing strategies have resulted in tremendous HMO industry growth. This has led to many new HMO entries and very intense competition in certain markets. As a result, demand for highly qualified executives, marketing professionals, and other key contributors has intensified. Mergers, restructuring, and the profit motive have also had a significant impact on pay philosophy, practice, and strategy.

Recent research indicates that HMOs have taken the following steps: they have formalized pay programs, emphasized total compensation, shifted to performance-based variable reward systems, adopted long-term incentives, and created special board committees to provide fiduciary overview. The data reveal that HMO management salaries are growing nearly twice as fast as wages for similar positions in other industries (12-percent versus 6-percent annual growth between 1984 and 1990). (See Exhibits 25–9 and 25–10.) Some of this increase can be attributed to the fact that HMO salaries lagged behind salaries in other sectors to start. Growth itself is also responsible for rising wages, since as an HMO gets bigger and more complex, so do the management jobs (see Exhibit 25–11).

HMOs have increased annual bonuses and tied them more closely to specific operating results such as net enrollment growth, profit margins, and reserve levels. Sixty-one percent of for-profit HMOs now use long-term incentive plans to encourage more sophisticated budgeting and business planning. Officers and directors own between 20 percent and 30 percent of HMO stock, accumulated through equity programs such as stock options, performance plans, and special nonqualified deferred compensation (see Exhibit 25–12). The use of employment agreements in HMOs is up by 75 percent since 1985.

CONCLUSION

More rigorous performance appraisal has eliminated most weak management in the health care industry. The imposition of businesslike

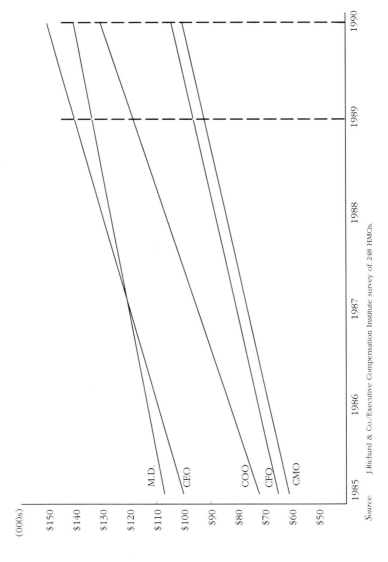

EXHIBIT 25-9
Five-Year Base Salary Trends, 1985 – 1990

(000s)

$150
$140
$130
$120
$110
$100
$90
$80
$70
$60
$50

M.D.

CEO

COO

CFO

CMO

1985   1986   1987   1988   1989   1990

Source: J.Richard & Co./Executive Compensation Institute survey of 248 HMOs.

EXHIBIT 25-10
Five-Year *Total Cash* Compensation (Salary + Bonus) Trends

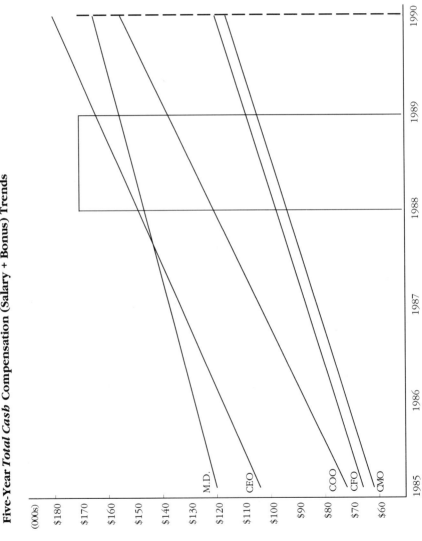

Source: J. Richard & Co., surveys 1985–1990.

EXHIBIT 25-11

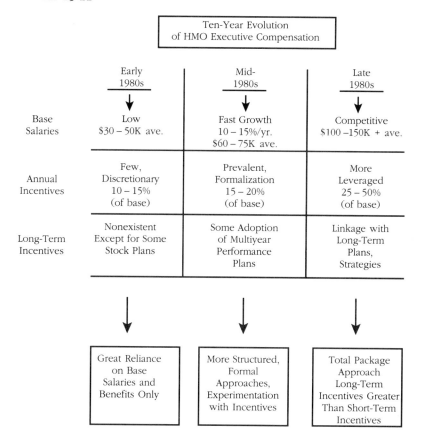

	Early 1980s	Mid-1980s	Late 1980s
Base Salaries	Low $30 – 50K ave.	Fast Growth 10 – 15%/yr. $60 – 75K ave.	Competitive $100 –150K + ave.
Annual Incentives	Few, Discretionary 10 – 15% (of base)	Prevalent, Formalization 15 – 20% (of base)	More Leveraged 25 – 50% (of base)
Long-Term Incentives	Nonexistent Except for Some Stock Plans	Some Adoption of Multiyear Performance Plans	Linkage with Long-Term Plans, Strategies

Great Reliance on Base Salaries and Benefits Only	More Structured, Formal Approaches, Experimentation with Incentives	Total Package Approach Long-Term Incentives Greater Than Short-Term Incentives

Ten-Year Evolution of HMO Executive Compensation

policies has produced the executive responsibility common to other sectors.

This is not to say that there is one simple solution or approach to executive compensation in health care. The environment is volatile, increasingly risky, and competitive. The differences between health care and business in the industrial sector have almost disappeared with the introduction of profit motivation, new board attitudes, managerial expertise, and strategic executive pay approaches.

The compensation programs discussed in this chapter are not without problems. A significant amount of board and executive time will be needed over many years to ensure successful implementation of new ideas. Institutions must learn to deal skillfully with shareholders and the

EXHIBIT 25-12
Stock Ownership/Equity Participation in Publicly Owned HMOs*

HMO	Total Shares Outstanding	Number of Shares Owned by Officers & Directors	Number of Officers & Directors	% of Total Outstanding Shares
1	6,408,000	3,963,950	6	61.6%
2	16,448,000	3,072,501	16	29.0
3	4,835,697	1,956,061	9	40.5
4	22,800,000	14,364,000	19	63.0
5	4,813,478	153,290	18	3.2
6	4,875,654	469,070	21	9.6
7	4,900,820	258,882	24	5.3
8	7,082,300	415,600	6	6.0
9	5,102,367	1,136,991	14	22.0
10	13,898,629	3,377,485	16	24.2
Average	9,116,495	2,916,783	15	Weighted Average 32.0% Median 23.1%

*All publicly held HMOs (Proxy/Annual Report Survey).

public in order to deflect the kind of criticism that is directed at executive pay in other industries. Most boards of trustees and executives want to link management compensation more effectively to real performance.

BIBLIOGRAPHY

Browdy, J. D. *Health Care Executive Compensation: Principles and Strategies.* Rockville, MD: Aspen Publishers, 1983.

Connors, T. D. *The Nonprofit Organization Handbook.* New York: McGraw-Hill, 1980.

Henderson, R. R. *Health Care in the United States.* New York: Metropolitan Life, 1982.

Longest, B. B. *Management Practices for the Health Professional.* Reston, VA: Reston, 1984.

McConkey, D. D. *MBO for Nonprofit Organizations.* New York: AMACON, 1975.

Steinforth, A. W. *Topics in Health Care Financing.* Rockville, MD: Aspen Publishers, 1980.

U.S. Chamber of Commerce. *A Primer for Hospital Trustees.* Washington, DC, 1984.

Unterman, I., and Davis, R. H. "The Strategy Gap in Not-For-Profits." *Harvard Business Review* (May–June 1982), pp. 30–40.

APPENDIX

Case Study: Health Care Providers, Inc.

Health Care Providers, Inc. (HCP), a not-for-profit, multi-institutional health services organization owned by Health Services Corporation, instituted incentive compensation plans for two different levels of its management.

First, an incentive plan was developed for the unit heads of all of the operating hospitals within HCP. Annual incentives depended on how well the CEO accomplished objectives established jointly by the hospital board of directors, the corporate senior vice president, and the CEO. Objectives had to be specific, reasonable, and achievable. Both the goals and the criteria that were used to judge whether they had been met were stated in writing. No changes were allowed during the year, even if ensuing events made the goals appear either too stringent or too liberal. The CEO furnished progress reports to the chairperson of the board and the senior vice president at least once a quarter.

The maximum bonus was 30 percent of base salary as of the start of the year. (The CEO's salary had to be within an established range before he was eligible for the bonus.) To receive an award, the officer had to achieve a performance rating of "proficient" or higher. Performance was evaluated according to guidelines set out in a CEO compensation manual.

Participants in the plan could choose to receive bonuses in cash, contributions to a tax deferred annuity, a separate deferral plan, or individually negotiated alternatives.

All but one of the unit heads earned a bonus payment in each of the years that the plan had existed. Bonuses ranged from 12 percent to 28 percent of base salaries. The two years the plan had paid out were HCP's best years of financial performance and overall development.

The plan was modified to make a portion of incentive compensation dependent on the performance of the entire corporation. After several years, the incentive plan was extended to include senior management of HCP. Designed by an executive compensation planning firm, the senior-management version incorporated many of the ideas of the CEO plan. It offered up to 35 percent of base pay in bonuses.

Each executive's award was based on a combination of factors. The relative weights given to organizational and personal performance were determined for each executive separately depending on job responsibilities. (For example, if an executive's duties were primarily corporate, 75 percent of his performance rating might be based on corporate results.)

Two organizational goals were chosen at HCP: to improve surplus throughout the corporation, and to improve systemwide productivity. Individual objectives were developed by the executive and reviewed by the CEO. No more than two individual goals could be added to the organizational goals.

The first payout under the senior-management incentive plan ranged from 15 percent to 25 percent of base pay. A long-term financial performance improvement plan was also created. Payments were based on a rolling three-year average return on investment. Features of the plan included the following:

Senior managers could earn up to 20 percent of their base pay.

A threshold was established each year by the executive committee of the board, below which no payout was made.

For payout, the year's performance had to exceed by 1 percent the rolling three-year average ROI for HCP. For example, if the company averaged an ROI of 8.3 percent in the first three years, in the fourth year HCP would have to achieve an ROI of 9.3 percent to generate payments.

As is evident, each year of successful performance raised the threshold for the following year.

HCP was studying the possibility of adding other three-year averages as measures of performance.

The nine senior corporate managers of HCP responded to the new plan by giving much attention to financial performance and systemwide objectives. In addition, they attempted to accomplish their individual goals, although, since these were "stretch" objectives, they were more difficult to achieve.

HCP was engaged in a number of general/limited partnership ventures, and made limited partnership units available for purchase by senior officers of the corporation. In addition, HCP spun off a medical trading company, a sales and marketing arm for services, and the products of other small medical companies. A trading company was formed with the assistance of private equity capital on a shares-of-stock basis. Senior officers of HCP were allowed to buy blocks of the shares ($20,000 per block). Additional ownership in HCP's proprietary enterprises would be offered to senior officers in the future.

PART III-C

Executive Compensation in Financial Services

26

STRATEGIC EXECUTIVE COMPENSATION IN FINANCIAL SERVICES

W. Donald Gough

INTRODUCTION

The financial services sector, as the backbone of our economy, requires a proper balance in rewarding executives for risk-taking profitability and for conservative financial stability. Tipping the scale too far in either direction can cause dysfunction in many economic sectors. Thus the selection of programs to compensate executives in banks, S&Ls, mortgage banks, life and property/casualty insurance companies, and credit/leasing companies, as well as in investment banking and securities firms, must be done thoughtfully and in such a way as to support the business strategy approved by boards of directors.

In the 1980s, the financial services sector changed profoundly in some ways. New products, like universal life and mortgage-backed securities, and the proliferation of mutual funds have dramatically increased business for some companies. Mergers, takeovers, and diversifications have reshaped the entire industry, taking many firms like Xerox, General Electric and the Travelers beyond the bounds of their traditional businesses. Many of these changes were driven by a need to increase profitability or capitalize on management strength. Yet in other ways, it is business as usual: culturally and organizationally, most banks, insurance companies, and thrifts remain conservative, bureaucratic, and security-oriented. And their executive compensation programs reflect this conservatism: fixed pay (salary and benefits) dominates compensation policy, while incentives, either short- or long-term, are used sparingly.

The conservative pay policy may be a result of a long-term view, or it may reflect the difficulty of measuring performance in financial services firms. The practices of certain companies can help us understand the difficulty and provide guidance in selecting a compensation program that supports a firm's business strategy.

Clearly, the most important question facing the boards of most financial services companies in the foreseeable future is, "What strategy will enable us to maintain financial stability (or even survival) and improve profit performance in the changed and changing market environment of our industry?" After the board answers this question, it should ask, "What strategy will ensure that we maintain and motivate our executive team and properly reward them when we achieve the objectives of our business strategy?" The business strategy should emphasize annual profitability and long-range asset-value stability; the executive compensation program should provide a complementary emphasis on annual and long-term pay.

UNIQUENESS OF FINANCIAL SERVICES FIRMS

Although these questions can be asked in any large corporation, there are certain characteristics of the financial services sector that differentiate it from manufacturing, retailing, and other service companies. For example, in manufacturing, decisions relate to the level of capital to be invested in plant and equipment, the amounts of working capital, and the return on the assets invested relative to the cost of acquiring capital. In many cases, the profitability or success of the capital investment decision is known within a short period of time, i.e., one to three years. In service businesses, the economics are easy since the profitability realized from a new client or new account can be quickly determined by subtracting expenses from revenues. (The economics of the investment banking and securities sector of financial services are similar to those of most service businesses. For example, revenues for an investment banking firm generally are determined as a percentage of the value of the transaction, e.g., an initial public offering of stock. Profits are what is left after expenses such as the compensation of the employees and the costs of office space, printing, and telecommunications are paid. Generally, this calculation is made at year end and accounts for the large bonuses paid to the senior partners or executives of securities and investment banking firms.)

Financial services economics are more complicated. Often, the profitability of a transaction is not known for an extended period of time. For a bank, the profitability of a loan is not known until that point in the future when the loan has been paid off (or defaulted). In the leasing business, profitability is not known until the lease is terminated and the residual value of the asset is determined. In the commercial property and casualty insurance business, the profitability of the liability business put on the books in a given year is undetermined until fifteen or even twenty years later when all the losses incurred against the policy have been paid. In a life insurance company, it may take forty or fifty years after a life policy is purchased to determine whether a profit was made. The question for a board compensation committee member who is attempting to reward executives for doing the right thing is, "How can rewards be based on performance when the 'right thing' is not known until five, ten, or even fifteen years after the original decision was made, and perhaps as long as fifty years later?"

A property and casualty insurance company is a useful model to illustrate the complexity of the financial services sector. On the surface, the business appears to be straightforward. For a specified price or premium rate, the customer purchases a contract that obligates the insurance company to pay for any loss that may occur during the life of the policy, which is typically one year. The customer pays an annual premium. The company subtracts from that premium all expenses it incurred to obtain that customer (typically the commission paid to a broker or agent), home office expenses, any loss from accidents or losses occurring in the contract year (amounts both paid and reserved to be paid), and any loss adjustment expenses (to insurance adjusters and lawyers). The resulting amount is the company's underwriting profit. The primary objective is to manage premium rates relative to expected losses to maximize underwriting profit.

Managing a book of business, however, is more complicated, because of the *timing* of the various events. First, premiums do not always begin at the first of the year. Therefore, for a new policy that begins in July, half of the premium revenue will be counted in the present year and half in the next year. (In statutory accounting, a premium is not counted as "revenue" until it is "earned"; in effect one-twelfth of the annual premium on a policy is "earned" each month. That is why a growing company always has a larger written premium value, i.e., the amount paid for one policy year of coverage, than earned premium value.) Second, the *actual* cost of the loss for an accident that occurred in one year may not be known until several years later. For example, under a worker's compensation policy, an individual could take five to ten years—or even longer—to fully recover from an accident. Therefore, a determination of whether a profit was earned on policies written or put on the books in one year may not be known for two, three, or maybe six years. For a book of general liability insurance, the determination of profitability may take as long as fifteen or twenty years while such court cases as asbestos claims or toxic waste disposal drag on and on. The profit (or loss) shown by a property and casualty insurance company in one year may be the result of business that was put on the books in the prior year or even before the prior year if the company has not taken sufficient reserves for the expected loss payments. The compensation-related question is, "Does the underwriting profit reported in one year on a statutory basis fully reflect the performance of the executive group for that year?" The answer in most cases is, "Maybe!" Specifically, if there have been no additions to reserves for prior-year losses and no additional reserves need to be taken in subsequent years for losses occurring in the present year, then it does reflect the performance of the executive group.

The economics are further complicated when reserves are considered. An insurance company must have sufficient capital or "surplus" to be in business. Such surplus is known as stockholder's equity in stock companies and policyholder's surplus in mutual insurance companies. In addition to this basic surplus, cash from premium payments is held in reserve until losses are actually paid. The total reserve capital is generally invested in fixed-income securities, e.g., bonds, that mature when the loss is expected to be paid. Insurance companies manage their cash flow so that extra cash is invested in bonds, stock securities, or, in some cases, real estate financing. They expect to earn interest on the cash flow, which actuaries consider in determining the premium rate to charge for a particular risk. The "net earnings" reported annually by an insurance company takes into account not only its realized underwriting profit (earned premium less expenses and losses incurred and reserved), but also interest earned on the invested capital from surplus and loss reserves. It also reports any gains realized from the sale of appreciated assets, i.e., realized capital gains. It does not report, as part of its statutory P&L statement, any unrealized capital gains (or losses).

Given this situation, what is the right performance measure to use for determining the pay of the executive group of a property and casualty insurance company? What measure or measures relate to the strategy of the business? What measure truly reflects the contribution of the marketing and underwriting executives? The chief executive officer? The head of the investment group?

It is this determination of performance that is the most difficult in financial services firms. Whether the financial services company is a bank, insurance company, S&L, leasing firm, or mortgage company, the performance of the executive group over a given year is not clearly measurable. For many financial services companies, there are too many unknowns to determine the level of performance in any one year. Because of the difficulty of measuring performance, incentive compensation for executives of financial services firms has been uncommon historically. Recently, however, incentives have been on the increase as companies attempt to link pay to financial performance or become more sophisticated in the measurement of performance.

FUNDAMENTAL ISSUES

There are certain fundamental questions underlying the design of an executive compensation program in a financial services company. These are:

- Should pay be related to performance? If so, how should performance be defined—by stock price performance, accounting measure performance, cash flow performance, underwriting performance (now or later?), investment performance, strategic performance, functional performance, or by some other measure?
- Does owning stock in the entity cause executives to take a longer-term view? Should executives be compensated as if they were partners—sharing successful annual results but with minimal income when the business is not successful?
- How does one communicate desired executive behavior through the compensation program? What is desired behavior—conservative and proven decision making or risk taking on a new product or marketing idea?
- When should the retention/attraction objective override paying for performance? How important is it to pay executives over the market rate to retain the executive team when financial performance in a given year is poor, perhaps as a result of decisions made three or four years ago?
- How do you assure fair and equitable treatment among the executive ranks when part of the organization is involved with sophisticated investment banking transactions and another part is involved with simple asset leasing? Should there be an overall corporate executive compensation strategy, or should the strategy vary by organizational unit—for example, should those responsible for investing corporate assets be paid more than those selling/underwriting the product?

CURRENT PRACTICES IN FINANCIAL SERVICES

Some of these issues, while not unique to the financial services industry, have become particularly important as consolidation occurs and it becomes difficult to tell the difference between a bank, an insurance company, and a securities/investment banking organization. (Current regulations require a distinction between banks and insurance companies, but there are some gray areas since bank holding companies own insurance agencies and insurance holding companies operate credit and bank loan-related operations.) What are financial services companies doing? As consolidation and restructuring of companies within the financial services sector has occurred, the cost of the *best* executive talent has increased. Movement of these executives from one company to another is accompanied by increased compensation levels, both in salary and incentive compensation opportunity. Moreover, in the securities industry sector, in just a few years the bull market and company acquisition trends have resulted in investment managers and bankers earning levels of compensation that historically had only been realized by movie stars and top athletes. These changes put upward pressure on the levels of pay for executives and changed the perceptions of individuals concerning what constitutes a fair level of pay for their contributions. As might be expected, pay for executives in the insurance and banking sectors has increased at a greater rate than that of executives in manufacturing, retailing, and other service businesses. However, the tables can turn quickly when profitability falls, companies downsize or even file for bankruptcy (e.g., Drexel Burnham), and management talent is readily available. Thus, maintaining pay competitiveness is an important consideration that must be constantly examined.

START WITH WHERE YOU ARE

Because of the "blending" taking place in the financial services sector, the selection of a comparison group of companies for determining pay involves more than just defining a group of banks of similar size or a group of insurance companies that are primarily in the same business. It is not unusual for senior executives to move from a reinsurance company to the securities division of a mutual insurance company. Insurance executives have moved easily from the property and casualty sector to a company made up of leasing, mezzanine financing, investment banking, and securities brokerage operations. In fact, the Xerox Financial Services unit was put together by an individual with limited insurance experience. The criteria for selecting a peer group should relate to what the business does today and where it is going in the future.

A market rate for each executive position can be established by applying statistical techniques to the available data. Generally, the technique should yield a dollar amount correlated with a scope-of-responsibility factor or factors associated with the position. In the banking industry, for example, the scope-of-responsibility factor for the CEO position is the asset size. For an insurance company, it is generally the net written premiums, but it could include the asset size as well. For investment banking and securities brokerage operations, it is generally the overall fee revenue. For credit and leasing organizations, it is the annual asset volume on leases transacted for the year. To determine the relevant rate for a given organization, the level of pay associated with the current scope-measure size would determine the current market rate. Or, in cases where significant growth is expected, the scope measure could be the level expected in two or three years, implying that the level of executive talent required now would be one that could manage a much larger organization in the future.

By knowing a fair market rate, one is in a better position to determine what the appropriate rate of pay should be for the executive group. The financial services sector is always making judgments on a fair rate for the products and services that it is providing, and it relies on available numerical data to make a business decision. Banks and leasing/credit companies decide on loan rates based on their cost of capital and what competitors are charging. Insurance companies establish premium rates based on what actuaries indicate are proper charges for anticipated losses, but they are often swayed by premium rates charged by the competition. Underwriters and loan officers are trained to make judgments based on what is perceived to be a fair charge for the service provided. Thus, it is not surprising that executives in financial services firms believe that such judgment can be extended to the area of executive compensation and that they can establish a fair rate of pay for the value they provide to the organization. It is important, therefore, that the analysis of data be as systematic and structured as actuarial projections so that board compensation decisions are perceived as fair and equitable by the individuals affected.

RELATING PAY TO PERFORMANCE

In some financial services organizations such as investment banking and investment management firms, pay can be directly related to performance—primarily because performance is easy to measure. Many Wall Street investment banking firms operate as partnerships. A fee is typically charged for the services performed. The fee could be a percentage of the value of the deal or an underwriting premium on a new stock issue. After office costs such as rent, utilities, support staff, and other personnel costs are subtracted from all fees received, the partners share the profits. In some cases, the partners take their "profits" out of the business on an annual basis; in other cases, they leave the profits in the partnership for reinvestment, which might include, for example, taking an equity position in the business for which they are arranging financing. If the value of the equity investment increases, then the value of each partnership share increases.

In this example, the business is driven by the deals that a partner brings to the business. In very simple terms, the larger the deal, the larger the fees. The compensation for the executive in this case is simple and linked directly to the first fundamental strategy, i.e., if the partner obtains more and higher fees, then the partnership will be in a position to realize larger profits. The second fundamental business strategy is to invest in good deals, i.e., those with high returns over a long period of time. This will result in increasing the value of the partnership. Since the executives are the owners, it does not matter to them how much they are paid annually. What matters most is the increasing accumulation of their net worth and the ability to take dollars out of the partnership whenever necessary to meet their financial needs. "Cashing in" on the value created means an individual partner taking his or her share of the accumulated wealth of the firm out of the partnership. In general, if the partnership allocation percentages reflect the fee income produced by each partner, then the compensation to each partner is perceived as being fair. Because partnership pay is linked directly to the value created by each partner, questions of the value contributed by the executive rarely arise.

In a bank or insurance company, in almost all cases, the executives are employees of the company under contract—implicitly or explicitly—to manage the company for a level of compensation that generally increases annually. (The exceptions include Saul Steinberg of the Reliance Insurance Group and Warren Buffet of Berkshire Hathaway, who are more than just executives.) If given a choice, in most instances these executives would like to have a deal similar to that of the partners in an investment banking firm. Who could blame them? Who wants to take the risk associated with what can happen to the business in the future? Most publicly held corporations, however, do not give the executive a choice. Executives are typically provided with a balance in their pay between current cash and compensation based on stock price appreciation (and often dividend payments in a dividend paying company). The board compensation committee in these companies, after deciding on the level of pay, must decide on the mix among the various compensation elements. It must determine the extent to which performance should be measured by changes in stock price versus performance determined through financial measures or strategically important events such as an acquisition, divestiture, or change of business mix.

Executives in banks, insurance companies, and other financial services companies cannot be paid totally in shares of stock. There is a need for a periodic cash flow to cover normal living expenses—even for executives. (There are a number of owner/managers with significant wealth who take a small or no salary and receive most of their living expense income from stock dividends.) Therefore, it is logical that executives receive an annual cash compensation amount. But the amount should be variable relative to the performance of the executive and the contribution that his or her decisions make to increasing value for the shareholder. Thus, performance should be measured by more than just stock price. Pay should be based on the return that management can realize on the equity that shareholders have invested in the business. Thus, return on equity should be an important factor in determining the incentive pay of executives, in particular the return on equity of the company compared to peer companies, even if it is determined that net earnings against plan is a simpler measure. For example, the target level of net earnings for the year could be established from peer group historical ROE performance as applied to company equity.

SHOULD EXECUTIVES HAVE AN OWNERSHIP INTEREST IN THE BUSINESS?

To ensure that executives' behavior exhibits a properly balanced long-term view, against short-term financial stability (or survival), financial services executives should be encouraged or even required to have a significant stock ownership (or simulated stock ownership) position until retirement or termination of employment with the company. Executives' net worth must be tied up in the long-term success of multiyear loans, adequate premium rates, and sufficient reserves for losses, and of investment practices that provide reasonable returns without inordinate risk. Thus, bank executives should own significant levels of stock to ensure that they realize the impact of sound loan underwriting, aggressive marketing strategy, attention to customer service, and reasonable fees for transactions. Insurance executives need to be held accountable for sound underwriting practices, reserve adequacy, and the investment of reserves and surplus to produce an underwriting profit, investment income, and capital gains (both realized and unrealized) that are in excess of the cost of equity capital to the corporation. They should be compensated as if they were partners in the business, but required to leave a portion of their partnership earnings in the business in the form of stock ownership. Ownership *is* magic in providing the right long-term view, and the compensation program strategy in most cases needs to be based on attaining this objective. Annual cash could be taken out of the business by the executive in those years when earnings are good, but retained in the business in those years—which inevitably occur in financial services—when earnings are poor. However, by properly balancing stock ownership opportunity and gains from stock ownership with annual cash opportunities, desired executive behavior can be reinforced through the compensation program.

IS PAY-FOR-PERFORMANCE ALWAYS RIGHT?

Pay-for-performance should not be the primary issue when building or rebuilding the executive group of a financial services firm. A large salary, guaranteed bonus, and/or guaranteed stock payment, e.g., restricted stock, may be needed to attract the executive talent required to move in a new direction or restructure an existing business. For example, there are not many executives who truly understand the reinsurance business. If planning suggests that reinsurance is an important business channel, large, guaranteed levels of compensation will have to be paid to executives in this area. But because profitability will not be known for five to eight years after initial marketing efforts, annual pay cannot be based solely on annual financial earnings. Rather, performance must be determined by the quality of decisions about the type of business to reinsure and decisions about premium pricing/underwriting. Most board members have insufficient knowledge and data to evaluate such decisions. Consequently, pay levels will need to be driven by the *potential* value that the executive has to the business and the going rate of pay for executive talent in the reinsurance industry in general. The board can estimate the potential value by determining the level of annual pay associated with the current and future premium volume and providing a level of long-term compensation opportunity commensurate with that level of pay. The magnitude of the executive's ultimate net worth would then be dependent on the ultimate profitability of the business written during that year.

A DIVERSIFIED INSURANCE COMPANY EXAMPLE

Over the years, companies have used various approaches to compensate executives in an attempt to align pay with business strategy. A well-known, large diversified insurance company has minimized the use of annual incentives at the executive level. Its compensation program for senior executives is linked to proven executive value over the long term. Rewards are provided through significant stock ownership and participation in a highly lucrative program with payouts based on appreciation in company stock price and dividend payments. The culture, carefully orchestrated by the chief executive officer, places a high value on sustained underwriting profitability, as measured by the loss ratio on each line of business and combined ratio for a business unit, and innovative thinking in approaching new markets and developing new products. Small annual successes are rewarded, but those rewards are not as significant as the rewards from participation in the elite executive group compensation program or from promotions that frequently occur for the better performers. By traditional measures of executive compensation, salaries, annual incentives, and even stock option grants may be at or possibly below competitive levels of pay. However, when the values realized from stock price growth, dividend performance, and a unique nontraditional net worth building program are included, pay is positioned to be significantly above competitive medians.

In this company, performance expectations are not communicated through a formal annual executive incentive plan. Performance expectations are communicated in the budgeting and long-range planning processes, and throughout the year as profitability is closely examined on an ongoing basis. The pay system provides rewards that reinforce the business strategy by providing significant pay when performance contributes to sustained profitability resulting in increased stock price performance.

PROPERTY AND CASUALTY COMPANY EXAMPLE

In another example of linking pay to business expectations, a diversified property and casualty insurance company wanted to affect executive behavior and decision making after a change in management. Historically, the company operated with an entrepreneurial management style, delegating significant decision-making authority to executives in each of its business units. Initially, this approach appeared to be working well as outstanding earnings were reported under insurance accounting provisions. However, as the losses began to mature and actual loss payments exceeded what was initially reserved, reported earnings began to suffer. So the company restructured itself.

The new management team wanted business-unit management to employ a strategy that encouraged an adequate premium rate for the risk and resulted in a return-on-equity level that met the requirements of the new owner. The annual earnings results, using conventional insurance accounting, did not adequately reflect management's performance against its earnings and ROE goal, even when measured over a three-year period. There were two primary reasons for this inadequacy:

- Current earnings results were being negatively influenced by the additional reserving required to cover the losses from the business written by former management several years earlier.
- The adequacy of the premium rate charged for a risk in any one policy year cannot be determined until three to six years after the policy year is over, when losses have had an opportunity to mature.

To focus management on improving the premium rate charged for the risks currently underwritten and on measuring the adequacy of the rate charged on these risks (and not prior risks), a new long-term incentive plan was developed and implemented. The plan employs a three-year performance period. Because actual performance over these three years is not known until loss reserves have more fully developed, it is measured at the end of an additional three years after the original performance period. Specifically, earned premium and operating expense are determined over the three-year performance period. Actual losses and loss reserves for "accidents" occurring in the three-year performance period are measured three years after the end of the performance period, with estimates made at the end of the third, fourth, and fifth years. Partial payments to the participating executive group are made after the initial three-year performance period based on these estimates. Furthermore, any reserve for losses occurring prior to the three-year performance period is excluded in determining payout under the long-term incentive plan so that current management is not penalized for underwriting decisions made by the previous management. A new six-year program begins every three years.

The payout under the plan is based on attaining an absolute level of financial performance that relates to a required return-on-equity level. However, within the property and casualty insurance sector, the actual level of performance may be contingent on circumstances beyond the control of management. These circumstances typically influence the industry in general. To reflect such circumstances in the long-term incentive plan, the amount determined from absolute performance is modified to reflect *relative* performance. Thus, if management does better than a peer group, it realizes more in the long-term payout than it would by measured absolute performance results. Conversely, if performance is worse than that of the peer group, management realizes less than that indicated by measured absolute performance. Although this relative performance dimension adds to the complexity of the program, it is perceived to be fair by the owners, as well as by the participating management group.

In this case, the compensation program for the executive group was clearly developed to advance the business objective of maximizing the premium rate on business written. The justification for such premium rates was the high quality of customer service provided—both to the independent agent and to the insured. Well-defined, nonfinancial strategic decisions and actions supporting the customer service strategy that the company believes is important to realize the appropriate financial results are considered when measuring executive performance in the annual incentive plan. Under this plan, payout is based on actual results against evaluation criteria identified for a number of nonfinancial performance areas, as well as on the underwriting profit of the business unit.

REGIONAL BANK HOLDING COMPANY EXAMPLE

In the 1980s, consolidation through acquisition was the guiding principle in the banking industry; it was a rare bank that did not look to acquire or be acquired. One such regional bank holding company was particularly concerned about losing a number of its key executives to either a major money center bank or another large regional bank holding company in its geographical area. Through acquisitions of its own, good lending practices, and efficient backroom operations in the parent and acquired banks, its return on equity and return on assets were at levels exceeding the median or average of comparators by a significant margin. Such financial performance usually attracts executive recruiters looking for management talent to turn around a bank or other financial services company that has not experienced the same financial success. This bank corporation believed that it was particularly vulnerable to being acquired and was concerned that many executives would not wait until an acquisition to look for alternative employment. Moreover, management had determined that there were strategically important milestones that the bank needed to achieve if it was to maintain its superior financial performance. For example, it needed to consolidate the backroom operations of all banks in the holding company, improve computer systems, centralize commercial lending decisions on major loans, and create a greater sense of customer service among all employees.

The executive compensation strategy linked to these business objectives was threefold:

1.   Provide above-median total compensation, most of it in long-term incentives, and make payout contingent on remaining as an executive in the corporation.

2.   Base the magnitude of long-term incentive compensation opportunity on return-on-equity performance relative to a peer group of companies and on corporate stock price, with a portion of long-term pay related to dividend performance.

3.   Focus on annual earnings objectives and achieve strategic milestones through the annual incentive plan, and position to provide above-market compensation when performance meets above-market performance expectations.

A key to the strategy of the bank is the long-term incentive plan. It uses three elements to encourage and simulate stock ownership. As in most other bank holding companies, stock options are provided to a broader group of executive employees. These options provide compensation rewards if the stock price increases as a result of continuing earnings growth. They also provide for significant rewards in the event that the holding company is acquired by another bank corporation. In addition, for the senior executive group, performance shares are provided where the number of shares awarded is dependent on the holding company's return-on-equity rank in a peer group of bank corporations of similar asset size. This element keeps top management focused on maximizing return on equity while recognizing that the overall level of profitability is dependent on the overall health of the economy and discount rate, which should affect all banks similarly. With the reward for relative ROE performance paid in shares, the compensation value to the executive is also dependent on stock price. The third element, dividend units, is used as a means of reminding executives that they are in a stock ownership position and that dividend performance is based on sustaining a high level of earnings. With long-term incentive awards that are above the median of levels typically provided to executives within bank corporations of similar size, this bank corporation was able to attract a few selected executives from money center banks and retain other key executives during a period of much anxiety from threatened acquisition.

SUMMARY

What is essential in developing a strategic executive compensation program in financial services is a clear understanding of the underlying nature of the business and of what must be done to maximize value to the owners of the business. This means understanding the financial facts and what management can do to affect financial results. The programs developed must have a strong business rationale, yet be perceived by participants as fair and by owners as increasing shareholder or policyholder value. In financial services, where underwriting, lending, and investment decisions require executive judgments on fairness and value on an ongoing basis, the issues of executive compensation program design often become emotionally, if not technically, complex. Successful financial services executives believe their judgment is pre-eminent and that such judgment carries over to compensation decisions. But these decisions should be based on fact and evaluated on how they help improve or reinforce the performance of the organization. The executive group is the key to financial success in the financial services sector, both in the short and long term. The executive compensation program needs to keep both perspectives in balance since today's profits may be realized at the ultimate expense of the company in the long term.

PART III-D

Executive
Compensation
in
Restructurings
and Buyouts

27

THE LEVERAGED BUYOUT: OWNERSHIP AS COMPENSATION

Carl Ferenbach

MANY PEOPLE THINK OF a leveraged buyout as primarily a financial transaction, the replacement of equity with debt in a company's capital structure. But an LBO is also a reorganization of an existing corporation into a form that so alters the relationship between financial risk and reward that it must lead to a reexamination of operating risk and reward.

Clearly, a company that is recapitalized with debt must be managed differently from one that is financed by equity. Interest payments and principal reduction are contractual obligations and must receive top priority. Corporate strategies, therefore, must stress husbanding resources and using assets in the most efficient ways possible to ensure meeting two goals: the repayment of debt and creation of value through improved operations.

In order to engender the responsibility and accountability to deal with the special risks of an LBO, the sponsors or buyers invariably turn to management ownership. Including top managers in the owning group as a reward for managing financial risk has proven to be a wonderfully simple way to improve the chances for success. All other forms of management compensation in an LBO are secondary.

THE POTENTIAL REWARDS OF AN LBO

A leveraged buyout is the acquisition of an existing business by a new corporation or partnership formed for that purpose. Most LBOs are organized by financial entrepreneurs who either control or have direct and easy access to the debt and equity capital needed to complete the acquisition. LBO transactions almost always include as owners a group of key senior managers of the enterprise. These managers typically receive three kinds of equity interest in the new firm: an initial ownership position that they purchase themselves; additional promoted or subsidized shares received at the time of the acquisition; and incentive equity in the form of stock options that are earned if the company exceeds the goals set forth in the business plan.

Unless they have significant personal resources, top company officers rarely are able to acquire control of the LBO. Occasionally however, because of a low stock price relative to a large pool of assets or because the business requires a management-led turnaround, a so-called bootstrap can be accomplished whereby a commercial finance company or asset-based lender supplies the debt. With such an arrangement, management may be able to acquire control.

Most leveraged buyouts are purchases of divisions or subsidiaries of major corporations, or of privately or closely held firms. The managers of such divisions or companies usually have not accumulated great wealth. A leveraged buyout represents their principal opportunity to be owners of the company that they operate and to create large estates for themselves.

The easiest way to understand how wealth can be generated with limited resources is to examine a hypothetical acquisition of a sound business. If Company X earns operating profits (before interest and taxes) of $15 million and expects moderate growth (6 percent to 10 percent annually) during the next five years, its capital structure might be organized in a leveraged buyout for $100 million as follows:

Capitalization of Company X
    ($000s)

Senior debt	$60,000
Subordinated debt	30,000
Common stock	10,000

The forecast statement of income might be as follows:

Projected Income of Company X
    ($000s)

	Year One	Year Two	Year Three	Year Four	Year Five
Revenues[a]	$100,000	$107,000	$114,490	$122,504	$131,079
Operating profit	15,000	16,050	17,174	18,376	19,662
Interest expense[b]	9,900	9,541	9,083	8,513	7,819
Taxes[c]	1,836	2,343	2,913	3,551	4,263
Net income	3,264	4,166	5,178	6,312	7,580

a. Seven percent annual growth rate
b. $90 million of debt at average cost of 11%
c. Thirty-six percent

If the company invests 3 percent of sales annually in new plant and equipment, which is equivalent to its yearly depreciation, and it does not have significant requirements for working capital to achieve growth, its cash flows will be as follows:

Projected Cash Flow for Company X
            ($000s)

	Year One	Year Two	Year Three	Year Four	Year Five
Net profit	$3,264	$4,166	$5,178	$6,312	$7,580
Depreciation	3,000	3,000	3,000	3,000	3,000
Capital expenditures	3,000	3,000	3,000	3,000	3,000
Change in working capital	0	0	0	0	0
Free cash	3,264	4,166	5,178	6,312	7,580
Cumulative debt retired	3,264	7,430	12,608	18,920	26,500

With these prospects, the investors customarily offer management the opportunity to acquire what they can afford to buy for cash. It would be typical for a group of seven to ten managers to purchase 10 percent of such a company for $1 million. The balance of the equity would be acquired by the sponsor, the subordinated noteholder, and possibly by the senior creditor.

The sponsor and the creditors generally offer management additional equity for free. This typically represents between 5 percent and 10 percent of the ownership in the firm. Under current tax laws, the grant is usually in the form of ten-year options to purchase stock at the founders' price. Since the options will only be exercised in the event of a transaction that enables the holder to sell the stock at a profit, the grant represents a promoted interest. The options vest over a three- to five-year period, during which the holder must remain in the company's employ.

A second incentive plan tied to a specific performance target often is added in a leveraged buyout. One common variety, used in our hypothetical example, grants options that are vested only if the aggregate operating profit for the first three years equals or exceeds a predetermined target. The target is normally the forecast that management has developed as part of the sale. This plan permits management of Company X to acquire another 5 percent of the company.

If the owners decide to sell the firm at the end of year five for the same multiple that they paid for it (6.5 times operating profit), the enterprise will have a value of $127,803,000. After retirement of the remaining senior and subordinated debt, $64,303,000 will remain for the shareholders. Management's direct investment will be worth $6,430,300. Its option or free stock and its incentive stock each will be worth $3,215,150. Therefore, management's entire interest will equal $12,860,600, for which $1,000,000 was invested. The sponsors who paid $9 million for 80 percent of the company will have earned a 42 percent internal rate of return. The transaction will be counted a financial success.

THE BUSINESS PLAN AND ITS DEMANDS

The key to every leveraged buyout is the business plan, which usually is developed as part of the seller's information. All the critical variables in the financing and operating of the LBO for some time to come are developed from the business plan: debt arrangements and terms, equity requirements, management's share of the equity, and performance targets.* The ability of the firm to meet the targets specified in the business plan will determine future cash compensation and the level of new investment in the company.

Although the business plan is developed by management, all of the investors usually are held accountable by the corporation's creditors if debt repayments are not made. Hence, both the buyer/sponsor and management should have confidence in the plan and agree on what steps they will take if its targets are not met. They should also understand what each may wish to do if the company exceeds the plan's performance goals.

For the owners of equity in a leveraged buyout, particularly for management, the requirements of the business plan are both a stick and a carrot. The stick will flail them if they cannot meet their obligations under the debt agreements, but they will get the carrot if they succeed. Both possibilities lead managers to take a critical look at operations. When they do, they typically prune redundant management positions and staff. They develop capital budgets that enhance existing productive assets but forego new or risky ventures. They adopt a business strategy that emphasizes service to customers but does not make provision for extra demand. Man-

---

*All of the shareholders (management, buyer/sponsor, and any creditors) also enter into a shareholders' agreement at the time of the acquisition. This agreement covers the purchase of stock and the terms of the options, as well as the disposition of a manager's shares if he or she leaves the company. The cashing-out provisions of the shareholders' agreement will be discussed in detail in the section "The Decision to Seek Liquidity."

agers who have become accustomed to having room for error find that their livelihood now depends on greater attention to detail.

Participants in LBOs often discover assets and/or operations that are worth more to someone else than to them. The decision to sell unnecessary or poorly performing assets is usually made quickly. Longer-term questions that may eventually confront those in control of an LBO, especially a successful one, are how to raise additional capital for growth and when to seek liquidity for their investment.

If management owns a large equity interest in an LBO, it has good reason to care about the outcome of strategic decisions. In many public companies the interests of the management and the shareholders often are not aligned by common ownership, making it difficult to settle disagreements constructively. The management of an LBO, on the other hand, has a powerful incentive to resolve problems quickly. (Resolution usually is based on shareholder consensus.) Because of the importance of aligning the rewards to managers with the performance of the company, *the most significant compensation decision that the buyer/sponsor will make is what ownership stake to offer management.*

THE STRUCTURE OF MANAGEMENT OWNERSHIP

A variety of circumstances can affect management compensation in an LBO: whether the acquisition is hostile or friendly; whether the sale is an auction or negotiated one-on-one; whether the present management will be let go or retained. If the management is part of the deal, existing contracts and compensation programs (salaries, bonuses, pensions, health benefits, stock options, and so forth) will have weight in the determination of executive pay.

Let us assume that Company X has been a subsidiary of a larger parent and has a management team in place that has performed effectively and wants to participate in a leveraged buyout. The executives have no contracts and received most of their compensation in the form of salary, bonus, and benefits. In these fairly typical circumstances, several questions arise: How much money does the management group have to invest? How eager is it to invest? Is it willing to stand behind the business plan? How many managers want to participate? How do they want to allocate the stock among themselves? Each question is important to both the debt and equity participants in a leveraged buyout.

Broadly speaking, there are two schools of thought on how much of their personal resources managers should be required to invest in an LBO. According to some, managers should pledge everything they own and borrow as much money as they can to purchase their position. They should receive little incentive equity. If the company fails, so will the managers, totally. According to a more moderate view, a reasonable portion of personal savings is adequate to offer a meaningful incentive, since failure will not only cost the manager his savings but also his reputation and opportunities for future employment. Management's willingness to commit personal resources to the LBO and to stand behind the business plan are particularly persuasive influences on the buyer/sponsor's decision to provide promoted stock and additional equity as a reward for meeting or exceeding performance targets.

The credibility of the business plan represents an interesting problem for both managers and the LBO investors. At the stage when managers are negotiating their own participation in a leveraged buyout, they face a conflict. In light of their continuing fiduciary obligation to the existing owners, managers should produce an aggressive plan to achieve a high price for the sale. Yet, as buyers, they will have to live up to the plan in order to meet its credit terms, and they will have to achieve the plan's targets in order to realize their own potential equity stake. As investors, the managers want to present a conservative business plan to get a lower price for the buyer.

For outside investors who do not really know how this game is being played, the simplest rule of thumb is to lower the effective purchase price by seeking more direct investment from management (and offering a smaller promoted interest) if the business plan forecasts a rate of growth in operating income that is greater than that achieved historically. Managers' option plans also should be contingent on the achievement of business plan performance goals.

Another interesting and important group of questions concerns the composition of the management group. Which managers significantly influence operating outcomes and therefore should be included? How should the company compensate those who are not included? How should stock be allocated among the participants?

A buyer/sponsor may choose to be involved in these decisions or to let management make them either unilaterally or with the approval of the compensation committee of the new company's board of directors. Experience suggests that management's answers will be influenced heavily by existing compensation standards, as well as by the chief executive's willingness to use equity as a management tool to move key people in new directions. Most buyer/sponsors, on the other hand, want the top two or three executives to be highly motivated and therefore highly paid.

Buyers' preferences aside, the allocation of equity among managers tends to be determined by the corporate culture. In some companies, ownership is limited to a few key managers who control most decision making. Other companies that are more democratic include a much larger group. Some chief executives allocate equity broadly in the belief that it is their best chance to refocus management efforts on the new corporate objectives of debt retirement and value creation and the greater attention to detail needed to achieve them.

The owners of equity eventually become recognized as a key group within the company, a group that aspiring managers want to join. Leaving room to include new managers is an important and difficult problem for founders of an LBO, because stock is allocated at the price on the acquisition date. Future sales to managers beyond the initial investor group, therefore, are difficult to accomplish. New participants can be brought into the option plans, but in the minds of the original manager/investors, the newcomers may be second-class citizens because they did not make a direct investment.

INCENTIVE EQUITY

Invariably, managers feel that their contribution to the success of the company they run warrants more of a promoted interest than the outside investors are willing to grant them, particularly given the financial risk of an LBO. One way both parties can achieve their goals is to agree to make additional stock options contingent on performance that surpasses the targets of the business plan.

There are many criteria for performance that are suitable for determining incentive equity; one simple standard is to make the vesting of options depend on achievement of the forecast aggregate earnings before interest and taxes (EBIT) for the first three years. The choice of EBIT as a measure is based on its universal acceptance as one of the components in a valuation equation. This equation values equity interests at a multiple of EBIT less debt outstanding at the time measured. (Our hypothetical company was valued at 6.5 times EBIT.) By offering incentive equity, the buyer/sponsor is expressing willingness to share value in excess of expectations with management, provided management creates the value.

CASH COMPENSATION

There are different approaches to setting salaries for the managers of a company reorganized as a leveraged buyout. Practices range from cutting salaries to conserve cash, to placing more emphasis on performance-oriented bonuses, to leaving the old plans in place undisturbed, to actually increasing current pay. In analyzing this decision, the buyer/sponsor must keep several objectives in mind:

1. Equity should be more important to management than current pay.
2. Cash must be conserved.
3. Managers must not be distracted by either an excess or a lack of cash compensation.

The buyer/sponsor who insists on lowering cash compensation in the belief that equity represents an irresistible golden handcuff runs the risk that the managers' lowered standard of living will distract them from the important tasks at hand. Conversely, overpaying management will reduce the important incentives inherent in the equity. A bonus plan that is keyed to EBIT (so that it is consistent with the incentive stock plan) and possibly to one or more additional ratios important to short- and medium-term performance in the company's industry best fits everyone's needs.

Most LBOs also have comprehensive medical plans and one or more forms of retirement plans. Often the former owner who installed the plans insists that the buyer continue to provide the same or similar benefits. These plans are of sufficient concern to the management and employees that it would be foolish for the buyer to do otherwise.

NONOWNING MANAGERS

Establishing cash compensation that will motivate those not included in the ownership is important to an LBO's success. Managers often can be made to feel they are a part of the inside group if they are allowed to participate in a performance-based bonus pool along with the investors.

For consistency, the cash compensation that nonowning managers receive can be keyed to the same performance standards that are used for the equity group. Although the equity group may choose to make only small annual adjustments to its current compensation in order to conserve cash and set a standard for cost control, the nonequity group must receive total compensation that is fully competitive with industry standards. Keeping this group involved in the company is important to senior management for the obvious reason that companies are only as good as their people, as well as for the not-so-obvious reason that in a successful LBO the managers with equity often retire or leave the company after the outside investors exit or cash out. The value of the company (and the owning manager's investment) will depend partly on the capability of the next generation of management.

THE DECISION TO SEEK LIQUIDITY

Among the difficult decisions that the owners of a leveraged buyout make is when and how to realize the value of their equity by going public, selling out, or recapitalizing. If this decision is precipitated by a need for more capital because the business is growing, it is generally easy to choose to go public. However, outside investors may want to cash out of a successful company, putting them in conflict with management desiring to maintain the status quo. When all has gone reasonably well, this situation is likely to arise sometime during the five years after the leveraged buyout.

When the buyer/sponsor controls the company (with or without the subordinated noteholders), it can decide to sell unilaterally, by means that may not accommodate management. For instance, most management groups do not like auctions that are designed to maximize value. They often prefer a limited, selective process in which they themselves may be buyers, plowing their profits from the sale back into the new acquisition. Under these circumstances, management's ability to control information gives it a decided advantage.

Professional owners approach this problem in a variety of ways. Most are fiduciaries for an investment pool and feel obligations to their limited partners. On the other hand, most readily acknowledge management's critical role in creating a successful leveraged buyout and therefore seek consensus on the form of sale. Whether the decision is to auction or to negotiate privately, the management investor group will receive financial benefits.

The shareholders' agreement, entered into at the time of the leveraged buyout, specifies the conditions for shareholder liquidity. It states who can initiate negotiations, who can participate and for how much, and how a public equity offering must be conducted. The agreement also provides for the disposition of a manager's stock if he or she leaves the company for any reason.

Generally, it is agreed that all owners have the right (but not the obligation) to take part in an exit—whatever the form—pro rata. Coupled with this right is a come-along/take-along provision that in effect says that the controlling shareholder may initiate a sale but must permit all other shareholders to cash out as well. In partial exits, which typically take the form of public offerings but can involve a sale to a third party, companies often can take advantage of a repurchase right that supercedes any other bid as long as the company's repurchase offer is highest.

The shareholders' agreement almost always requires that the stock held by managers who leave the company while it is still closely held must be resold to the company or to the other shareholders. This rule ensures that the stock is available only to other insiders.

The price the owners will pay for a manager's stock depends on the reason for departure. A manager who quits voluntarily is entitled to a return of his or her investment at either its purchase price or at book value, whichever is lower. The same is true for a person dismissed "for cause," which usually means for criminal activity or negligence. If a manager dies or is permanently disabled, his or her stock is repurchased at fair market value (determined by pre-agreed formula or by selection of investment bankers if the company is not public). The same applies to the shares of a manager dismissed by the board of directors for reasons other than cause.

SIGNODE CORPORATION: A CASE EXAMPLE

The leveraged buyout of Signode Corporation stands out among many similar transactions as a compelling example of how cash-based performance targets can be used to accomplish specific strategic goals quickly. At Signode, a leveraged buyout was used to make the transition from the paternalistic culture that had carried over from two generations of founder/owner management to a more competitive culture.

A public corporation, Signode was the leading producer of strapping and strapping systems used in industrial packaging. The company manufactured both the machines and tools and the steel and plastic strapping materials. Signode had diversified its primary business to include fasteners for commercial and residential construction, other construction-related products, industrial marking products for inventory control, and a line of plastic bags employing the zip-lock technology for which a subsidiary held the patent.

When Signode was threatened by a corporate raider, the management realized that a leveraged buyout could help the company move to a new phase of development. When management entered into the LBO in August 1982, it adopted several goals: (1) to reduce inventories and overall working capital, while continuing to service customers effectively; (2) to address the secular decline in its steel strapping business; and (3) to develop new products using technologies well known to Signode.

The acquisition by Signode Industries was completed for approximately $450 million. Management purchased 18 percent of the company for $2,700,000. Thirty-two managers bought 9 percent of the new company for cash and received another 9 percent of the fully diluted common stock in the form of incentive options. Because few of the managers had the money to buy their stock, a local bank loaned them the money necessary for the purchase.

Two incentive compensation plans were installed: a short-term or annual plan, and a long-term or three-year rolling plan. Management shareholders agreed to apply the proceeds of the short-term plan to reducing the loans they had taken to purchase their shares. The proceeds of the long-term plan would be used to exercise their stock options.

The short-term incentive plan had one performance standard: cash flow, defined as net income before depreciation but after capital expenditures and changes in working capital. Simple thresholds were used that presumed proper debt service. From the thresholds a pool was created that could reach a maximum of 50 percent of the eligible group's salaries. The plan was administered by senior management using a performance appraisal system, and was reviewed by the board of directors.

Payments from the long-term plan were predicated on a debt-to-total-capitalization test, made for the first time at the end of the third year. The goal of the plan was to reduce the corporation's financial risk by reducing debt while building equity through earnings. The plan also provided the means for management shareholders to exercise their options. In addition to the owner/managers, a group of nonowning managers whose decisions could affect results was included in this plan.

All three compensation schemes succeeded. Although the first year of operation was difficult in several of Signode's markets, management achieved its goal of reducing working capital. As a result, the short-term plan rewarded the participants so that both corporate and personal debt were reduced significantly.

Management also made progress on its other goals, particularly the development of new products. The company set up venture teams to bring fresh thought to new uses for existing technologies. Several new products made it to market over the ensuing three years. Debt reduction continued and after the third year the long-term plan also made attractive awards because of a safer capitalization.

As the fourth anniversary of the leveraged buyout approached, management asked the board to form a committee of independent directors to consider future alternatives for the company's capital. After extensive deliberation, the outside owners followed the preference of the management group and negotiated a merger with a leading manufacturing company. All of the shareholders sold their stock for cash at a substantially higher price than they had paid for it. By means of a leaner balance sheet, stronger capitalization, and new products that were beginning to contribute to operating income, Signode managers had increased the value of the equity for the benefit of all the shareholders, including themselves.

APPLICATION OF LBO TECHNIQUES TO PUBLIC COMPANIES

Public companies have begun to use management ownership in an effort to generate the discipline and incentives of an LBO. Among a number of models used by public companies, two are most common. The first is a leveraged recapitalization (leveraged recap), by which the corporation repurchases as much as 80 percent to 90 percent of its equity with the proceeds from bank loans and high-yield bonds. Because the company does not become private, the public can retain an interest in the leveraged company. Management can increase any existing ownership through the grant of new options similar to those issued in an LBO.

Other corporations, such as the Henley Group (a company spun off by Allied-Signal Corporation), have sold management a significant equity interest paid for with low-cost loans keyed to performance. (In its first two years of operation, Henley spun off all or parts of three businesses, broke itself into two companies, made two acquisitions, and engaged in a contest to acquire Santa Fe Southern Pacific. Few other diversified companies have managed their assets as aggressively.)

CONCLUSION

While the leveraged buyout is a transaction in which the replacement of equity with debt alters the financial risk inherent in the enterprise, it is also a transaction in which governance of the corporation is shifted to a small group of professionals and to managers dedicated to the future of its core business. The essence of management compensation in the LBO form is ownership. Although other forms of remuneration are important, particularly for the nonowning group, the focused strategies needed to succeed and create value in a leveraged situation depend on management's ability to manage cash flow to pay debt and still invest in the business. Those who organize and invest in leveraged enterprises have found that the best way to motivate management to follow these strategies is to include them as beneficiaries of success.

28

THE EMERGING ROLE OF THE MANAGEMENT INVESTOR IN CORPORATE RESTRUCTURINGS

Frederic W. Cook and Matthew P. Ward

MANAGEMENT OF AMERICAN BUSINESS has come full circle. In the beginning, the founders of enterprises were also the owners and managers. Their vision and drive created basic industries and technologies. Later, owner-managers were replaced by professional managers who had greater technical skills but who lacked a meaningful ownership stake in the company. Recently, as a result of the surge in corporate restructurings, professional managers have taken on substantial personal investments in their employers. Occasionally, managers themselves initiate these transactions. Major changes in the ownership or capital structure of their businesses offer management an opportunity to significantly increase its at-risk investment to an extent that might not otherwise have been justifiable. To succeed, the new management investors must blend the drive and commitment of the founders with the technical proficiency required in today's complex business world.

THE MODERN INVESTOR

The matrix below illustrates the interrelationship of four basic characteristics of investors:

	Active Investor	Passive Investor
Employed Investor	④	③
Financial Investor	①	②

Investors are either "active" or "passive," and they are either employed by the company they are investing in or they are not employed (i.e., they are "financial" investors). When enterprises begin, capital comes from active investors of both types: entrepreneurs (employed) and venture capitalists (financial), who contribute time and energy to make their investment pay. As the company matures, active investors are replaced by passive financial investors: individuals and institutions such as pension plans or mutual funds.

Although both active and passive investors have a financial interest in raising a stock's value, only the active investor can assist in enhancing its value. Most employees who own shares in their employer are *not* active investors, because the amount they own is small. Nor does potential ownership, regardless of amount, affect behavior. Stock options, the most popular vehicle to enhance management ownership, are really only a passive investment. Even a huge option grant, say five times annual compensation, is not likely to alter a manager's passive investor behavior because there is no *real* investment, commitment, or downside risk. Fundamental change in the ownership or capital structure of an enterprise, on the other hand, creates the need for changed management behavior.

In practice, the designers of stock-based compensation plans avoid the issue of capital structure entirely. The source of shares for these plans is typically either Treasury shares or newly issued shares as the board determines from time to time. The designers just do not care where the shares come from; the plans are considered neutral appendages to companies' capital structures. You can bet that the founder-entrepreneurs would have cared a great deal.

A new breed of active investors has arrived on the scene. Some are employees and some are outsiders, and together they have created a new age in corporate management. Previous notions of acceptable competitive practice are being challenged aggressively. The new investors see easy prey in established, mature enterprises characterized by low profitability and stock price, high labor costs, and conservative balance sheets.

The first to draw public attention were hostile financial investors like Carl Icahn, Samuel Heyman, Saul Steinberg, Ronald Perelman, and Irwin Jacobs. All purchased large stakes in established companies with a view toward taking control and selling off assets (the bust-up strategy), or putting the company into play and being bought out at a profit by another company (a white knight) or by the company itself (greenmail). The early leveraged buyout leaders such as Kohlberg Kravis Roberts & Co., Forst-

man Little, and Wesray were also active financial participants in the restructuring of corporate America. They specialized in buying out passive
investors, including employees.

Companies responded to these developments with numerous *defensive
strategies* designed to protect the companies and their managers: staggered
board elections, by-law changes, various poison pills, employment contracts, golden parachutes, and rabbi trusts. Clever names, but not such
clever strategies. The hostile investors succeeded because the shareholding public supported, or at least acquiesced in, the basic premise that
fundamental changes were required to awaken the sleeping giants of corporate America. It would take active management investors to combat the
hostile buyer and such management investors materialized.

Active management investment is an *offensive strategy* to maintain independence and increase shareholder value without third-party intervention. So far it has consisted of the following:

- Management-led LBOs
- Public recapitalizations
- Partial public offerings
- Divestitures or spinoffs
- Leveraged employee stock ownership plans (ESOPs)

MANAGEMENT-LED LBOS

Donald Kelly of Beatrice Companies and Edward Finkelstein of R.H.
Macy & Co., were both initiators of and active participants in LBOs of
their companies. Although management has participated in hundreds of
these transactions, it has initiated few. (See Exhibit 28–1 for examples of
substantial increases in management ownership achieved via management-led LBOs.) The financial restructuring of the enterprise (low equity
and high debt), combined with management's huge ownership position
(real stock, not stock options), gives management the incentive and imperative to manage an enterprise differently and more profitably in the
future.

PUBLIC RECAPITALIZATIONS

Essentially, a public recapitalization is a leveraged buyout of most but
not all of the shares held by passive investors. Public investors cash in part

EXHIBIT 28-1
Management Ownership before and after LBOs in Representative Firms

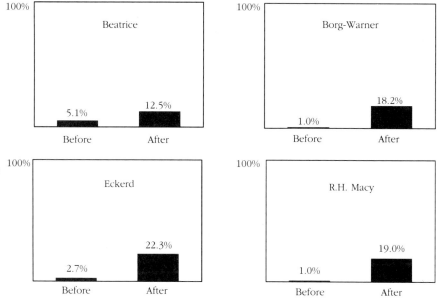

Source: Compiled by Frederic W. Cook & Co. from SEC public disclosure documents.

of their holdings but continue as equity investors in the "new," highly leveraged entity. Again, management's stake is substantially increased (see Exhibit 28–2). The companies borrow money or sell assets to pay public investors cash for a portion of their share value. The remainder is converted to a new, smaller equity piece ("stub" equity). Instead of cash, employees receive new equity representing a significant multiple of (e.g., five times) their current holdings.

PARTIAL PUBLIC OFFERINGS (PPOS)

A partial spinoff of shares of a subsidiary by a parent not only establishes a public market for the subsidiary's stock, but provides an investment op-

EXHIBIT 28-2
Management Ownership before and after Recapitalizations in Representative Firm

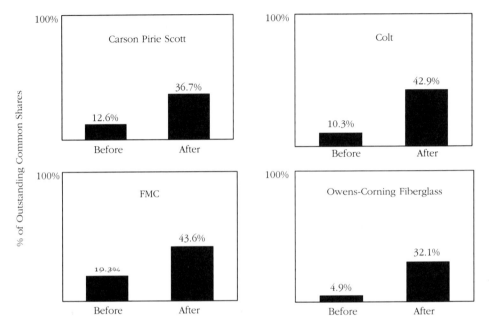

Source: Compiled by Frederic W. Cook & Co. from SEC public disclosure documents.

portunity for management as well. Although the parent retains an ownership interest—sometimes a majority—management and other employees typically hold a large stake too (see Exhibit 28–3). As part of the going-public process, managers can convert their parent company equity into shares of the new entity. In addition, they often receive large, up-front grants or purchase opportunities intended to provide a significant incentive for success and to build investor confidence via prospectus disclosures that those charged with managing the enterprise have a parallel stake in its future.

EXHIBIT 28-3
Ownership of Representative Partial Public Offerings

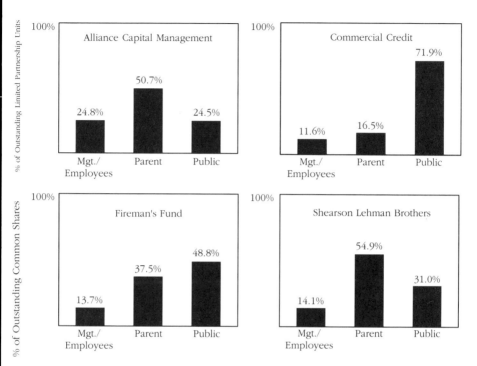

Source: Compiled by Frederic W. Cook & Co. from SEC public disclosure documents.

SPINOFFS

Sometimes a parent company completely divests itself of a subsidiary, either through an outright sale of shares to the public or by way of a special dividend of subsidiary stock to parent shareholders. The method for increasing management ownership is identical to PPOs and, as shown in Exhibit 28–4, the entity is truly freestanding.

LEVERAGED ESOPS

As tax-qualified employee benefit plans, leveraged ESOPs are not strictly vehicles for enhancing management investment in a company.

EXHIBIT 28-4
Ownership of Representative Spinoffs

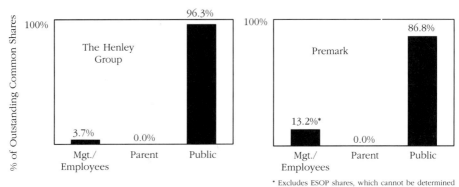

* Excludes ESOP shares, which cannot be determined

Source: Compiled by Frederic W. Cook & Co. from SEC public disclosure documents.

However, because of their unique tax advantages, ESOPs have been used by companies as a financing tool in combination with the strategies outlined above to decrease public ownership and, correspondingly, increase the ownership and voting power of all employees (including management). The partial public offerings of Fireman's Fund and Shearson Lehman Brothers and the spinoff of Premark included ESOPs as part of the overall management investor strategy.

An ESOP trust is created to acquire shares for allocation to the individual accounts of employees. The company (or the ESOP, with the company's guarantee) can borrow the funds required to purchase the shares at favorable rates because lenders need only recognize 50 percent of the interest as income. Company contributions of cash and shares (up to certain limits), and both principal and interest on ESOP debt, are tax deductible. Dividends paid are also deductible when allocated to individual accounts or used to repay ESOP debt.

All of these offensive strategies increase shareholder value through a major change in the ownership or capital structure of a company. Management either initiates or participates significantly in the restructuring. In the process, managers emerge as active investors. Not only is their stake in the organization's success much larger than before, but the equity compensation program requires their at-risk commitment. When the dust settles, a company managed by passive investors has been almost instantly transformed into an actively managed enterprise with an important risk/reward equity program.

DESIGN ISSUES

To successfully complete the transformation to active management, re-structuring requires:

1. A significant investment opportunity in the restructured entity, *and*
2. Management's willingness to change its behavior in ways necessary to meet the challenge and opportunity of invigorating the business.

Compensation professionals play a pivotal role in achieving both of the above. Three fundamental rules should guide the compensation experts:

1. From the very beginning, there must be collaboration between compensation strategists (who know incentive principles) and financial strategists charged with the restructuring.
2. The management equity program *must* represent a very large, at-risk investment. Outright ownership on the order of 15 percent to 25 percent of total shares is called for if managers are to regard themselves as real owners. Numbers of this magnitude are much higher than usual and require a suspension of competitive rationale. Substantial ownership is only justified if the program is truly at-risk (i.e., the manager's career and personal finances are on the line) and not risk-free like stock options, restricted stock, and performance shares.
3. Other aspects of total compensation may have to be altered. Administration of base salaries may need to be tightened up; annual incentives might shift from being goal-driven to being results-driven; performance measures might shift from accounting profits to cash flow; stock options and other risk-free long-term incentives are likely to be replaced by the new active management investor program; and SERPs, perks, and other management entitlements may give way to a new cost consciousness and spirit of teamwork throughout the ranks.

CONCLUSION

The New Perspective: Incentives, Not Windfalls

Collaboration among financial, legal, and compensation professionals is easier said than done, particularly in LBO transactions. Perhaps because of the sheer magnitude of the financial work involved in LBOs, compensation planning has usually taken a back seat to the resolution of financial and legal issues. Another reason for the low priority given compensation issues may be the influence of outside parties with significant ownership positions and decision-making power. Often the level of management participation is a function of how much ownership the outside LBO firm is willing to share. The individual managers' shares (and options) are allocated only after an acceptable level of management participation is determined.

However, with the exception of LBOs, corporate restructurings do lend themselves to thoughtful human resource and compensation planning from the outset. Which restructuring alternative to choose and how to treat prerestructuring compensation arrangements are crucial decisions. The underlying principle should be that the transaction should create an incentive, but *not* a windfall. Similarly, all elements of the firm's compensation and benefits program must be altered to enable it to recognize each individual's sacrifice or contribution to the repayment of the debt and to recognize the more efficient allocation of scarce resources resulting from the transaction.

A leaner organization requires a leaner overall compensation package and a more cost-conscious executive mindset. Fixed compensation costs must be minimized. Large equity positions must motivate not only because of the possibility that managers will get rich but also because of the possibility that they will go broke (or at least suffer a little bit). The risk in the equity program for management investors must be something of an all-or-nothing proposition, much the same as it was for the founder-entrepreneurs.

Existing programs and practices that are not in keeping with this new risk perspective have to change. Such changes are fundamental prerequisites to the success of the restructuring transaction. The evidence overwhelmingly demonstrates that American corporations are undergoing a radical transformation in their capital structures. An equally radical transformation of compensation and benefit programs is essential to the survival and success of those companies.

29

EXECUTIVE COMPENSATION IN SPINOFFS

Robert C. Ochsner

SPINOFFS WERE RELEGATED to the back closet of corporate finance for much of the postwar era: they were seldom used and little discussed, even in textbooks. During the massive restructuring of American corporations in the 1980s, spinoffs have come to life as a means both of altering capital structure and of changing a company's strategic product mix.

A spinoff often creates the need for major surgery on executive compensation programs. This chapter discusses the compensation problems of several types of transactions that currently are lumped together as spinoffs:

- Classical separation of a controlled subsidiary by distribution of the subsidiary's stock directly to the parent's shareholders;
- Public sale of all or part of the subsidiary's stock, usually at full value without preference to the parent's shareholders;
- "Packaging" of a group of subsidiaries into a form of holding company prior to either distribution or public offering; and
- Separation, usually by public offering, of a joint venture owned by two or more companies.

Although the capital market conditions preceding a spinoff and the effect of a spinoff on the parent's strategy are interesting parts of the drama, I will concentrate on the situation faced by the new company after separation.

The distinctive characteristic of a spinoff is an orphaned feeling. By their nature, subsidiaries are systematically denied the corporate adolescence enjoyed by most startup companies. They do not have complete internal functions: neither finance, personnel, data processing, law, planning, nor, often, even R&D. Subsidiaries do not have to communicate with stockholders, the SEC, the IRS, or the financial community. Instead, they are subject to review (often known as "hell week") during which line managers demand more profit and corporate staff specialists grill on details. This environment does not foster development of a cadre of real managers.

Then comes independence, often with little warning because of financial or strategic considerations unrelated to the subsidiary's readiness to function in the "real world" of adult corporations. Subsidiaries are often talented children, especially in marketing, product development, and operations, but they lack experience in handling their own money, planning their future, or simply living within the ambiguous rules of adult society. The skills required to design, install, and administer the executive compensation program (including expertise in SEC law, FASB regulations, taxation, and record keeping) are rarely present in a spinoff company and probably must be acquired—and acquired quickly—from the outside. Developing these skills internally should be an objective of the post-spinoff transition period.

Because of a subsidiary's immaturity, human resource strategy in a spinoff should have these priorities:

- To retain one (or more) key levels of management until the corporation can determine its own destiny—probably a period of three to five years.
- To distribute both rewards and status in a flexible way so that they will be available to support the rapid creation of a culture distinctive to the company.
- To make enhancement of shareholder value, measured by market value of the stock, the only way to earn above-market levels of pay.
- To keep the program simple and communicate it clearly.

In trying to accomplish these objectives, compensation planners must address the following questions when designing pay programs for a spinoff:

1. *How much of the executive compensation structure should be fixed by the parent before the spinoff?* The answer seems to depend on whether the stock is being distributed to shareholders or sold to the public. In public offerings, underwriters press for including top-management employment contracts and stock options in the prospectus, as is done in an initial public offering. Spinoffs that are accomplished by distribution to shareholders rely less on predetermined compensation arrangements.

Size also counts: managements of spinoffs with multibillion-dollar market capitalizations, that might be presumed to need such help less, are more likely to have the bargaining power to get advance assurance of future compensation. Deals of this type might be seen as corporate "wills," but to the extent that they try to enforce the parent's wishes far beyond the spinoff, such provisions are unlikely to have much force—unless, of course, they turn out to provide a windfall. This possibility, together with the need for flexibility mentioned earlier, argues strongly for less predetermination of executive compensation.

An exception might be made in spinoffs that have limited capacity to set their own compensation course for the first several years, like smaller product-line spinoffs in the apparel and home furnishings industry. Food companies acquired many of these firms in the 1970s, but they found the strategic fit was poor. When they were spun off individually to maximize their value, most of them had sales volume of $100 million or less and only a few hundred employees. In cases like these, a very simple, understandable job classification and compensation structure should be "willed" to the spinoff. Typically, this includes (a) a graded salary system at or below the large company market, (b) an annual incentive pool based on cash flow generation over the "nut" of cost to run the business and service the debt, and (c) an equity position for the management group totaling 5 percent to 15 percent of the outstanding stock with a three- to seven-year vesting lock-in.

2.   *What is the appropriate comparison group for determining executive compensation in a spinoff?* For companies using a formal job evaluation or classification plan, this question becomes, "Will some of our management jobs get bigger after the spinoff?" Although the answer is usually yes for a limited number of jobs, there is another side of the coin. To get bigger after a spinoff, job classifications must start relatively small. Before raising grade levels, make sure that the existing levels appropriately reflect subsidiary status. For companies using "market pricing" compensation surveys, it will be difficult to assign an extra market-value factor to salaries since most of the jobs surveyed probably come from publicly owned companies.

3.   *Who should be included in the executive group?* In practice, this has ranged from only the CEO—which looks suspiciously like a case of greed—to three, six, fifteen, and even forty or more top managers. Planners should consider the strategic importance of the jobs, the relative difficulty of replacing incumbents, and the extent to which jobs rely on teamwork.

It is important to remember that the strategic framework for a spinoff is the first three to five years, rather than the full planning horizon of an existing business. In one spinoff in the steel business, for example, several dozen department heads were included in the executive group. They were not likely to be lured away by competitors (the industry was too depressed), but they were essential to producing the short-term cash flow from operations needed to pay off debt and make the spinoff a success. The group was a coherent one: All of the incumbents were males aged forty-five to sixty-two with twenty or more years of company service and annual compensation of about $75,000. Many were eligible to retire immediately, and a number had minority stock interests, which appreciated significantly in the spinoff. Because the subsidiary had not grown over the previous fifteen years, no replacements had been trained internally. Given the industry's uncertain long-term future, it was essential to show these executives that they were important and to provide enough economic incentive to make it clearly worthwhile for them to put in another three to five years. This was done through stock awards and options with a value of about $150,000 per individual if the stock doubled from the offering price within five years, a reasonable possibility if the company's internal financial projections were met. Each individual had to invest (and hold) about $25,000 in stock to join the program.

Focusing on an executive group allows planners to concentrate on two or three dozen managers and a limited time period. This makes it possible to think about executives as people—and to design a compensation program that will retain and motivate them to meet short-term strategic goals. (Attraction is not initially a priority of the spinoff's program. Few outside hires will be needed; those who are hired can be treated as individual cases.)

4.   *What performance targets will really measure management's value-added to the spinoff?* In every spinoff we have seen, the executive group received a stock-oriented incentive for the intermediate to longer term. This allowed managers to benefit from increases in shareholder value, regardless of their cause, and usually did so with little or no actual investment of their own capital required.

The problem comes in replacing the parent's bonus plan with an annual incentive geared to the needs of the spinoff—because the parent's bonus may have extended well beyond the executive group. If stockholders agree to sandwich this layer of compensation between salaries and the longer-term stock incentive, they want it to stand for something more than a salary improvement or a profit-sharing pool, since profits will be reflected in stock prices. Strategically speaking, the annual incentive in a spinoff should reflect *management's current contribution to the quality—not the quantity—of future profits.* This initially difficult concept, always lurking in the background of true incentive plans, is particularly important in a spinoff for two reasons: (a) The practice of setting goals and implementing plans to achieve them must be stimulated if it is to grow in a former subsidiary, where goals were largely set for management from outside, and (b) belief that there is a future, and that it is in the hands of management as a group, must be created and reinforced as an integral part of the spinoff's new management process.

This sounds difficult because most established businesses have had little practice in real operational planning. It is a big change for a spinoff because most corporate incentive plans are so bad, with little risk and no real relationship to performance. In every case where top management has shown determined leadership, the organization has been able to develop this kind of incentive within two to three years. Doing so requires choosing a measure of performance that truly reflects the spinoff's short-term goals. In the steel spinoff, a plan using the appropriate measures was adopted: (a) cash flow from operations (rather than accounting earnings, some of which may come from noncash sources, and therefore cannot reduce debt load), and (b) return on assets employed, which encourages reductions in inventories and working capital and strengthens the company's ability to withstand business downturns. Success in penetrating the market, developing products, enhancing human resources, and improving financial and data processing systems can figure in the incentive calculations for managers in those areas.

5. *How can the other parts of total compensation—salary, benefits, and perquisites—be reshaped to fit the needs of a spinoff?* These programs actually account for the largest part of executive compensation cost, and their costs tend to grow more or less automatically, regardless of performance. Many spinoffs inherit programs from former parents that are modeled on the "big is beautiful" theory of compensation popular among American companies in the 1970s and early 1980s. Shareholders of the spinoff and, most important, its board will probably view exorbitant salaries, benefits, and perquisites as unnecessarily expensive and likely to send the wrong signals to management and other employees. However, they prove extremely hard to control, much less to reduce.

Executive salaries and perquisites may even experience upward pressure in a spinoff, because the new jobs are seen as larger and having higher status. Former subsidiary managers may hunger for the rewards that were enjoyed by executives of the parent. This delicate situation is difficult to handle well in the midst of a spinoff.

It is best to adopt a simple but conservative approach: If cuts are to be made, they should be made at the outset, for it will be even more difficult to make them later. The salaries and benefits adopted should reflect the compensation position of the spinoff measured against the appropriate competitive market. The inherited program may be totally inappropriate to the industry in which the spinoff must compete, or overly burdensome for the available personnel resources.

GOALS FOR TRANSITION TO INDEPENDENCE

Although these problems call for immediate corrective action, usually the extra layer of fat is not removed surgically but allowed to melt away over a transition period of about three years. During this time, spinoffs should try to develop a permanent philosophy of total compensation and to ensure that program scope and costs are controlled. The rules for the transition period might include these points:

- No salaries should be reduced, but increases should occur only for bona fide promotions or major enlargements in position.
- Benefit programs outside the core (life, health, disability, and retirement) should be candidates for discontinuance, particularly those that pay an average of less than 10 percent of base pay to more than 10 percent of the employee population.
- Employee contributions should be increased to cover at least 50 percent of all future benefit cost increases that are caused by external factors.
- The costs and benefits of executive perquisites should be examined with a goal of dropping the least useful programs and strengthening the most useful programs within one year.
- No benefit or perquisite liberalizations should be adopted except as specifically provided above.

After the transition, the organization's compensation philosophy might evolve into this:

> We recognize that employees are the company's most important asset. We are committed to a compensation program that supports the company's business objectives and complements programs for training and development of our human resources.
>
> Our compensation program is built around five principles:
>
> 1. Levels of base pay will be monitored so that they are reasonable vis-à-vis the marketplace.

2. Total pay, including bonus, incentive, and other pay programs, will exceed the average to the extent that our employees excel in producing and selling better products than does our competition.
3. The pay of every employee will relate to the way he or she performs and will reflect the perception of others about how the employee meets job responsibilities.
4. Our benefit programs will be restricted to areas where the company, through its greater purchasing power or because of tax rules, can provide needed coverage better than the individual employee.
5. All compensation and benefit programs will be simple so they can be fully understood by employees and fairly administered for everyone.

Long-Term Incentives (LTI)

Exhibit 29–1 details how executive stock was used as a long-term incentive in a cross-section of spinoffs in the mid-1980s. Several conclusions emerge from these data:

• Long-term incentives in spinoffs, unlike other compensation programs, are really the result of "deals" struck during separation negotiations.
• The deals do not exhibit a clear pattern, in terms either of size or of the type of stock used.
• Some boards prefer to make grants after the stock is trading publicly, others favor making grants before the spinoff, and some adopt a mixed approach.
• It is difficult to determine the total number of managers covered by the programs, and the size of allocations is usually not available beyond the top five.

Exhibit 29–2 outlines one long-term incentive plan. The spinoff company was capitalized at fifty million shares and bought out in an offering at $20 per share, for total market capitalization of $1 billion. Three percent, or 1.5 million shares, was reserved for issuance under the LTI plan. The plan included authority to grant stock options and restricted stock. For flexibility, long-term cash awards of performance units and phantom stock were also permitted, but no such awards were contemplated in the initial grant cycle.

Initial grants covered a three-year period and involved combinations of stock options and restricted stock. The option exercise price was the initial

EXHIBIT 29-1
Use of Executive Stock in Spinoffs

Spinoff (Parent)	Date	Industry	Sales $ millions	% of Stock Outstanding	Description
Ryder (Pie)	9/85	Trucking	888	18.5	Option plan after trading begins
Kenner Parker (General Mills)	8/85	Toys	638	5.6	Option plan after trading begins (includes 0.2% in contractual options to CEO)
				0.1	Contractual restricted stock to CEO
Crystal Consolidated (General Mills)	9/85	Sportswear	481	6.7	Option plan after trading begins
				0.7	Options to top 2; 92% to CEO
				1.4	Restricted stock plan after traditional; 5-year vesting
				0.4	Restricted stock to top 2; 85% to CEO
Advo-System (John Blair)	9/86	Direct mail	450	4.4	Option plan at market after distribution
				8.7	Restricted stock; 60% to CEO & CFO at 33 cents/share; 3-year vesting
Wood Bros. Homes (City Invest)	10/85	Home builder	187	9.7	Option plan at market after distribution
				12.8	Stock appreciation rights (includes 2.6% contractual to CEO)
Sunbelt Nursery (Pier 1)	11/85	Retail nursery	126	3.2	Sold to key employees at $7.50 on 10-year 9% notes
				6.6	Option plan at fair market value (includes 2.1% already granted)
Henley Group (Allied-Signal)	5/86	Diversified manufacturing & services	3,340	0.9	Stock participation grant to 38 employees; 3-year vesting
				2.8	1986 stock plan (options, restricted stock, stock appreciation rights)
				4.5	Company-financed stock purchase; includes 0.9% by CEO
Coca-Cola Enterprises (Coca-Cola)	10/86	Soft drinks	2,922	2.1	Stock option plan after offering
				0.14	Option to top 4 at offer price
				0.7	Restricted stock plan; no fixed vesting
Aristech Chem (USX Corp)	10/86	Chemical	789	5.3	Options at or above market (includes 1.1% to executive officers before closing)
Commer Credit (Control Data)	10/86	Financial services	1,130	0.7	Sold to CEO at 15% discount 1 month before offer
				11.6	Options—Immediate grants at offering price minus underwriters' discount (includes 7.0% reserved for CEO)

Source: Data compiled from public sources by Hay Management Consultants.

EXHIBIT 29-2
Outline of XYZ Corporation Long-Term Incentive Plan

Effective date	December 15, 1987
Expiration date	December 31, 1992
Types of awards	Stock options, restricted stock, long-term cash payments
Eligible employees	Specifically designated key executives and managers
Plan administrator	Compensation committee of the board of directors
Maximum number of shares	1,500,000 (3% of outstanding shares)
	Conditions of Initial Grant
	Stock Options
Type	Nonqualified
Length	10 years
Exercisability	1/3 each on 12/15/88, 12/15/89, and 12/15/90
Lapse	5 years after retirement or disability, 1 year after death, 1 month after any other termination of employment
Exercise	For cash or by tender of shares of company stock
	Restricted Stock
Lapse of Restrictions	1/3 each on 1/5/89, 1/5/90, and 1/5/91. Plan administrator can accelerate lapse for good reason.
Forfeiture	Any stock still restricted is forfeited on termination of employment except by death or disability.

Source: Data compiled from public sources by Hay Management Consultants.

offering price; attempts to use a lower price after an offering is underway face both practical and legal barriers. Option exercise began on December 15 each year, while the restricted stock lapsed on the following January 5. The dates reflect the different tax status of the two vehicles. Stock options are taxed when they are exercised, so the December 15 date provided a choice of two tax years if the executive wanted to exercise right away. Restricted stock is taxed on the date restrictions lapse, so January 5 provided the maximum time for tax planning.

Exhibit 29–3 shows the distribution of initial awards under the XYZ Plan, which included seven executives. Below the corporate level, the company was divided into a number of separate operating units. Expanding the eligibility to one more level was not feasible; it would have increased the number of participants to about forty. However, each of the second group of managers was considered for option awards on the basis of individual performance and career potential; about 100,000 additional options were bestowed in this manner.

The salaries and annual bonuses, shown in Exhibit 29–3, were kept conservative for top management in order to accent the desirability of the LTI, which was relatively generous. In fact, there was little or no increase

EXHIBIT 29-3

XYZ Corporation Executive Compensation Architecture Initial Long-Term Incentive Grant
(000s of shares)

Job No.	Title	Job Points	Alternative A		Alternative B		Salary Midpoint ($000)	Target Bonus ($000)
			Nonqualified Options	Restricted Stock	Nonqualified Options	Restricted Stock		
1	Chairman/CEO	4,700	200	100	200	100	250	100
2	President/COO	3,100	80	40	80	40	175	50
3	VP Marketing	2,300	20	10	60	—	135	35
4	VP European Operations	2,200	20	10	60	—	130	30
5	VP American Operations	2,100	20	10	60	—	125	30
6	VP Finance	1,800	10	5	30	—	105	20
7	VP Administration	1,700	10	5	30	—	100	20
	Totals		360	180	520	140	1,020	285

in salaries at the point of the spinoff. (Compensation had been broadly competitive for division or subsidiary jobs and had no LTI component.)

Exhibit 29–4 compares alternative long-term incentives for jobs 3, 4, and 5 at XYZ Corporation. The alternatives were considered for all but the top two jobs. Because of the size of grants to these two executives, a mix of restricted stock and options was awarded in order to allow them to be able to exercise their options and still maintain stock ownership. The psychological value of providing similar funds to other executives had to be weighed against the accounting consequences of alternative A, which required the company to accrue compensation expense for the restricted stock. This would reduce earnings during the initial spinoff period and depress the market price of the stock. (Under present accounting rules, options require no charge to earnings if the exercise price is at least equal to the market price on the grant date.) Thus, oddly enough, alternative B may result in higher values for both the executives and the other stockholders.

As Exhibit 29–4 shows, the preferable alternative for the executive depends on the future price of the stock. The numbers of shares were chosen so that at a price between $20 and $40 per share (the range of market prices expected during the first three years), they represent a fair trade-off for the executive.

The percentage of equity dedicated to create long-term incentives for management is a board decision that should be based on the size of the key group, its other compensation, the amount of net worth it is believed to possess, and the market value of the company. Most of the time the final decision will fall in the broad range of 2 percent to 20 percent, with asset-intensive companies at the lower end of the range. The following table gives a rough rule of thumb for the relationship:

Sales/Assets	Management Percentage
10:1	15–20
5:1	10–15
2:1	5–10
1:1	2–5
1:2	1–2

Special circumstances can easily dictate a different percentage for any given company, however. For example, smaller companies may push at the top end of the ranges and larger companies at the bottom end simply because of the absolute number of dollars involved. Plans that award restricted stock will tend to give fewer shares, while those offering options give more. However, the value of an option share is between 25 percent

EXHIBIT 29-4
Pretax Value of LTI Grants

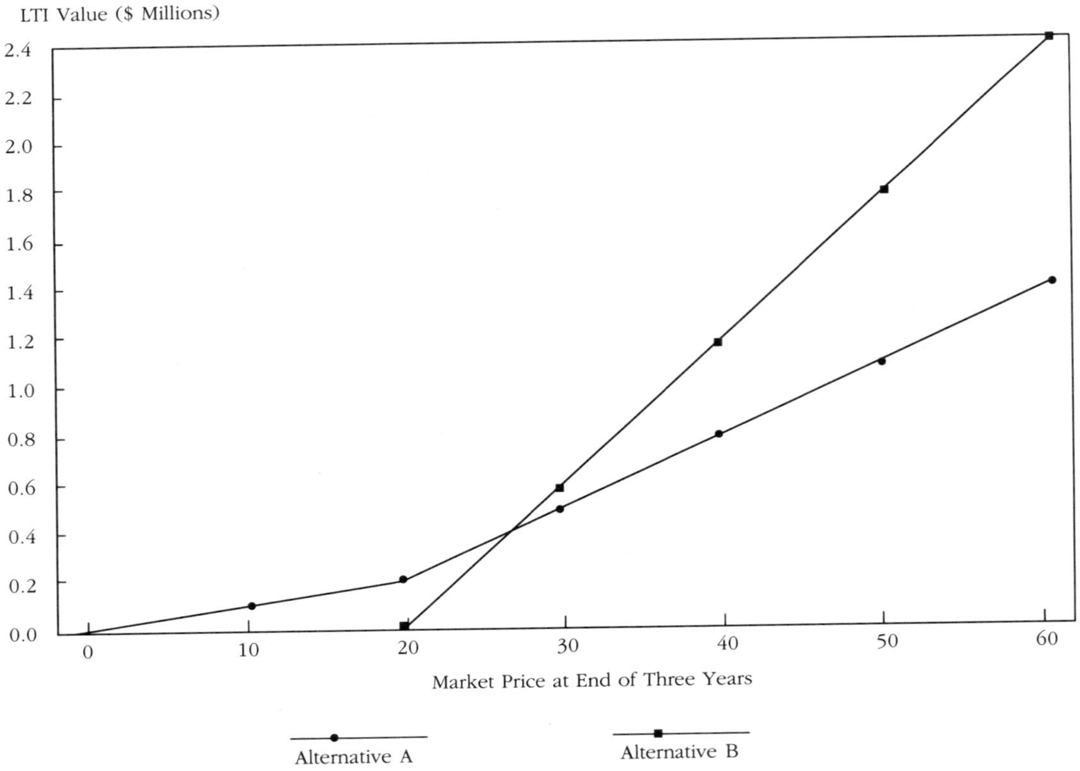

LTI Value ($ Millions)
2.4
2.2
2.0
1.8
1.6
1.4
1.2
1.0
0.8
0.6
0.4
0.2
0.0
0
10
20
30
40
50
60
Market Price at End of Three Years
Alternative A
Alternative B

and 50 percent of the exercise price (if it is priced at market on the grant date) depending on its length and exercise terms and the characteristics of the stock. Thus, as in Exhibit 29–4, fewer shares of restricted stock may have greater actual value to the executive.

We have seen what it takes to create a successful executive compensation plan in a spinoff. Two principles emerge:

- Keep it as simple as possible. There will be no time to administer complex plans or plans that are not well understood in the aftermath of a spinoff.
- Provide plenty of equity to management, but go through the decision process to make sure it goes to the right group: those who will wield decision-making power after the spinoff.

The most important thing to keep in mind when designing executive compensation plans in spinoffs is that the situation demands creativity. It is important to avoid stereotyped solutions, especially during the initial transition period to corporate adulthood.

30

STRATEGIC EXECUTIVE COMPENSATION IN CORPORATE VENTURES

James W. Fisher, Jr., and Richard A. Furniss, Jr.

WEBSTER'S NINTH NEW COLLEGIATE DICTIONARY defines *venture* as "an undertaking involving chance, risk, or danger; especially, a speculative business enterprise." In business usage, the term implies unusually high growth and profits if the experiment is successful. Compensation in a venture offers managers the opportunity to earn above-average rewards in return for committing themselves to above-average risk of receiving low (or no) compensation.

This chapter considers compensation in new ventures within established corporations. We will discuss how pay systems in a corporate venture can borrow ideas from the stand-alone startup, yet also conform to central compensation structures.

TYPES OF VENTURES

The term venture can be applied to the labors of a lonely inventor toiling at night in a garage, or to the plans of a huge corporation entering a new market segment. Although the two situations are quite different, they have much in common and in many ways differ only in degree.

It may be useful to view ventures on a spectrum. Compensation plan design can have a great deal to do with where a particular venture falls on the spectrum (see Exhibit 30–1).

Clearly, the spectrum cannot be used precisely, but we have found that the exercise of determining where a new project falls can be useful in helping corporations determine what kind of a venture they really want to create. For example, many corporations apply the term venture to what is essentially a new product development effort. Such ventures rely on corporate manufacturing, distribution, human resources, and so forth; the parent provides all necessary capital within budget. Management usually

EXHIBIT 30-1
Spectrum of Venturing

	Degree of Venturing	
	Low	High
Resources Available	Multiple resources freely available and used traditionally	Capital is primary resource; limited corporate commitment
Venture Management Authority	Limited authority	Complete authority over all functional areas
Range of Freedom	Limited latitude in achieving objectives	Free to use resources in any way to achieve goals
Influence of Parent	Significant guidance from parent	Limited outside guidance or support
Objectives	Multiple interim objectives well defined and near term	Financial success only goal
Venture Management Commitment	Limited identification with activities; positions regarded as "assignments"	Achieving goals an all-consuming passion
Risk/Reward Opportunity	Limited; few unknowns	High; few precedents

has an escape route in the event of failure. Such a project would fall to the left on the spectrum and have comparatively low risk/reward compensation opportunities.

The joint venture typically falls in the middle of the spectrum. Each parent usually contributes a share of corporate resources (e.g., a new technology, administrative services, capital), but management is granted considerable freedom to operate (and fail) and a relatively high risk/reward opportunity.[1]

At the right of the spectrum is the pure stand-alone venture, where the investor supplies only capital, there are few constraints on management action, and the highest risk/reward opportunity occurs.

ISSUES IN VENTURE COMPENSATION

Once a corporation has decided how much venturing it wants to undertake, the compensation designer must address several key issues.

Competitive Environment for People

The first step is to establish a realistic picture of the labor market. Where will the venture obtain its staff? How much do the people the venture intends to hire earn in their present positions? How do they make their money? These are sometimes thorny issues if the venture's competitive environment is (or is touted to be) different from the corporation's mainstream business.

Degree of Risk

Next, the degree of risk managers will face should be established, because it has a direct bearing on the reward opportunity management will expect. The corporate executive who asks to transfer to a new subsidiary with an open door back to the parent should expect less than someone who decides to start his or her own company from scratch.

Measures and Timing of Success

The compensation planner must establish milestones and a schedule so that both the executives and the corporation agree on what constitutes success and when it will be measured. For typical stand-alone ventures, success is when the company goes public or is acquired. For corporate ventures, success can be the achievement of other objectives: rollout, market share, sales volume, FDA approval, pilot plant startup, profit, ROE, and so forth.

For any venture, there is a limit to the patience of the investor, and perhaps a limit to the market opportunity. Therefore, a range of acceptable time horizons must be established for milestones and ultimate success. An important aspect of the decision is to determine when the venture should begin to make the transition to an ongoing business. This turning point is important not only for strategic purposes, but also for human resource management, since new types of compensation plans may be required to promote the behavior appropriate to a maturing business.[2]

As design proceeds, planners should keep in mind that executives typically prefer low risk, high reward, and eternal patience from the shareholders. Investors, on the other hand, prefer a minimal investment, quick payout, and, if projections are not met, a change of personnel. The art of compensation design is to reconcile the two sets of desires.

REQUIREMENTS OF GOOD COMPENSATION SYSTEMS

Good venture compensation systems do the following.

Link Reward to Performance

The best system is one in which the reward comes when the venture succeeds, however success is defined. Stand-alone ventures often use stock or stock surrogates as the primary, or perhaps only, measure of performance. Although fine in theory, this approach may not always work for corporate ventures. Success may not be measurable in financial terms, as, for example, when a venture aims to launch a new product that will eventually be put into the mainstream. In other cases, success may take so long that the payout is too remote to act as an incentive. For these reasons, corporate ventures often must use other devices to link pay and performance. We will describe them later.

Balance Executive and Shareholder Risk Appropriately

Even though the concept of dividing risk between management and shareholders is widely accepted, there is no law that requires that the executive's personal risk/reward situation be the same as that of the shareholder. In many cases, equating the two is *not* a good idea and can lead to the wrong management behavior. Managers can be forced to be too conservative, because the downside of the risk is so awful (loss of all personal net worth, career in ruins) or they can be impelled to take too much risk because the upside is so attractive. The solution is to develop a plan that encourages executives to take the risks the corporation wants taken. This means consideration of a safety net for failure (e.g., adequate base salary, employment contracts, rehiring by the parent); and for success, a payout that is handsome, but perhaps not the riches of Croesus.

Provide "Progress Payments" as Milestones Are Met

Because most corporate ventures do not provide the unlimited upside reward potential that a stand-alone startup does, sound incentive design principles require periodic payouts as targets are met. The big reward can come at the end, but such milestones as reaching the break-even point, winning minimum market share, or achieving a profit threshold should result in management awards.

Accommodate Contingencies

Planners of ventures (and most other things) hope that their undertakings will turn out successfully. In new businesses, however, a single outcome is unlikely. A corporation may be acquired before its venture reaches viability, for example, and the new owner may kill the enterprise. Or, a new president may cancel or fail to encourage a project that he or she inherits. Sometimes projects fail at what they set out to do, but succeed brilliantly at something else. In other cases, the company fires one or more of the original venture executives before the compensation plan reaches maturity.

A proposed compensation plan should be tested under various possible scenarios, not just the ideal "planning case." If long-term financial success is the primary objective, for example, it would be a mistake to tie incentives to strategic milestones that may become irrelevant as the business plan changes; management reward in such cases should be based solely on shareholder gain. To reduce the chance of key executives leaving, a plan can be designed so that the bulk of the long-term gain comes at the end, and is forfeited by premature resignation. On the other hand, if the intent is to protect management from corporate mind-changing, plans can be designed to pay out as milestones are reached, rather than at the end.

DESIGNING THE PLAN

The basics of all compensation plans are salary, benefits, annual incentives, and long-term incentives.

Base Salary

Salary in a stand-alone venture is the least important element of compensation; capital-building is far more crucial. Similarly, in a corporate venture, the fixed portion of pay should be deemphasized so that the executive team focuses on the incentive and what it takes to earn it. Accordingly, there may be no salary increase associated with a transfer from the corporate mainstream to a venture (although this is not always the case).

Benefits and Perquisites

Corporate ventures typically provide the parent's benefits for their staff. Although the program may be more generous than a stand-alone startup might provide, there are several reasons for *not* adopting separate, more modest health care, disability, and pension plans.

1. Staff may be transferred back and forth between the parent and the subsidiary.
2. The parent's group rates often provide lower costs than a small venture could obtain, particularly when administrative costs are considered.
3. Tax-qualified benefit plans (especially health care) are a tax-effective way to deliver compensation to employees.
4. Eliminating a pension plan could create excessive risk and anxiety for the executive.
5. Subsidiaries with fewer than fifty employees typically are not permitted to provide separate tax-qualified benefit plans.
6. In the total picture, benefit costs for executives are far outweighed by salary and incentives.

Perquisites, on the other hand, should be limited in a corporate venture. Venture managers should keep their eyes on the ball, not on the country clubs and cars. Ventures also tend to have an egalitarian climate that discourages the use of obvious privileges for senior executives.

Annual Incentives

One general principle of incentive plan design is particularly useful in ventures: senior executives should be rewarded for developing and implementing a successful strategy (doing the right job); below the top, executives should be rewarded primarily for implementing the strategy developed at the top (doing the job right).

The use of annual bonuses varies in ventures. Stand-alone ventures may not pay annual incentives to senior executives, focusing instead on the long term. One reason is that a stand-alone venture either succeeds or fails. Success is measured by the creation of an enterprise whose stock has value, typically after several years. Creating this value during the startup phases requires no annual inducements.

Annual bonuses are more common in corporate ventures, however, particularly those at the lower end of the venturing spectrum with regard to risk/reward opportunity. Annual performance targets can be set by the parent and progress toward corporate objectives measured, perhaps subjectively. Executives transferred from the mainstream are accustomed to annual awards and count on them for maintaining a standard of living.

Individual performance should be measured rigorously, of course, and awards should be based closely on performance of the venture.

Because there may be no profit in the early years, bonus pools may have to be funded as an additional cost. They are tied to the achievement of strategic or individual objectives, rather than considered as the traditional share of profits.

Low-level staff in ventures generally should also be on an annual bonus plan to support the hard and creative work needed in such an effort. Bonus plans in a venture often reach to lower levels of employees than they do in the parent company or in more established companies in the same industry. Although no one should get rich from bonuses, a variable form of compensation is desirable, if for no other reason than to reduce fixed costs.

Long-Term Incentive Measures

Viability   Conventional wisdom says that the chance to earn long-term wealth is the reason people join ventures. The long-term incentive is what makes millionaires, inspires seven-day work weeks, creates the great industrial dynasties of our country. In truth, of course, making money is only part, sometimes a small part, of what drives the entrepreneur. Nevertheless, the lack of an appropriate long-term incentive can impede the effort to attract and retain the best people; a well-designed system can support and encourage success. Because of the real and perceived importance of this portion of the compensation package, we will discuss it in some detail and provide examples of various approaches that can be used.

Most long-term incentive plans for venture executives are based on the concept of shareholder value. The vehicles used include stock ownership, options, phantom shares, performance units, and bonus pools. In designing plans, there are two important decisions: choice of performance measure and choice of vehicle.

The goal in selecting a measurement system is to be able to register a change in shareholder value. In most cases, a small number of factors—often only one or two—can approximate performance adequately. The following approaches are possible.

The performance of some ventures, especially corporate subsidiaries, is best measured by viability expressed in terms of revenue. To preclude deliberate underpricing in order to boost sales, profit thresholds may also be included. The two measures could be related by a matrix or formula to achieve the appropriate balance. Management will be encouraged to keep both factors in mind, although in early stages, more weight might be given to revenue.

Price/Earnings   Some plans try to simulate public ownership by establishing a hypothetical price/earnings ratio. The ratio can be derived from the stock market P/E ratio, that of comparable companies, or from key financial ratios such as earnings growth and ROE. The resulting P/E ratio is then multiplied by earnings to derive a total value for the venture.

Economic Value   The most sophisticated approach, and the most theoretically correct, is to measure the value created by the venture for its shareholders. Economic models have been developed by academicians, securities analysts, and strategic planners that relate real return on investment to risk-adjusted cost of capital (or expected return). The result is a theoretical premium or discount to book value that represents the "intrinsic" or economic value of the enterprise to a rational investor. A simple formula derives the premium or discount by comparing actual return on investment to required return, and multiplying the ratio times book value. Another approach is to discount expected future profit, the result being the present value of the business.

The results of such calculations should be compared to the performance of the parent(s) in order to determine the value created by venture management for the corporation's shareholders.

Strategic Milestones   Many corporate ventures tie long-term incentives to objective strategic goals. This is appropriate when full profitability cannot be achieved until many years after inception, or when the venture is not meant to be profitable on a stand-alone basis. Examples of milestones include pilot plant operation, threshold market share, or FDA approval.

Market Value   The ultimate measure of success in virtually all independent ventures, and even in some corporate ventures, is the market value of the enterprise, revealed at either a public offering or sale of the business. After all, the monetary value of a business is what a buyer will pay for it. If market value can be determined perhaps by a valuation carried out by an independent appraisal expert or investment banker, that may be the best measure of success.

Long-Term Incentive Devices

Once the measurement system has been chosen, it is relatively straight-forward to tie compensation to it. The commonly used devices outlined below are right out of the basic compensation menu.

Performance Units

1. Units granted to each participant at outset of cycle.
2. Target value of units set at a target performance level.
3. Units' value at above or below target set either by a theoretical approximation of shareholder value or by judgment regarding relative importance of each.
4. Units valued at maturity according to actual performance during the period (see Exhibit 30–2).
5. Units usually have no value if performance fails to reach minimum on either scale.

Phantom Shares

1. Notional shares established, valued, and granted to each participant.
2. Initial share value equals a base value, often initial shareholder investment.

EXHIBIT 30-2
Value of Performance Units According to Sales and Profit Margin

		Sales ($ millions)		
		$10	$15	$20+
Profit Margin	15%	$100	$125	$150
	10%	$ 75	$100	$125
	7%	$ 50	$ 75	$100

EXHIBIT 30-3
Phantom Share P/E Multiple Matrix

		ROE		
		10%	15%	25%
Profit	20%	12×	17×	20×
	15%	10×	15×	17×
Growth	10%	7×	10×	12×

EXHIBIT 30-4
Phantom Share Valuation Formula

$$\text{Value} = \frac{\text{Average ROE}}{\text{Cost of Equity}} \times \text{Book Value}$$

3. Share value at maturity derived from formula or matrix. Exhibits 30–3 and 30–4 illustrate this approach. (Appendix I of this chapter discusses a phantom share plan in a new venture.)
5. Final payout can equal change in value (simulates options) or total value (simulates grants of shares).

Bonus Pool

1. Milestones set and calibrated to target payouts; e.g., percentage of participants' salaries, set according to competitive practice but probably higher to reflect venture risk/reward.
2. Actual results determine pool.
3. Pool awarded on predetermined basis to participants. (Appendix II discusses a bonus pool program used by Air Products.)

Options/Purchase/Grants

1. Actual shares valued at outset, usually at book value.
2. Options granted, shares sold or granted to participants with vesting provisions to prevent sale before either the lapse of time (e.g., five years) or a specific event (e.g., public offering or sale).
3. If no sale or public offering, shares can be put back in company after vesting at book value.

CONCLUSION

There are many acceptable approaches to venture compensation, and a full range of proven tools are available to address various situations. While appropriate remuneration can contribute to venture success, it is crucial to view compensation as a subset of the broader issues discussed in this chapter. The main source of failure in venture compensation is lack of resolution of the broader issues. If compensation matters per se appear to be the focus of extreme attention, the other key issues are probably being neglected. Worse, the key issues may constitute a conscious or subconscious (hidden) agenda. If the underlying issues are in focus, on the other hand, compensation can be relatively simple.

NOTES

1. Designing compensation for joint ventures almost always leads to even more hazards than designing compensation for freestanding or wholly owned ventures. The usual conflict between mature and fledgling, and managerial and entrepreneurial outlooks is often aggravated by a clash between at least two well-developed sets of compensation systems and philosophies. Furthermore, despite the crucial role pay can play in influencing the affairs of the joint venture, compensation planning generally receives secondary or belated consideration.

2. Long-term incentive design should work not only during the initial phase but also during likely future phases of the venture. In the flush of optimism when a new venture is launched or a promising small acquisition is brought in, it is fun to focus on compensating for success. If success does occur, it is helpful to have laid the groundwork for an eventual transformation of the venture and its employees into mainstream participants in the parent's portfolio.

This transition often means that the original management team and the organization, culture, and operating climate have to change. In many cases, a significant shift to the left on the venture spectrum beings to occur, and sometimes the original executives have to leave. Accordingly, some corporate venture incentive plans are designed to end at the transition and be replaced with the parent's conventional program.

APPENDIX I

Corporate Venture in a Subsidiary

A large industrial company developed a computer-based system to support an internal manufacturing function. The company believed that the system had commercial potential, but recognized that there was virtually no possible synergism between the parent and the proposed new product. It therefore formed a separate subsidiary.

The subsidiary was staffed with data processing specialists, headed by an experienced, entrepreneurial general manager from the parent. One of his first acts was to move the subsidiary's offices to a separate location, with totally different and considerably more austere decor.

A separate salary structure was then established, with pay grades based on data processing industry practices rather than the parent's industrial scales. All professionals were eligible for annual bonuses (unlike employees at the parent), based partly on personal performance and partly on the subsidiary's results. The ratio of corporate to personal performance increased at higher management levels. Senior executives' bonuses were based 70 percent on corporate results.

The cornerstone of the venture's compensation plan was a long-term plan based on performance units coupled with book value options. The plan was designed to reward executives for creating value for the parent, both in the initial startup phase and into maturity.

Various compensation elements worked as follows:

Performance units were valued on a matrix with revenue on one axis and profit margin on another, each measured over three years. Target performance resulted in a value per share of $100 at the end of three years—or sooner—if key milestones were met.

At the end of the first cycle, the book value plan (see below) remained.

Book value options were granted in tandem with the phantom shares. The venture was intended to pay no dividends and it was anticipated that the venture might in fact need additional funding from the parent, in which case the number of book value shares might be adjusted to reflect the new capital.

As the venture became profitable, earnings would be retained for further growth or paid to the parent. Regardless, the share price would increase, so that cash paid to the parent would not negatively affect executives.

If the venture were sold or taken public, the options would become options on real stock. It was expected that the market value would be considerably greater than book value and result in a significant reward.

Vesting would occur over five years, or sooner if milestones were met. The tandem link to the performance units would cancel one if the other were exercised. Therefore, after three years the executive would have the choice of receiving cash from the performance unit plan or forfeiting it and holding the options.

APPENDIX II

Venture Compensation at Air Products

Air Products' venture compensation program is an example of the deliberate integration of organization, executive compensation, and staffing with strategy. Present in three ongoing ventures, the program was also used in a project that was dissolved and in one that was divested. Air

Products' approach is suitable for "close-in" ventures that are intended to grow into major businesses generally resembling the others in the corporation's portfolio.

The venture compensation program is used only in projects that involve new technology as well as new markets. The senior executive must report to both the vice president of research and development and a venture board. Each venture board is chaired by an Air Products group vice president (a line officer), generally the one to whose group the venture will be assigned if it becomes a major business. The board also includes other high-level executives selected for their ability to advise the venture, give it resources, influence the right people to join it, and give it some protection from overcontrol by Air Products' normal systems.

Only the top manager of the venture is eligible for the compensation program (other unique programs are in effect at lower levels). The venture manager's salary grade is consistent with Air Products' normal position evaluation system (which gives unusually large problem-solving and know-how credit to positions charged with growing small organizations into large ones within a compressed time frame). Salary range, stock options, management bonus opportunities, and benefits are also within normal Air Products standards. Staying within the standard minimizes discontent on the part of parent company employees and give comfort to and eases repatriation for venture managers, who normally come from within Air Products and have a "round-trip ticket."

A fund is established annually that consists of 25 percent of the manager's combined salary and management bonus. Several specific milestones are negotiated between the manager and his or her board. Each objective is worth a specified percentage of the total fund. The annual milestones and weighting are approved by various executives. Payout for achievement of particular objectives occurs swiftly. For instance, if 35 percent of the award depends on whether the pilot plant is running successfully by August 1, and that happens, payout takes place within a few days. Milestones have been stringent, and typical payouts have been closer to 50 percent than to 100 percent of the annual fund.

If the enterprise does not succeed, the compensation and grade level of the venture manager do not represent obstacles to reassimilation. If the venture succeeds in becoming a major mainstream business, the manager's salary grade and compensation will grow accordingly and the venture bonus scheme will be replaced by a standard executive compensation package.

Air Products often adapts the venture compensation program to suit particular projects. Because the company builds a wall around each venture, it feels free to experiment and innovate in compensation systems, minimizing the degree to which each system can be cited as a precedent elsewhere.

Air Products works hard to control the transfer of unusual provisions tailored to unique enterprises to more routine environments in which they are inappropriate. Within the venture context, however, the special provisions bring excitement, responsiveness, and innovation. And, the mainstream business benefits from compensation ideas the company has been able to test in its ventures.

GLOSSARY*

Back-loaded stock option exercise restrictions A restriction that delays the ability of the holder to exercise an option until a time near the end of its term.

Beta A measure of a stock's volatility or riskiness. Beta compares the stock's movement to that of the stock market as a whole (as represented by the S&P 500 Index).

Book-value plan An incentive plan that awards actual or phantom stock (either restricted or unrestricted) on the basis of its book value rather than its market value.

Business plan (in an LBO) The financial and operating plan developed by management for the buyer's information. The business plan spells out debt arrangements, equity requirements, distribution of equity, and performance targets.

Buyer/sponsor The financial entrepreneur, group, or institution that organizes and invests in a leveraged buyout.

CAPM Capital asset pricing model, developed in the mid-1960s by economists John Lintner and William Sharpe. CAPM states that in evaluating a particular stock, investors demand a return that equals the risk-free rate of return, plus the normal risk premium for investing in equities generally times the risk factor (or beta) of the particular stock.

Cash appreciation rights The award of cash based on the increase in value of a closely held business. Cash appreciation rights are a means of retaining control of a company.

Cash out To liquidate ownership. In an LBO, the cash-out transaction (merger, sale, or public offering) allows investors to realize the value derived from a successful turnaround. Cash out also refers to a lump

---

*The authors wish to thank Robert Paul and Mark Meltzer, vice chairman and senior vice president, respectively, of the Martin E. Segal Company, for helpful comments on the early drafts of this glossary. The *Glossary of Compensation & Benefits Terms* by the American Compensation Association was also helpful.

sum distribution from a qualified defined-benefit pension plan prior to retirement but after vesting has taken place. (See also **Exit**.)

Cliff vesting   The one-time accrual of all benefits once a specified amount of time has elapsed. No benefit is vested before the designated time has expired.

Constructive receipt   The time at which the Internal Revenue Service deems compensation to be taxable, which is when the recipient is eligible to take or draw upon the compensation even if he or she decides not to do so.

Deferred stock grant   A company's promise to give the recipient a number of shares at the end of a specified period of time. The recipient pays nothing and collects dividends from the initial date of award. Taxes are due only when constructive receipt occurs.

Defined-benefit pension plan   A pension plan that specifies the level of benefits (or the method of determining benefits), but not the amount of company contributions. Contributions are determined actuarially on the basis of the benefits expected to become payable.

Defined-contribution pension plan   A pension plan that specifies the amount of company contributions, but not the level of benefits. The size of the pension is determined by how much is in the account at the time the pension becomes payable.

Delta stock   A form of restricted stock sold to executives at a formula price (fair market or book value less a specified dollar amount).

Discounted cash-flow valuation   A method of valuing a company or division. Anticipated cash flows are reduced using a risk-adjusted discount rate.

Discounted stock option (DSO)   A form of deferred compensation consisting of the right to purchase equity at a below-market price.

EBIT   Earnings before interest and taxes, often used as one measure of performance in LBOs (e.g., achievement of forecasted EBIT for the three-year period after the buyout).

ERISA   Employment Retirement Income Security Act of 1974, the law that introduced complex restrictions on pension plans. The act covers eligibility for participation; reporting and disclosure requirements; fiduciary standards for management of retirement funds; and establishment of the Pension Benefit Guarantee Corporation (PBGC).

ERISA Excess Plan   A type of pension plan for top executives only devised to restore benefits that were reduced by the enactment of ERISA. The company makes up the difference between what an executive accrues under the company pension plan and the amount he or she is allowed to receive under ERISA restrictions.

ESOP Employee stock ownership plan, under which all employees receive stock in their company, generally upon retirement or separation from the company.

EVA Economic value-added, a measure of a company's return on investment that exceeds what is predicted by the capital asset pricing model.

Evergreen contract A contract that does not expire.

Exit To liquidate ownership. In an LBO, the exit (by merger, sale, or public offering) allows investors to realize the profits on a successful turnaround. (See also **Cash out.**)

Flexible benefits Plan under which employees can choose among a number of elective benefits (within a certain dollar amount) after subscribing to the core package of health, disability, retirement, and death benefits.

Formula value stock Simulated stock, also called phantom shares, used to measure the performance of companies or business units that do not have publicly traded shares. The value of the stock is determined by special formula.

Founders' stock A form of stock sometimes offered to employees of new companies (such as startup companies with potential for rapid growth).

Full-value plan A long-term incentive plan that rewards for the achievement of financial objectives rather than for increases in stock value, EPS, or ROI.

Funding formula A company's definition of the performance level required for bonuses to be paid (threshold) and the percentage of profits above the threshold that will go toward bonuses (multiplier).

Gainsharing A variable pay scheme designed to reduce costs and improve profitability. Gains made through cost-cutting efforts of employees are shared with them.

Goal setting The practice of basing bonuses on the accomplishment of financial targets. Achievement of goals is often determined by preestablished formula.

Irrevocable trust Money held for employees that cannot be recalled by the company.

Job-based pay The practice of evaluating and ranking jobs into pay levels.

Junior stock Discounted, restricted stock that is convertible to common stock after a specified goal has been attained.

Leveraged recapitalization   A transaction whereby a public company buys back 80 percent to 90 percent of its equity using debt without becoming private. Also called leveraged recap.

Mega-grant   An offer of an exceptionally large amount of stock, usually to offset a relatively low salary in a company with huge growth potential.

Multiplier   The part of a bonus funding formula that defines the percentage of profits that will go to executives once a specific performance level (or threshold) has been reached.

Nonqualified stock option (NQSO)   A grant of stock options that is taxable to the recipient in the year it is exercised. Companies are permitted to deduct for tax purposes the option spread (the amount by which the market price exceeds the strike price value). The company receives the tax deduction at the time the executive receives income.

Normal award opportunity   The percentage of either base salary or salary-range midpoint paid to members of a bonus plan.

Offset   A deduction from a pension plan for Social Security benefits or benefits earned at previous jobs.

Option spread   The amount by which the value of an option grant at the time of exercise exceeds its value at the time it was awarded; determined by multiplying the number of shares exercised by the amount by which the market price per share on the date of exercise exceeds the option's strike price per share.

Performance shares   Shares earned if an executive achieves specified levels of performance. The grant usually increases with increasing levels of performance.

Performance unit   Cash earned by an executive at the end of a long-term performance period if certain preestablished financial objectives are achieved. Similar to performance shares, except that payments are not related to stock price and units are earned on the basis of internal financial performance measures.

Phantom shares   Stock simulated for a private company or a division of a public company in order to measure performance. Also called formula value stock, such shares require careful valuation of a company or division. Can also apply to units that mirror the price movement of a public corporation's stock.

Positioning   The practice of setting pay levels in relation to those of a peer group.

Premium-priced option   An option whose exercise price is above the market price at the time of grant.

Promoted interest   An advantage in the effective price paid for shares of stock by a favored group.

Qualified stock option   A stock option that meets the requirements established by the Internal Revenue Service on which the recipient is not taxed until the stock is sold.

Rabbi trust   A nonqualified fund for holding deferred compensation tax-free until either the company gives up the right to recall the money, the beneficiary collects, or the funds are made available to the general creditors of the company.

Restricted stock grant   A grant of stock for which the recipient pays less than market value or nothing. The executive is prohibited from selling the stock for a specified period (usually four or five years), but he or she does receive dividends and voting rights from the time of the award.

Revocable trust   Money (held for a beneficiary) that a company retains the right to recall.

Rucker Plan   A cost-reduction program in which employees share in specific cost savings that are due to their effort.

Scanlon Plan   A gainsharing program involving much employee participation in which employees share in specific costs savings that are due to their effort.

Secular trust   A fund for holding deferred compensation. Differs from a rabbi trust in that contributions are taxable to the recipient as they accumulate. Beneficiary collects when he or she retires.

SERP   Supplementary executive retirement plan, a nonqualified method of raising pension benefits for a person who does not spend his or her entire career with a single company, either by giving credit for extra years' service or guaranteeing a specified level of pension benefits after a minimum period of service.

Shareholders' agreement   The document in an LBO governing the purchase of equity, the terms of stock options, and cashing-out provisions. All owners, including outside investors, managers, and creditors, sign the agreement.

Sign-on bonus   A large cash or stock award granted at the time an employment contract is signed. Also called joining bonus.

Skill-based pay   The policy of paying an employee according to his or her skills and/or competence rather than according to a predetermined ranking of the job.

Stock appreciation rights (SARs)   The granting by a company of the right to collect an option spread (or profit) in cash without exercising the option. SARs allow company officers to collect on the gain in option grants without regard to the six-month restriction period that normally applies under Section 16(b) of the Securities Exchange Act of 1934. SARs may be granted in tandem with a stock option or on a stand-alone basis.

Stock grant   The issuance of stock with no restrictions or conditions.

Stock option   The right to purchase company stock at a fixed price for a specified period of time. The difference between the option price and the market price of the stock at the time of exercise constitutes the reward to recipients.

Strategic milestone   A financial, market share, or qualitative goal against which performance is measured for the purpose of awarding bonuses.

Strike price   The price at which options may be exercised. An out-of-the-money strike price is one that is set higher than the market price on the date of the option grant.

Subsidiary stock   Stock issued for the purpose of granting equity in a subsidiary to an executive. The executive is granted stock at its fair market value.

Super option   An unusually large option grant to a relatively small group of key executives.

Surrogate stock   *See* Phantom shares.

Swapping options   The practice of calling in options when the market price falls below the strike price and exchanging them for new options at a lower strike price.

Tandem plan   A long-term incentive plan whose payments can be made in either cash or stock at the discretion of the board of directors.

Tax-sheltered annuity (TSA)   A type of pension sponsored by nonprofit organizations that allows the accumulation of money for retirement. Employee compensation, up to a certain percentage, used to purchase a TSA is not taxed as income; the retired employee pays income tax on TSA payments. Also called tax-deferred annuity (TDA).

Threshold   The part of a bonus funding formula that defines the level of performance required before bonuses will be paid.

Total return to shareholders index   A measurement of shareholder value creation based on stock appreciation and dividends received by shareholders relative to those of competitors. Used to determine executive performance and reward.

Unbundled compensation   A plan under which executives are rewarded based on the performance of their business unit rather than of the company as a whole.

Value leverage The relationship between increases in pay and increases in performance.

Variable compensation The part of overall pay that is determined by performance. Typical variable compensation includes annual bonuses, options, and performance shares. Also called variable incentive pay.

Variable ratio reinforcement The use of rewards for significant achievements as they occur rather than on a predetermined schedule. Rewards are given immediately after achievements and are random in that their distribution is not predictable in advance.

ABOUT THE CONTRIBUTORS

Louis J. Brindisi, Jr., is senior partner of Strategic Compensation Associates and managing partner of its New York office. Brindisi directs executive compensation strategy assignments, working closely with senior corporate management and boards of directors of client companies to develop programs that lead to strategic implementation, performance optimization, and the creation of shareholder value. He was formerly senior vice president and director, Booz, Allen & Hamilton, where he conducted a major study, published in 1983, on corporate performance, executive pay trends, and shareholder value creation. Brindisi is on the Executive Advisory Committee of the William E. Simon Graduate School of Business Administration at the University of Rochester.

Seymour Burchman is national practice leader for executive compensation and principal at Sibson & Company, Inc., a management consulting firm in Princeton, New Jersey. He has written several articles for the Academy of Management Association and *Directors & Boards*.

Gerald W. Bush is professor and director of the masters in management of human services program at the Heller Graduate School, Brandeis University. He previously was a senior vice president, human resources, at Gulf Oil Corporation. Bush served as a board member of the New England Employee Benefits Council from 1984 to 1988. He is editor-in-chief of *Compensation and Benefits Management*.

Theodore R. Buyniski, Jr., is national practice counsel for executive compensation and senior consultant, Sibson & Company, Inc., a management consulting firm in Princeton, New Jersey. He was formerly director of compensation and benefit services, Ayco Corporation.

Frederic W. Cook is president, Frederic W. Cook & Co., Inc., a firm that provides management compensation consulting services to corporations. Prior to forming the firm, Cook was a principal with Towers, Perrin, Forster & Crosby, a firm he joined in 1966. He is the author of numerous articles on management compensation.

Graef S. Crystal is an adjunct professor at the Graduate School of Business Administration, University of California, Berkeley. He has written extensively on executive compensation topics, contributing frequently to the *New York Times*, *The Wall Street Journal*, *Fortune*, and other major business periodicals. In addition to his teaching and research activities, he publishes the "Crystal Report on Executive Compensation." Crystal has written four books, including *Questions and Answers on Executive Compensation: How to Get What You're Worth* (Prentice-Hall, 1984). He is a former regional president of the American Compensation Association and has been honored with a lifetime membership in that organization.

Evan B. Dean is senior vice president, Martin E. Segal Company, a benefits, compensation, and actuarial consulting firm. Formerly director of benefits at Xerox Corporation, he has served on the Conference Board Councils on compensation, executive compensation, and benefits.

Carl Ferenbach is general partner, Berkshire Partners, an investment banking firm with offices in New York and Boston that organizes and invests in friendly leveraged acquisitions. He was previously managing director of Merrill Lynch's White Weld Capital Markets Group, where he was responsible for developing and managing its mergers and acquisitions and leveraged acquisitions departments. He is the author of *Handbook of Investment Banking* (Dow Jones-Irwin, 1989) as well as several articles on leveraged buyouts.

James W. Fisher, Jr., is director, organization planning and human resources development, Air Products and Chemicals, Inc. He is the author of *Organization Structure* (1980) and *Compensation Responsibilities of Outside Directors* (1985) published by the National Association of Corporate Directors Board Practices, as well as articles in *Directors & Boards* and *Director's Monthly*. He is chairman of the committee on compensation, organization, and management succession for the National Association of Corporate Directors and serves on the board of directors of the Association for Management of Organization Design.

Fred K. Foulkes is professor of management policy at the School of Management, Boston University and director of its Human Resources Policy Institute. Prior to joining the faculty of Boston University, he taught at the Harvard Business School. He teaches courses in human resource management, public management, university and college administration, strategic management, and labor and personnel relations. Before teaching he was employed by the Chrysler Corporation and the New York Telephone Company. He is the author of numerous books and articles, including *Personnel Policies in Large Non-union Companies* (Prentice-Hall, 1980), and *Human Resources Management: Cases and Text* (with E. Robert Livernash) (Prentice-Hall, 1989), and has developed over 100 case studies. He is a consultant to several large companies and leads many executive development programs.

Richard A. Furniss, Jr., is vice president of Towers, Perrin, Forster & Crosby, a benefits consulting firm. He is the author of numerous articles, as well as a chapter in *Handbook of Business Strategy* (Warren, Gorham, & Lamont, 1984).

W. Donald Gough is managing principal at Sibson & Company, Inc., a management consulting firm in Princeton, New Jersey, where he oversees the firm's financial services client consulting activities nationally and manages a unit of principals and consultants. He also has served as the firm's practice director for executive compensation. Before joining Sibson in 1975, Gough served as director of marketing services for National Liberty International Corporation, and worked for Towers, Perrin, Forster & Crosby and E. I. du Pont de Nemours & Company. Gough has been a speaker for the American Management Association, the American Compensation Association, and various industry seminars.

Robert W. Keidel is a senior consultant at the Wharton Center for Applied Research, University of Pennsylvania. He also heads Robert Keidel Associates, a consulting firm based in Wyncote, Pennsylvania. He is the author of *Game Plans: Sports Strategies for Business* (Dutton, 1985; Berkeley, 1986) and *Corporate Players: Designs for Working and Winning Together* (Wiley, 1988), as well as numerous articles on organizational design and teamwork.

Richard A. Lambert is Peat Marwick Main Term Associate Professor of Accounting at the Wharton School, University of Pennsylvania. He does research in the areas of executive compensation, performance evaluation, and agency theory. He is on the editorial boards of the *Journal of Accounting Research, Journal of Accounting and Economics,* and *The Accounting Review.*

David F. Larcker is Ernst & Young Professor of Accounting at the Wharton School, University of Pennsylvania. His research interests include the design of executive compensation contracts and economic impacts of accounting policy. He is associate editor, *Journal of Accounting and Eco-*

nomics, and a member of the editorial boards of the *Journal of Accounting Research* and *Accounting Review.*

Edward E. Lawler III is professor of research at the University of Southern California School of Business Administration. In 1979, he founded and became the director of the university's Center for Effective Organizations, a research unit that works with companies to study organizational change. He is the author and co-author of over 100 articles and eleven books. Lawler is a member of many professional organizations and is on the editorial boards of several periodicals, including *Human Resource Management, New Management, Personnel,* and *Compensation and Benefits Review.*

Wesley R. Liebtag is a visiting professor at the Institute for Labor and Industrial Relations, University of Illinois, where he teaches a course in compensation practices. During his forty years at IBM he worked in marketing management and as the director of personnel programs. A resident of New Canaan, Connecticut, and alumnus of Ohio State University, he is currently on the board of directors of Empire Blue Cross, New York. He was a member of two price control panels under John Dunlop and was staff director of two quadrennial commissions on compensation in the Nixon and Carter administrations.

David J. McLaughlin is president of McLaughlin and Company, Inc., a business research and management consulting firm that specializes in human resource management, and managing principal of Sibson & Company, Inc. McLaughlin is also the executive director of the Senior Personnel Executive's Forum, a nonprofit association of the top human resource executives in some thirty multibillion-dollar companies. He is the author of *The Executive Money Map* (McGraw-Hill, 1975) and editor of two professional compendiums, *Executive Compensation in the 1980s* and *Compensation and Company Performance* (Pentacle Press).

Kenneth Mason is former president of the Quaker Oats Company and a former director of Rohm and Haas and Harper & Row. He retired from Quaker Oats in 1979 and from all other business commitments in 1987. He lives on the coast of Maine.

Fred W. Meuter, Jr., is managing principal, Fred Meuter, Jr. & Associates, a firm providing a wide range of executive compensation consulting services. Prior to establishing his own practice, Meuter had twenty-eight years of compensation and benefits experience, working at Xerox, 3M Company, Northrop, TRW, and Curtiss-Wright; for the sixteen years Meuter served as manager of executive compensation at Xerox, he was involved in a complete range of compensation activities and worked with the board's compensation committee. He previously served as chairman of the Conference Board's Executive Compensation Council. He has written extensively and is a frequent speaker on the subject of executive compensation.

George T. Milkovich is M. P. Catherwood Professor of Human Resource Management, Center for Advanced Human Resource Studies at the Industrial and Labor Relations School, Cornell University. He is the author of more than 100 publications dealing with strategic perspectives on human resource management, managing compensation and reward systems, discrimination, and computer applications to personnel decision making and human resource planning models. Milkovich is chairman of the National Academy of Science Committee on Performance Evaluation and Pay, and has served on the faculty of the executive development programs for the graduate schools of business at Berkeley, Columbia, Cornell, and Duke. He serves on the editorial boards of *Industrial Human Resource and Review, Human Resource Management Review, BNA/ASPA Handbook of Personnel/Human Resources*, and *Employee Responsibilities and Rights Journal*.

Robert C. Ochsner is director of compensation, Hay Management Consultants, in Philadelphia, Pennsylvania. His articles have appeared in *Handbook of Wage and Salary Administration* (McGraw-Hill, 1984) and *Handbook for Creative and Innovative Managers* (McGraw-Hill, 1987), as well as in *Compensation and Benefits Management*.

Bruce Overton now manages his own consulting practice. He was formerly a partner and national practice director for Ernst & Young compensation consulting group in Atlanta, Georgia and vice president of personnel, RJR Nabisco. Overton is the author of numerous articles on compensation practices and personnel management. He is a former chairman and president of the American Compensation Association.

Arch Patton is a retired director of McKinsey and Company, Inc. He served as chairman of the Presidential Commission on Executive Legislation and Judicial Salaries. A pioneer authority on executive compensation, he is the author of *Men, Money, and Motivation* (McGraw-Hill, 1961), as well as numerous articles.

Robert D. Paul is vice chairman, Martin E. Segal Company, a benefits, compensation, and actuarial consulting firm. He is the author of numerous articles on the subject of pension plans, and is co-editor of *Employee Benefit Handbook* (Warren, Gorham & Lamont, 1982) and *Postretirement Health Care Benefits* (Panel Publishers, 1988). He is on the board of trustees of the Employee Benefit Research Institute and is former chairman of the American Compensation Association.

Bonnie R. Rabin is associate professor of management at Ithaca College. She was previously assistant professor of industrial relations and finance at the University of Illinois, and has held positions at IBM, Peat, Marwick, Mitchell & Company, and the National Bureau of Economic Research. Her research on executive compensation has been presented before the American Compensation Association, the Academy of Management, and the Industrial Relations Research Association. Her current research interests include executive compensation and the application of financial models to compensation theory and personnel decision making.

J. E. Richard is an executive compensation consultant for J. Richard & Co., a consulting firm with clients in the health service and high-tech sectors. He was previously director of executive compensation services at Hay Associates. He is the author of several articles on the subject of executive compensation.

Samuel J. Silberman was director and member of the Executive Committee at Gulf + Western Inc., and chairman of its Compensation Committee. He was formerly chairman and chief executive officer of Consolidated Cigar Corporation. He is the author (with Philip A. Thompson) of *A New Yardstick for Profit Analysis* (Dun and Bradstreet, 1955).

Ray Stata is a founder of Analog Devices, Inc., and is currently president and chairman of the board. Stata is active in the high-tech industry and in public service. He was a founder and first president of the Massachusetts High Technology Council, where he helped devise and implement the Massachusetts Social Contract between state government and the high-tech industry. He is currently a member of MHTC's Executive Committee and chairman of its Technical Education Committee. Stata also served as a member of the Massachusetts Board of Regents of Higher Education and the Commission on Higher Education and the Economy of New England, a study group created by the New England Board of Higher Education. Stata has received three honorary doctorates and is a co-author of *Global Stakes* (Ballinger, 1982) and *The Innovators* (Harper & Row, 1984).

Matthew P. Ward is a consultant with Frederic W. Cook & Co., Inc., in Los Angeles, California, a firm that provides management compensation consulting services to corporations. He is the author of "Executive Compensation Changes" in *The Corporate Board* (Vanguard Press, 1988).

INDEX